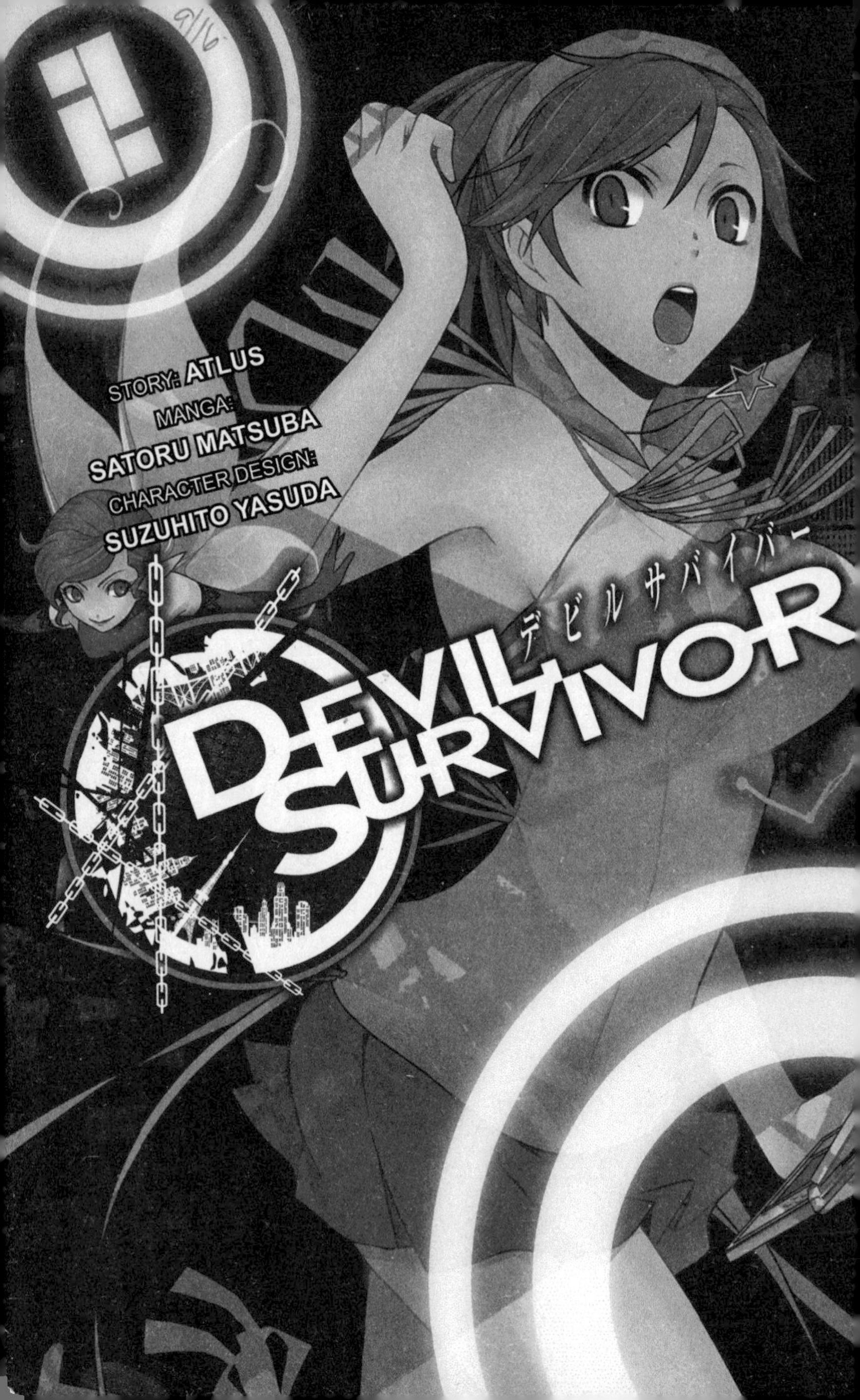
STORY: ATLUS
MANGA:
SATORU MATSUBA
CHARACTER DESIGN:
SUZUHITO YASUDA
デビルサバイバー
DEVIL SURVIVOR

MAIN CHARACTER

KAZUYA MINEGISHI
(KAZUYA)

Uses a portable gaming device known as a COMP to make contracts with demons after gaining the power to command them.

ATSURO KIHARA
(AT-LOW)

Kazuya's classmate and best friend. He's an aspiring programmer, and has been hanging with the big boys on the internet since he was in grade school.

NAOYA
(NAOYA)

Kazuya's cousin. He lost his parents at a young age and lived with Kazuya's family until last year. He's a known genius programmer with staggering insight.

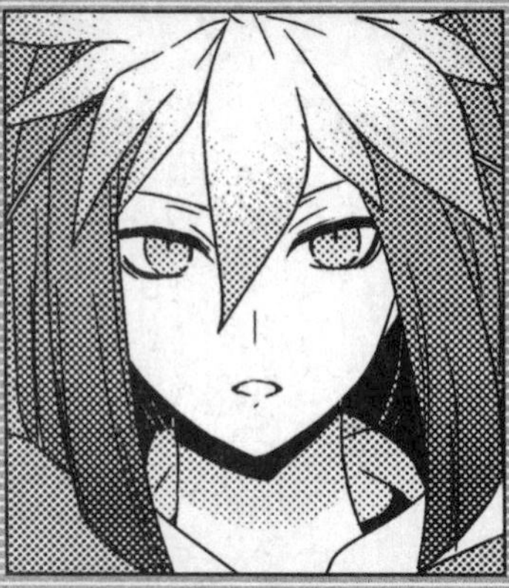

AMANE KUZURYU
(AMANE)

A priestess of the Shomonkai religious group. She can create barriers to prevent demons from approaching.

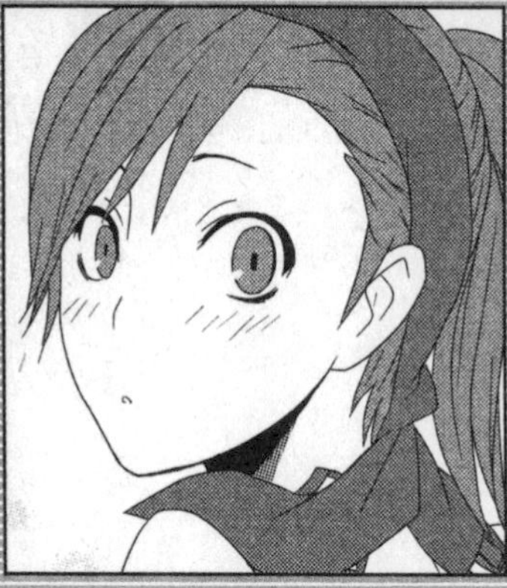

YUZU TANIKAWA
(YUZ)

A friend of Kazuya's since childhood. They currently attend the same high school.

STORY

FROM THE OBSERVER
SUBJECT LAPLACE MAIL

GOOD MORNING
HERE IS TODAY'S NEWS.

(1) AT AROUND 16:00, A MAN WILL **BE KILLED** IN AN AOYAMA, SHIBUYA-KU APARTMENT. THE WOUNDS ON THE ... WILL BE CONSISTENT WITH A... ATTACK BY A LARGE CARNIOROUS ...

(2) A LARGE **EXPLOSION** WILL OCCUR IN AOYAMA, MINATO-KU AT 19:00. THE CAUSE IS UNKNOWN.

(3) AT 21:00, A **BLACKOUT** WILL ... THE ENTIRE TOKYO ...LITAN AREA.

HAVE A NICE DAY.

DAY BEFORE (AN END TO THE ORDINARY)

At Naoya's request, Kazuya, Atsuro, and Yuzu arrive in Shibuya, where they receive the Laplace Mail newsletter—an email that predicts the future. The explosion and blackout mentioned in the email foreshadow the death of their peaceful days...

1ST DAY (Tokyo Lockdown)

After spending a night in the Aoyama Cemetery, Kazuya and his friends head to Shibuya to verify the accuracy of the newly sent Laplace Mail. What awaited them was something they couldn't have predicted: the Defense Force had locked down the entire area inside the Yamanote loop. The prophetic email had come true.

What destiny awaits our heroes, who are now trapped in an area crawling with demons...?! The 2nd Day (Any Way Out) is

CONTENTS

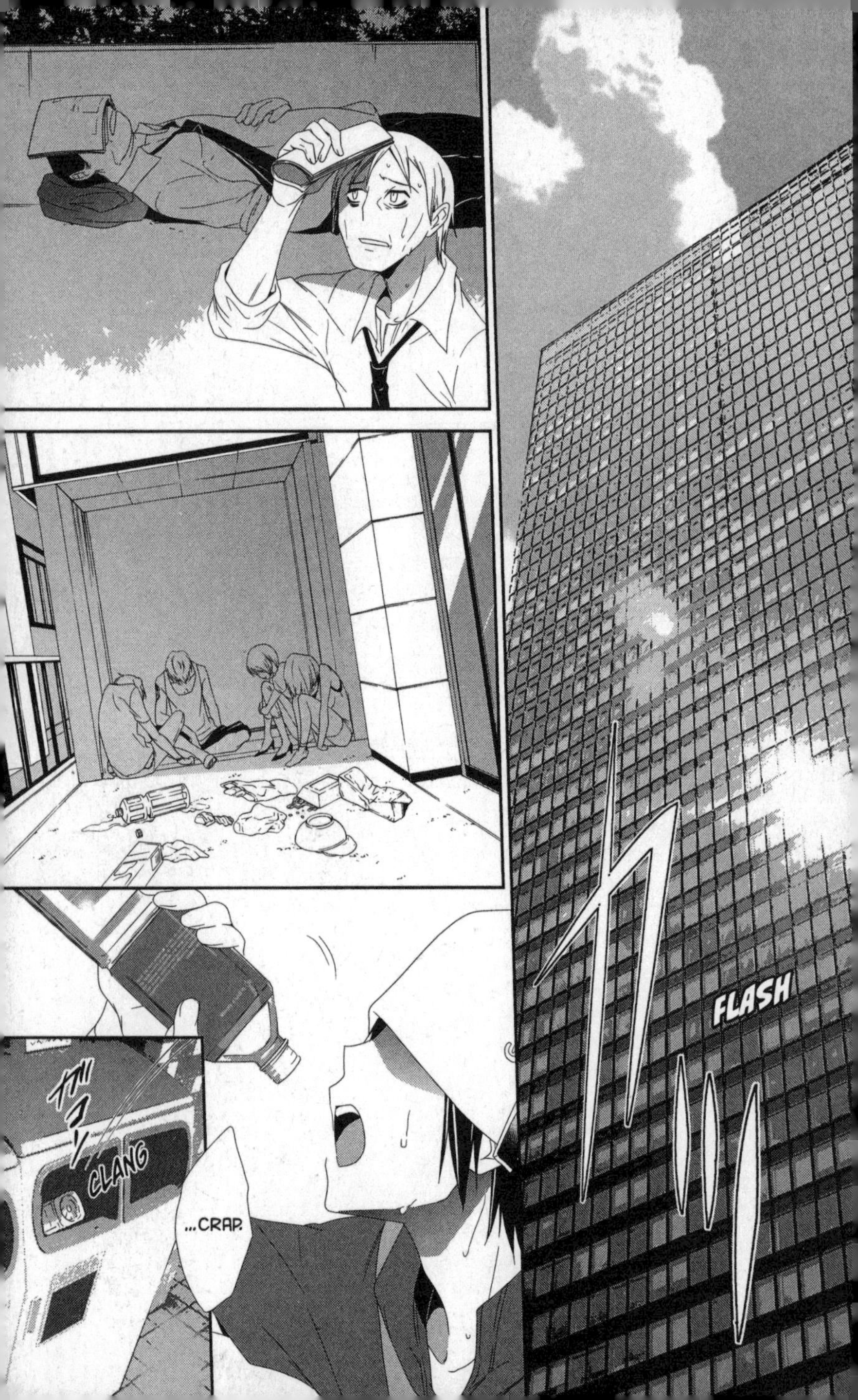
FLASH
CLANG
...CRAP.

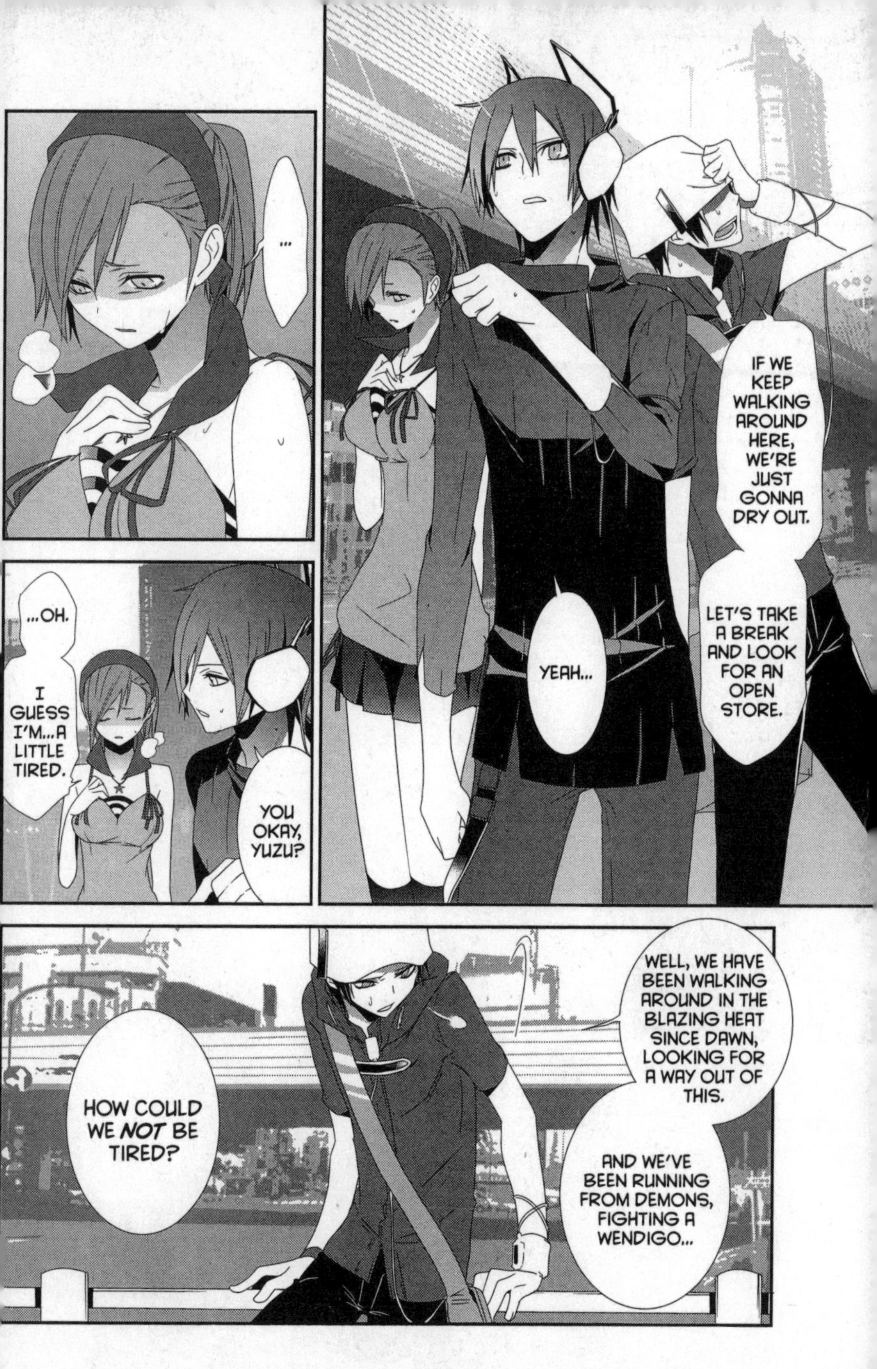
IF WE KEEP WALKING AROUND HERE, WE'RE JUST GONNA DRY OUT.
LET'S TAKE A BREAK AND LOOK FOR AN OPEN STORE.
YEAH...
...
YOU OKAY, YUZU?
...OH.
I GUESS I'M...A LITTLE TIRED.
WELL, WE HAVE BEEN WALKING AROUND IN THE BLAZING HEAT SINCE DAWN, LOOKING FOR A WAY OUT OF THIS.
AND WE'VE BEEN RUNNING FROM DEMONS, FIGHTING A WENDIGO...
HOW COULD WE *NOT* BE TIRED?

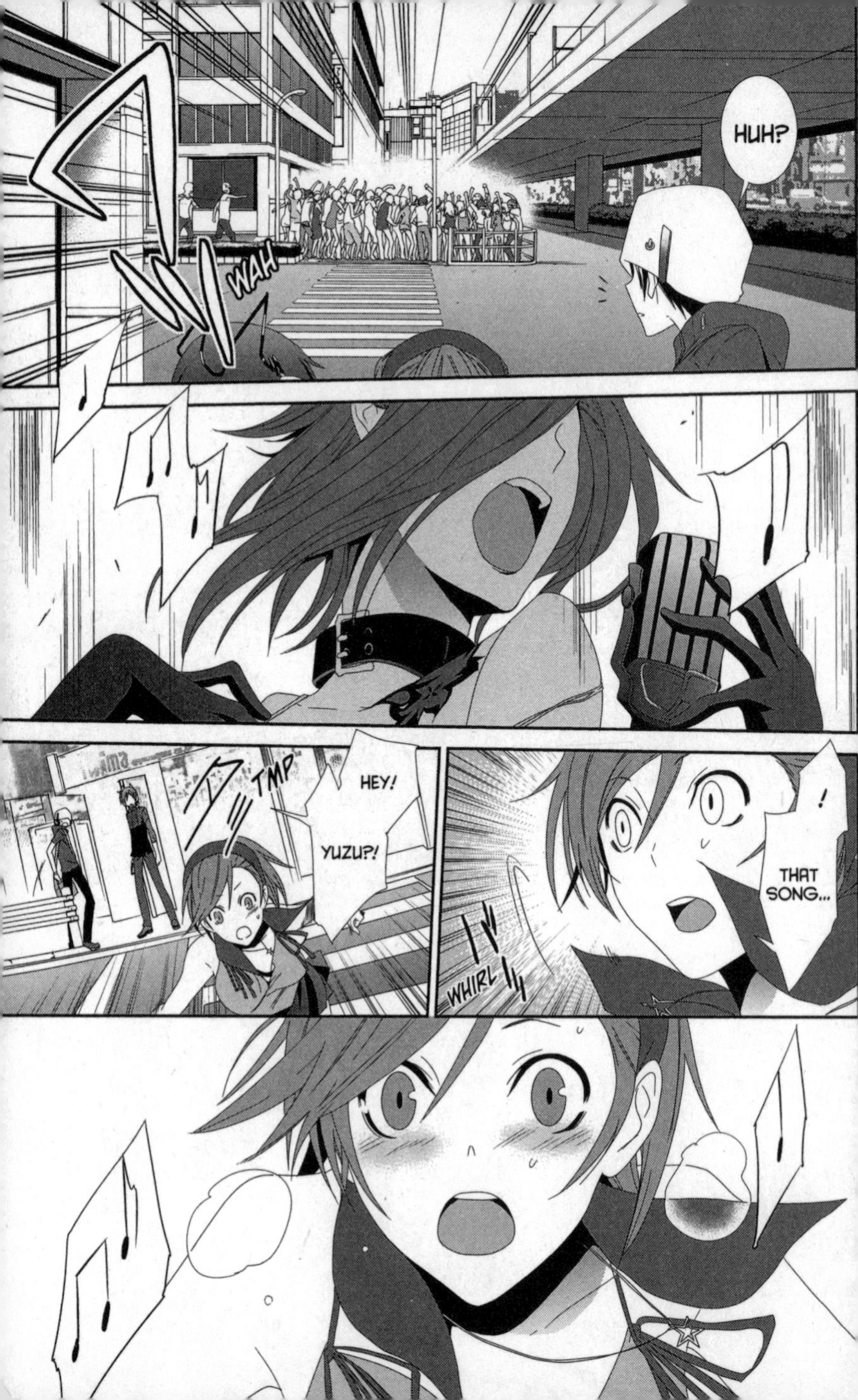
HUH?
WAH
!
THAT SONG...
WHIRL
HEY!
TMP
YUZU?!

SURVIVAL : 6   THE SONGSTRESS

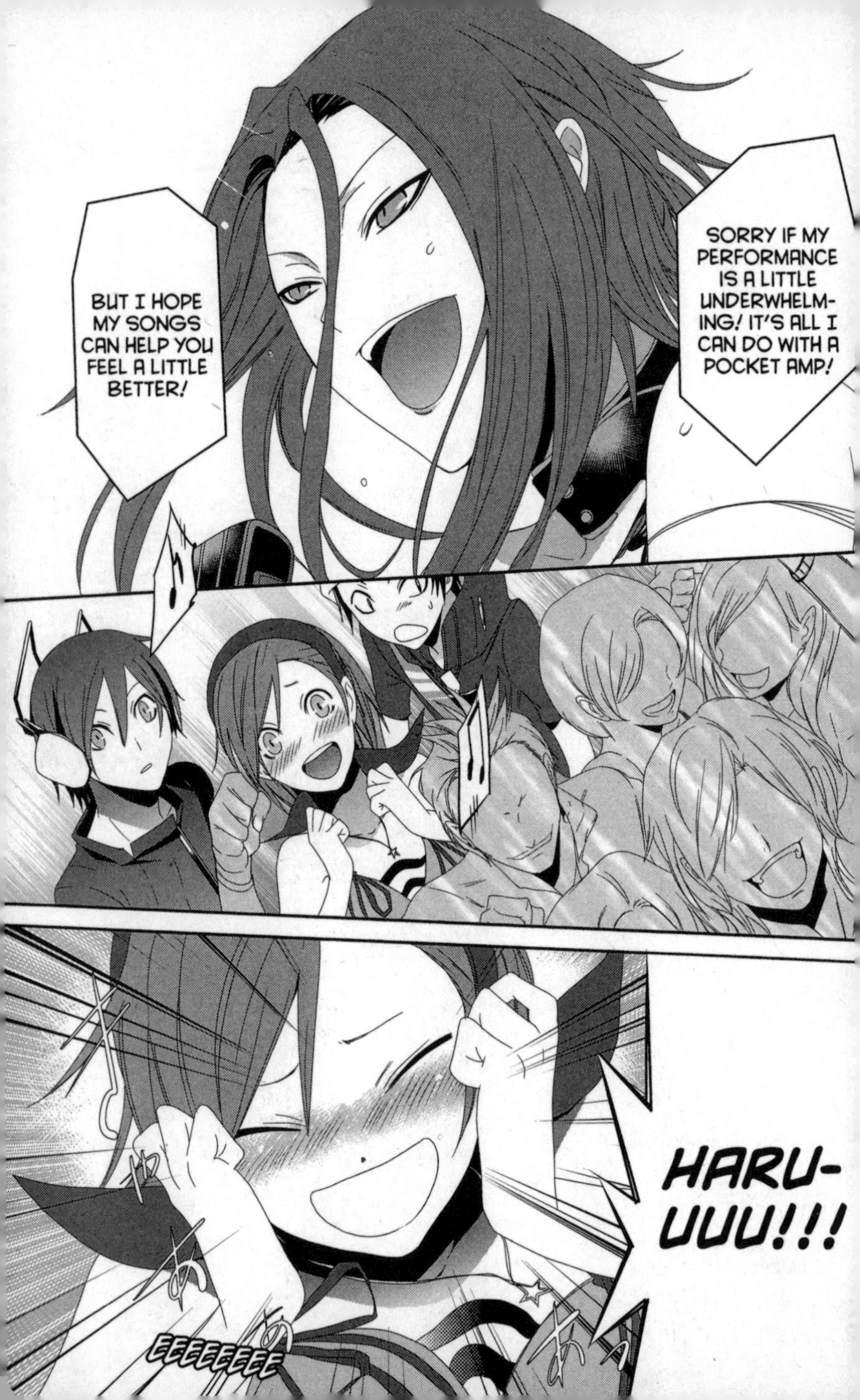
SORRY IF MY PERFORMANCE IS A LITTLE UNDERWHELMING! IT'S ALL I CAN DO WITH A POCKET AMP!
BUT I HOPE MY SONGS CAN HELP YOU FEEL A LITTLE BETTER!
HARU-UUU!!!
EEEEEEEE

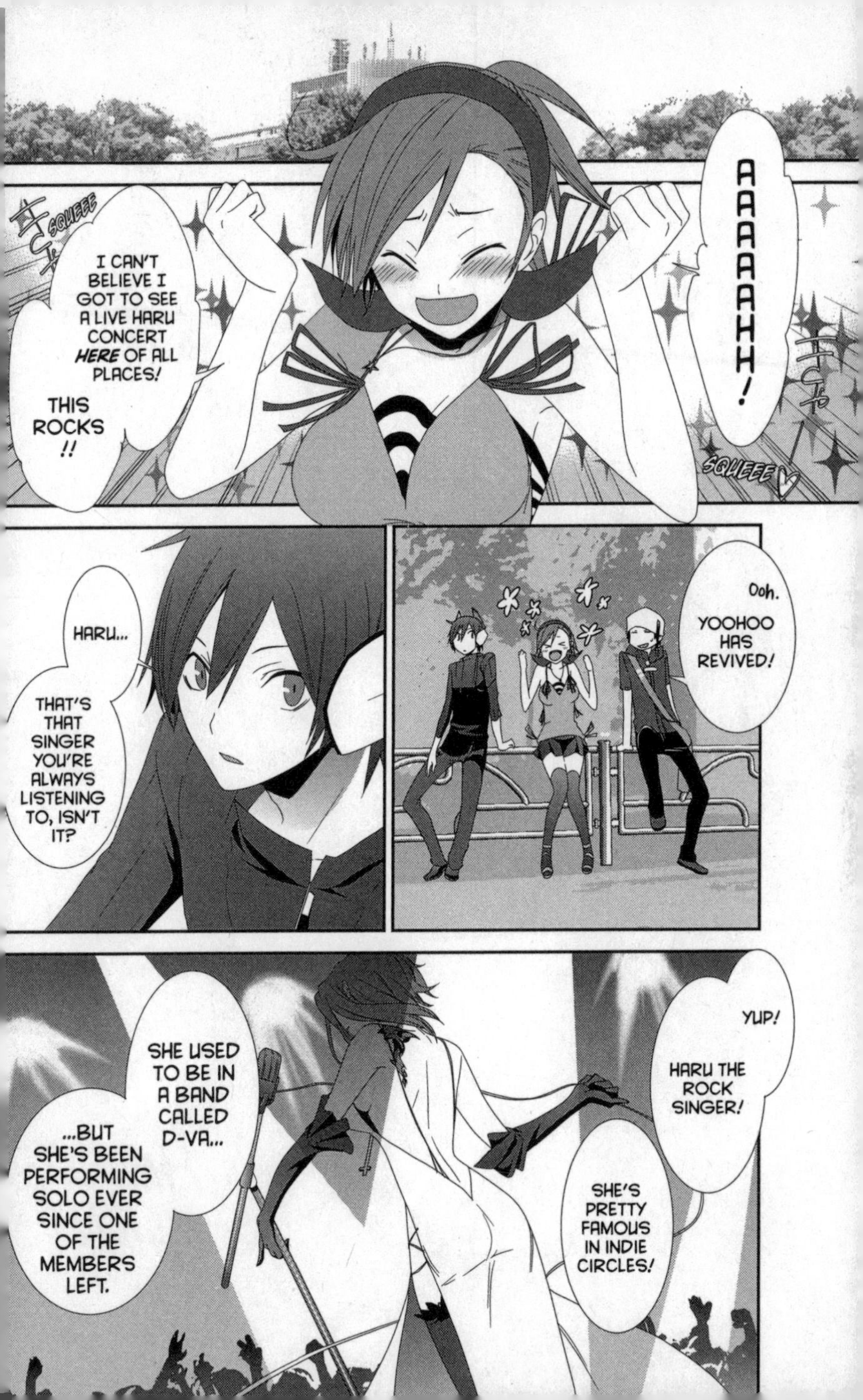
AAAAAHH!
SQUEEE♡
SQUEEE
I CAN'T BELIEVE I GOT TO SEE A LIVE HARU CONCERT *HERE* OF ALL PLACES!
THIS ROCKS!!
Ooh.
YOOHOO HAS REVIVED!
HARU...
THAT'S THAT SINGER YOU'RE ALWAYS LISTENING TO, ISN'T IT?
YUP!
HARU THE ROCK SINGER!
SHE'S PRETTY FAMOUS IN INDIE CIRCLES!
SHE USED TO BE IN A BAND CALLED D-VA...
...BUT SHE'S BEEN PERFORMING SOLO EVER SINCE ONE OF THE MEMBERS LEFT.

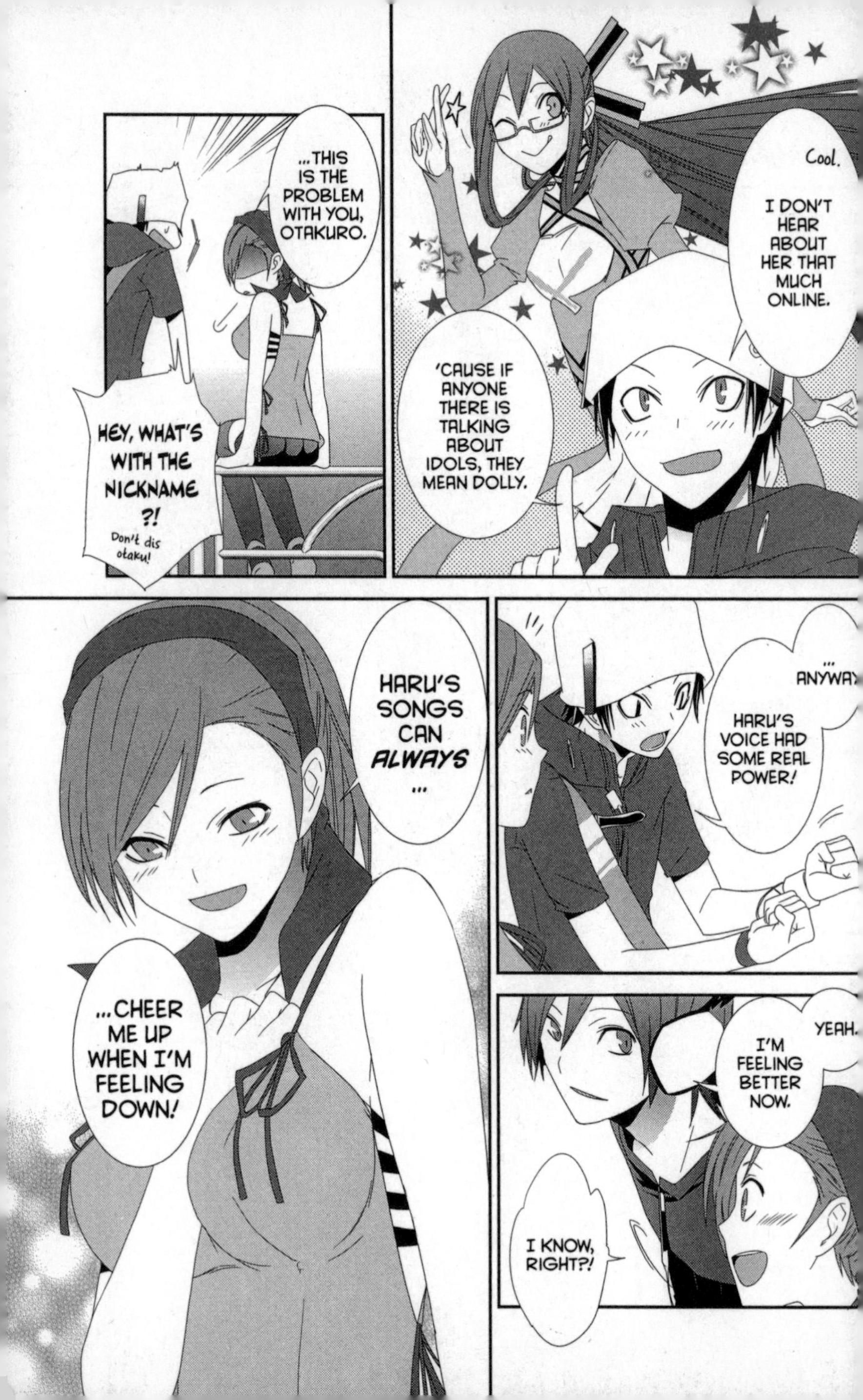
Cool.
I DON'T HEAR ABOUT HER THAT MUCH ONLINE.
'CAUSE IF ANYONE THERE IS TALKING ABOUT IDOLS, THEY MEAN DOLLY.
...THIS IS THE PROBLEM WITH YOU, OTAKURO.
HEY, WHAT'S WITH THE NICKNAME?!
Don't dis otaku!
... ANYWAY
HARU'S VOICE HAD SOME REAL POWER!
YEAH.
I'M FEELING BETTER NOW.
I KNOW, RIGHT?!
HARU'S SONGS CAN ALWAYS ...
...CHEER ME UP WHEN I'M FEELING DOWN!

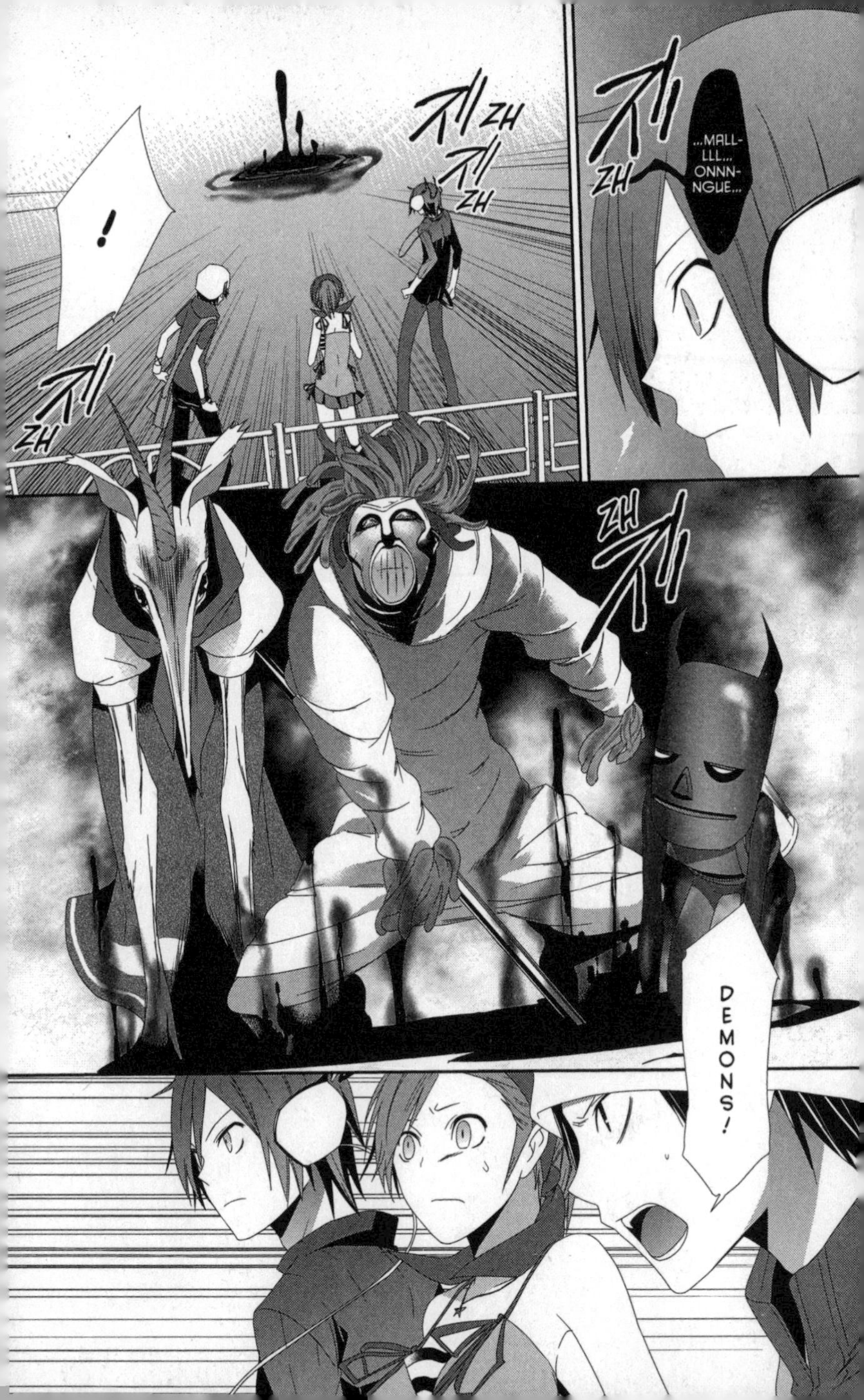

제
ZH
...MALL-LLL... ONNN-NGUE...
제
ZH
제
ZH
!
제
ZH
ZH
제
DEMONS!

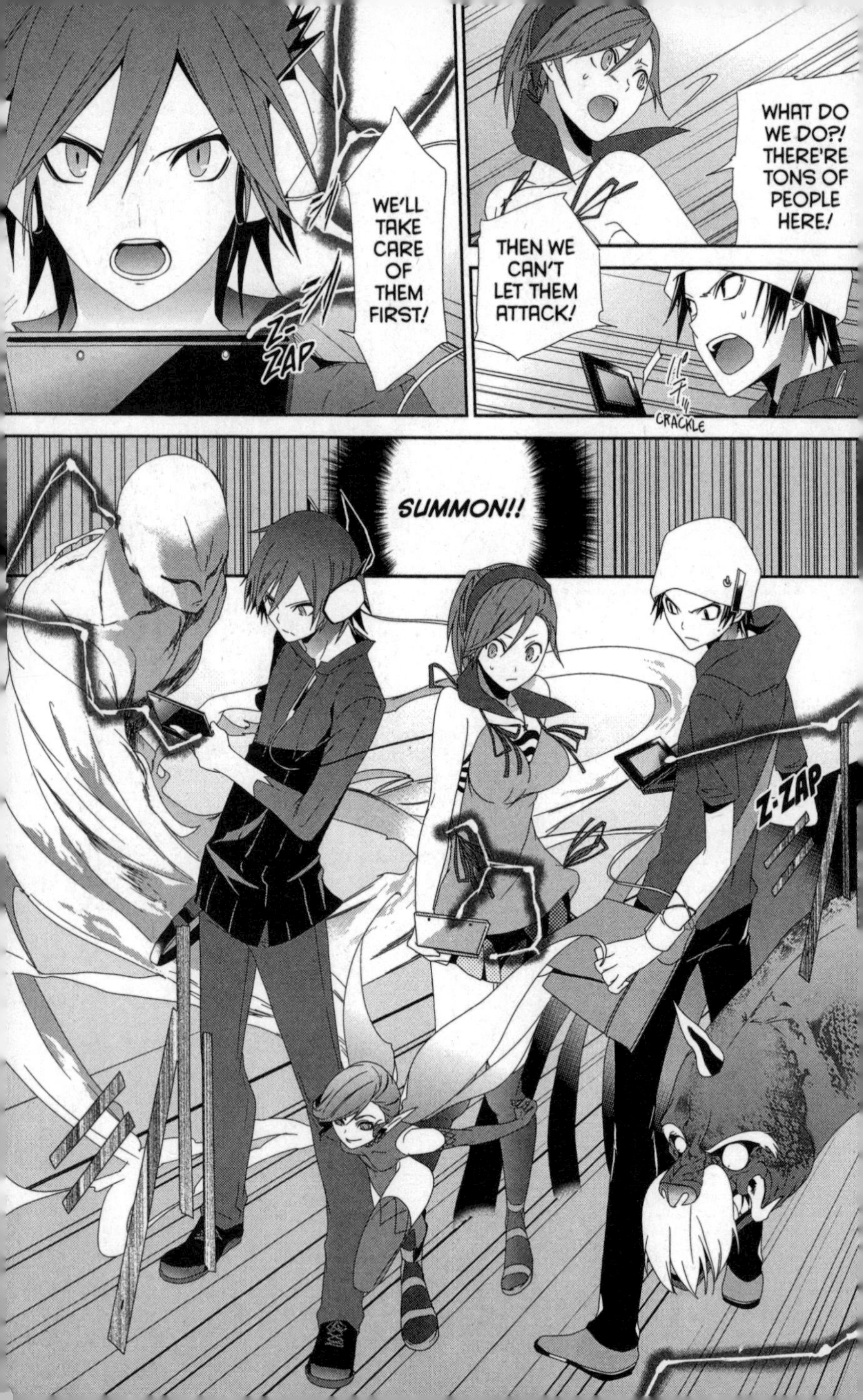
WHAT DO WE DO?! THERE'RE TONS OF PEOPLE HERE!
THEN WE CAN'T LET THEM ATTACK!
CRACKLE
WE'LL TAKE CARE OF THEM FIRST!
Z-ZAP
SUMMON!!
Z-ZAP

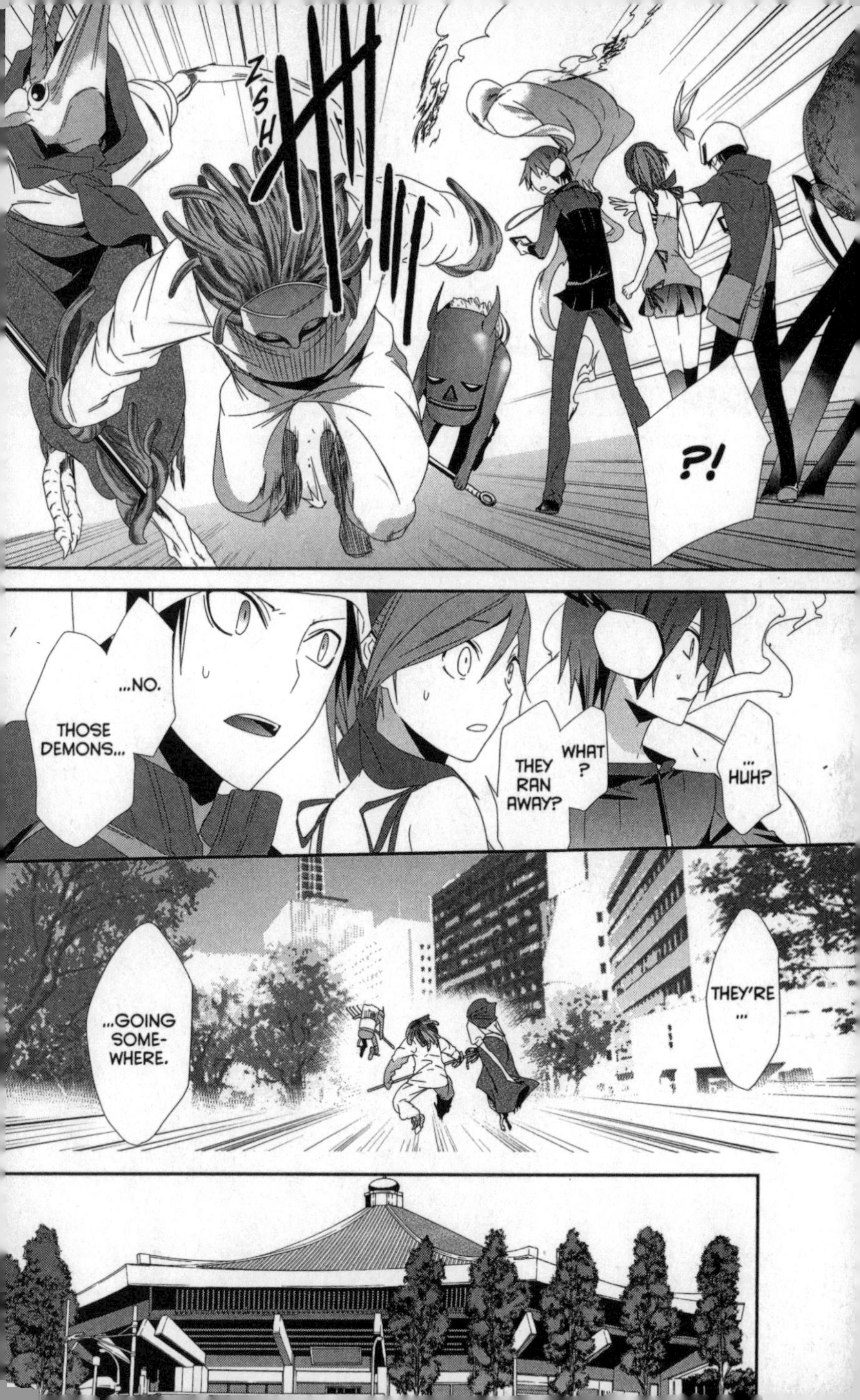
?!
ZSH
... HUH?
WHAT?
THEY RAN AWAY?
...NO.
THOSE DEMONS...
THEY'RE ...
...GOING SOME-WHERE.

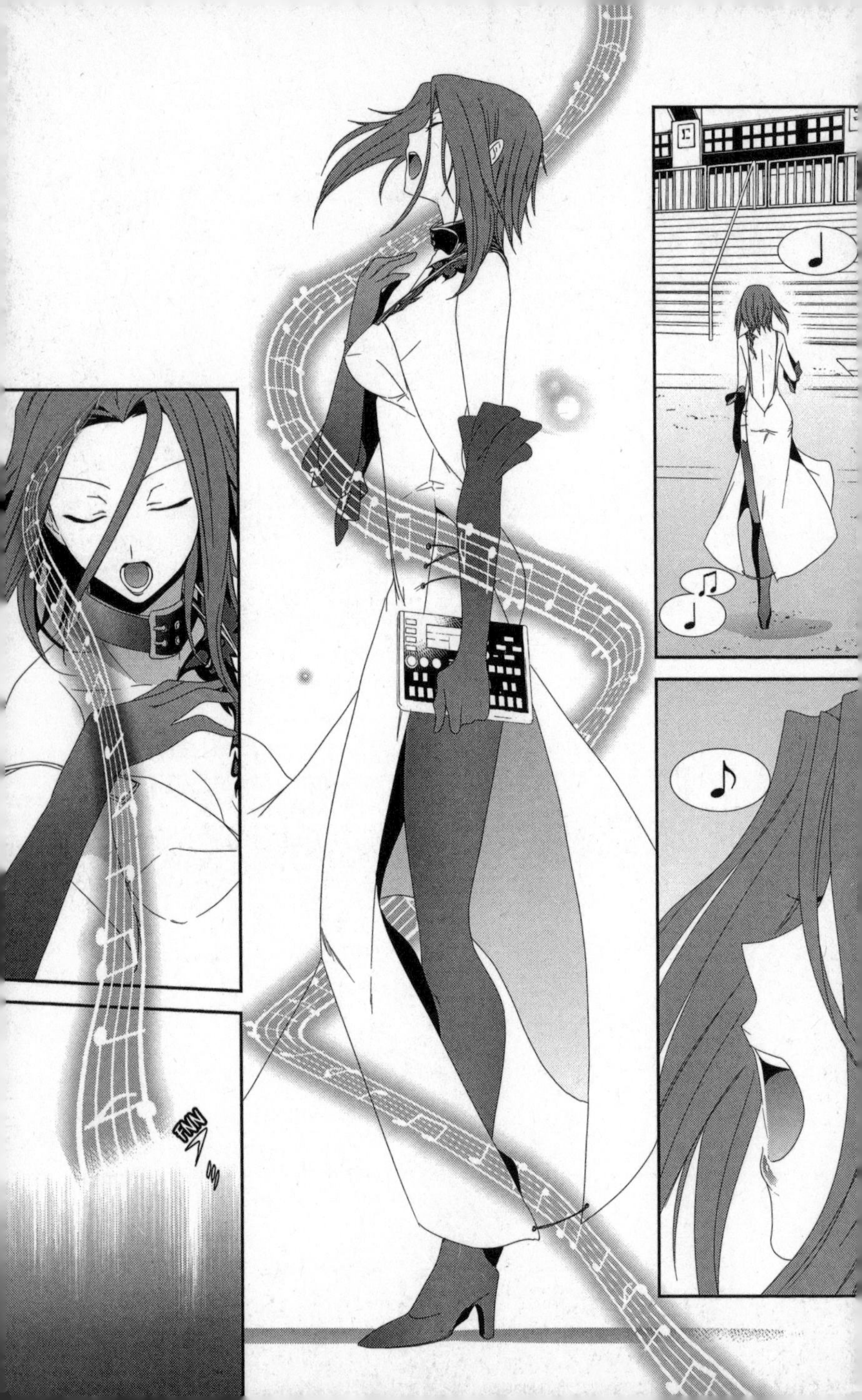
FNN

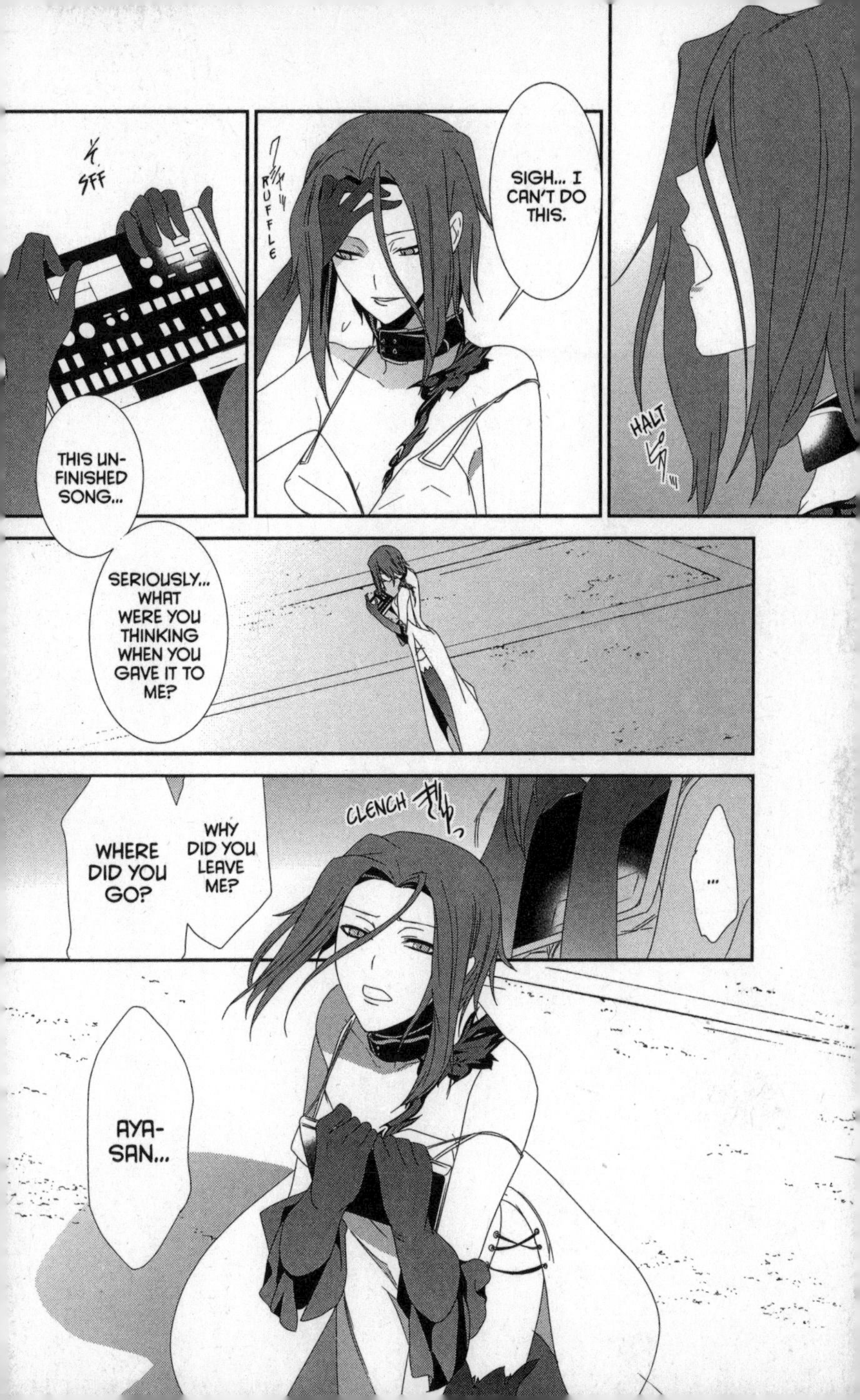
HALT
RUFFLE
SIGH... I CAN'T DO THIS.
SFF
THIS UN-FINISHED SONG...
SERIOUSLY... WHAT WERE YOU THINKING WHEN YOU GAVE IT TO ME?
...
CLENCH
WHY DID YOU LEAVE ME?
WHERE DID YOU GO?
AYA-SAN...

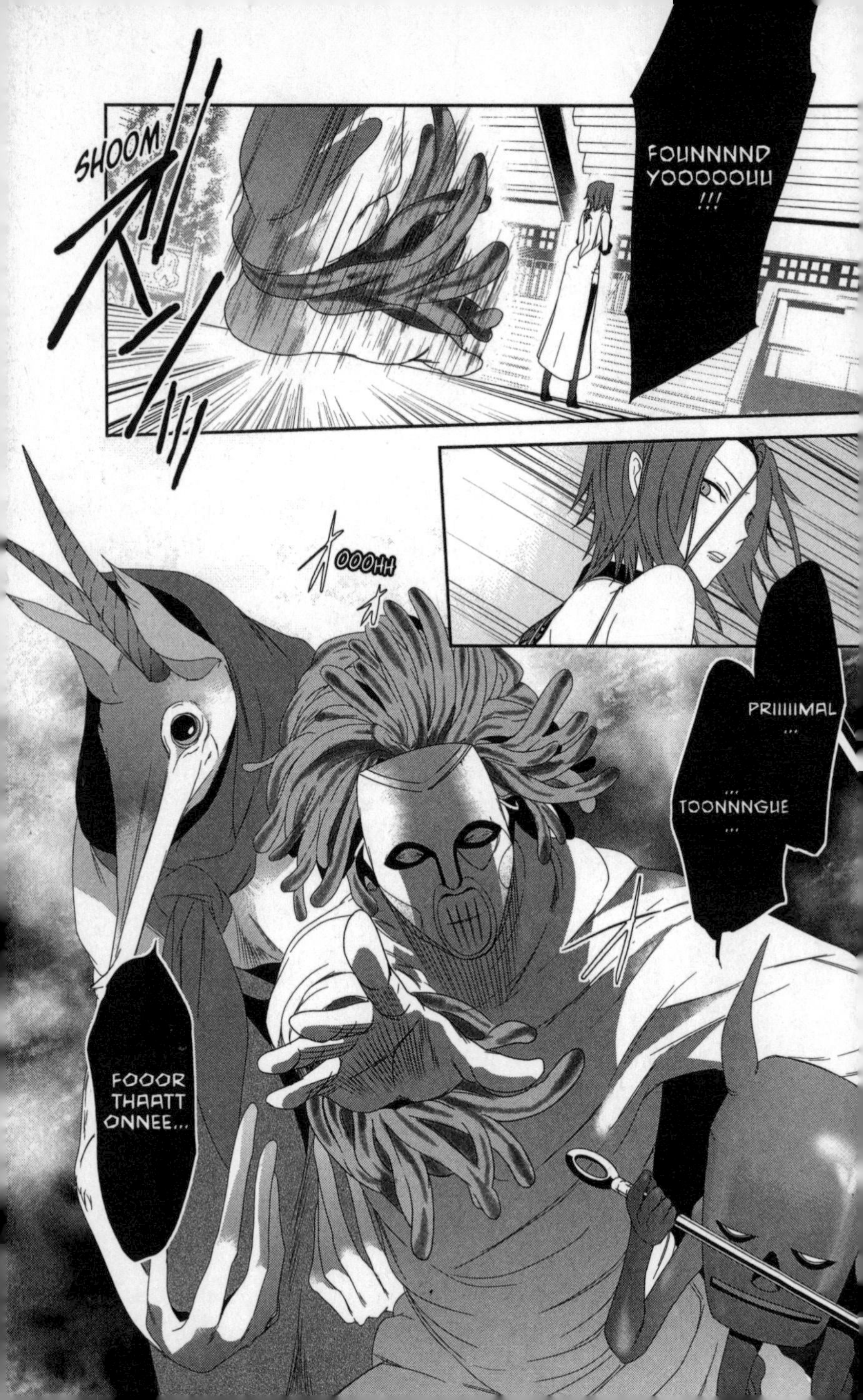
FOUNNNND YOOOOOUU !!!
SHOOM
OOOHH
PRIIIIIMAL ... ... TOONNNGUE ...
FOOOR THAATT ONNEE...

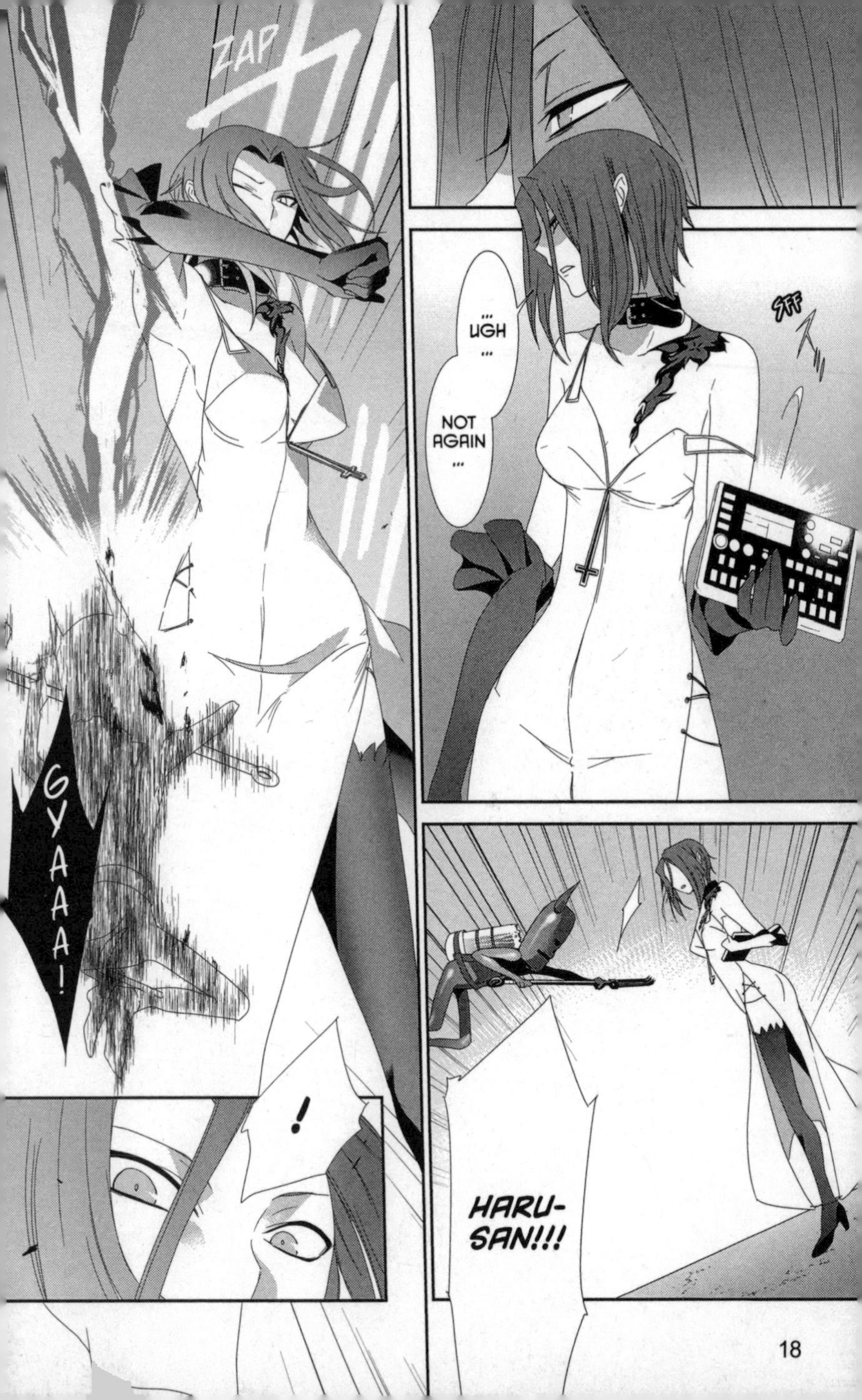
... UGH ...
NOT AGAIN ...
SFF
HARU-SAN!!!
ZAP
GYAAAA!
!

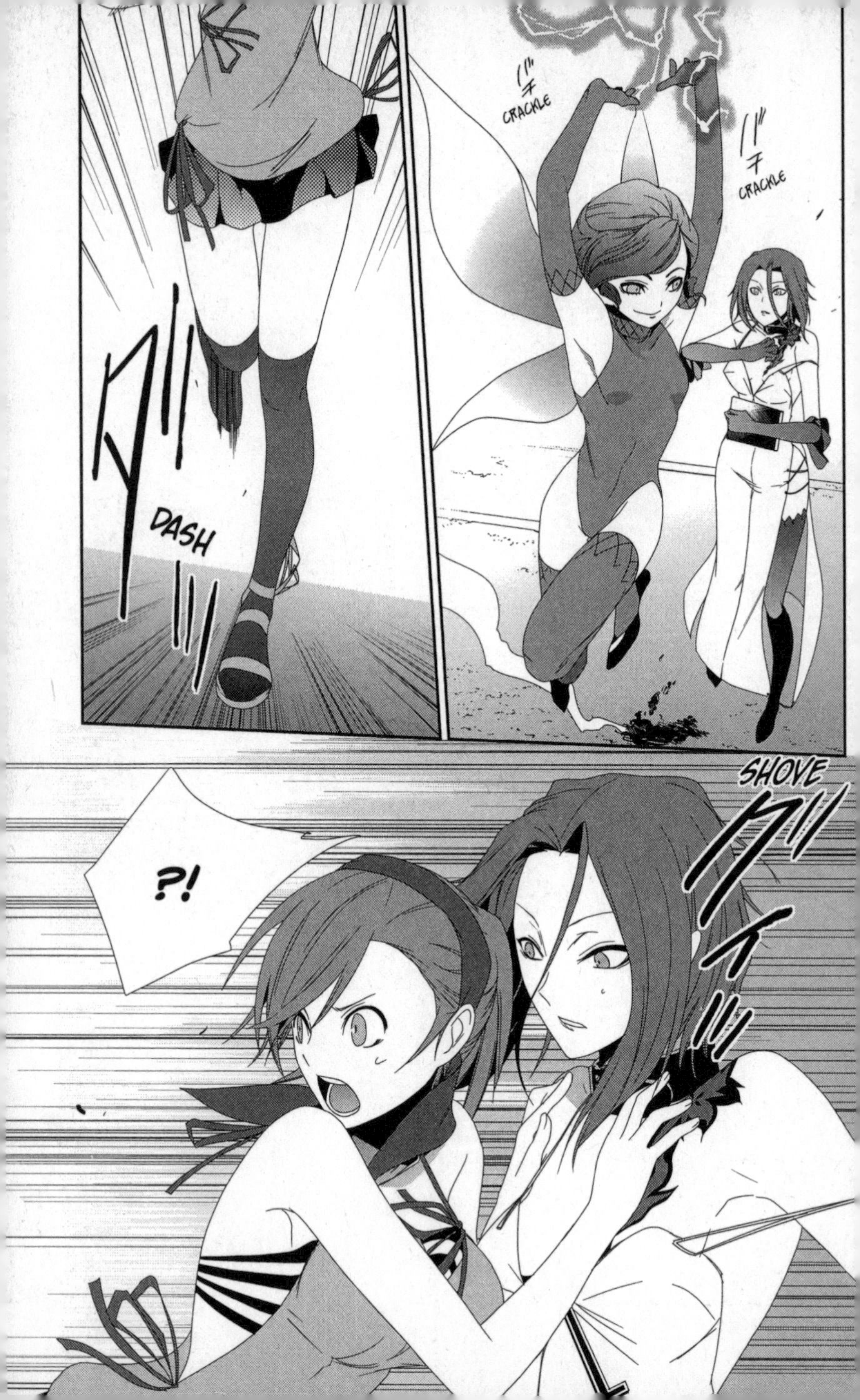

CRACKLE
CRACKLE
DASH
?!
SHOVE

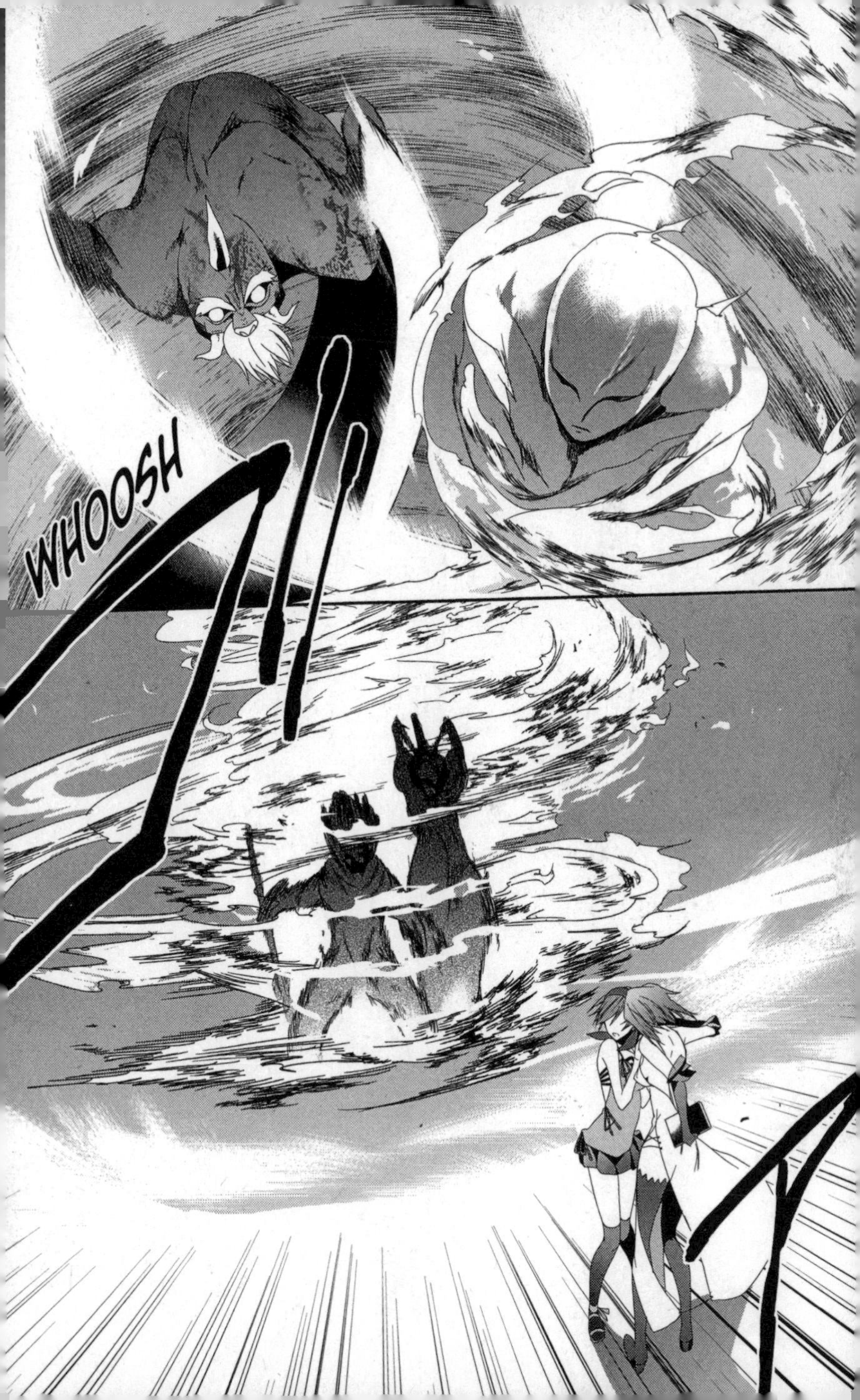
WHOOSH

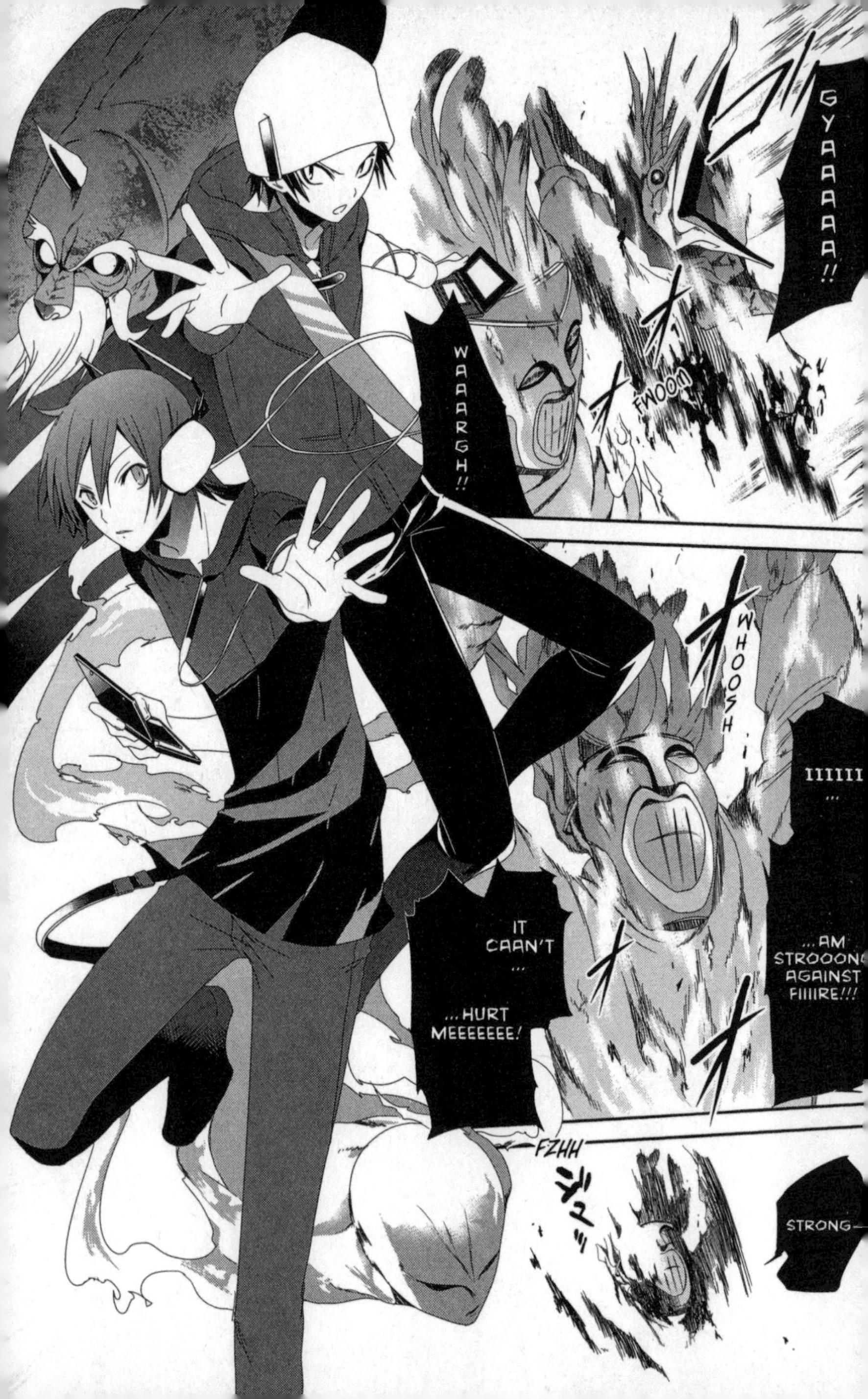
GYAAAAAA!!
FWOOM
WAAARGH!!
WHOOSH
IIIIII...
...AM STROOONG AGAINST FIIIRE!!!
IT CAAN'T...
...HURT MEEEEEEE!
FZHH
ジュッ
STRONG—

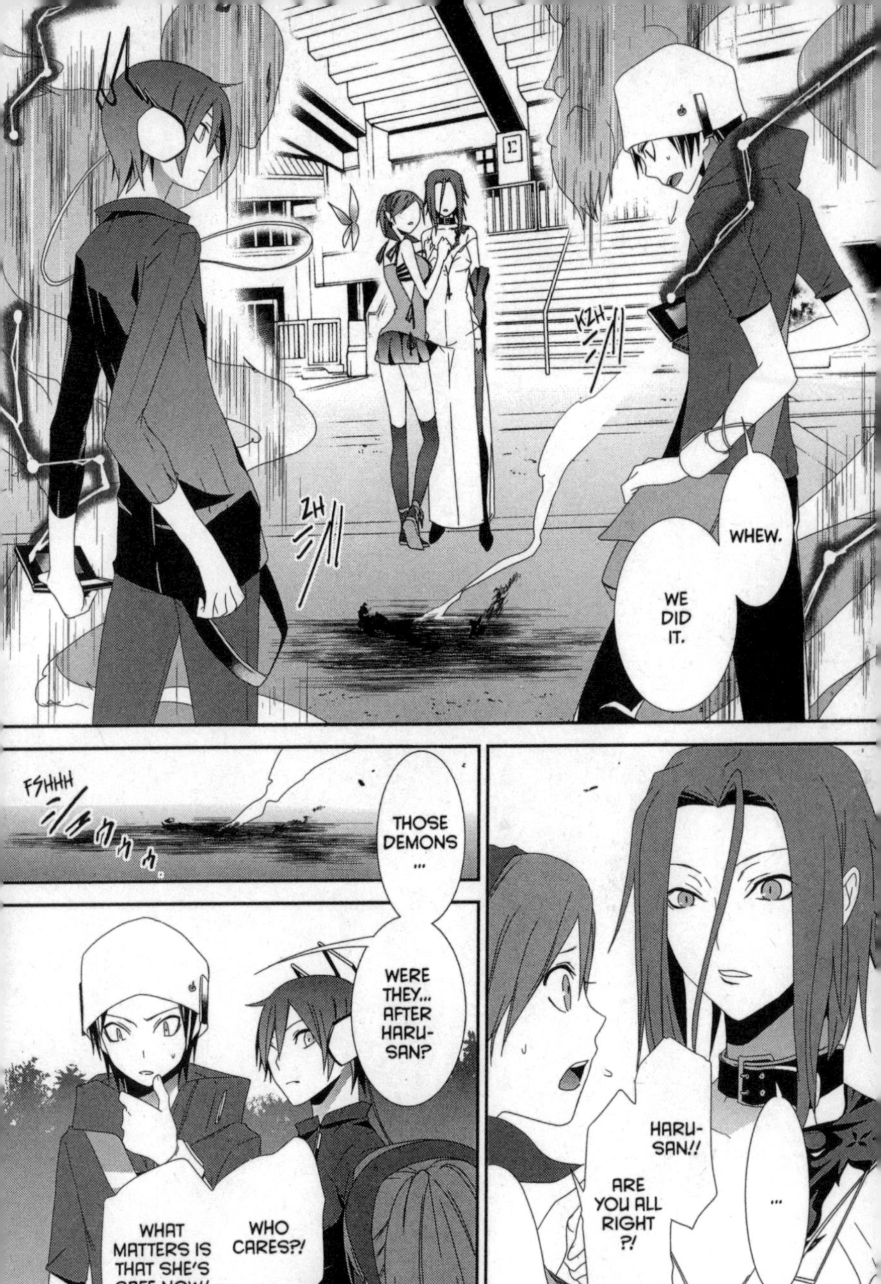
KZH
ZH
WHEW.
WE DID IT.
HARU-SAN!!
ARE YOU ALL RIGHT?!
...
FSHHH
THOSE DEMONS...
WERE THEY... AFTER HARU-SAN?
WHO CARES?!
WHAT MATTERS IS THAT SHE'S SAFE NOW!

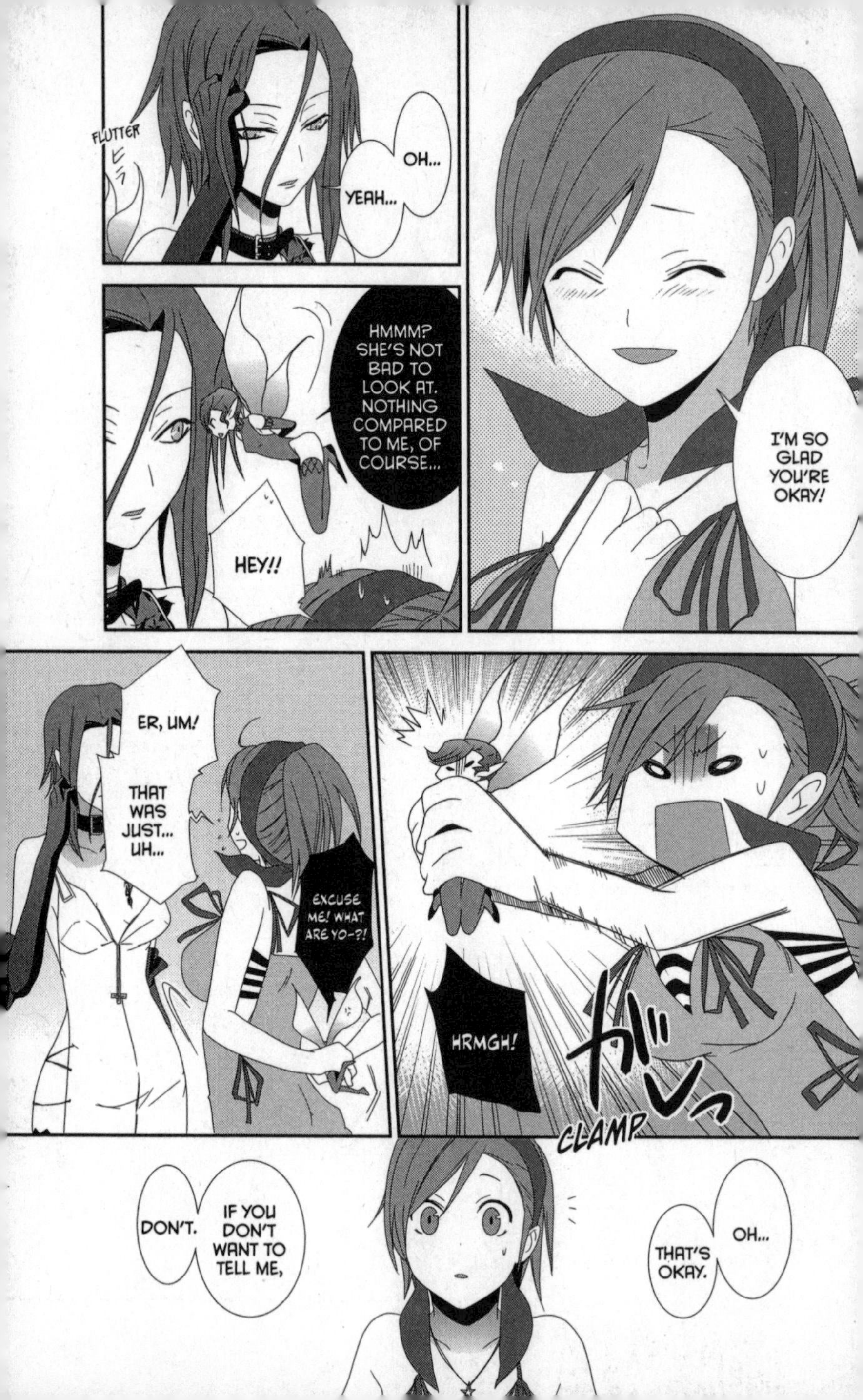
I'M SO GLAD YOU'RE OKAY!
FLUTTER
ヒラ
OH... YEAH...
HMMM? SHE'S NOT BAD TO LOOK AT. NOTHING COMPARED TO ME, OF COURSE...
HEY!!
HRMGH!
がしっ
CLAMP
ER, UM!
THAT WAS JUST... UH...
EXCUSE ME! WHAT ARE YO-?!
OH... THAT'S OKAY.
IF YOU DON'T WANT TO TELL ME,
DON'T.

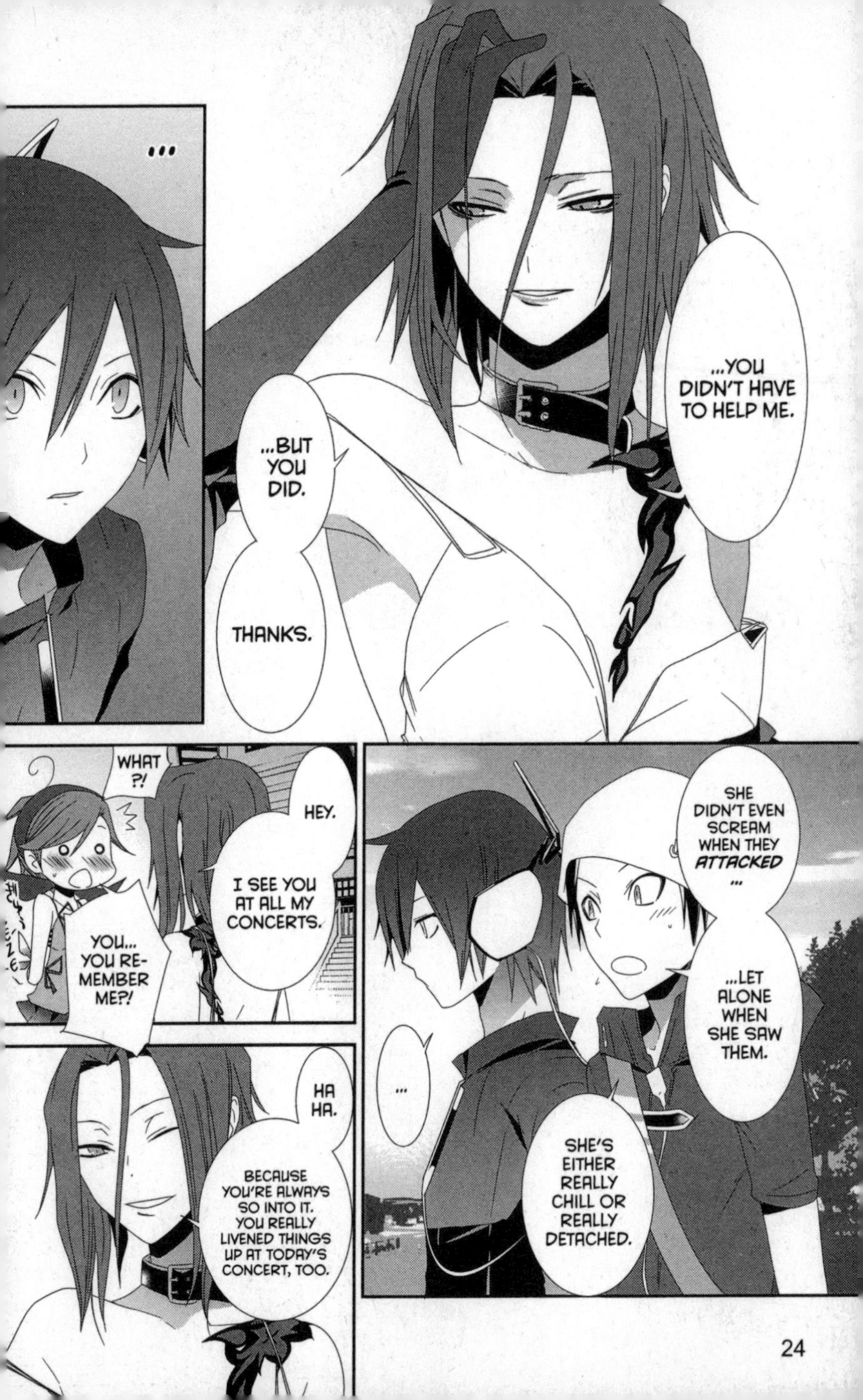
...YOU DIDN'T HAVE TO HELP ME.
...BUT YOU DID.
THANKS.
...
SHE DIDN'T EVEN SCREAM WHEN THEY *ATTACKED* ...
...LET ALONE WHEN SHE SAW THEM.
...
SHE'S EITHER REALLY CHILL OR REALLY DETACHED.
HEY.
I SEE YOU AT ALL MY CONCERTS.
WHAT?!
YOU... YOU RE-MEMBER ME?!
HA HA.
BECAUSE YOU'RE ALWAYS SO INTO IT. YOU REALLY LIVENED THINGS UP AT TODAY'S CONCERT, TOO.

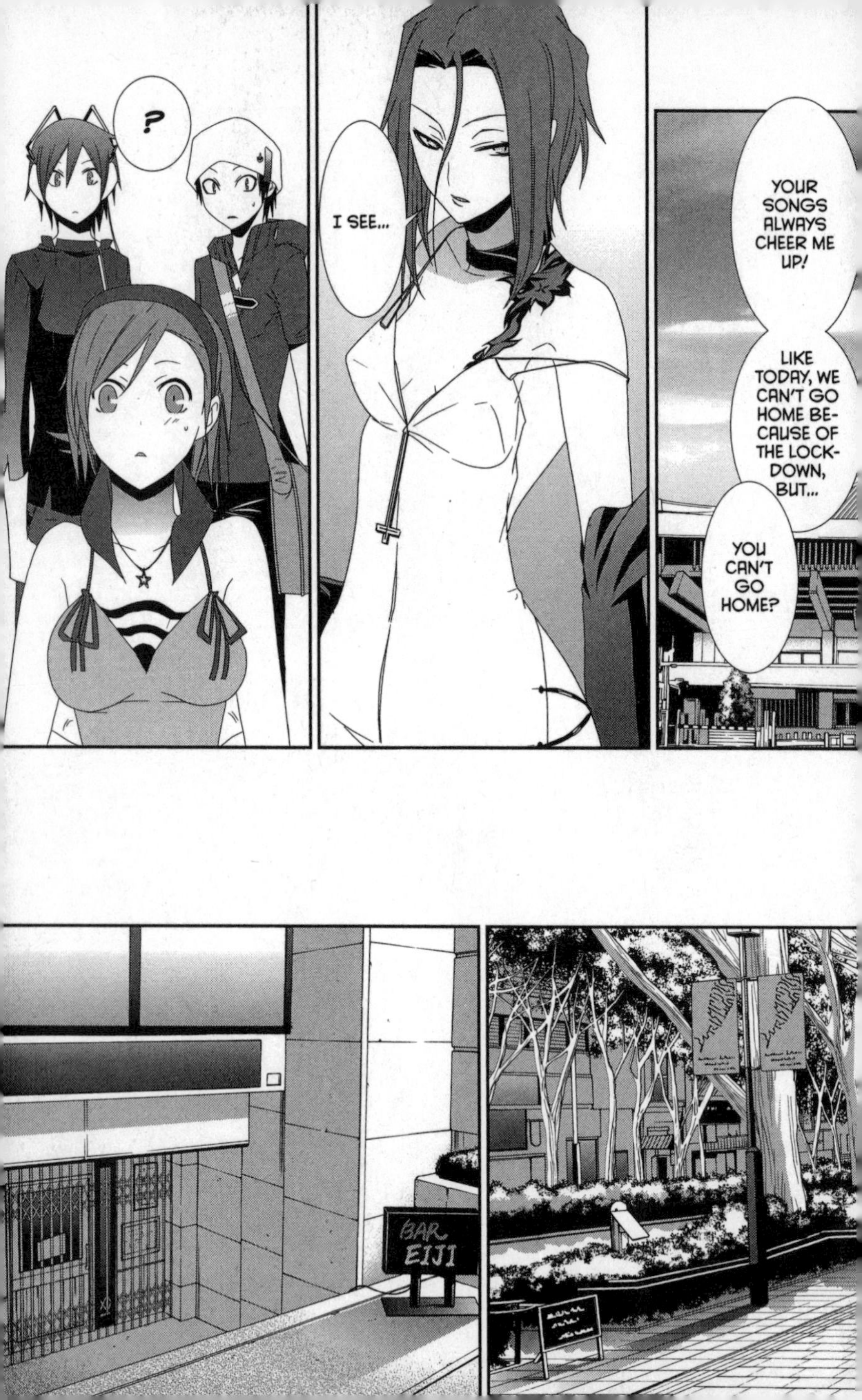
YOUR SONGS ALWAYS CHEER ME UP!
LIKE TODAY, WE CAN'T GO HOME BE-CAUSE OF THE LOCK-DOWN, BUT...
YOU CAN'T GO HOME?
I SEE...
?
BAR EIJI

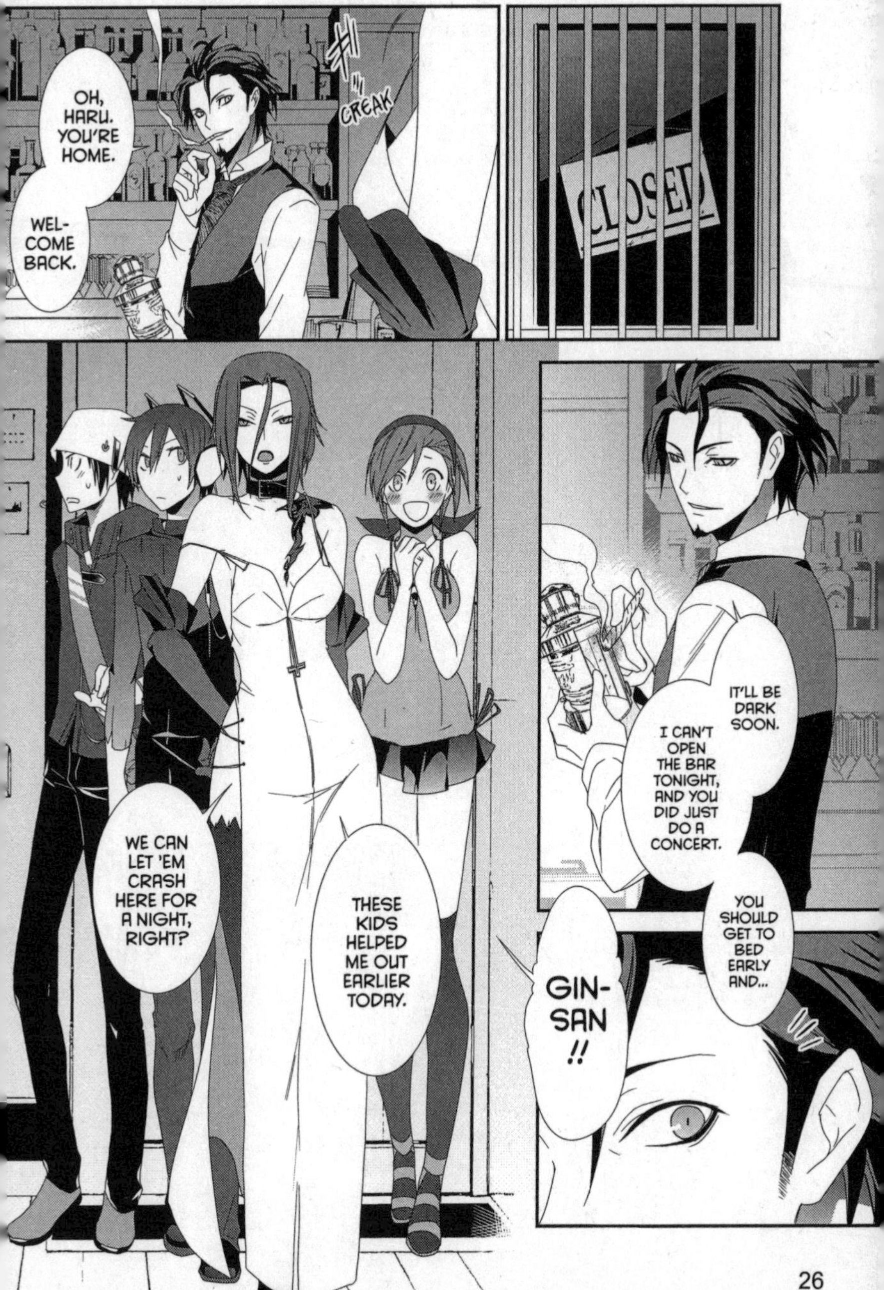
CLOSED
CREAK
OH, HARU. YOU'RE HOME.
WEL-COME BACK.
IT'LL BE DARK SOON.
I CAN'T OPEN THE BAR TONIGHT, AND YOU DID JUST DO A CONCERT.
YOU SHOULD GET TO BED EARLY AND...
GIN-SAN!!
THESE KIDS HELPED ME OUT EARLIER TODAY.
WE CAN LET 'EM CRASH HERE FOR A NIGHT, RIGHT?

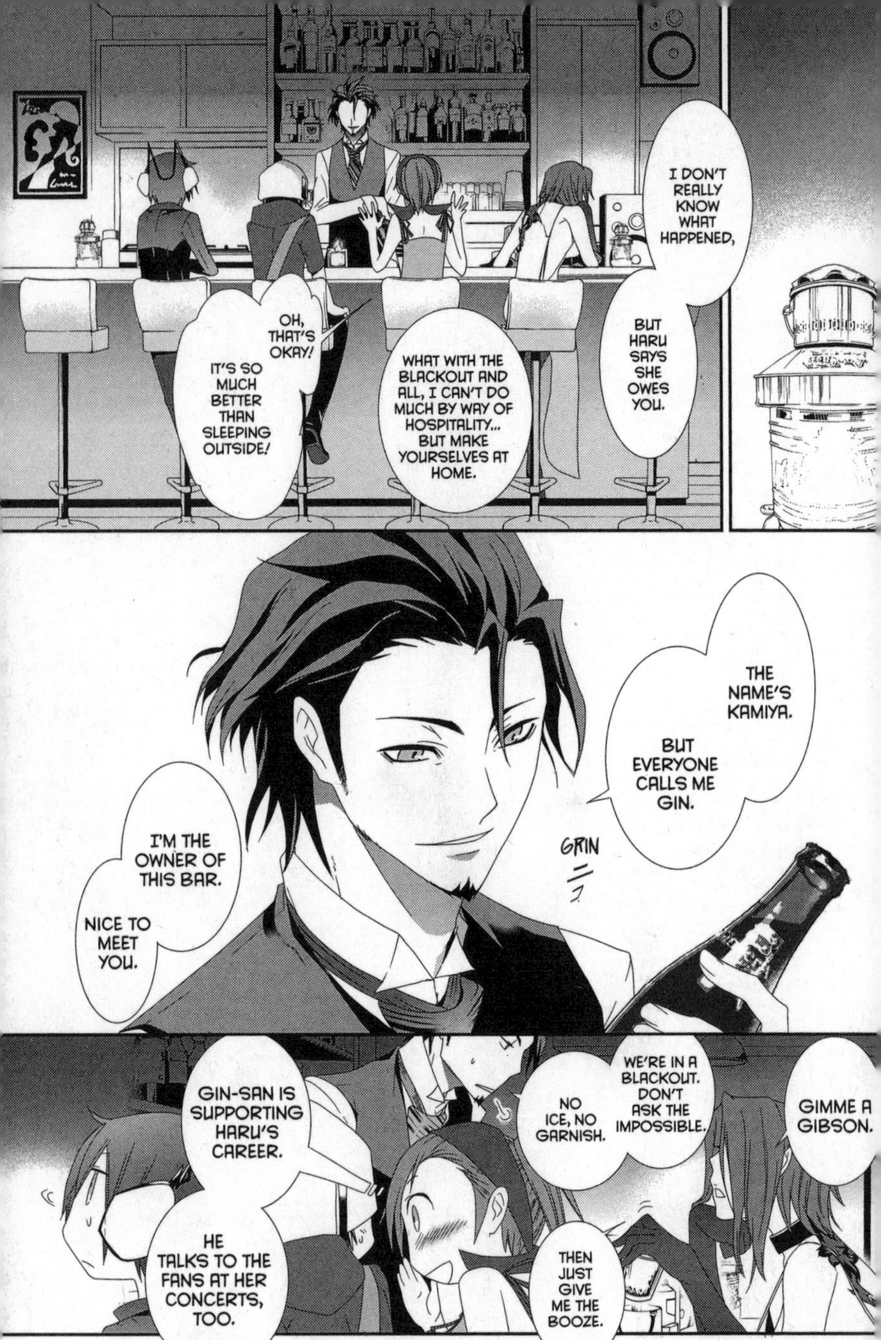
I DON'T REALLY KNOW WHAT HAPPENED,
BUT HARU SAYS SHE OWES YOU.
WHAT WITH THE BLACKOUT AND ALL, I CAN'T DO MUCH BY WAY OF HOSPITALITY... BUT MAKE YOURSELVES AT HOME.
OH, THAT'S OKAY!
IT'S SO MUCH BETTER THAN SLEEPING OUTSIDE!
THE NAME'S KAMIYA.
BUT EVERYONE CALLS ME GIN.
GRIN
I'M THE OWNER OF THIS BAR.
NICE TO MEET YOU.
GIMME A GIBSON.
WE'RE IN A BLACKOUT. DON'T ASK THE IMPOSSIBLE.
NO ICE, NO GARNISH.
THEN JUST GIVE ME THE BOOZE.
GIN-SAN IS SUPPORTING HARU'S CAREER.
HE TALKS TO THE FANS AT HER CONCERTS, TOO.

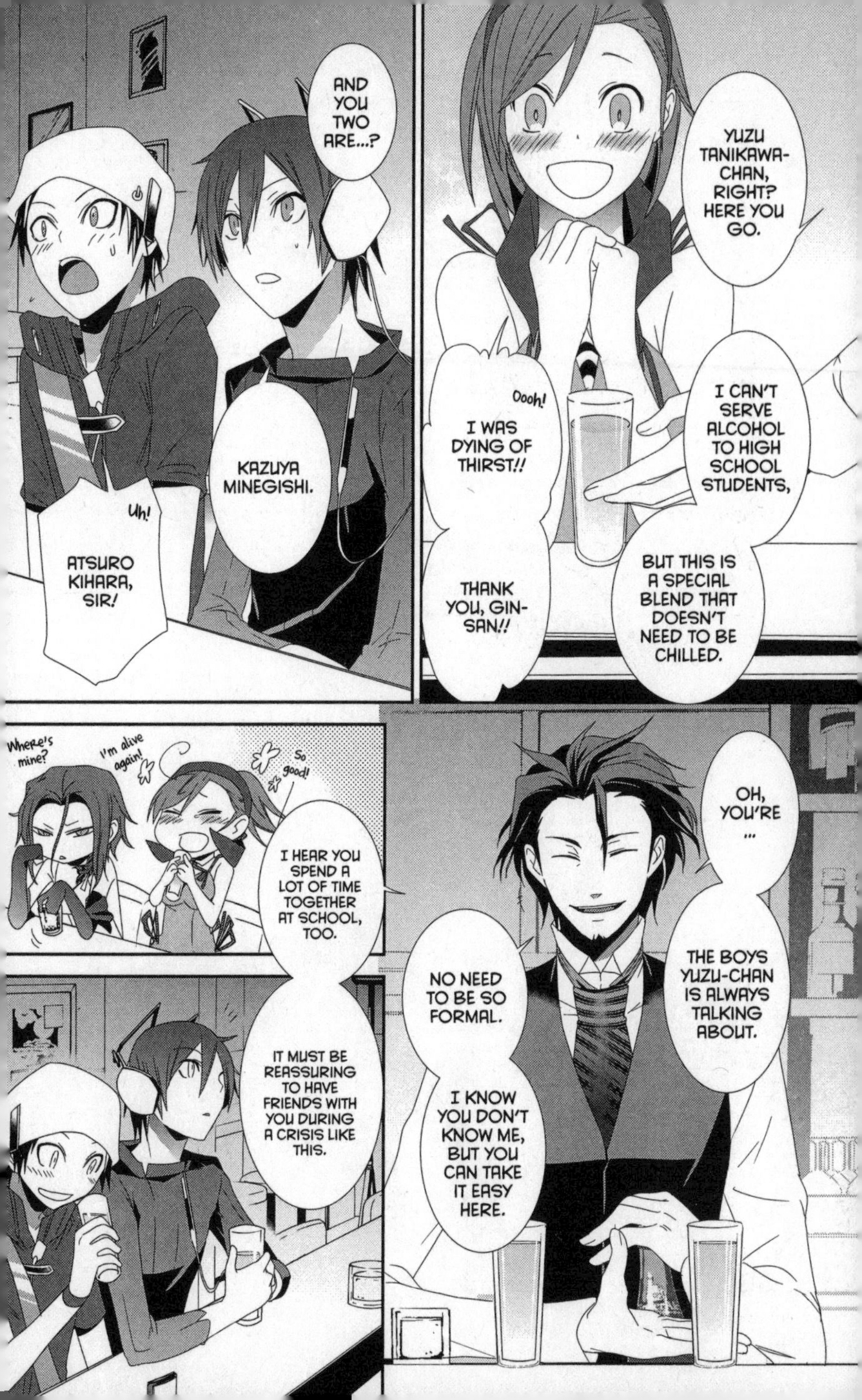
YUZU TANIKAWA-CHAN, RIGHT? HERE YOU GO.
I CAN'T SERVE ALCOHOL TO HIGH SCHOOL STUDENTS,
BUT THIS IS A SPECIAL BLEND THAT DOESN'T NEED TO BE CHILLED.
Oooh!
I WAS DYING OF THIRST!!
THANK YOU, GIN-SAN!!
AND YOU TWO ARE...?
KAZUYA MINEGISHI.
Uh!
ATSURO KIHARA, SIR!
OH, YOU'RE ...
THE BOYS YUZU-CHAN IS ALWAYS TALKING ABOUT.
NO NEED TO BE SO FORMAL.
I KNOW YOU DON'T KNOW ME, BUT YOU CAN TAKE IT EASY HERE.
So good!
I'm alive again!
Where's mine?
I HEAR YOU SPEND A LOT OF TIME TOGETHER AT SCHOOL, TOO.
IT MUST BE REASSURING TO HAVE FRIENDS WITH YOU DURING A CRISIS LIKE THIS.

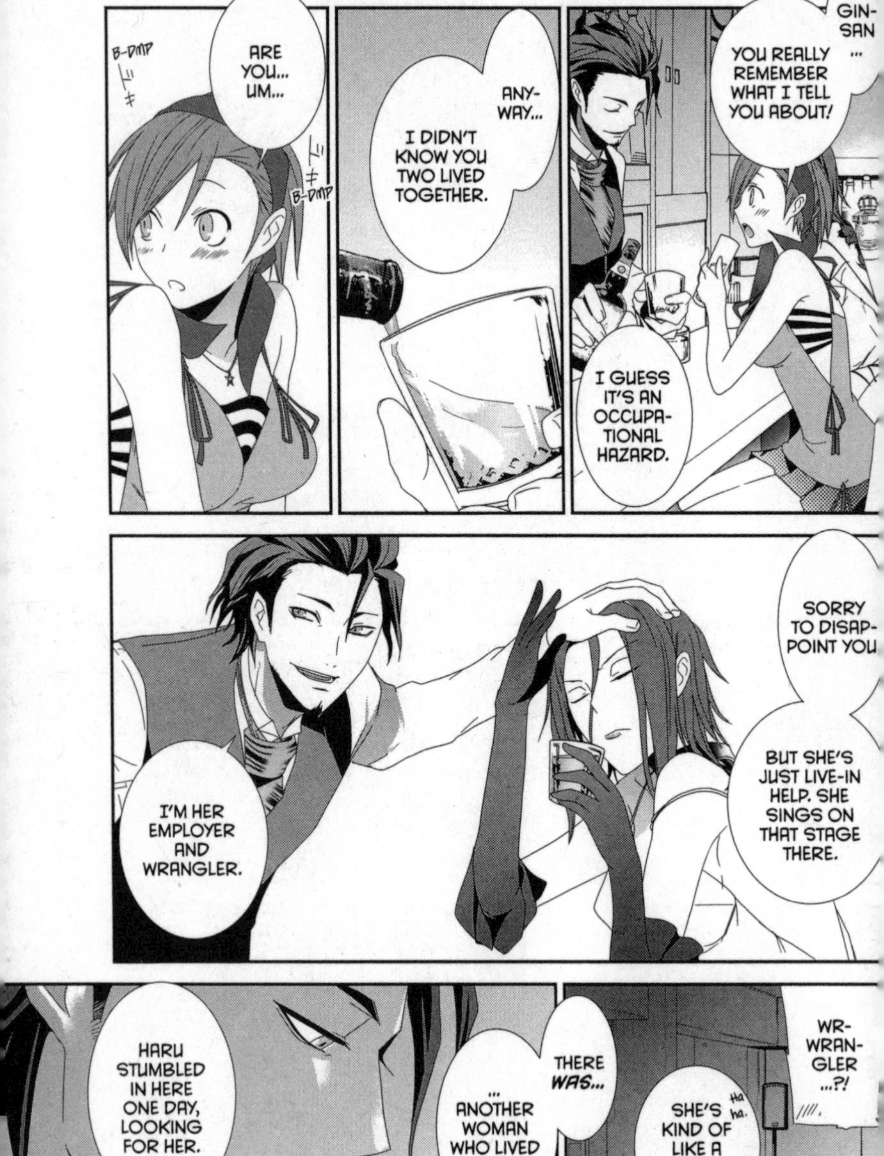
GIN-SAN...
YOU REALLY REMEMBER WHAT I TELL YOU ABOUT!
I GUESS IT'S AN OCCUPATIONAL HAZARD.
ANYWAY...
I DIDN'T KNOW YOU TWO LIVED TOGETHER.
ARE YOU... UM...
B-DMP
B-DMP
SORRY TO DISAPPOINT YOU
BUT SHE'S JUST LIVE-IN HELP. SHE SINGS ON THAT STAGE THERE.
I'M HER EMPLOYER AND WRANGLER.
WR-WRANGLER...?!
SHE'S KIND OF LIKE A STRAY CAT.
Ha ha.
THERE *WAS*...
...ANOTHER WOMAN WHO LIVED HERE.
HARU STUMBLED IN HERE ONE DAY, LOOKING FOR HER.

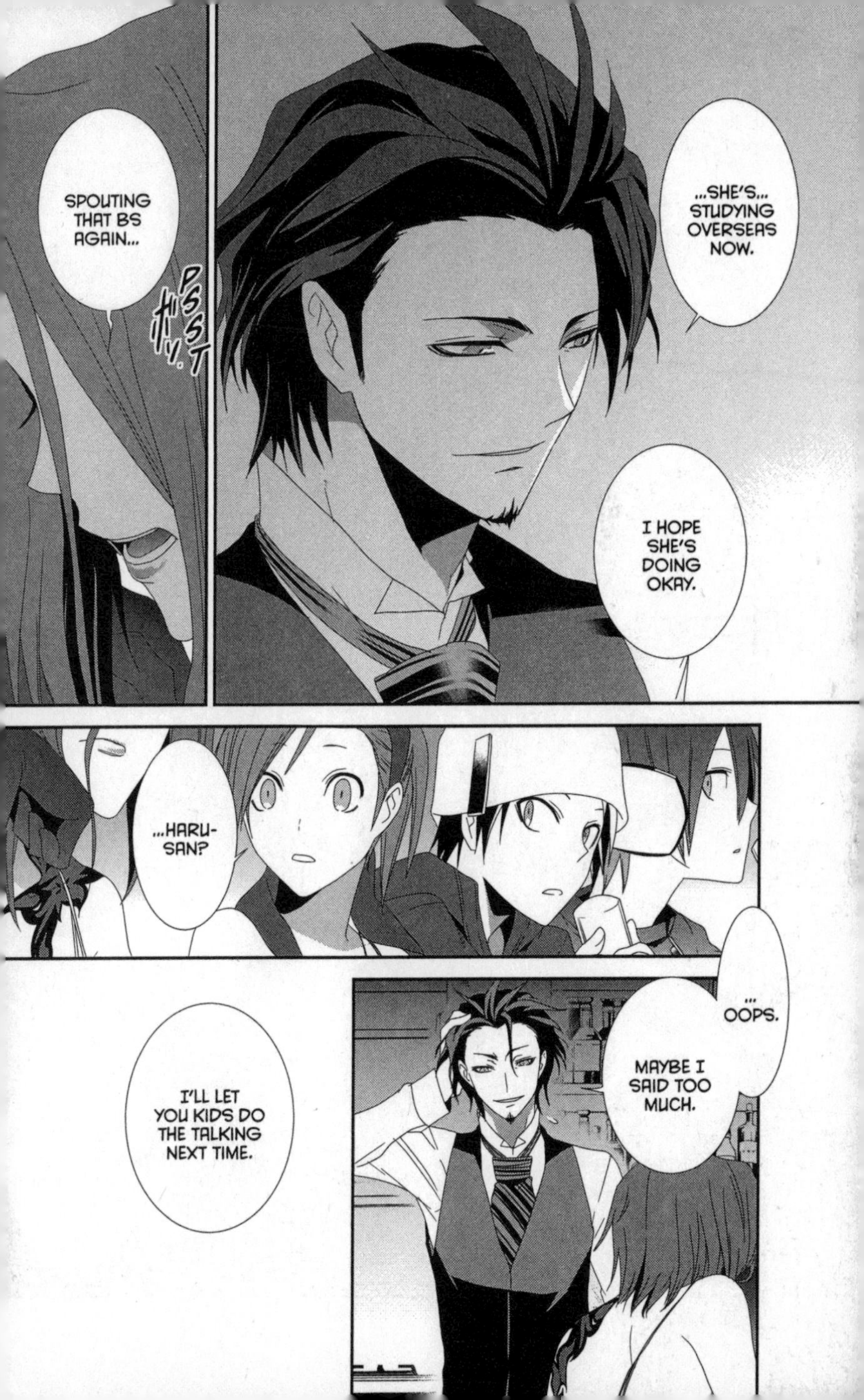
...SHE'S... STUDYING OVERSEAS NOW.
I HOPE SHE'S DOING OKAY.
SPOUTING THAT BS AGAIN...
PSST ボソッ
...HARU-SAN?
... OOPS.
MAYBE I SAID TOO MUCH.
I'LL LET YOU KIDS DO THE TALKING NEXT TIME.

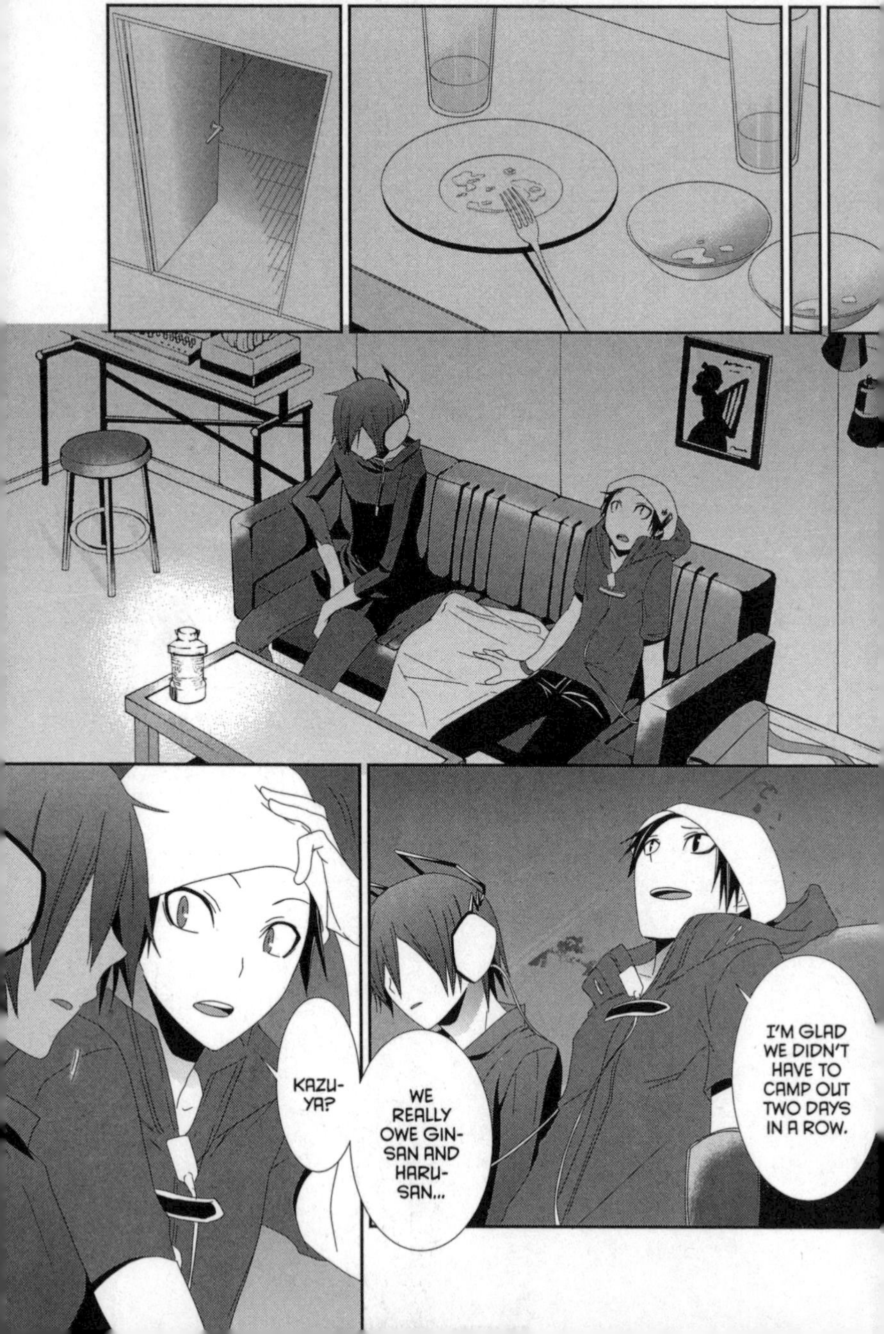
I'M GLAD WE DIDN'T HAVE TO CAMP OUT TWO DAYS IN A ROW.
WE REALLY OWE GIN-SAN AND HARU-SAN...
KAZU-YA?

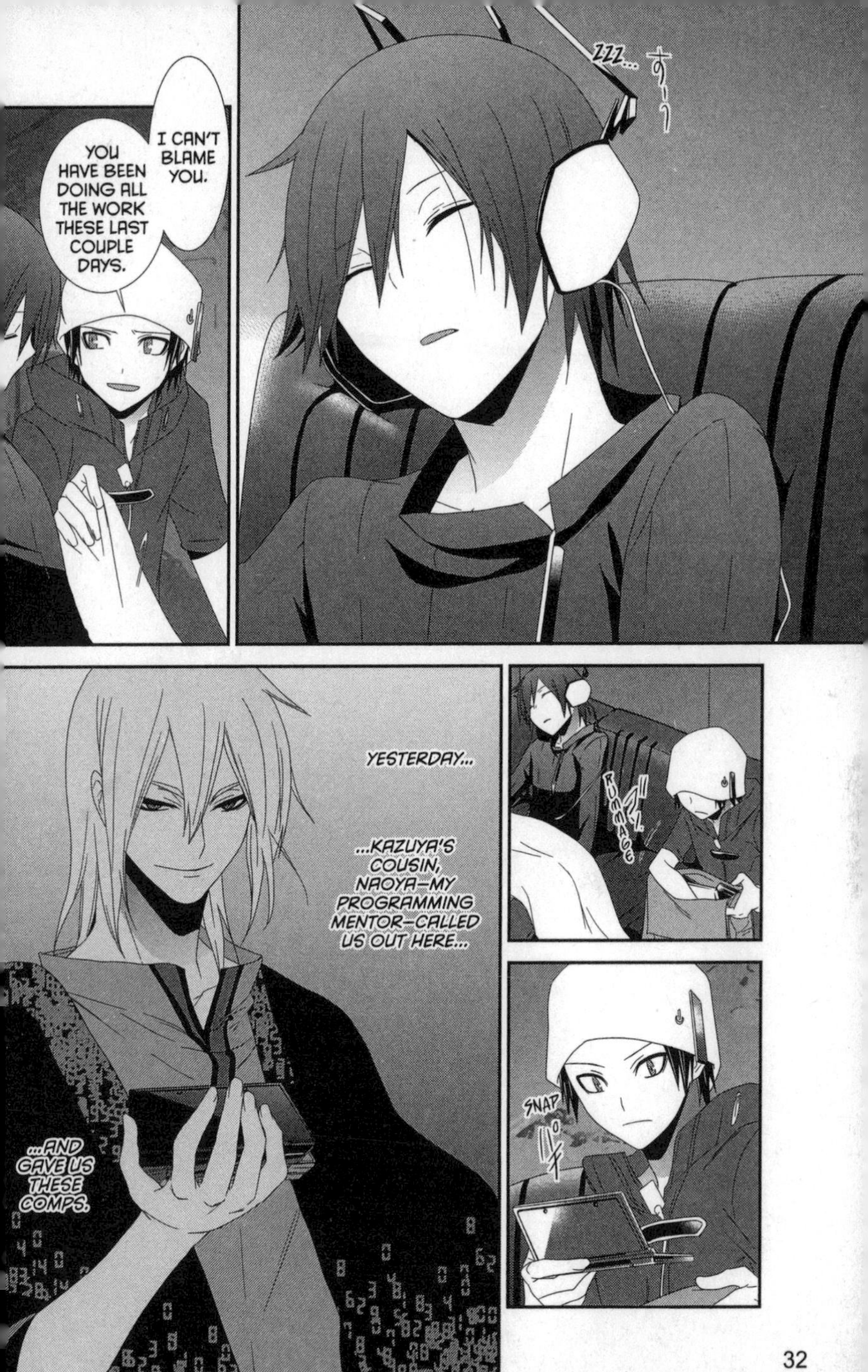
ZZZ...
I CAN'T BLAME YOU.
YOU HAVE BEEN DOING ALL THE WORK THESE LAST COUPLE DAYS.
RUMMAGE
SNAP
YESTERDAY...
...KAZUYA'S COUSIN, NAOYA—MY PROGRAMMING MENTOR—CALLED US OUT HERE...
...AND GAVE US THESE COMPS.

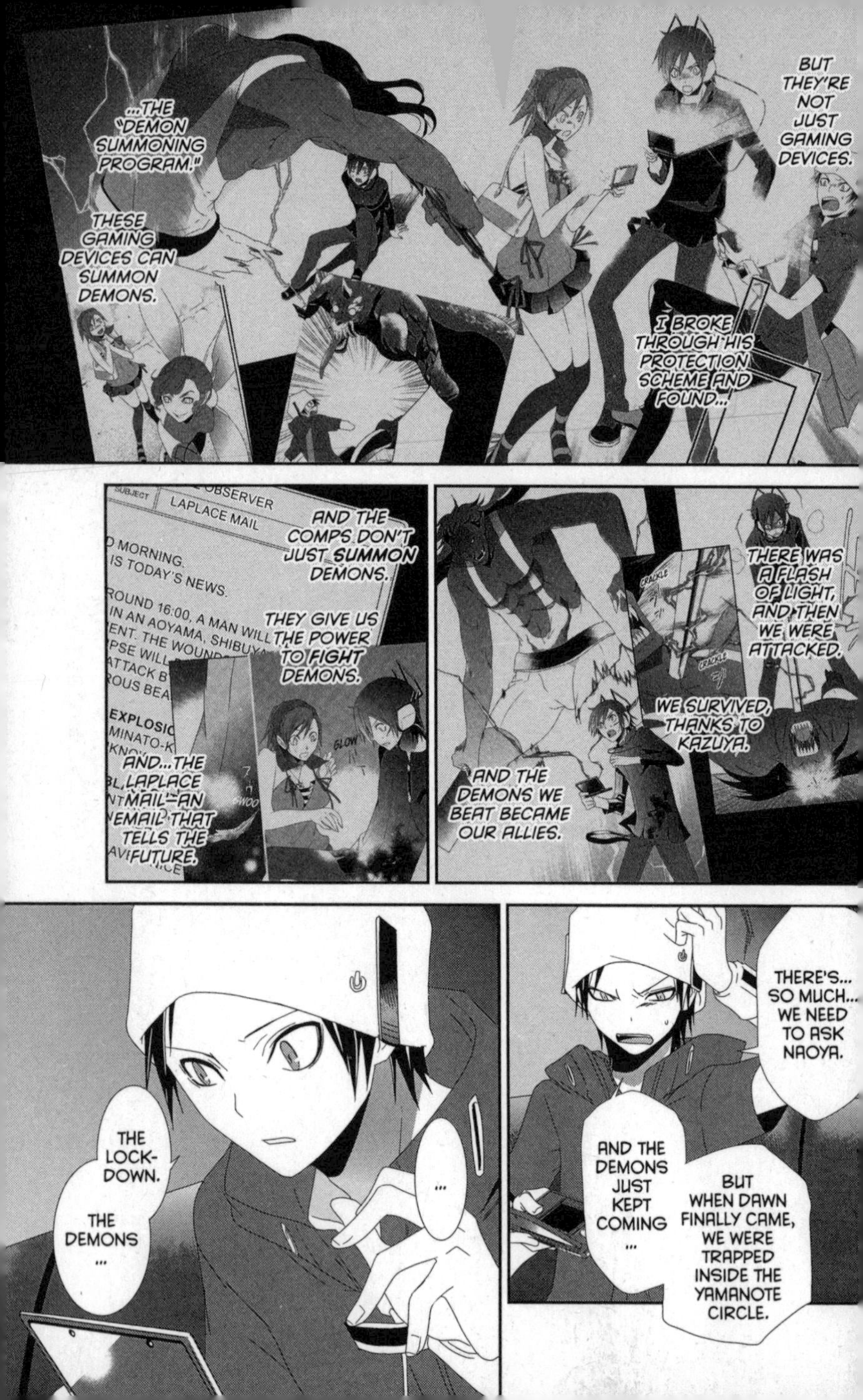
BUT THEY'RE NOT JUST GAMING DEVICES.
I BROKE THROUGH HIS PROTECTION SCHEME AND FOUND...
...THE "DEMON SUMMONING PROGRAM."
THESE GAMING DEVICES CAN SUMMON DEMONS.
THERE WAS A FLASH OF LIGHT, AND THEN WE WERE ATTACKED.
CRACKLE
CRACKLE
WE SURVIVED, THANKS TO KAZUYA.
AND THE DEMONS WE BEAT BECAME OUR ALLIES.
SUBJECT
OBSERVER
LAPLACE MAIL
AND THE COMPS DON'T JUST SUMMON DEMONS.
IS TODAY'S NEWS.
THEY GIVE US THE POWER TO FIGHT DEMONS.
GLOW
AND...THE LAPLACE MAIL—AN EMAIL THAT TELLS THE FUTURE.
THERE'S... SO MUCH... WE NEED TO ASK NAOYA.
AND THE DEMONS JUST KEPT COMING...
BUT WHEN DAWN FINALLY CAME, WE WERE TRAPPED INSIDE THE YAMANOTE CIRCLE.
...
THE LOCK-DOWN.
THE DEMONS...

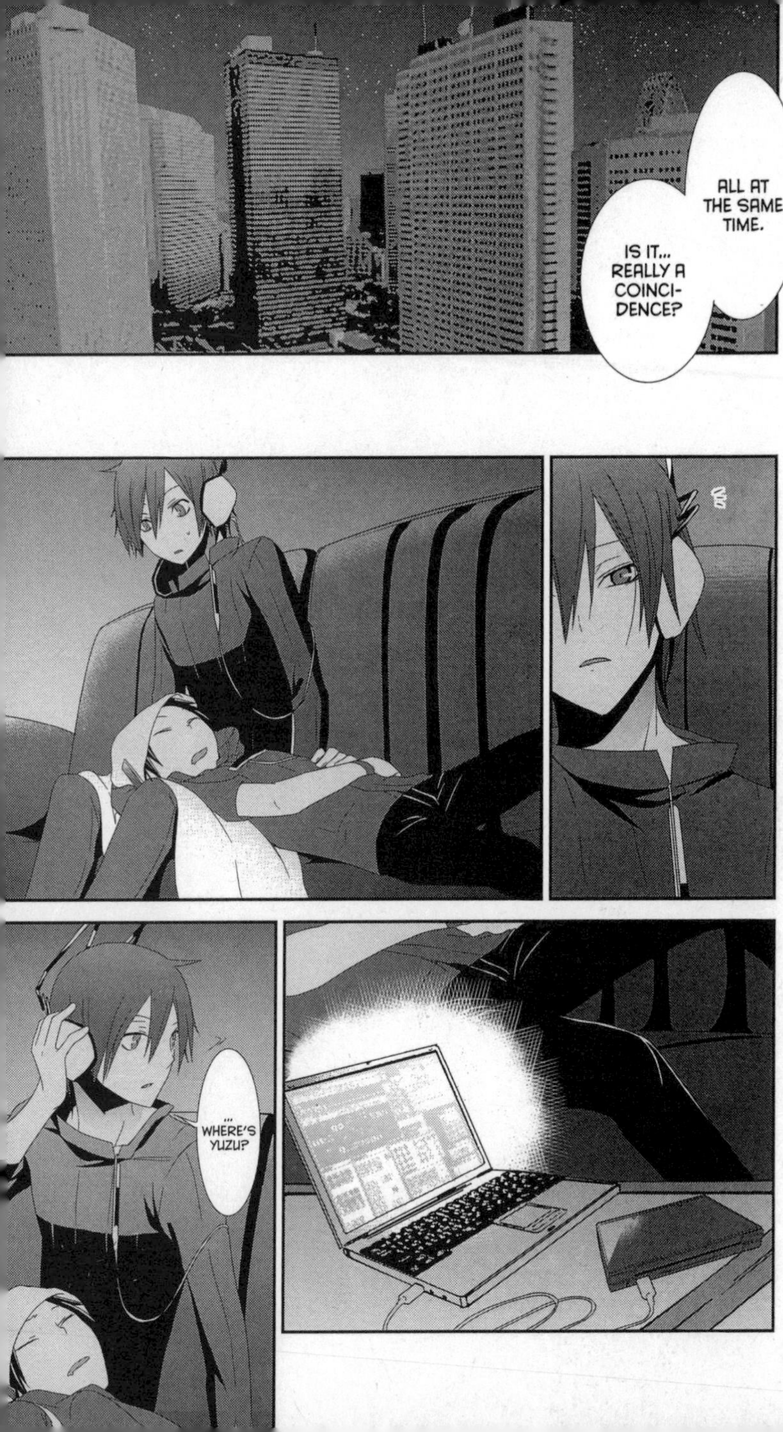
ALL AT THE SAME TIME.
IS IT... REALLY A COINCIDENCE?
... WHERE'S YUZU?

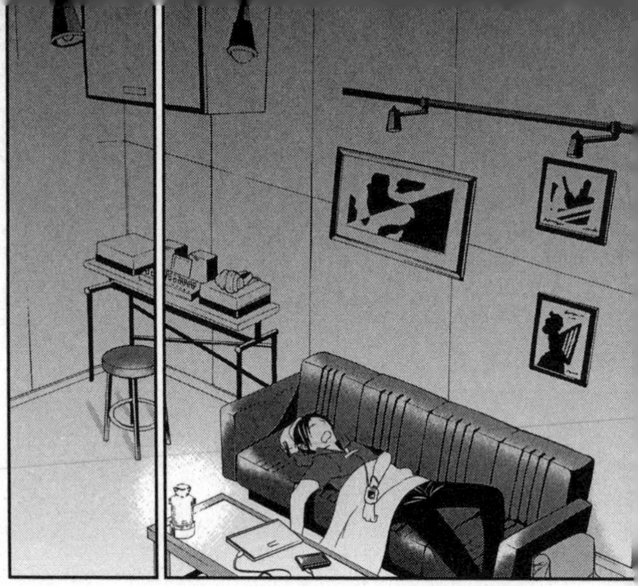

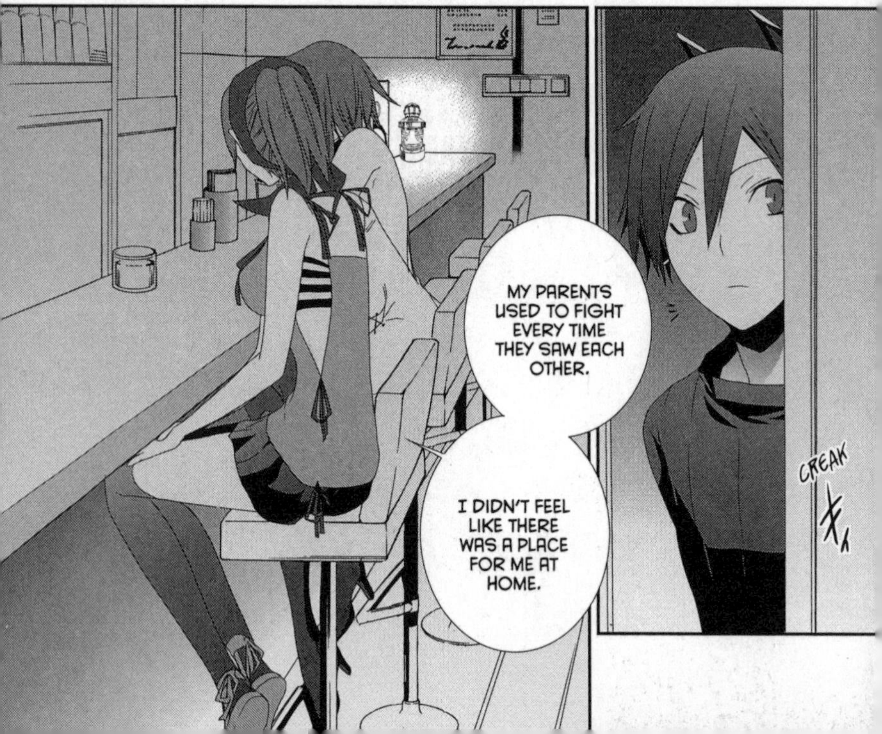
CREAK
MY PARENTS USED TO FIGHT EVERY TIME THEY SAW EACH OTHER.
I DIDN'T FEEL LIKE THERE WAS A PLACE FOR ME AT HOME.

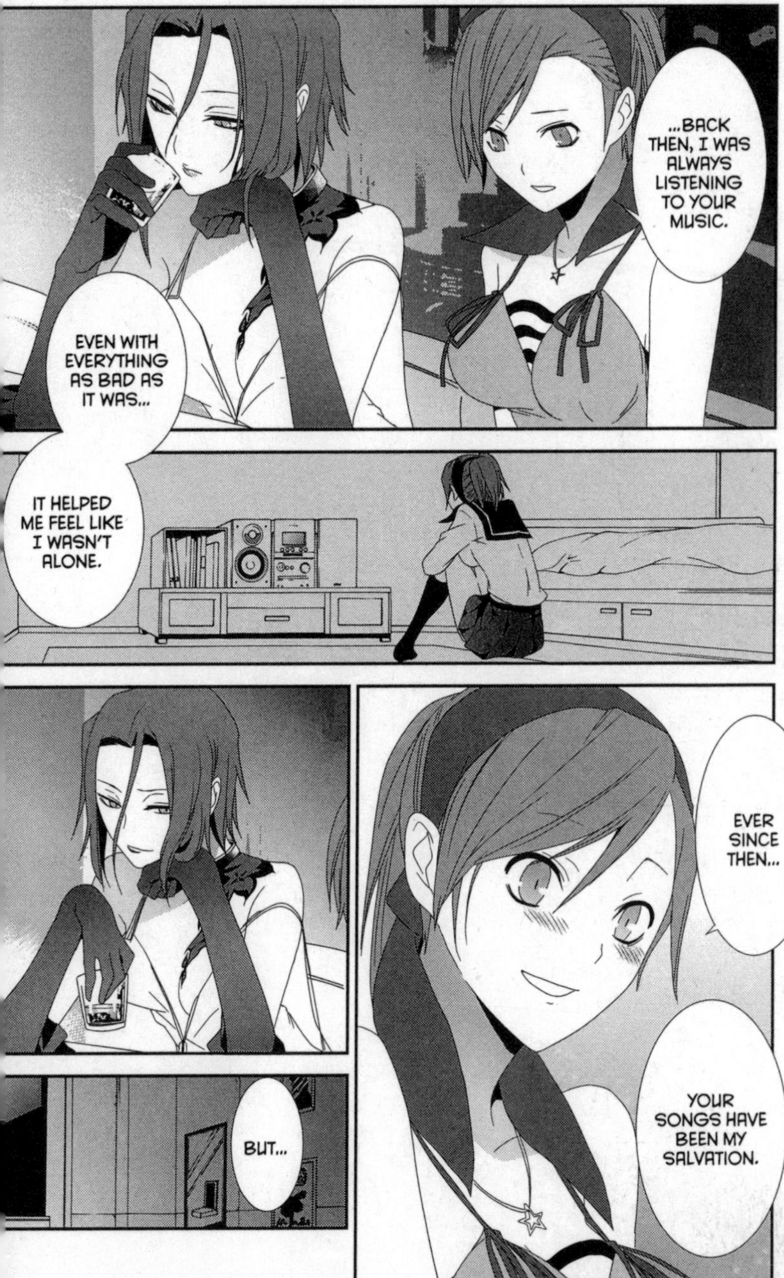
...BACK THEN, I WAS ALWAYS LISTENING TO YOUR MUSIC.
EVEN WITH EVERYTHING AS BAD AS IT WAS...
IT HELPED ME FEEL LIKE I WASN'T ALONE.
EVER SINCE THEN...
YOUR SONGS HAVE BEEN MY SALVATION.
BUT...

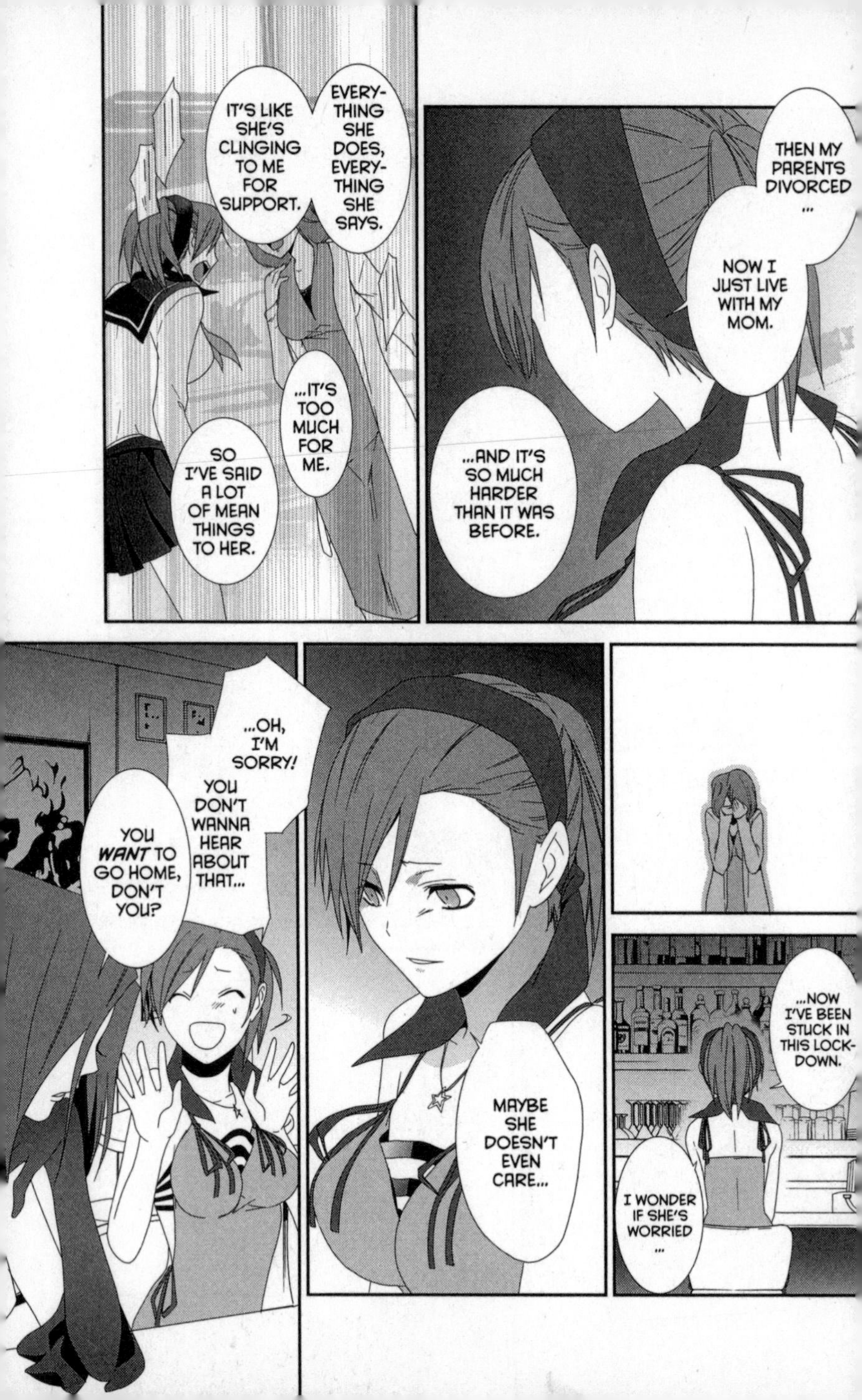
THEN MY PARENTS DIVORCED ...
NOW I JUST LIVE WITH MY MOM.
...AND IT'S SO MUCH HARDER THAN IT WAS BEFORE.
EVERY-THING SHE DOES, EVERY-THING SHE SAYS.
IT'S LIKE SHE'S CLINGING TO ME FOR SUPPORT.
...IT'S TOO MUCH FOR ME.
SO I'VE SAID A LOT OF MEAN THINGS TO HER.
...NOW I'VE BEEN STUCK IN THIS LOCK-DOWN.
I WONDER IF SHE'S WORRIED ...
MAYBE SHE DOESN'T EVEN CARE...
...OH, I'M SORRY!
YOU DON'T WANNA HEAR ABOUT THAT...
YOU *WANT* TO GO HOME, DON'T YOU?

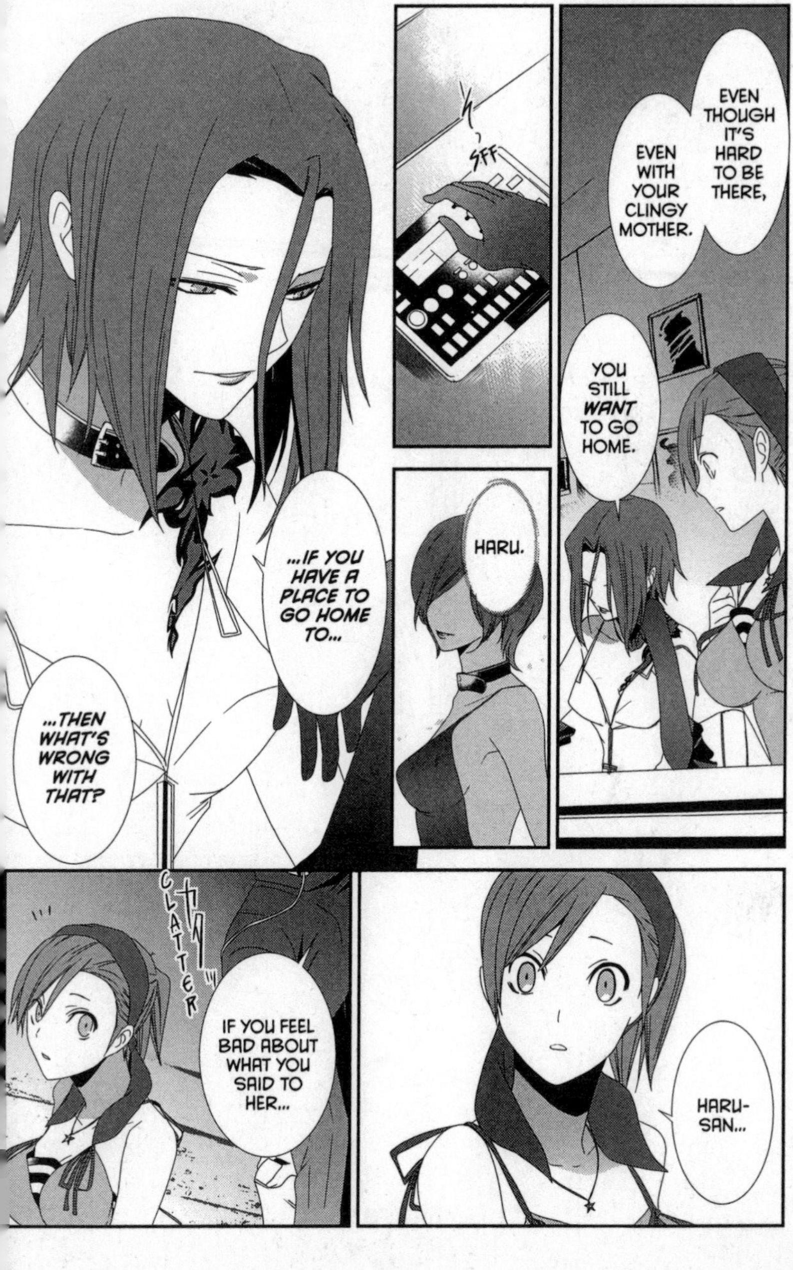
EVEN THOUGH IT'S HARD TO BE THERE,
EVEN WITH YOUR CLINGY MOTHER.
YOU STILL *WANT* TO GO HOME.
SFF
HARU.
...IF YOU HAVE A PLACE TO GO HOME TO...
...THEN WHAT'S WRONG WITH THAT?
HARU-SAN...
CLATTER
IF YOU FEEL BAD ABOUT WHAT YOU SAID TO HER...

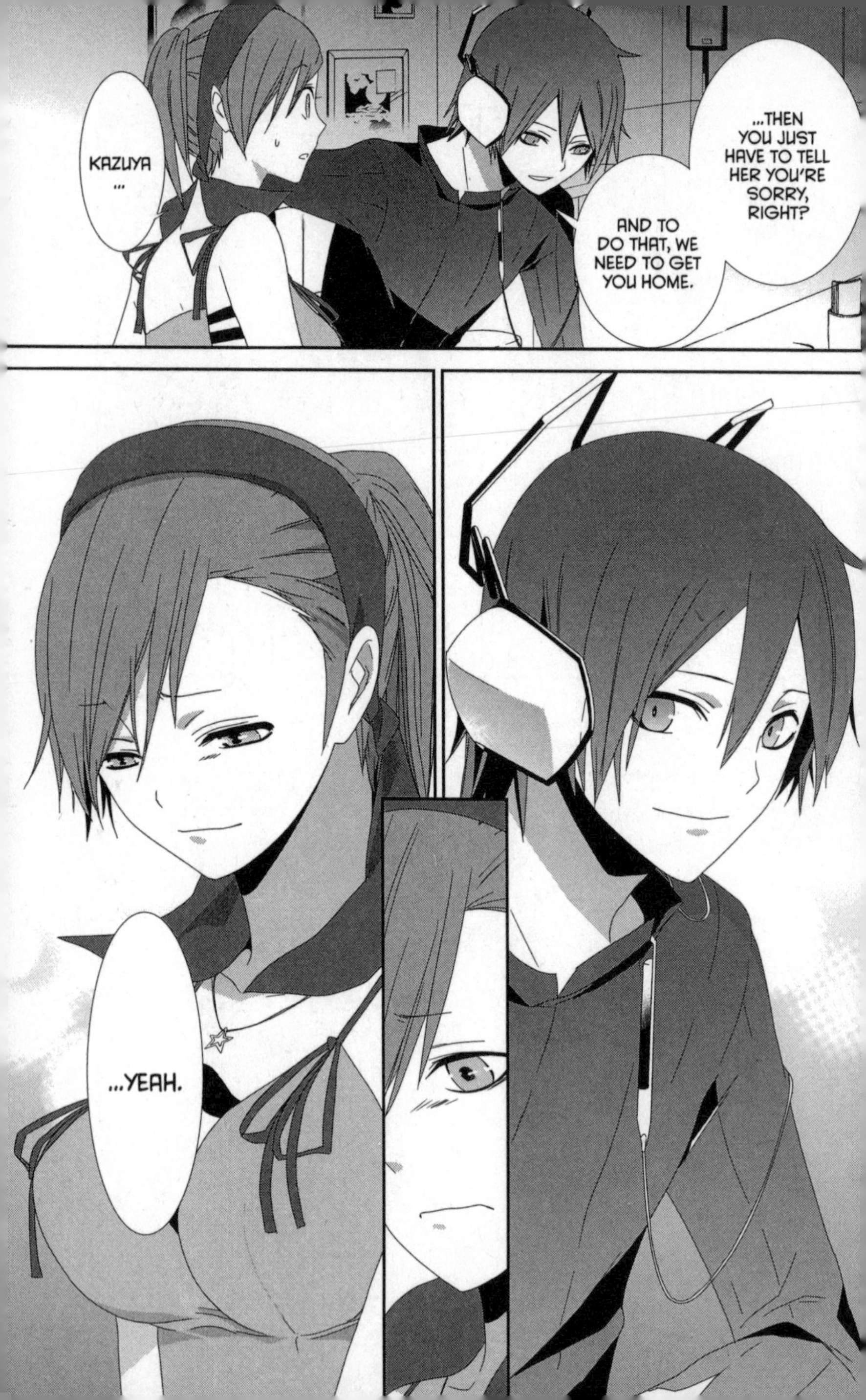
...THEN YOU JUST HAVE TO TELL HER YOU'RE SORRY, RIGHT?
AND TO DO THAT, WE NEED TO GET YOU HOME.
KAZUYA ...
...YEAH.

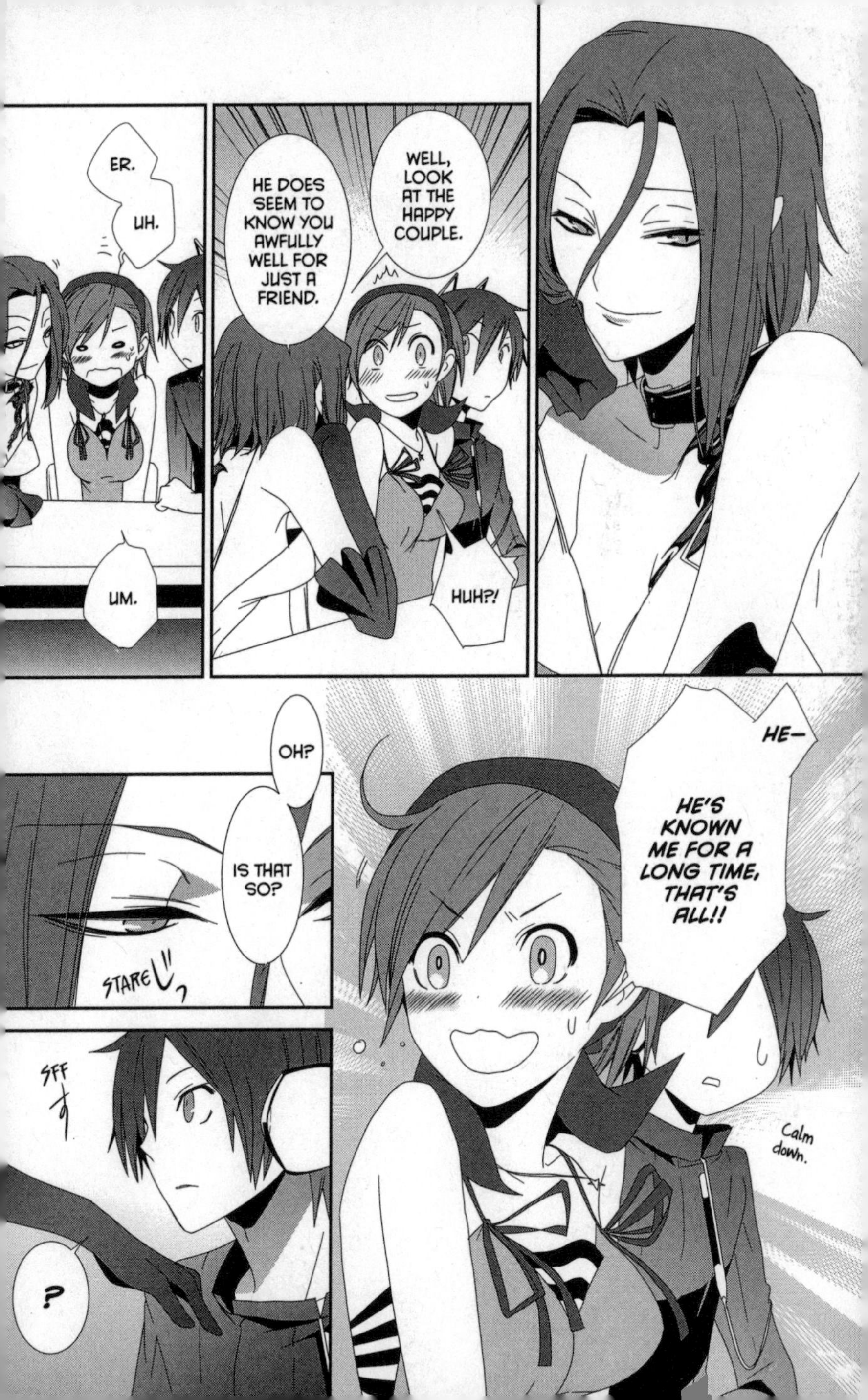

WELL, LOOK AT THE HAPPY COUPLE.
HE DOES SEEM TO KNOW YOU AWFULLY WELL FOR JUST A FRIEND.
HUH?!
ER.
UH.
UM.
HE—
HE'S KNOWN ME FOR A LONG TIME, THAT'S ALL!!
Calm down.
OH?
IS THAT SO?
STARE
SFF
?

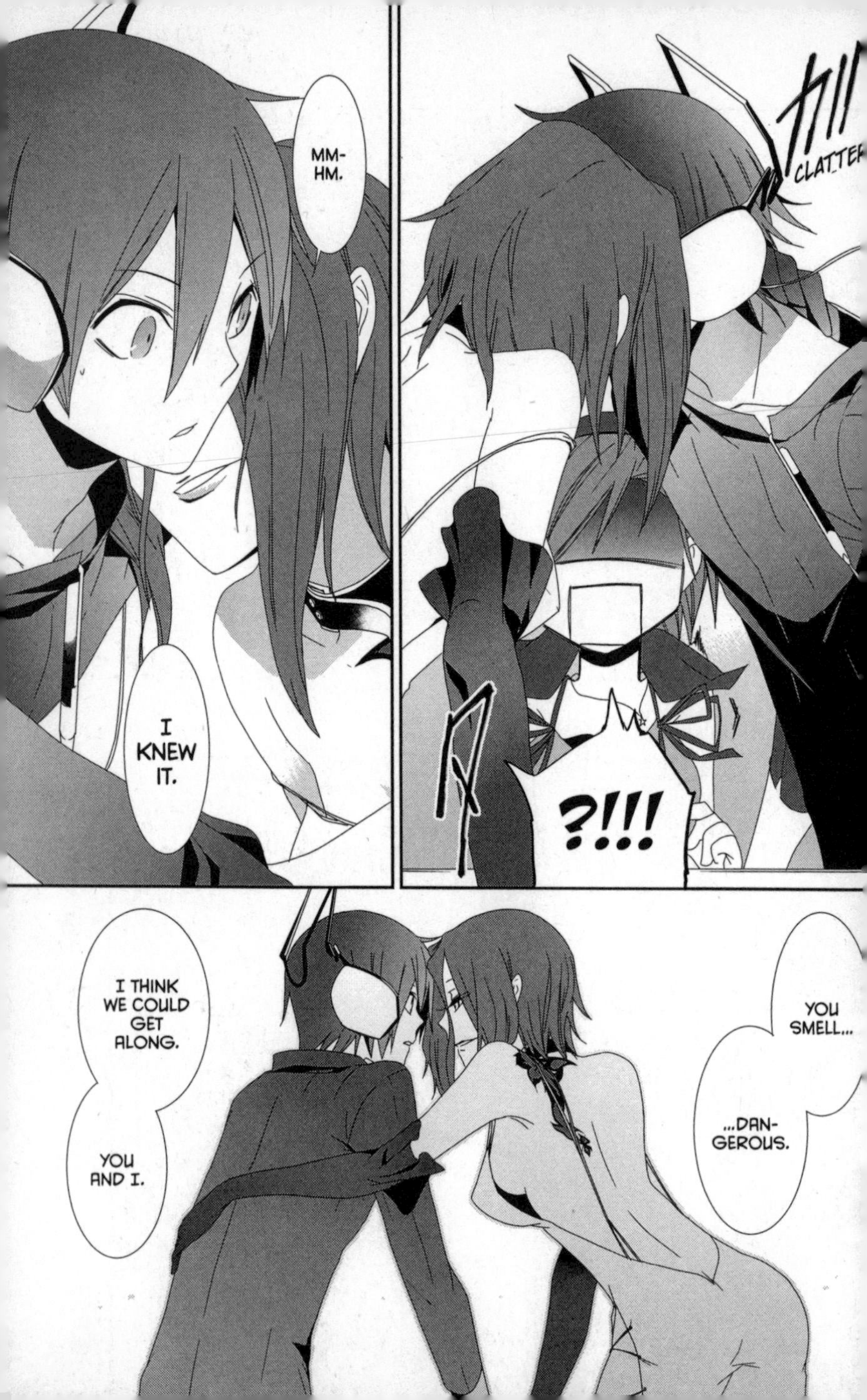
カリ
CLATTE
?!!!
MM-HM.
I KNEW IT.
YOU SMELL...
...DAN-GEROUS.
I THINK WE COULD GET ALONG.
YOU AND I.

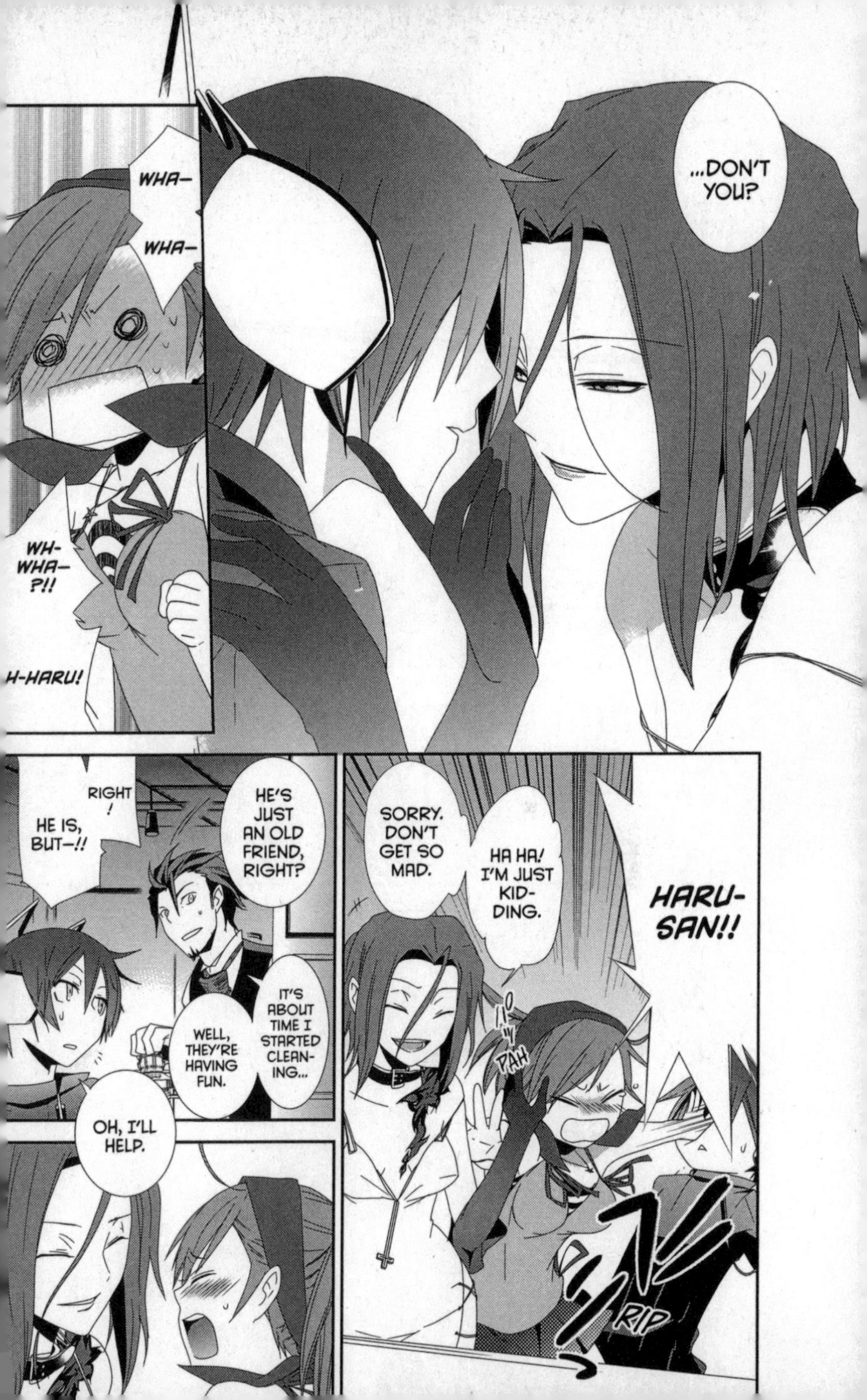
...DON'T YOU?
WHA-
WHA-
WH- WHA-?!!
H-HARU!
HARU-SAN!!
HA HA! I'M JUST KID-DING.
SORRY. DON'T GET SO MAD.
PAH
RIP
HE'S JUST AN OLD FRIEND, RIGHT?
RIGHT!
HE IS, BUT-!!
IT'S ABOUT TIME I STARTED CLEANING...
WELL, THEY'RE HAVING FUN.
OH, I'LL HELP.

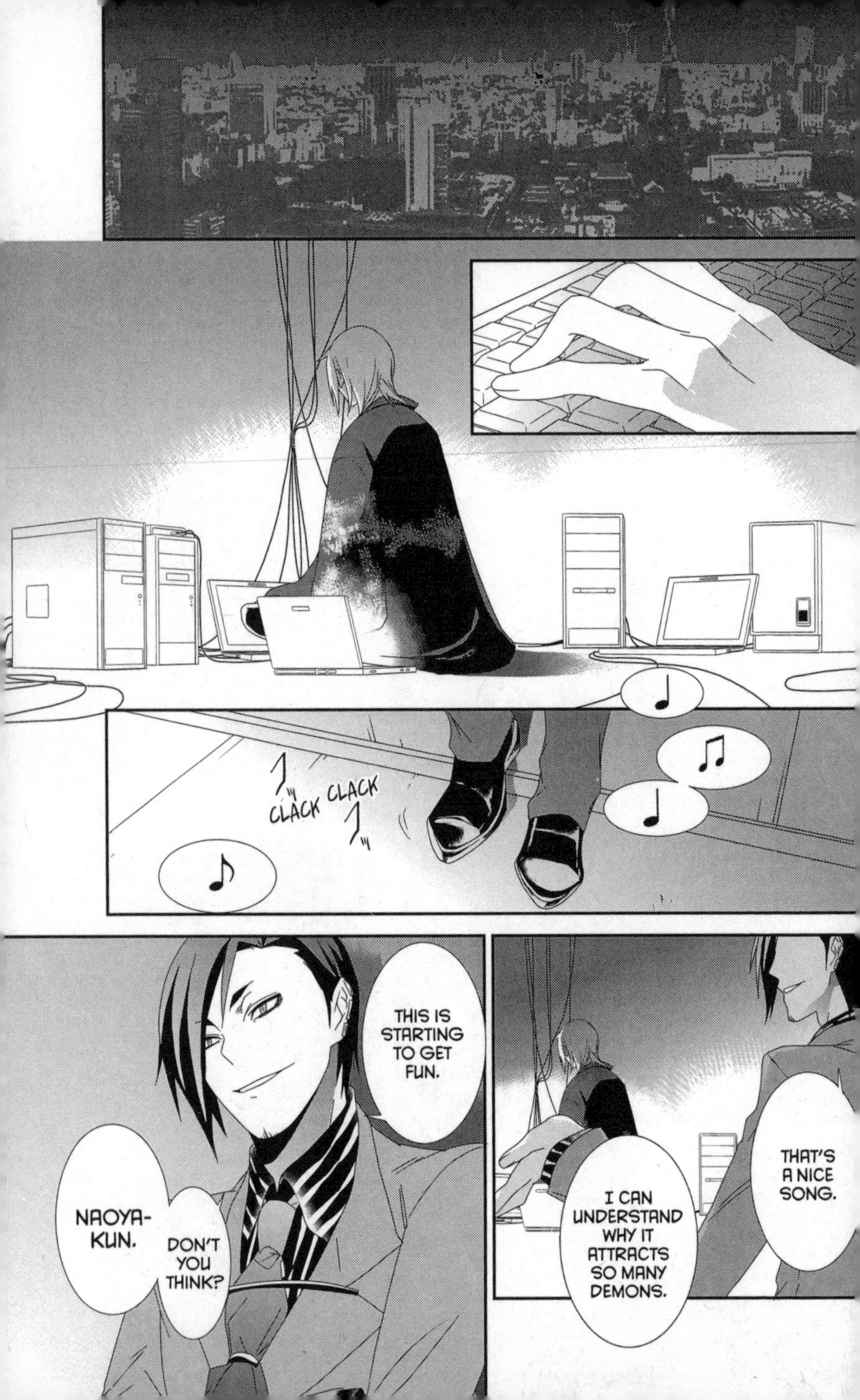
CLACK CLACK
THAT'S A NICE SONG.
I CAN UNDERSTAND WHY IT ATTRACTS SO MANY DEMONS.
THIS IS STARTING TO GET FUN.
NAOYA-KUN.
DON'T YOU THINK?

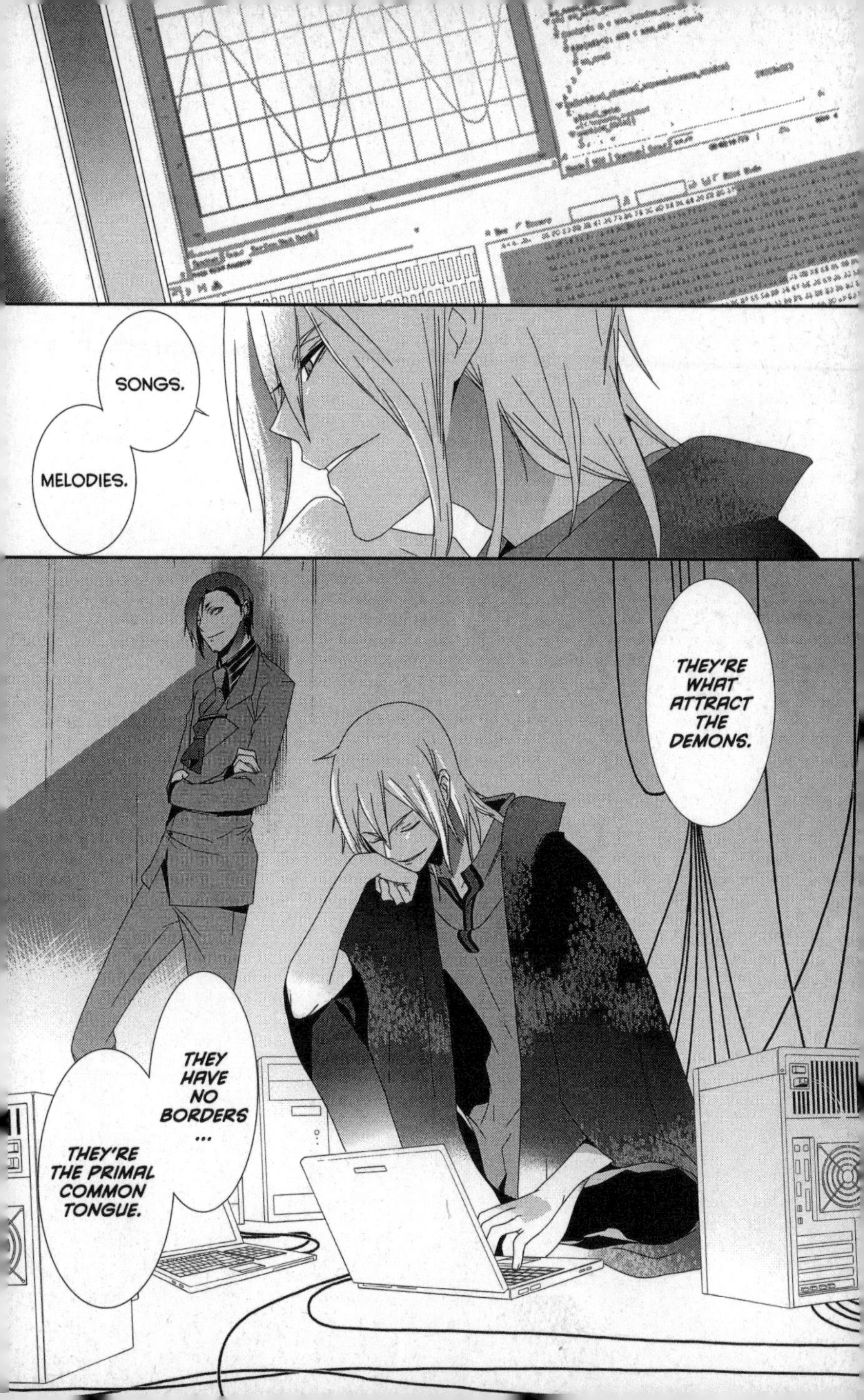
SONGS.
MELODIES.
THEY'RE WHAT ATTRACT THE DEMONS.
THEY HAVE NO BORDERS ...
THEY'RE THE PRIMAL COMMON TONGUE.

PROFILE

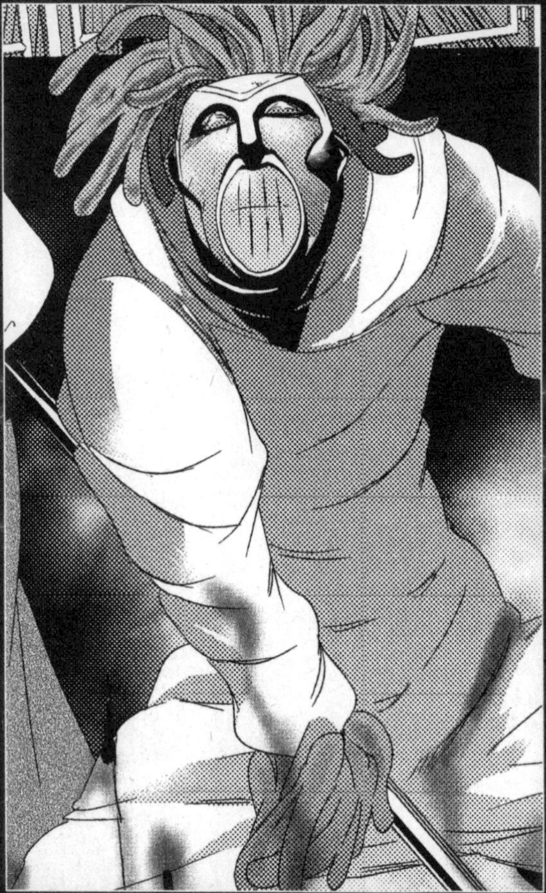

OGUN

A VOODOO SPIRIT BELIEVED TO BE A WAR HERO. HIS WORSHIP INCLUDES HIS FAVORITE DRINK, RUM. HE EXISTS IN VARIOUS FORMS, INCLUDING, OF COURSE, HIS ORIGINAL WARRIOR FORM, AS WELL AS THE FORMS OF SORCERER, GATEKEEPER, POLITICIAN, GUARDIAN OF FIRE, AND SACRIFICIAL VICTIM. HE ORIGINATED FROM THE NIGERIAN SPIRIT OF METALWORK, OF THE SAME NAME.

DEVIL SURVIVOR

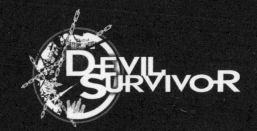

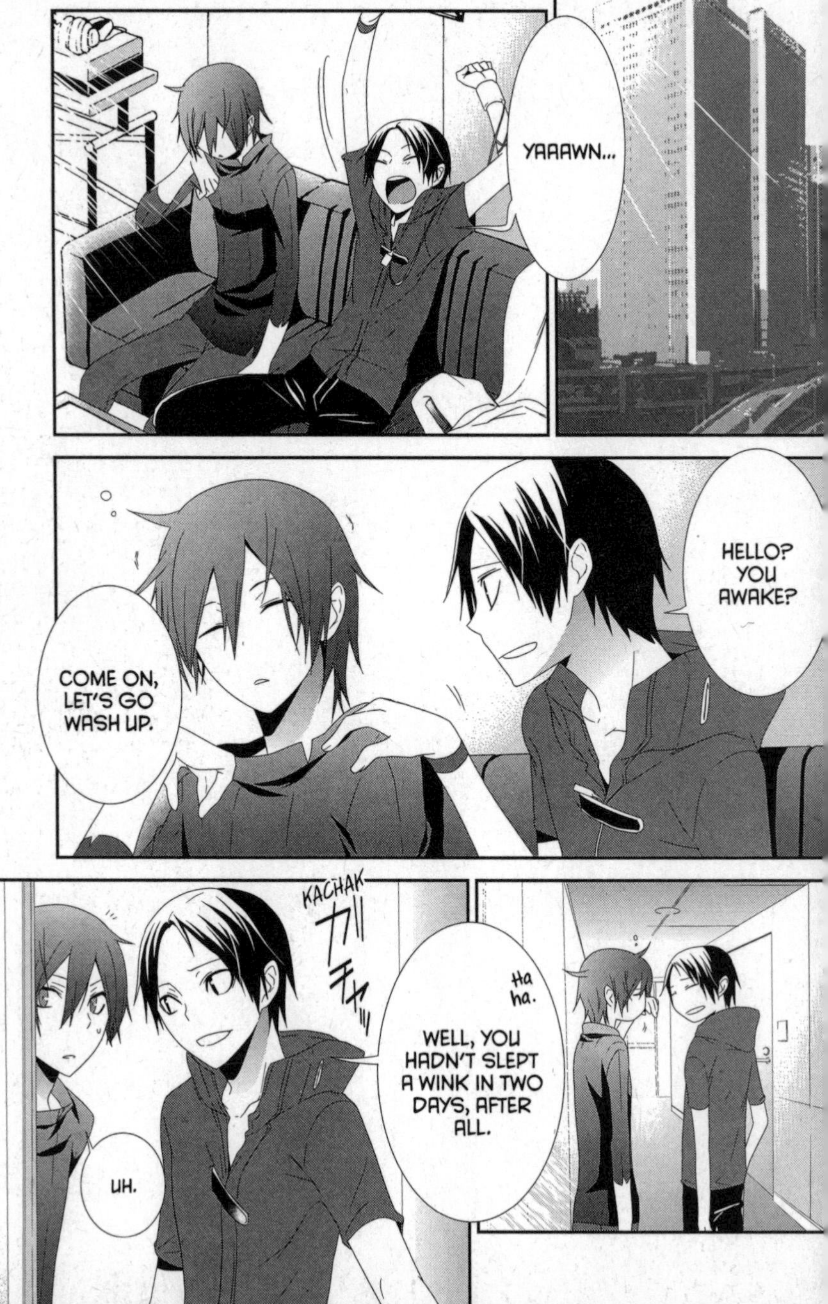
YAAAWN...
HELLO? YOU AWAKE?
COME ON, LET'S GO WASH UP.
KACHAK
ガチャッ
Ha ha.
WELL, YOU HADN'T SLEPT A WINK IN TWO DAYS, AFTER ALL.
UH.

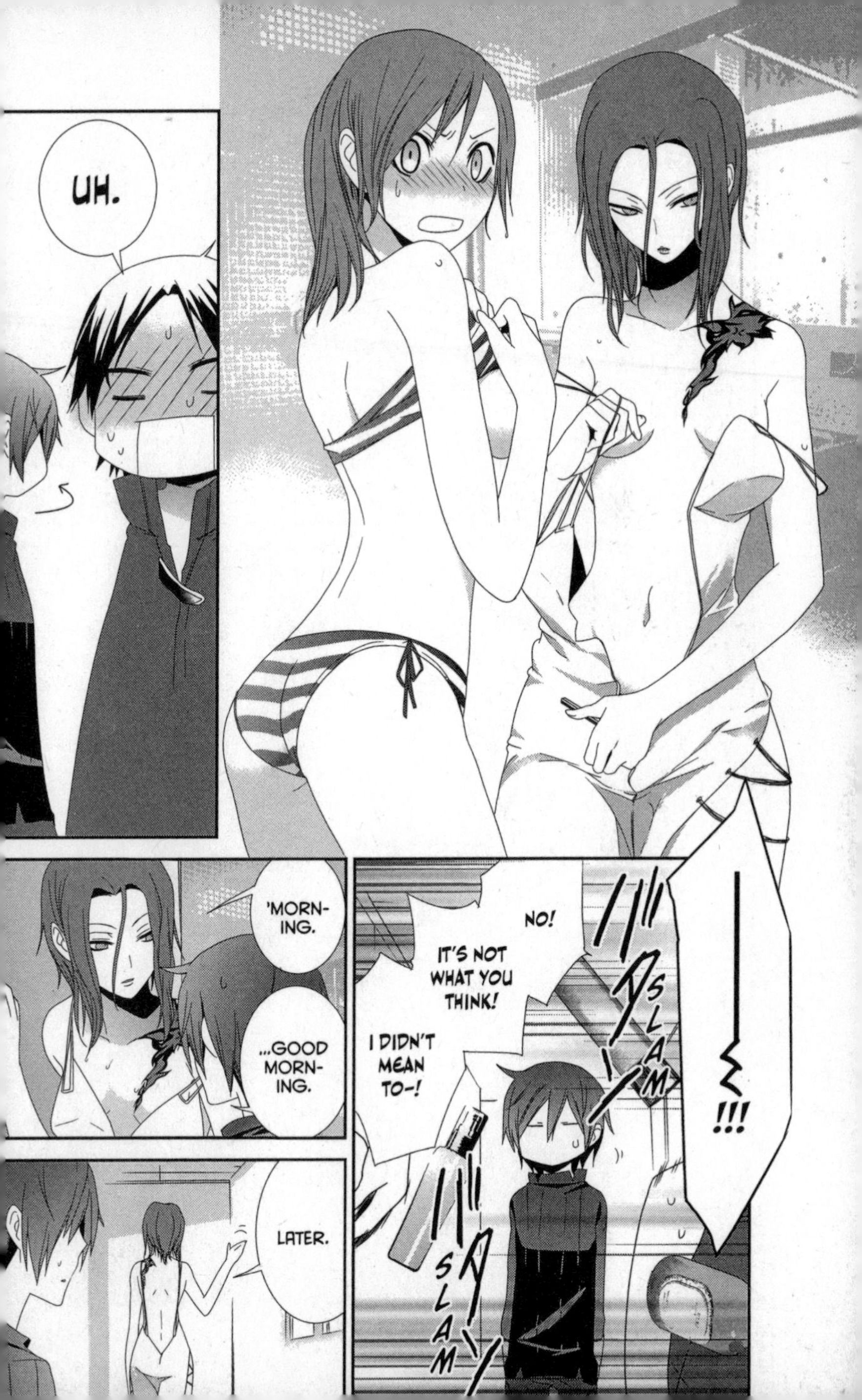
UH.
—!!!
SLAM
NO!
IT'S NOT WHAT YOU THINK!
I DIDN'T MEAN TO-!
SLAM
'MORN-ING.
...GOOD MORN-ING.
LATER.

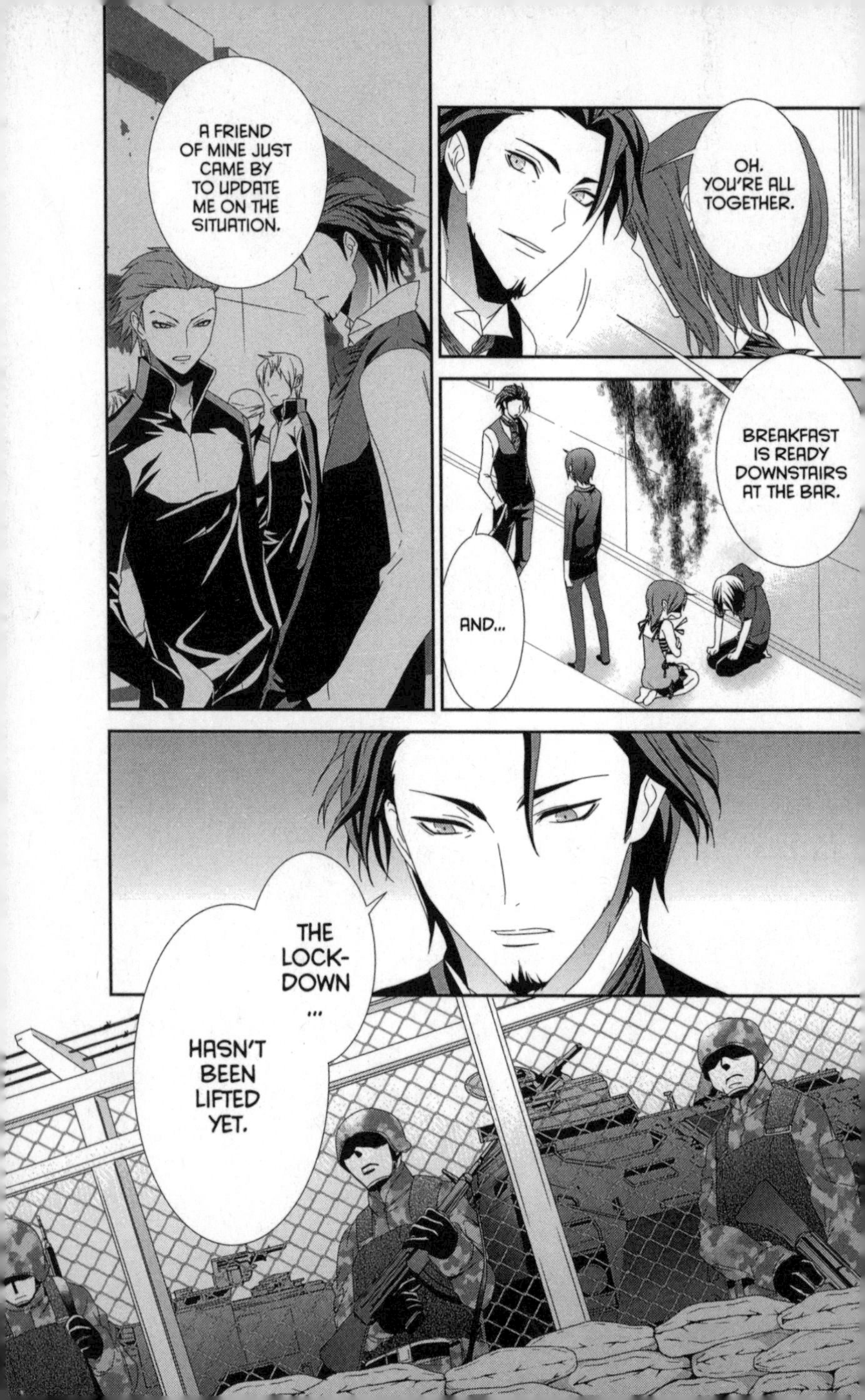
OH. YOU'RE ALL TOGETHER.
BREAKFAST IS READY DOWNSTAIRS AT THE BAR.
AND...
A FRIEND OF MINE JUST CAME BY TO UPDATE ME ON THE SITUATION.
THE LOCK-DOWN ... HASN'T BEEN LIFTED YET.

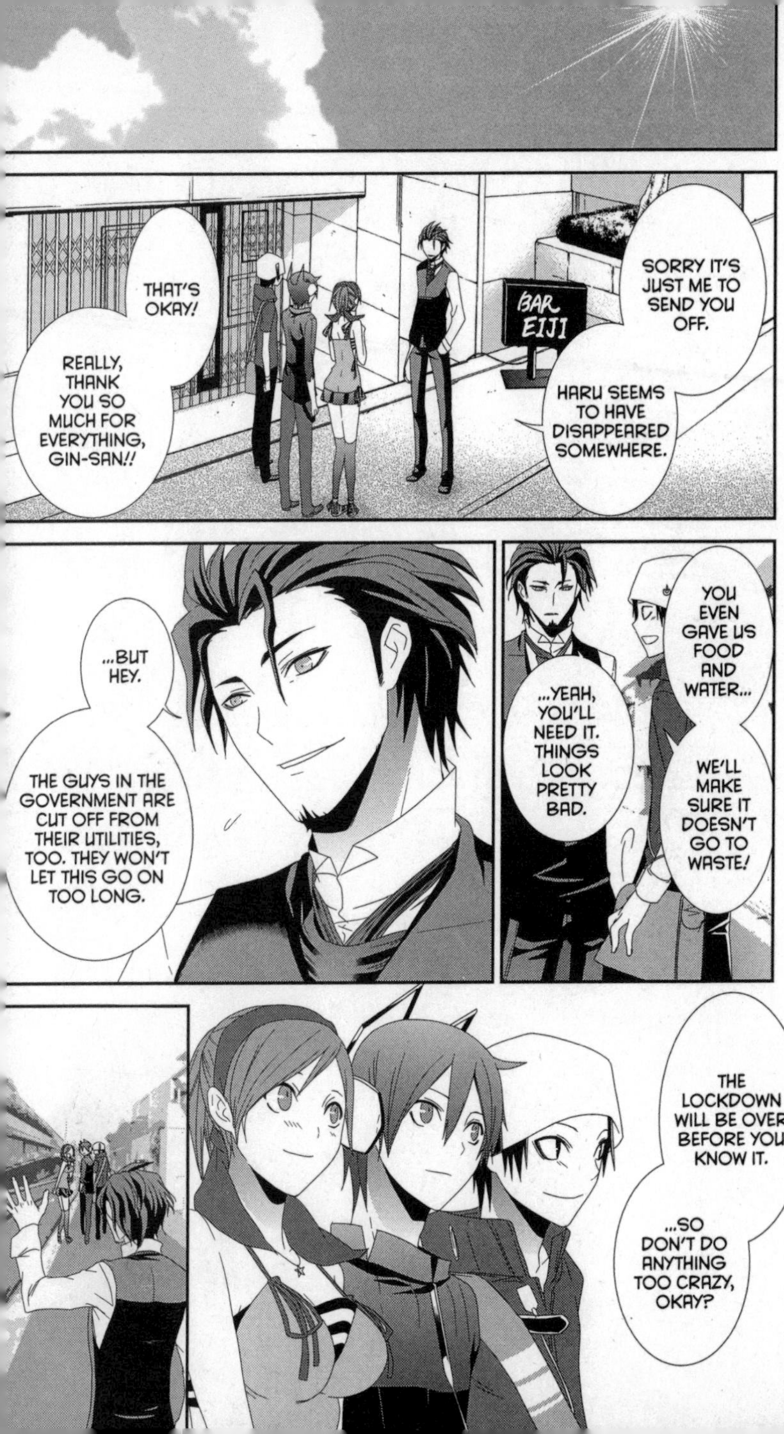
SORRY IT'S JUST ME TO SEND YOU OFF.
HARU SEEMS TO HAVE DISAPPEARED SOMEWHERE.
BAR EIJI
THAT'S OKAY!
REALLY, THANK YOU SO MUCH FOR EVERYTHING, GIN-SAN!!
YOU EVEN GAVE US FOOD AND WATER...
WE'LL MAKE SURE IT DOESN'T GO TO WASTE!
...YEAH, YOU'LL NEED IT. THINGS LOOK PRETTY BAD.
...BUT HEY.
THE GUYS IN THE GOVERNMENT ARE CUT OFF FROM THEIR UTILITIES, TOO. THEY WON'T LET THIS GO ON TOO LONG.
THE LOCKDOWN WILL BE OVER BEFORE YOU KNOW IT.
...SO DON'T DO ANYTHING TOO CRAZY, OKAY?

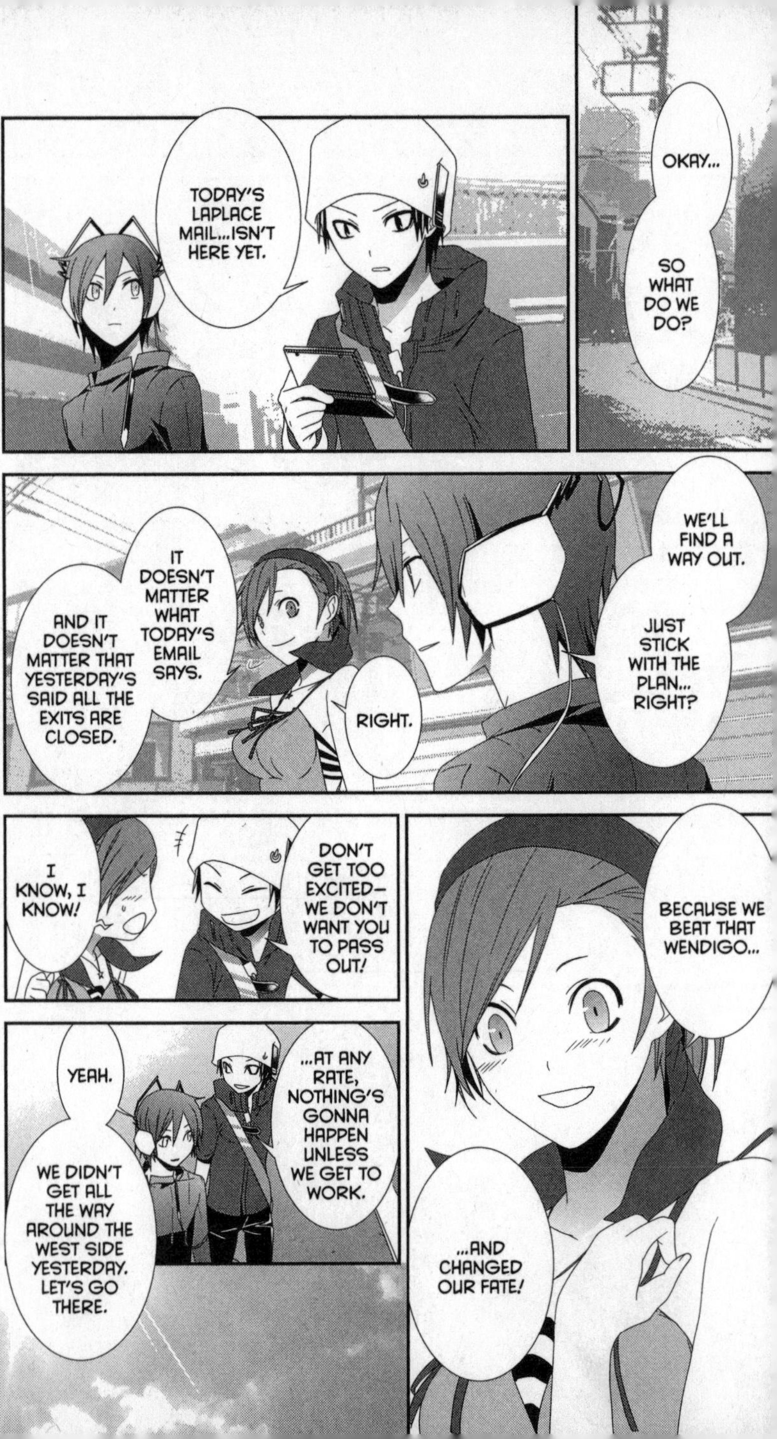
OKAY...
SO WHAT DO WE DO?
TODAY'S LAPLACE MAIL...ISN'T HERE YET.
WE'LL FIND A WAY OUT.
JUST STICK WITH THE PLAN... RIGHT?
RIGHT.
IT DOESN'T MATTER WHAT TODAY'S EMAIL SAYS.
AND IT DOESN'T MATTER THAT YESTERDAY'S SAID ALL THE EXITS ARE CLOSED.
BECAUSE WE BEAT THAT WENDIGO...
...AND CHANGED OUR FATE!
DON'T GET TOO EXCITED—WE DON'T WANT YOU TO PASS OUT!
I KNOW, I KNOW!
...AT ANY RATE, NOTHING'S GONNA HAPPEN UNLESS WE GET TO WORK.
YEAH.
WE DIDN'T GET ALL THE WAY AROUND THE WEST SIDE YESTERDAY. LET'S GO THERE.

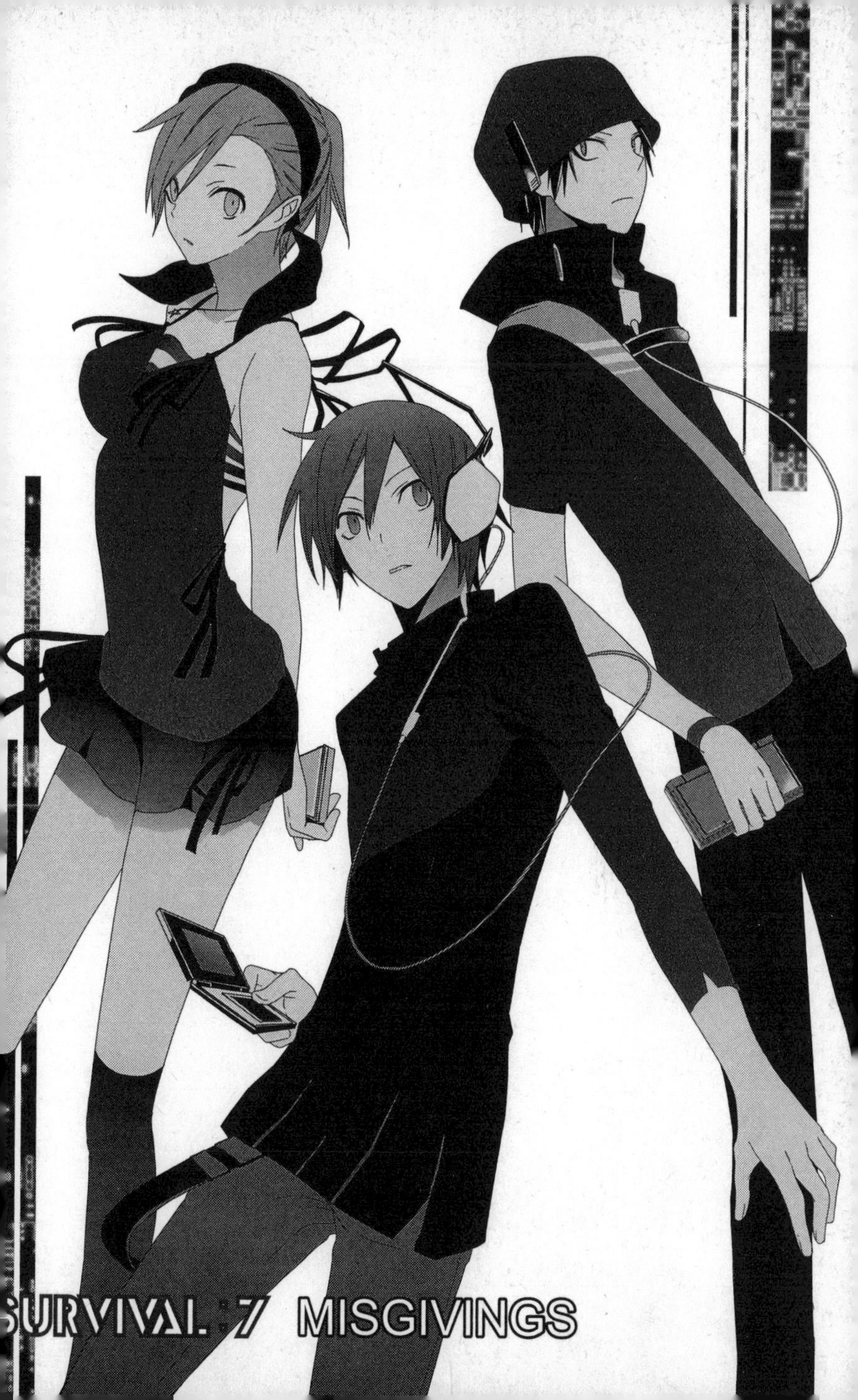

SURVIVAL: 7 MISGIVINGS

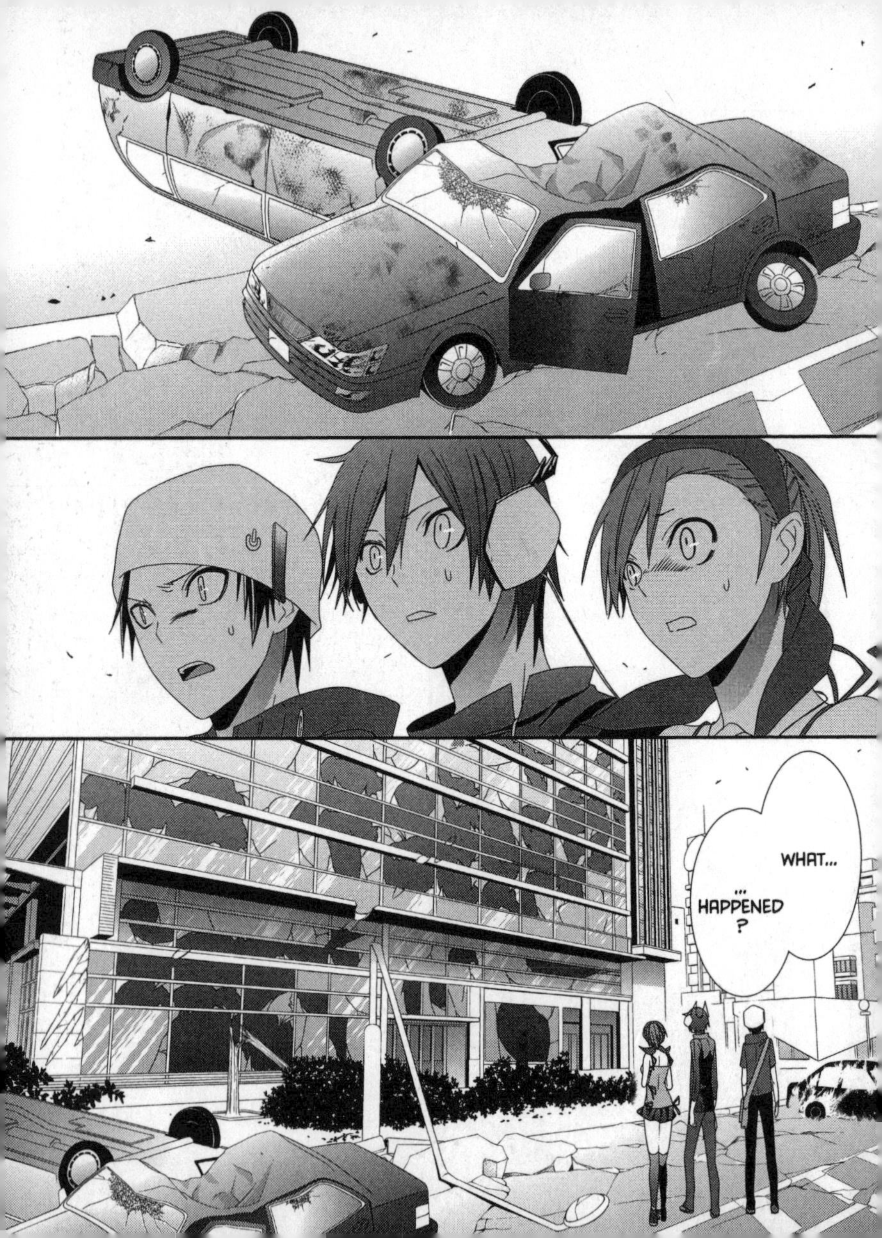
WHAT...
...HAPPENED?

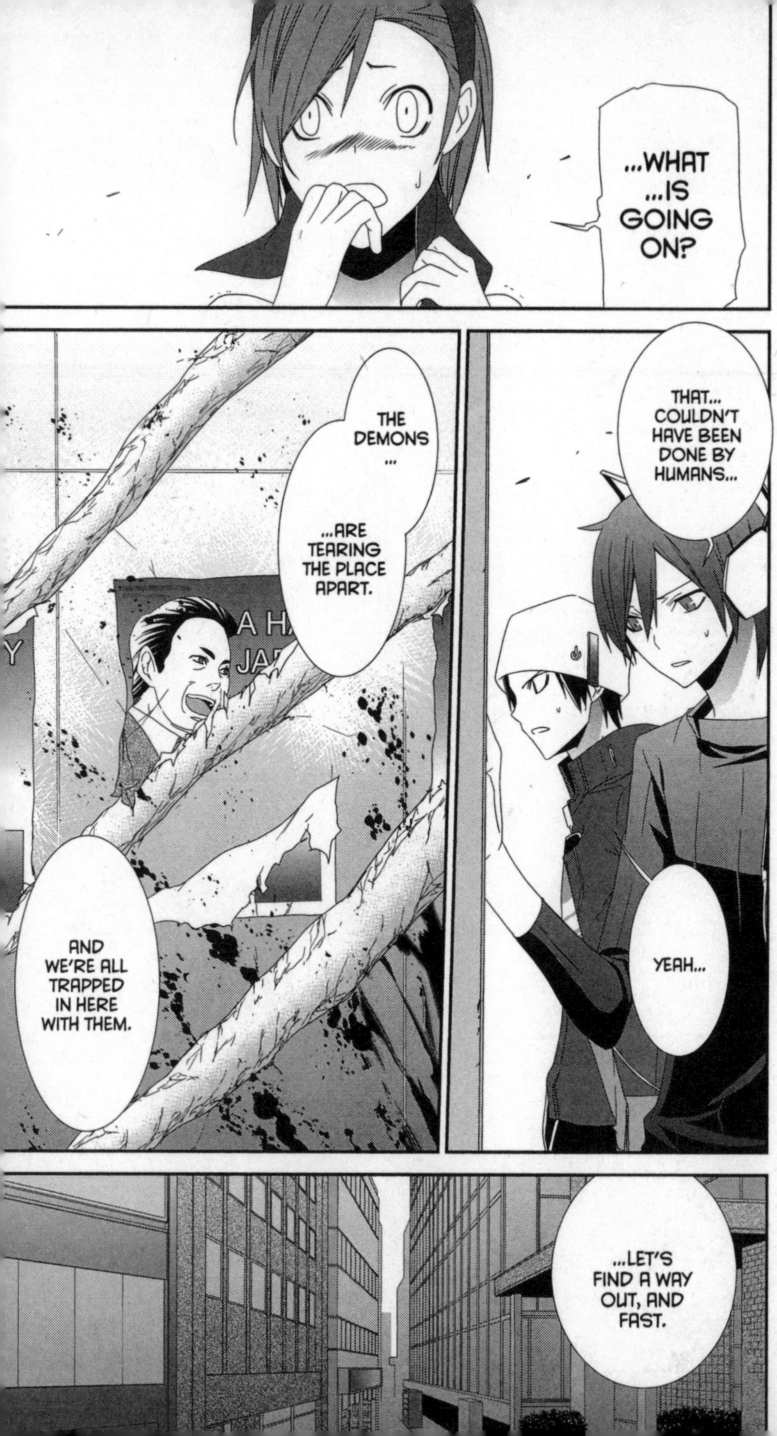
...WHAT ...IS GOING ON?
THAT... COULDN'T HAVE BEEN DONE BY HUMANS...
YEAH...
THE DEMONS ...
...ARE TEARING THE PLACE APART.
AND WE'RE ALL TRAPPED IN HERE WITH THEM.
...LET'S FIND A WAY OUT, AND FAST.

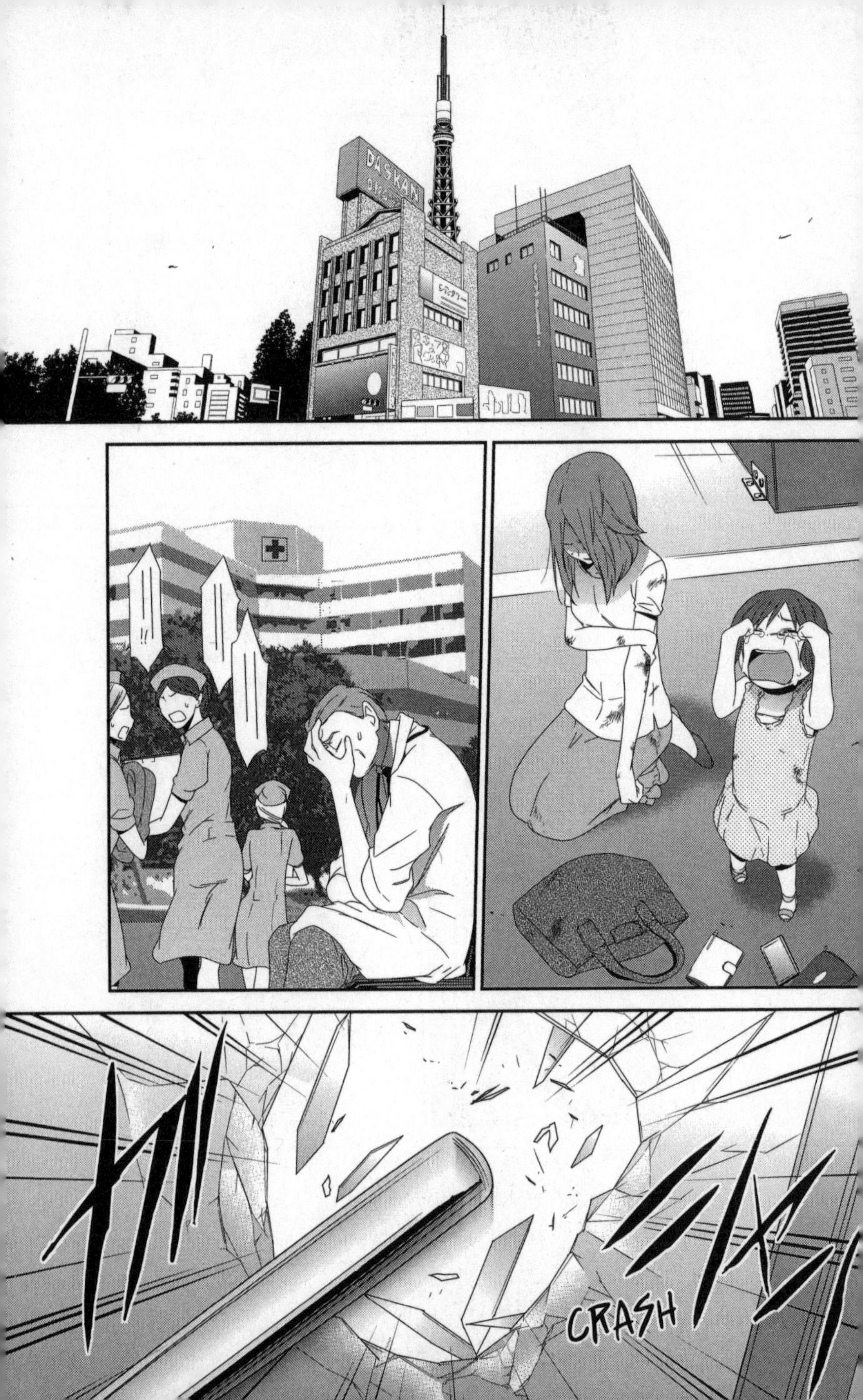
DASKAN
!!
CRASH

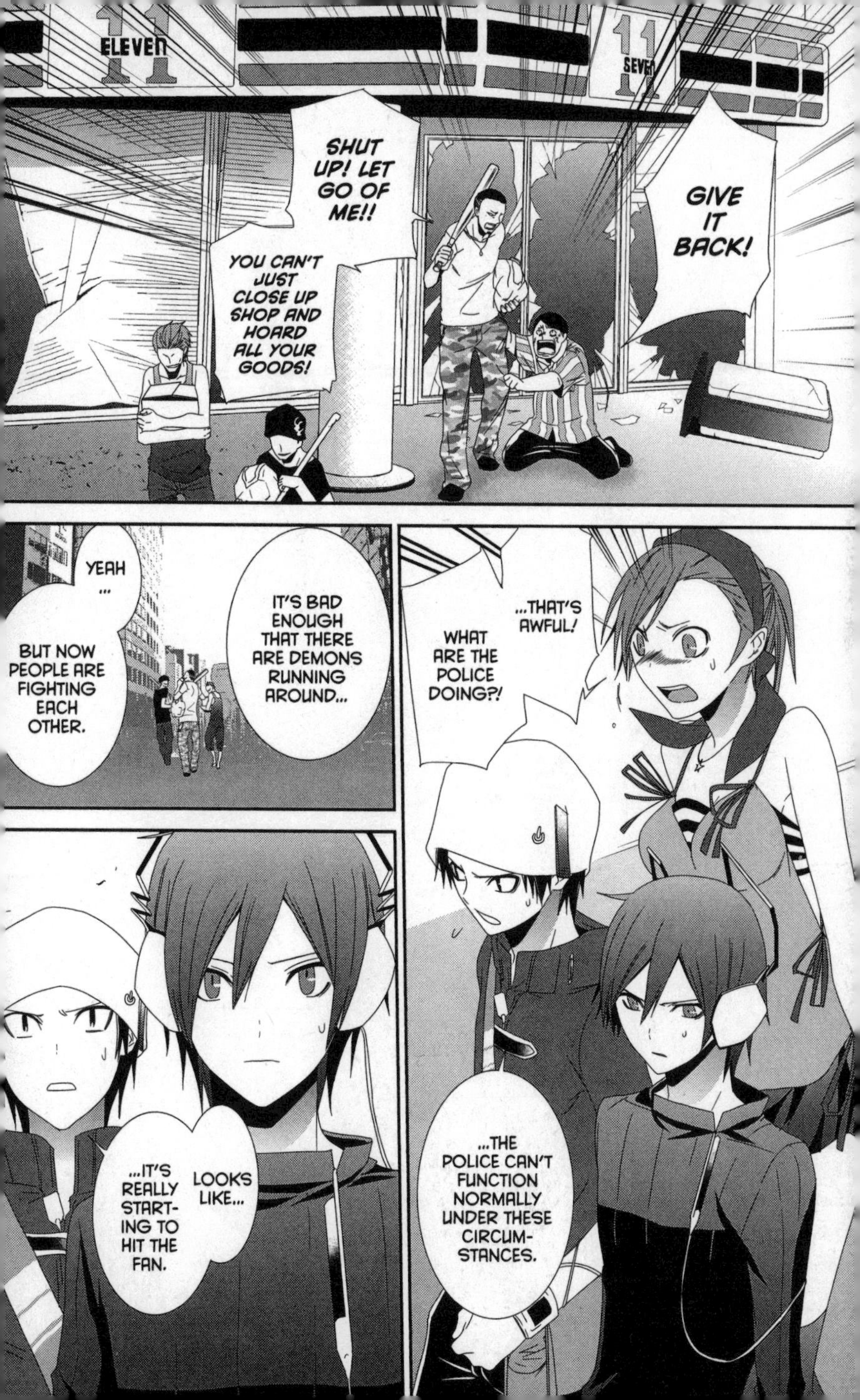
GIVE IT BACK!
SHUT UP! LET GO OF ME!!
YOU CAN'T JUST CLOSE UP SHOP AND HOARD ALL YOUR GOODS!
...THAT'S AWFUL!
WHAT ARE THE POLICE DOING?!
...THE POLICE CAN'T FUNCTION NORMALLY UNDER THESE CIRCUM-STANCES.
IT'S BAD ENOUGH THAT THERE ARE DEMONS RUNNING AROUND...
YEAH ...
BUT NOW PEOPLE ARE FIGHTING EACH OTHER.
LOOKS LIKE...
...IT'S REALLY START-ING TO HIT THE FAN.

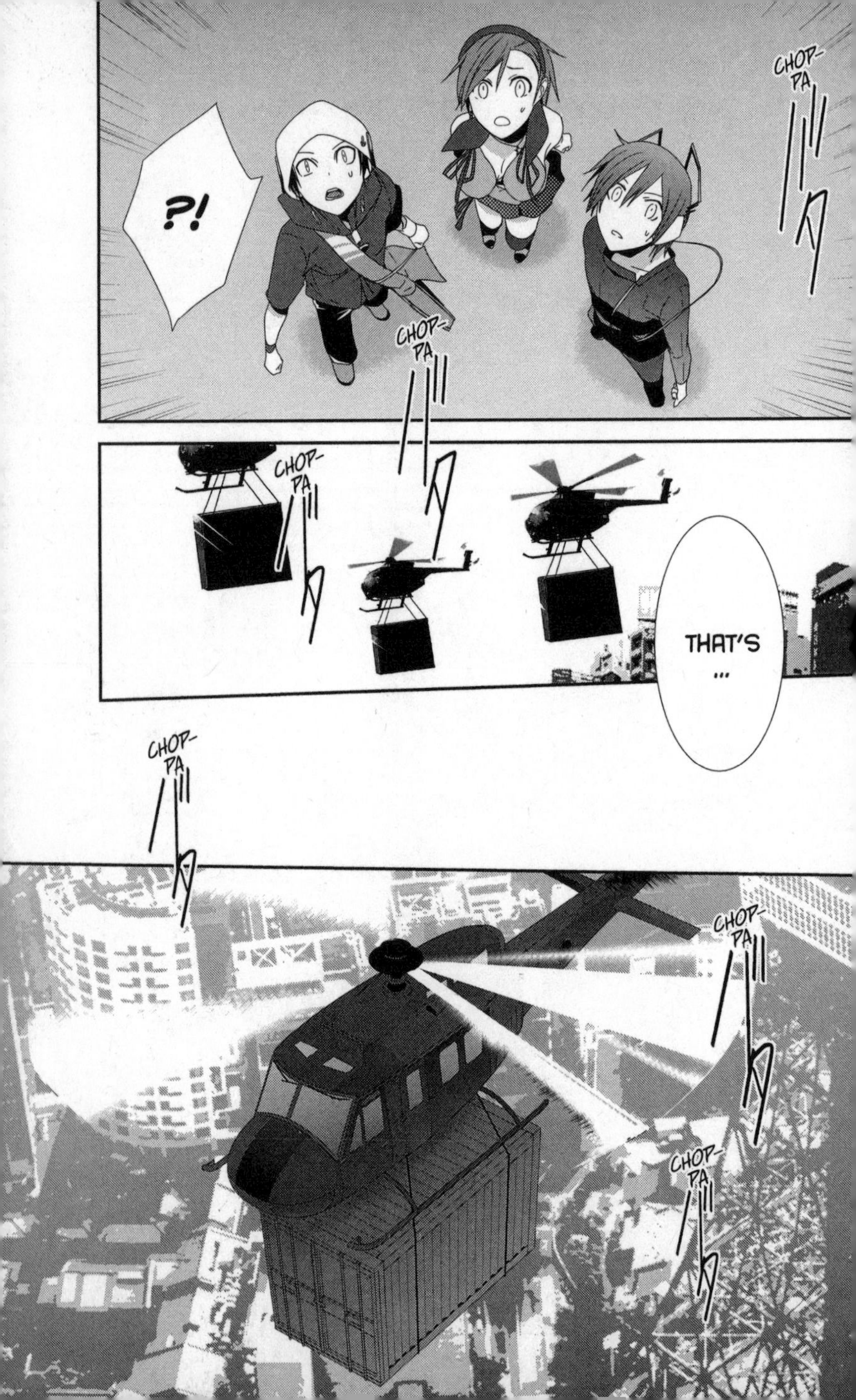
CHOP-PA
?!
CHOP-PA
THAT'S ...
CHOP-PA
CHOP-PA
CHOP-PA
CHOP-PA

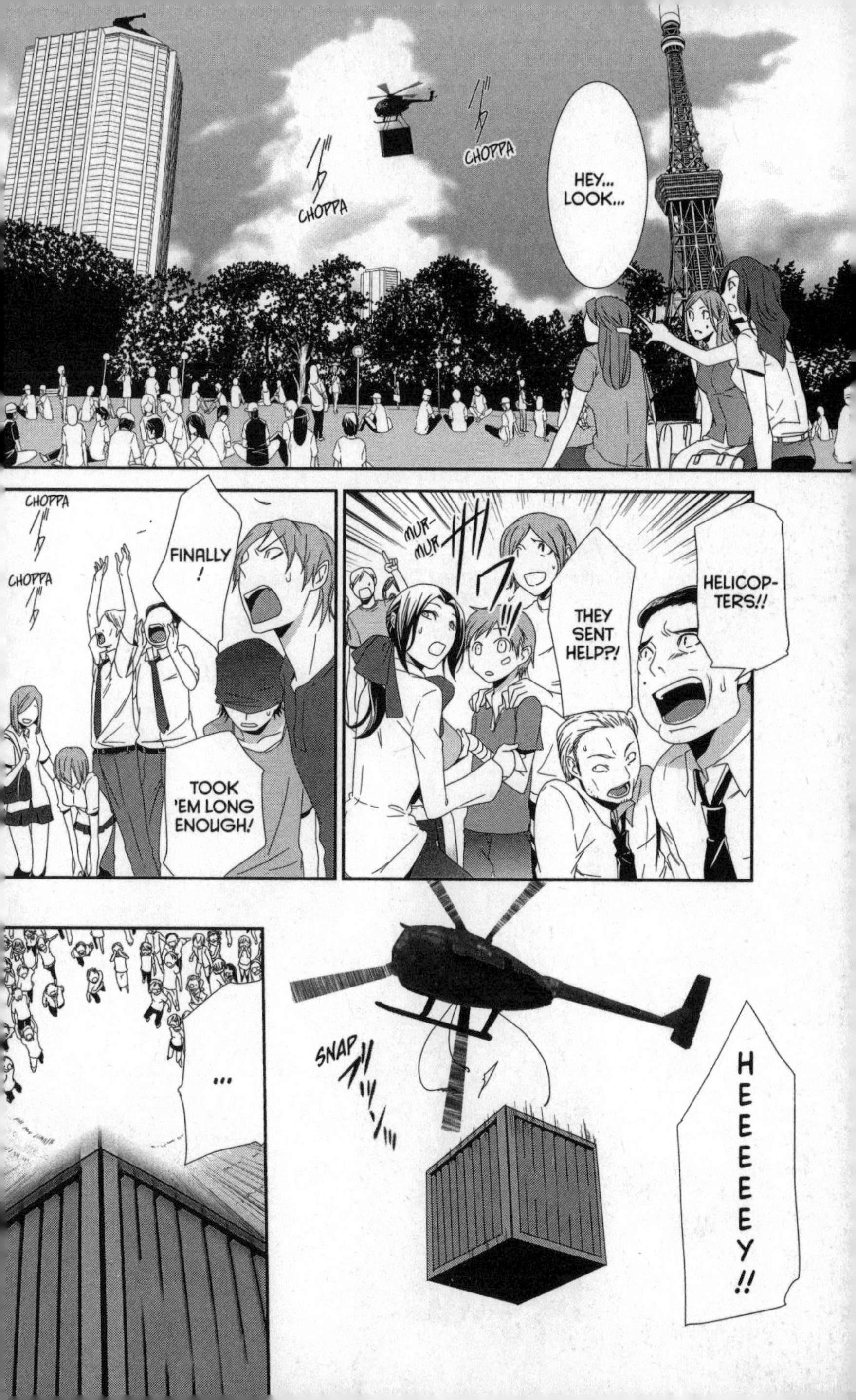
HEY... LOOK...
CHOPPA
CHOPPA
HELICOPTERS!!
THEY SENT HELP?!
MUR-MUR
FINALLY!
TOOK 'EM LONG ENOUGH!
CHOPPA
CHOPPA
HEEEEEY!!
SNAP
...

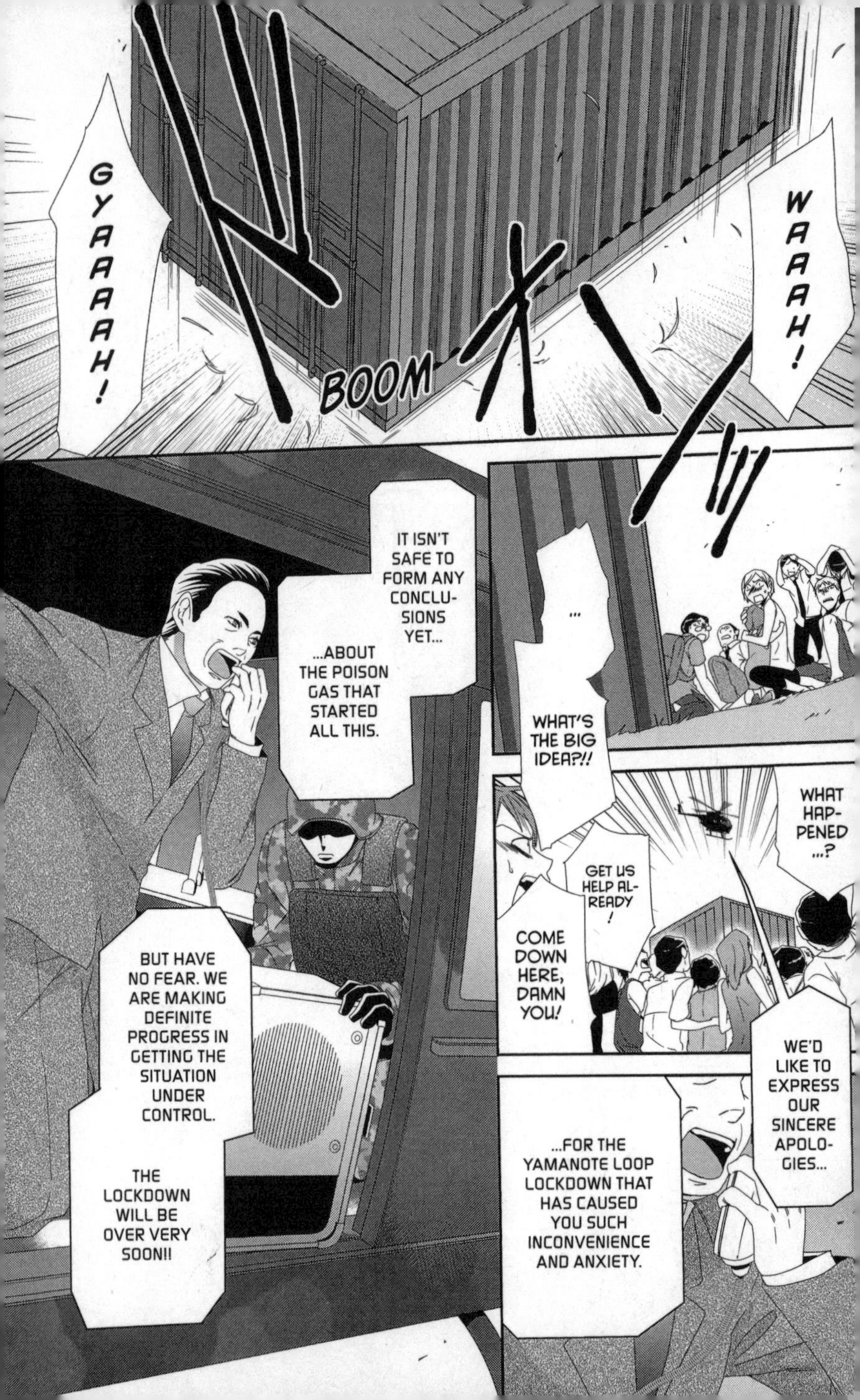
WAAAH!
BOOM
GYAAAAAH!
...
WHAT'S THE BIG IDEA?!!
WHAT HAPPENED ...?
GET US HELP ALREADY!
COME DOWN HERE, DAMN YOU!
WE'D LIKE TO EXPRESS OUR SINCERE APOLOGIES...
...FOR THE YAMANOTE LOOP LOCKDOWN THAT HAS CAUSED YOU SUCH INCONVENIENCE AND ANXIETY.
IT ISN'T SAFE TO FORM ANY CONCLUSIONS YET...
...ABOUT THE POISON GAS THAT STARTED ALL THIS.
BUT HAVE NO FEAR. WE ARE MAKING DEFINITE PROGRESS IN GETTING THE SITUATION UNDER CONTROL.
THE LOCKDOWN WILL BE OVER VERY SOON!!

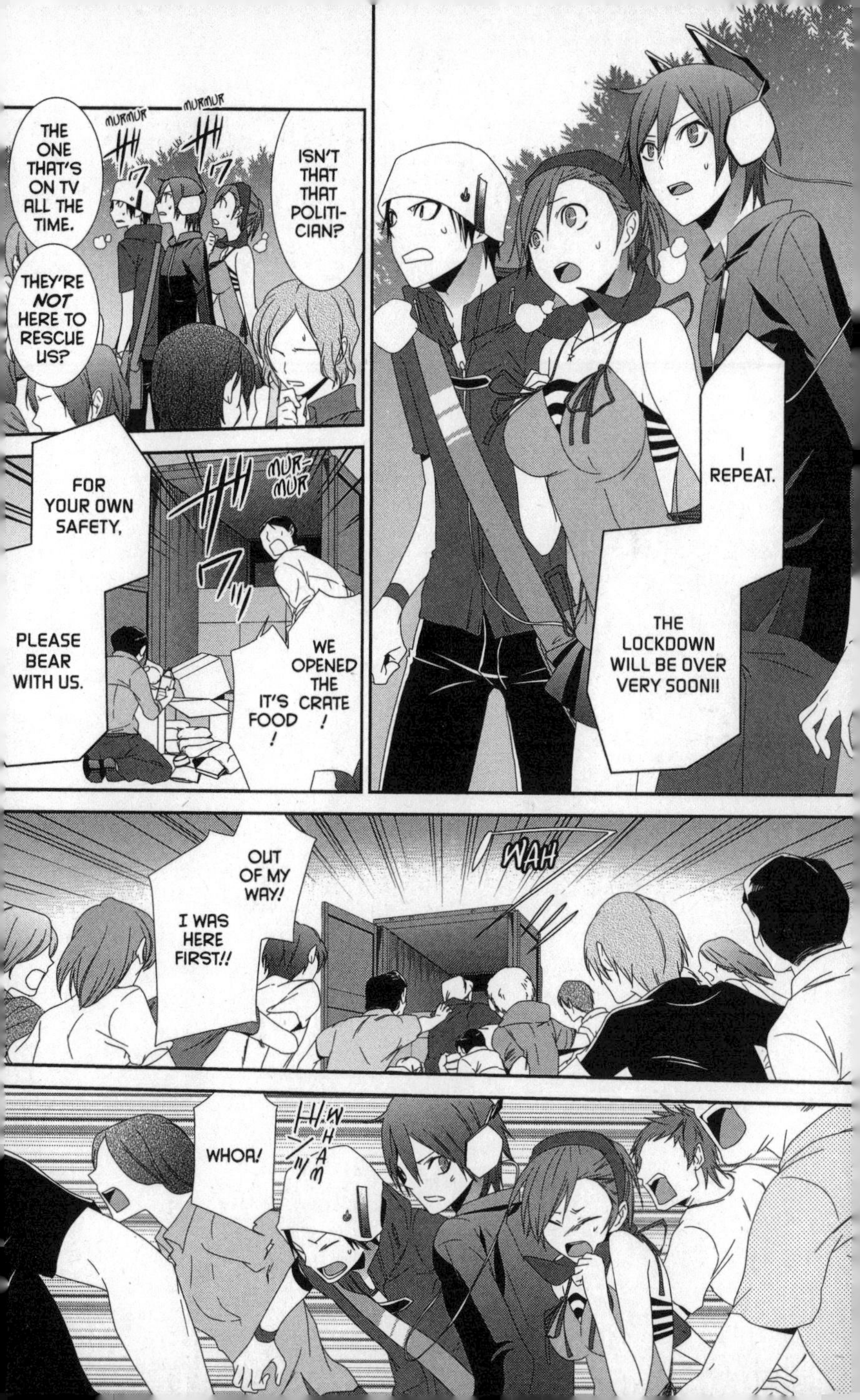
I REPEAT.
THE LOCKDOWN WILL BE OVER VERY SOON!!
MURMUR
MURMUR
ISN'T THAT THAT POLITICIAN?
THE ONE THAT'S ON TV ALL THE TIME.
THEY'RE *NOT* HERE TO RESCUE US?
MUR-MUR
WE OPENED THE CRATE!
IT'S FOOD!
FOR YOUR OWN SAFETY,
PLEASE BEAR WITH US.
WAH
OUT OF MY WAY!
I WAS HERE FIRST!!
WHAM
WHOA!

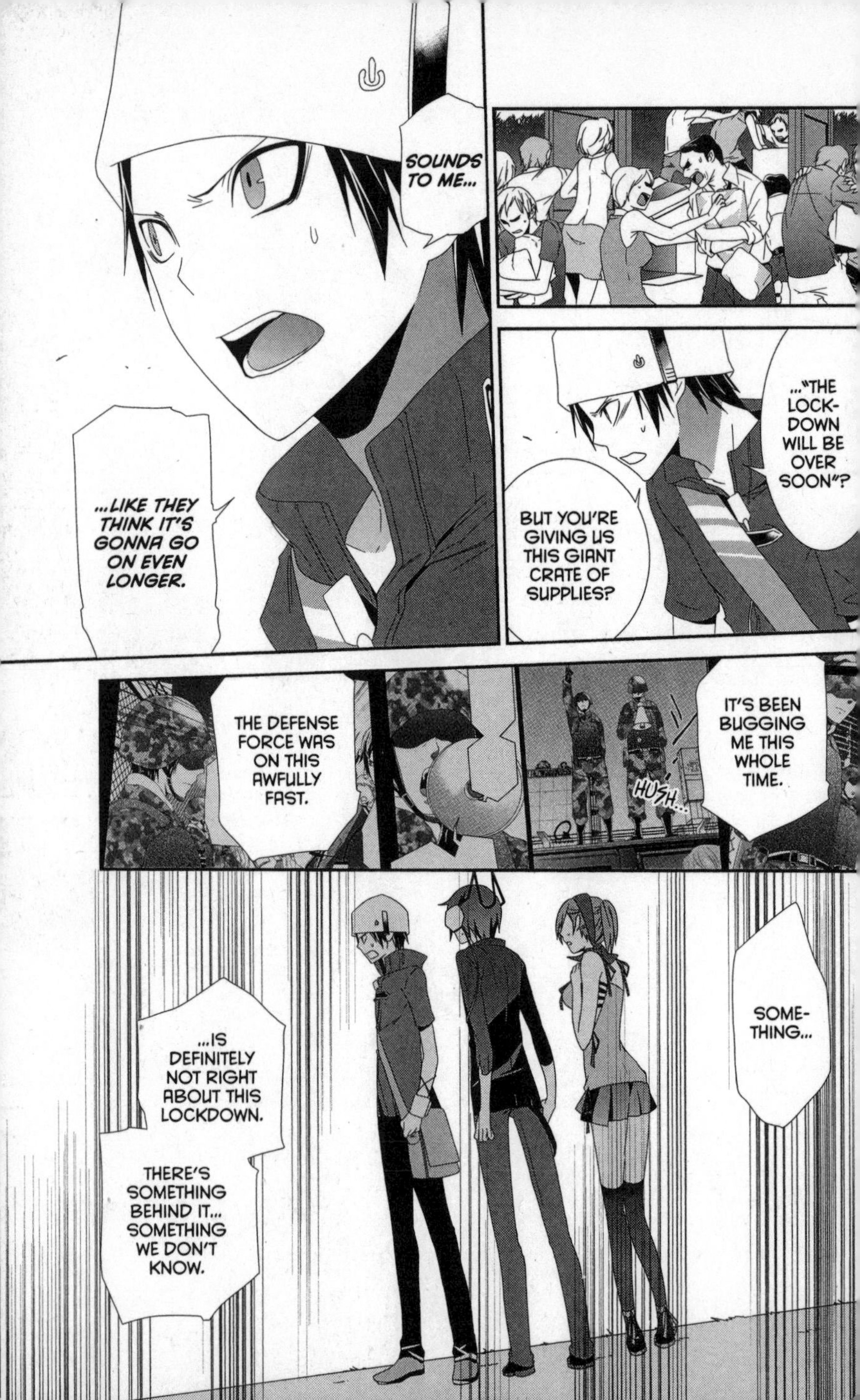
..."THE LOCK-DOWN WILL BE OVER SOON"?
BUT YOU'RE GIVING US THIS GIANT CRATE OF SUPPLIES?
SOUNDS TO ME...
...LIKE THEY THINK IT'S GONNA GO ON EVEN LONGER.
IT'S BEEN BUGGING ME THIS WHOLE TIME.
HUSH...
THE DEFENSE FORCE WAS ON THIS AWFULLY FAST.
SOME-THING...
...IS DEFINITELY NOT RIGHT ABOUT THIS LOCKDOWN.
THERE'S SOMETHING BEHIND IT... SOMETHING WE DON'T KNOW.

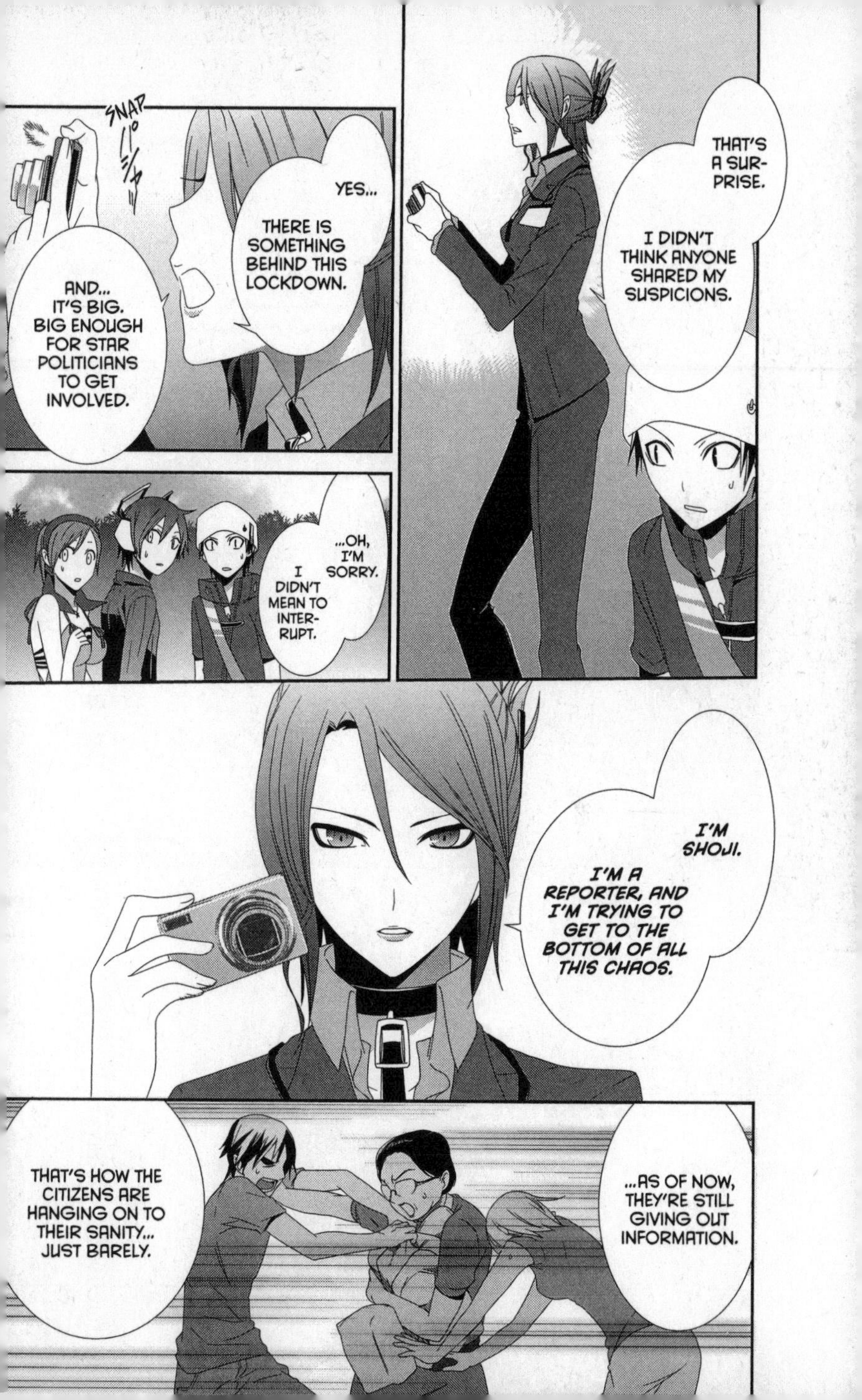
THAT'S A SUR-PRISE.
I DIDN'T THINK ANYONE SHARED MY SUSPICIONS.
SNAP
YES...
THERE IS SOMETHING BEHIND THIS LOCKDOWN.
AND... IT'S BIG. BIG ENOUGH FOR STAR POLITICIANS TO GET INVOLVED.
...OH, I'M SORRY.
I DIDN'T MEAN TO INTER-RUPT.
I'M SHOJI.
I'M A REPORTER, AND I'M TRYING TO GET TO THE BOTTOM OF ALL THIS CHAOS.
...AS OF NOW, THEY'RE STILL GIVING OUT INFORMATION.
THAT'S HOW THE CITIZENS ARE HANGING ON TO THEIR SANITY... JUST BARELY.

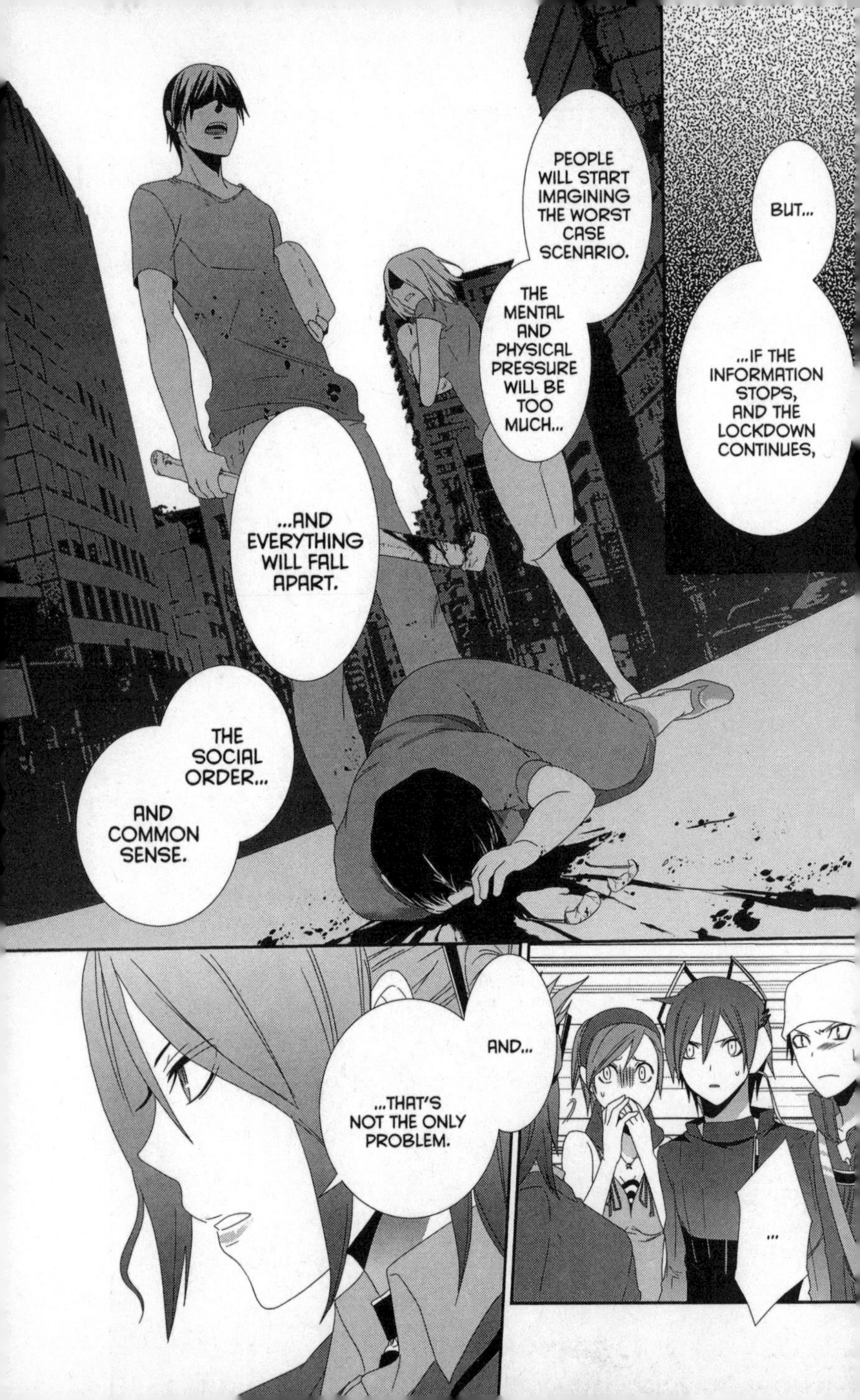
BUT...
...IF THE INFORMATION STOPS, AND THE LOCKDOWN CONTINUES,
PEOPLE WILL START IMAGINING THE WORST CASE SCENARIO.
THE MENTAL AND PHYSICAL PRESSURE WILL BE TOO MUCH...
...AND EVERYTHING WILL FALL APART.
THE SOCIAL ORDER...
AND COMMON SENSE.
...
AND...
...THAT'S NOT THE ONLY PROBLEM.

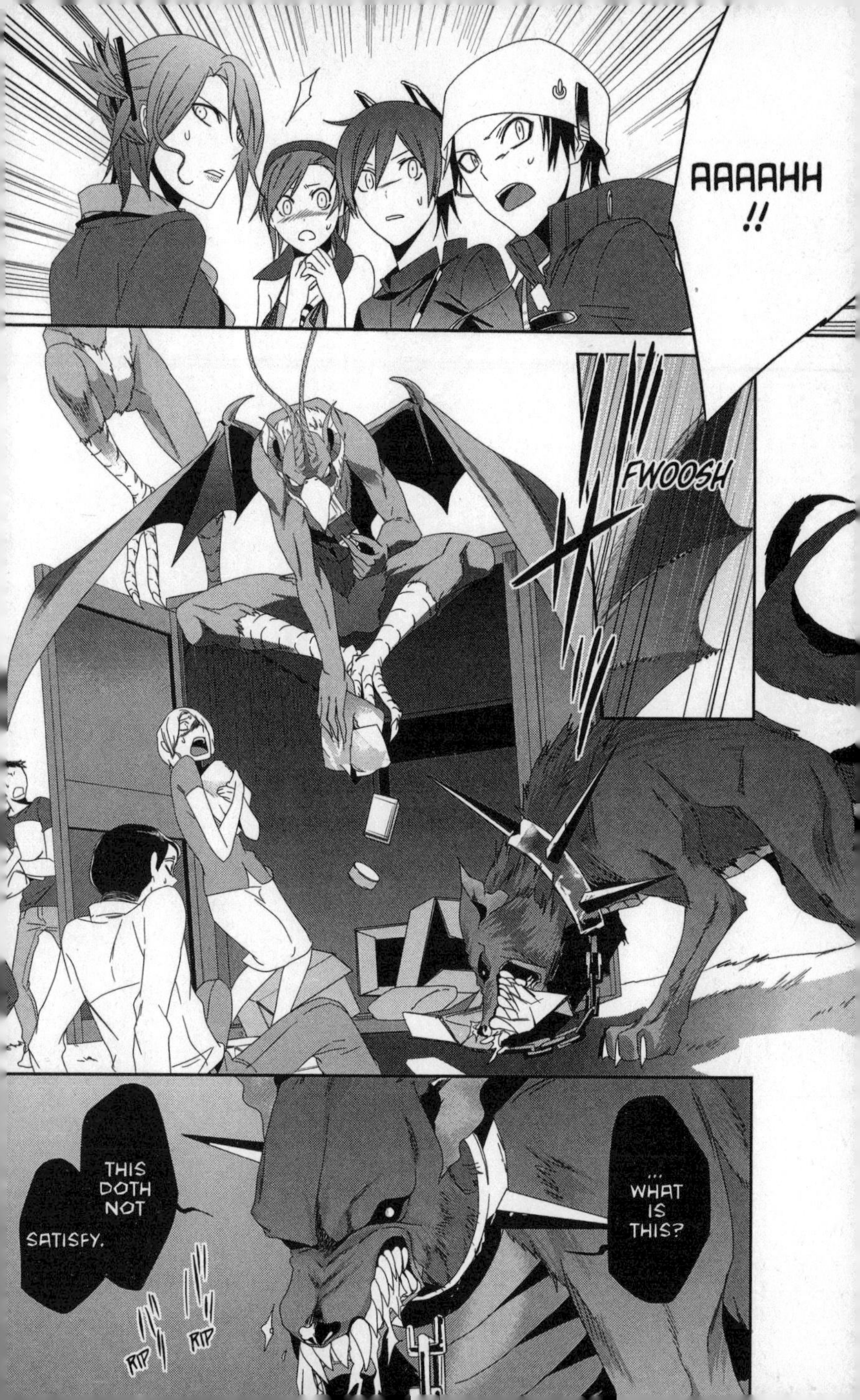
AAAAHH!!
FWOOSH
...WHAT IS THIS?
THIS DOTH NOT SATISFY.
RIP RIP

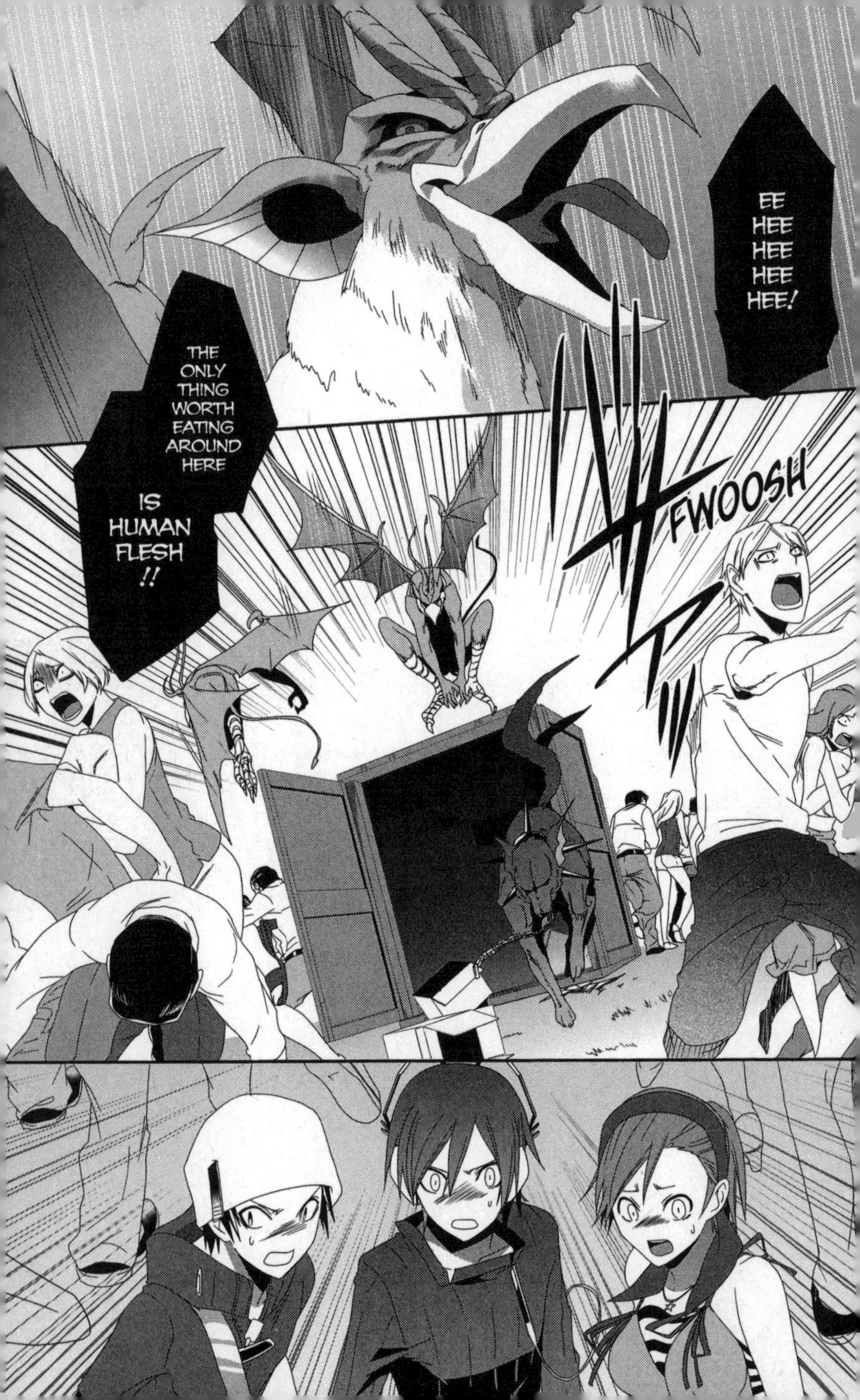
EE HEE HEE HEE HEE!
THE ONLY THING WORTH EATING AROUND HERE
IS HUMAN FLESH!!
FWOOSH

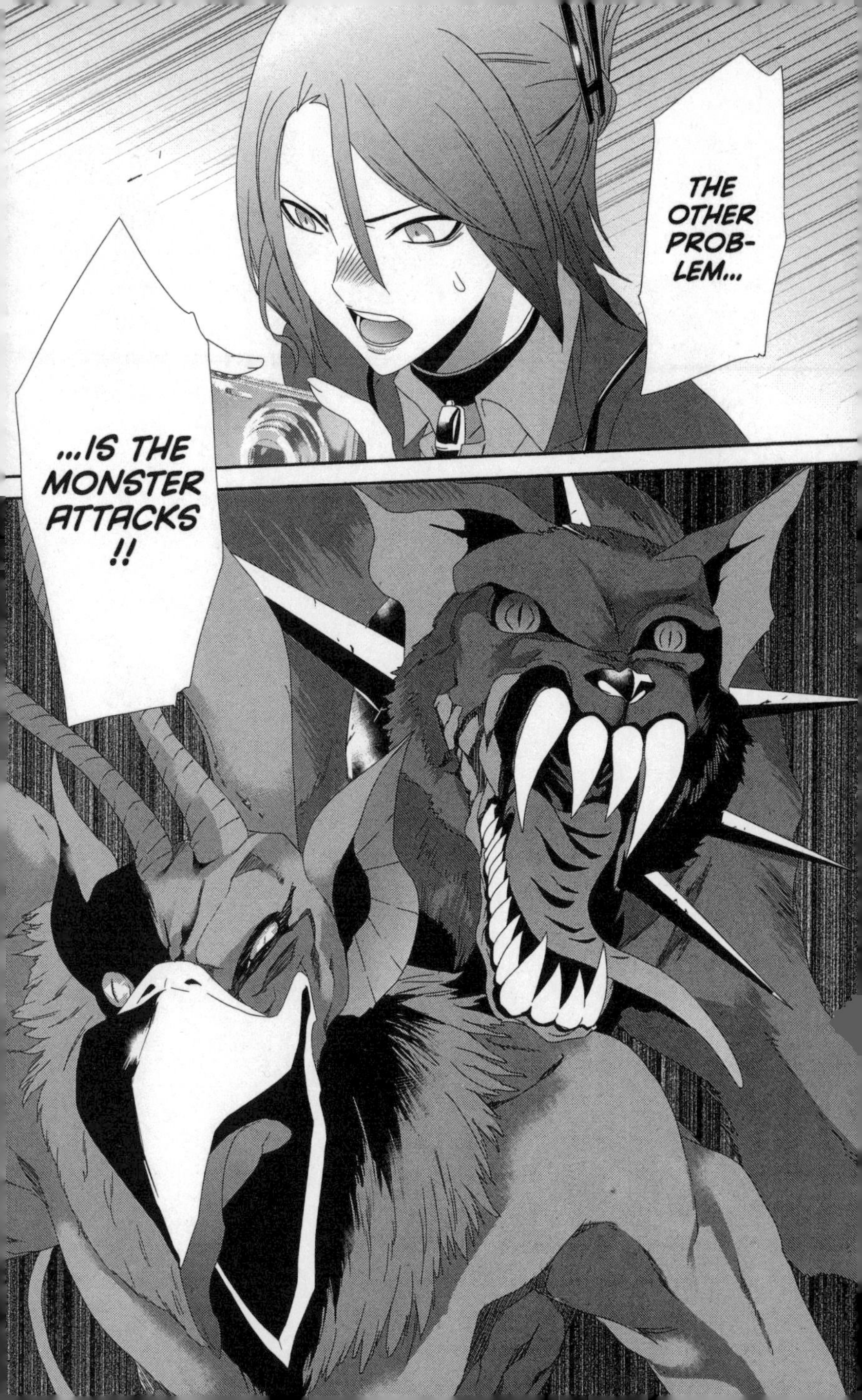
THE OTHER PROB-LEM...
...IS THE MONSTER ATTACKS !!

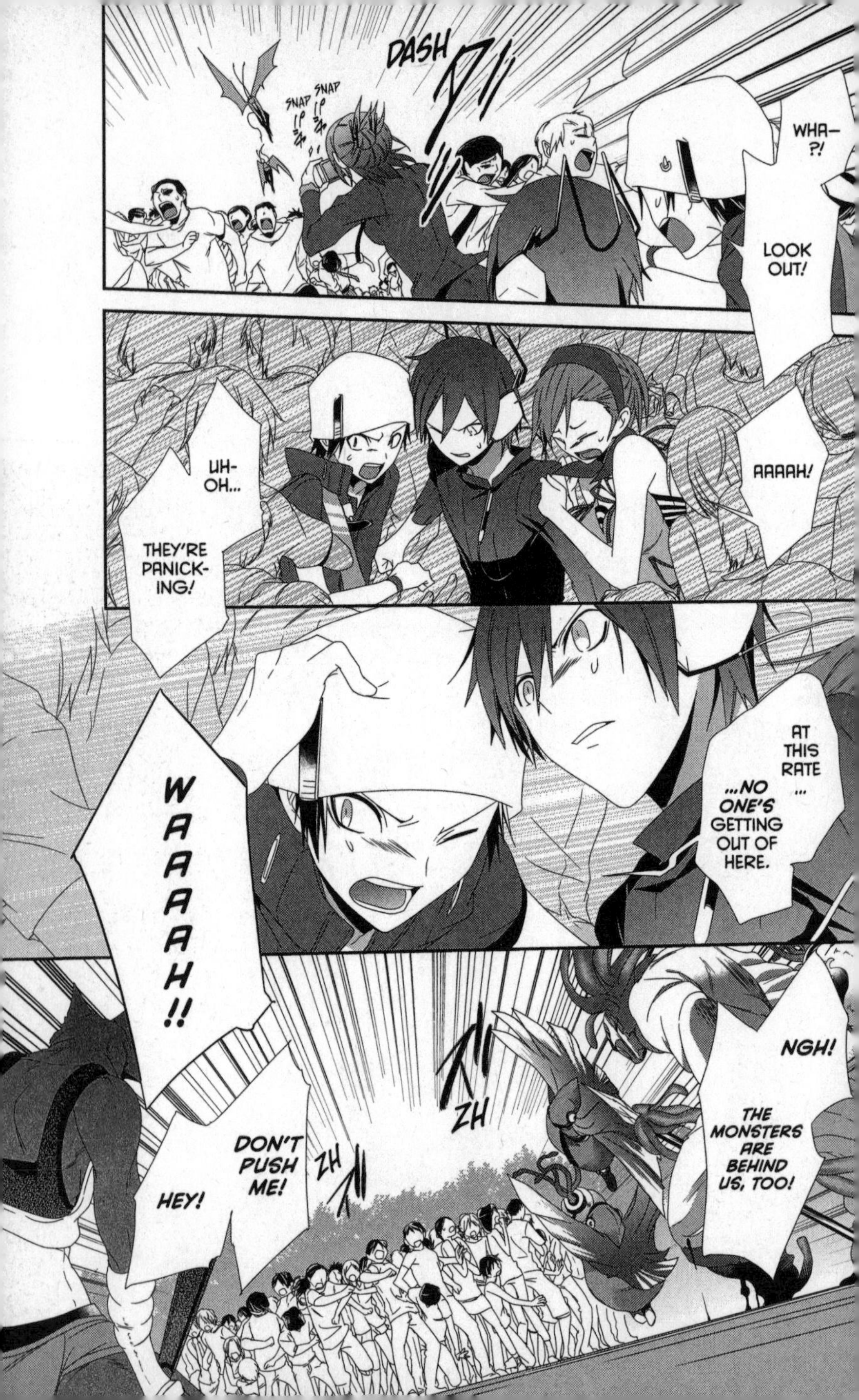
WHA—?!
LOOK OUT!
DASH
SNAP SNAP
AAAAH!
UH-OH...
THEY'RE PANICKING!
AT THIS RATE...
...NO ONE'S GETTING OUT OF HERE.
WAAAAAH!!
NGH!
THE MONSTERS ARE BEHIND US, TOO!
ZH
ZH
DON'T PUSH ME!
HEY!

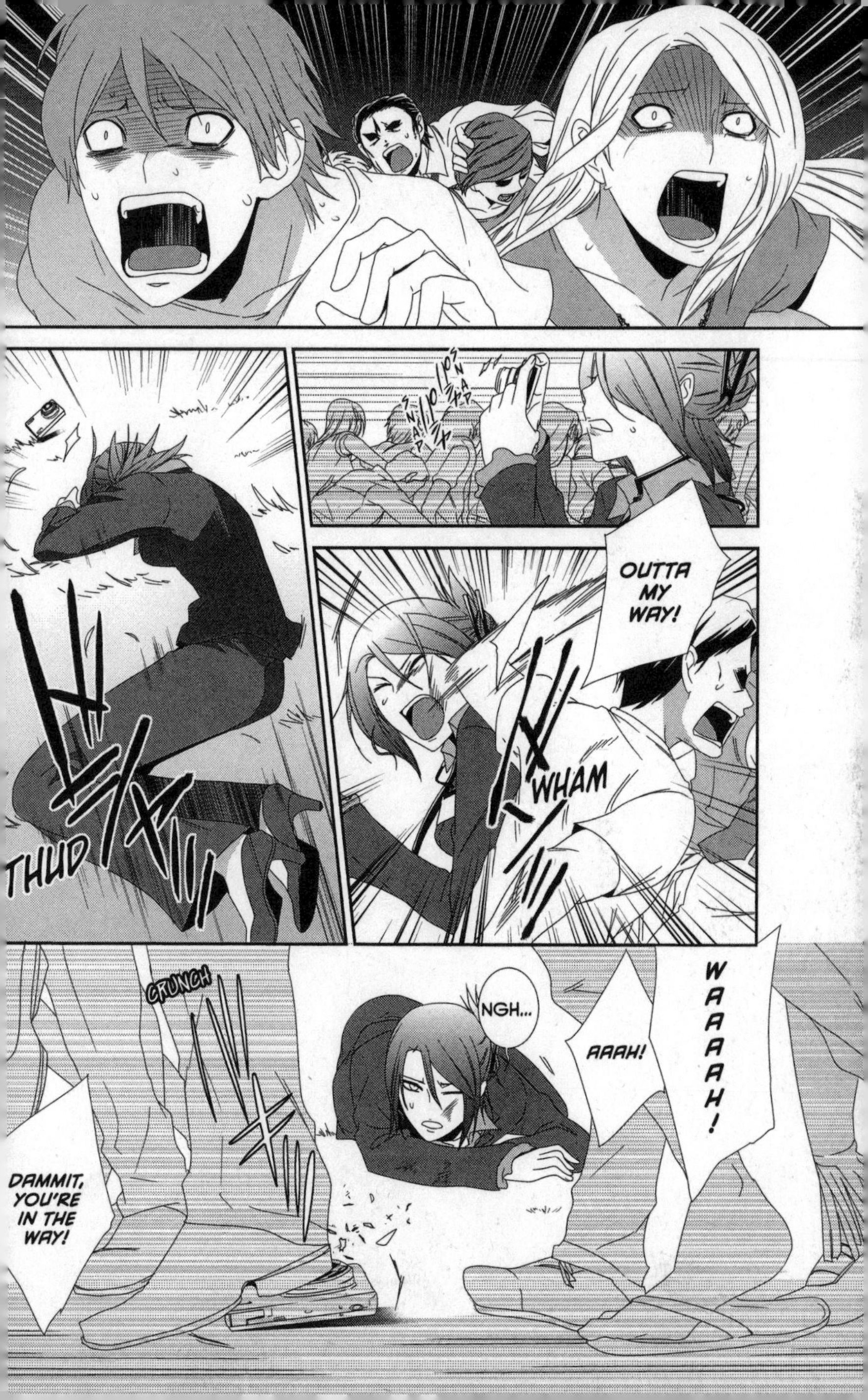
SNAP
SNAP
OUTTA MY WAY!
WHAM
THUD
WAAAAAH!
AAAH!
NGH...
CRUNCH
DAMMIT, YOU'RE IN THE WAY!

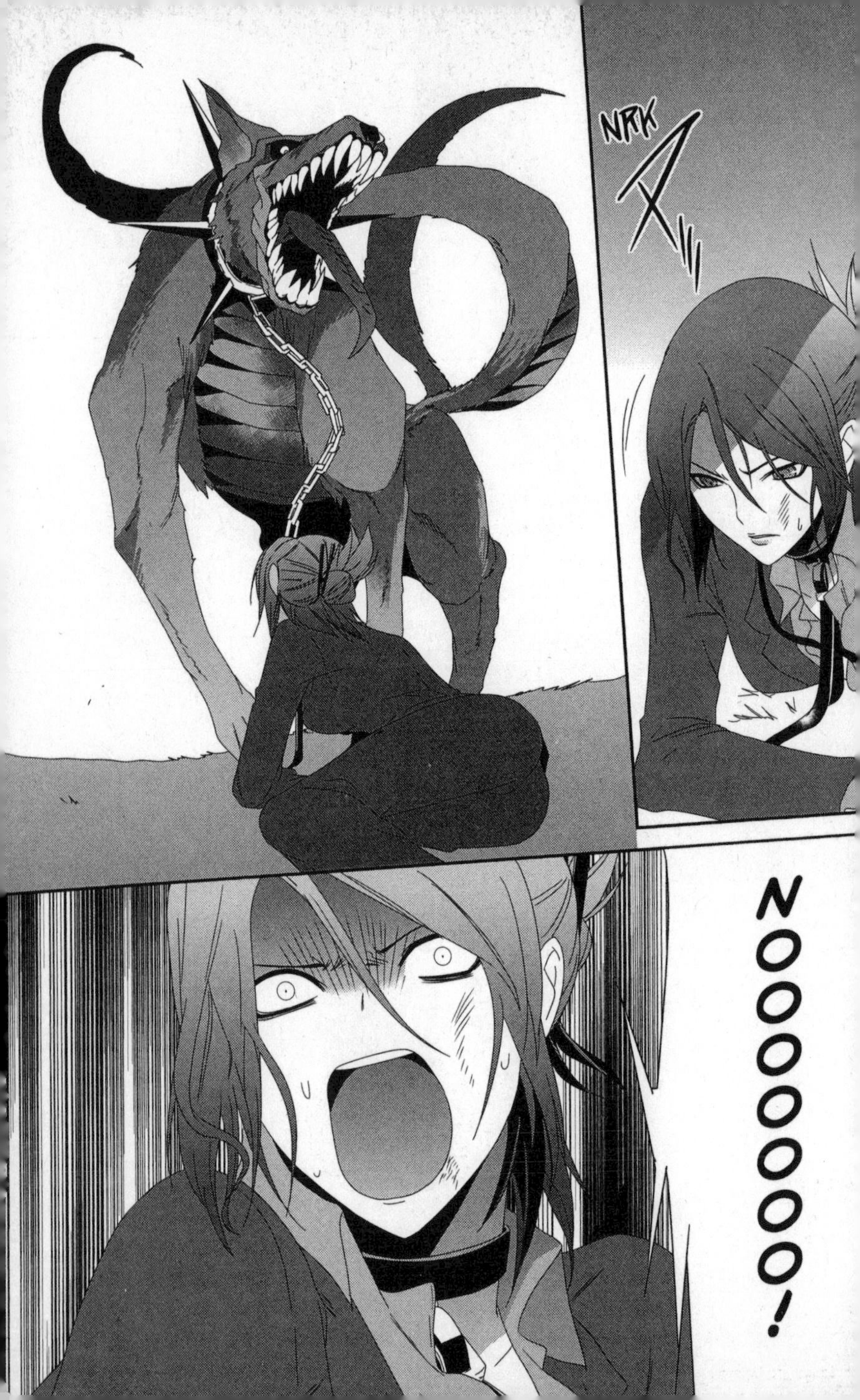
NRK
NOOOOOOOOO!

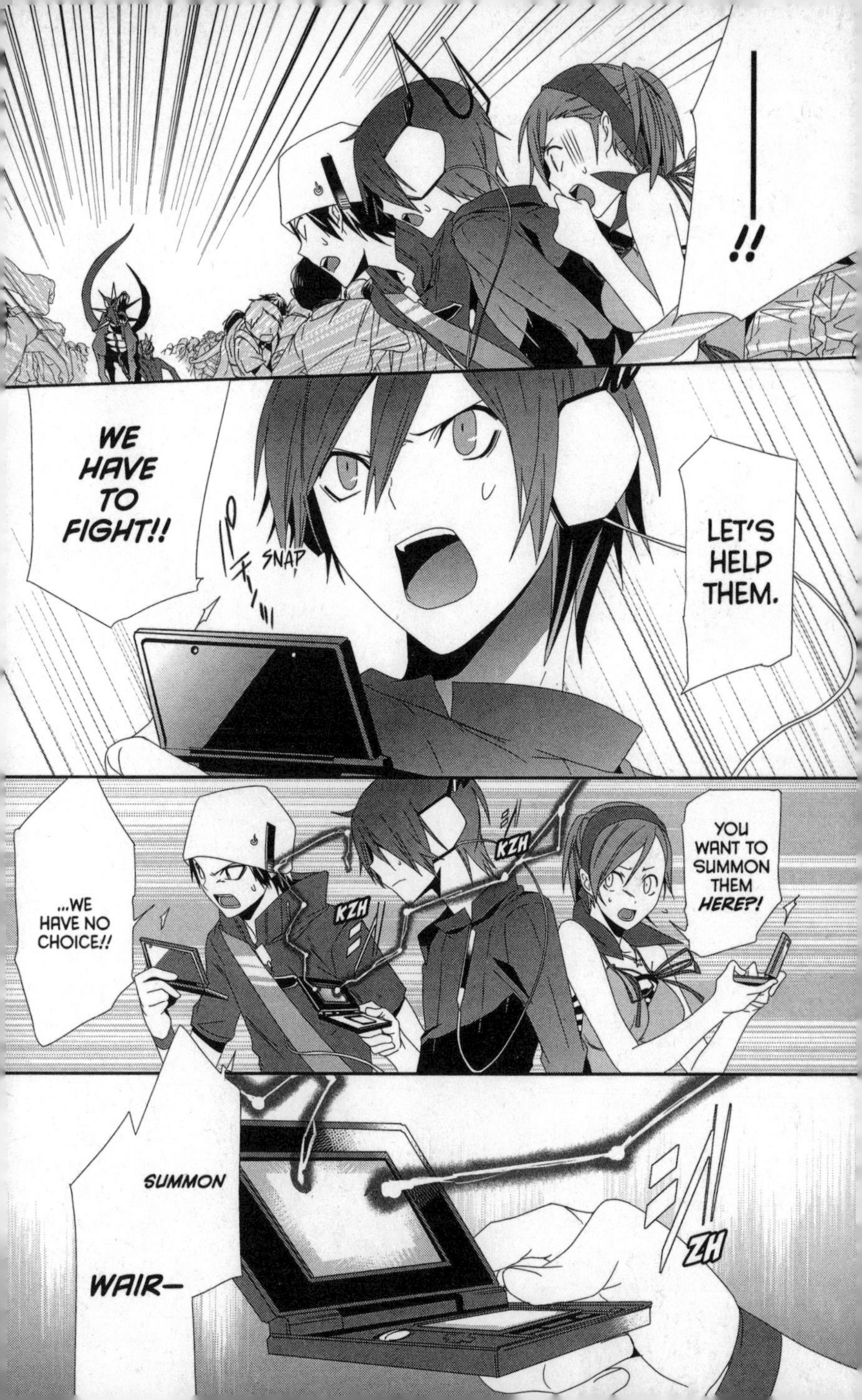
—!!
LET'S HELP THEM.
WE HAVE TO FIGHT!!
SNAP
YOU WANT TO SUMMON THEM HERE?!
KZH
KZH
...WE HAVE NO CHOICE!!
ZH
SUMMON
WAIR—

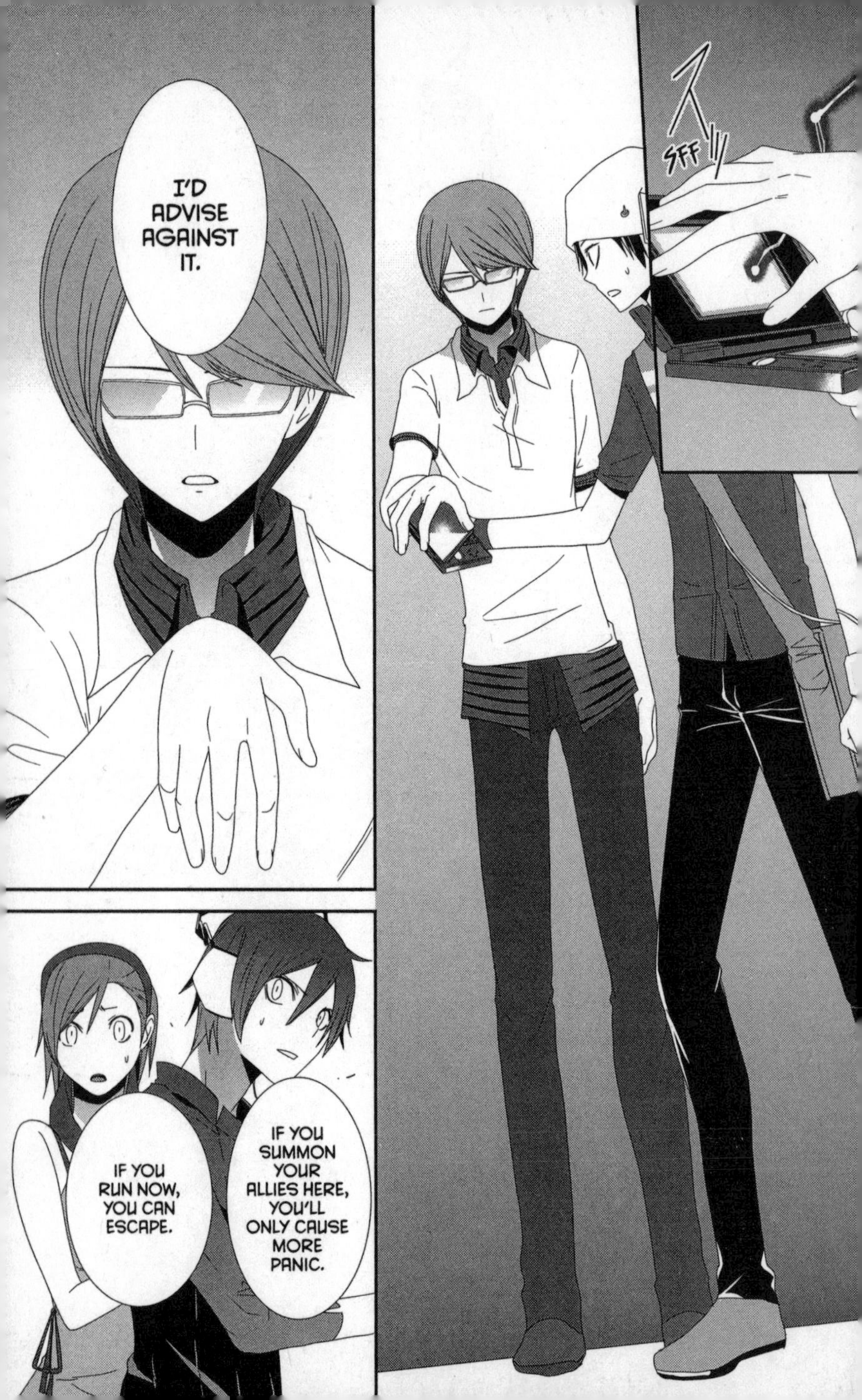
SFF
I'D ADVISE AGAINST IT.
IF YOU SUMMON YOUR ALLIES HERE, YOU'LL ONLY CAUSE MORE PANIC.
IF YOU RUN NOW, YOU CAN ESCAPE.

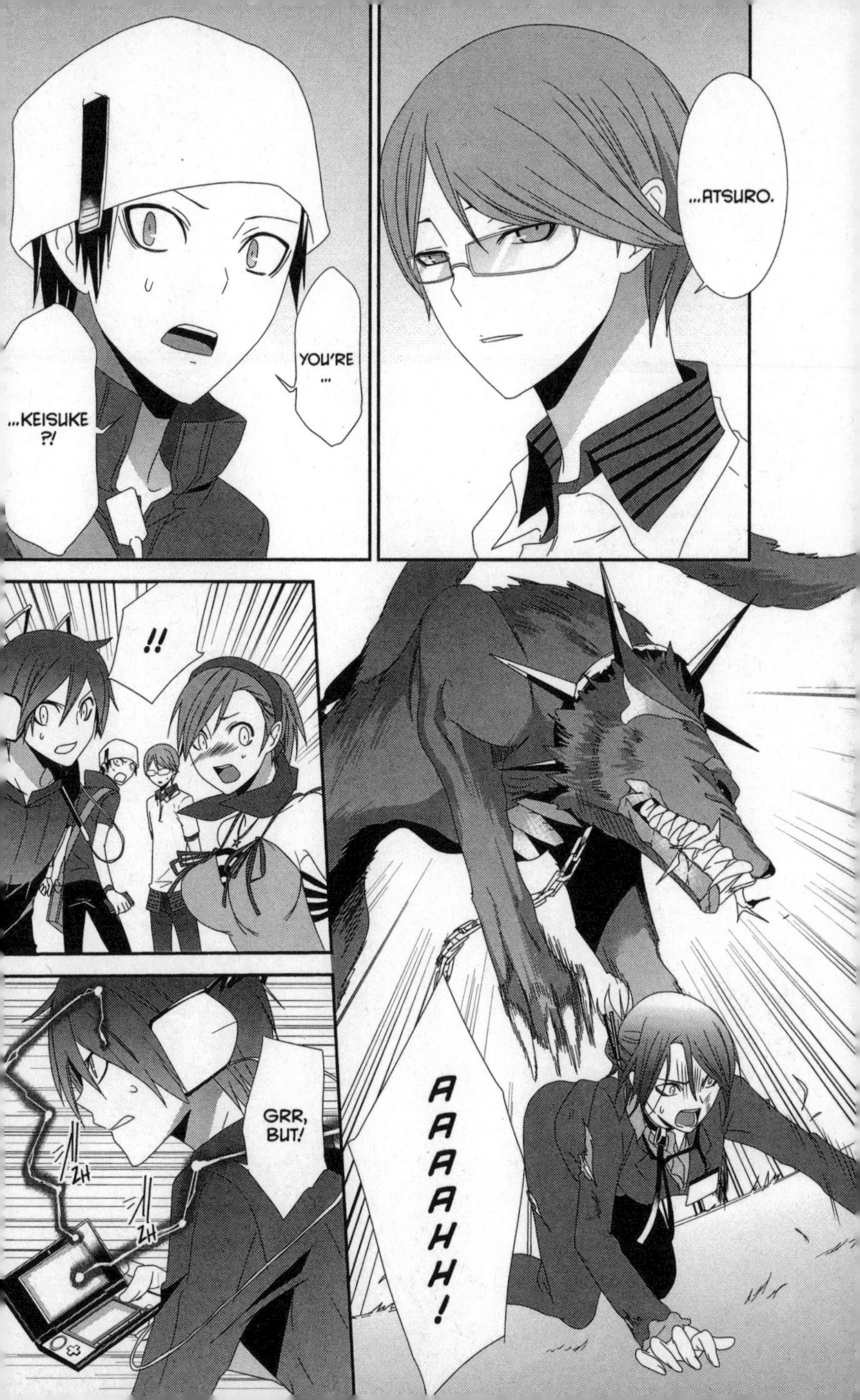
...ATSURO.
YOU'RE ...
...KEISUKE ?!
AAAAAHH!
!!
GRR, BUT!
ZH
ZH

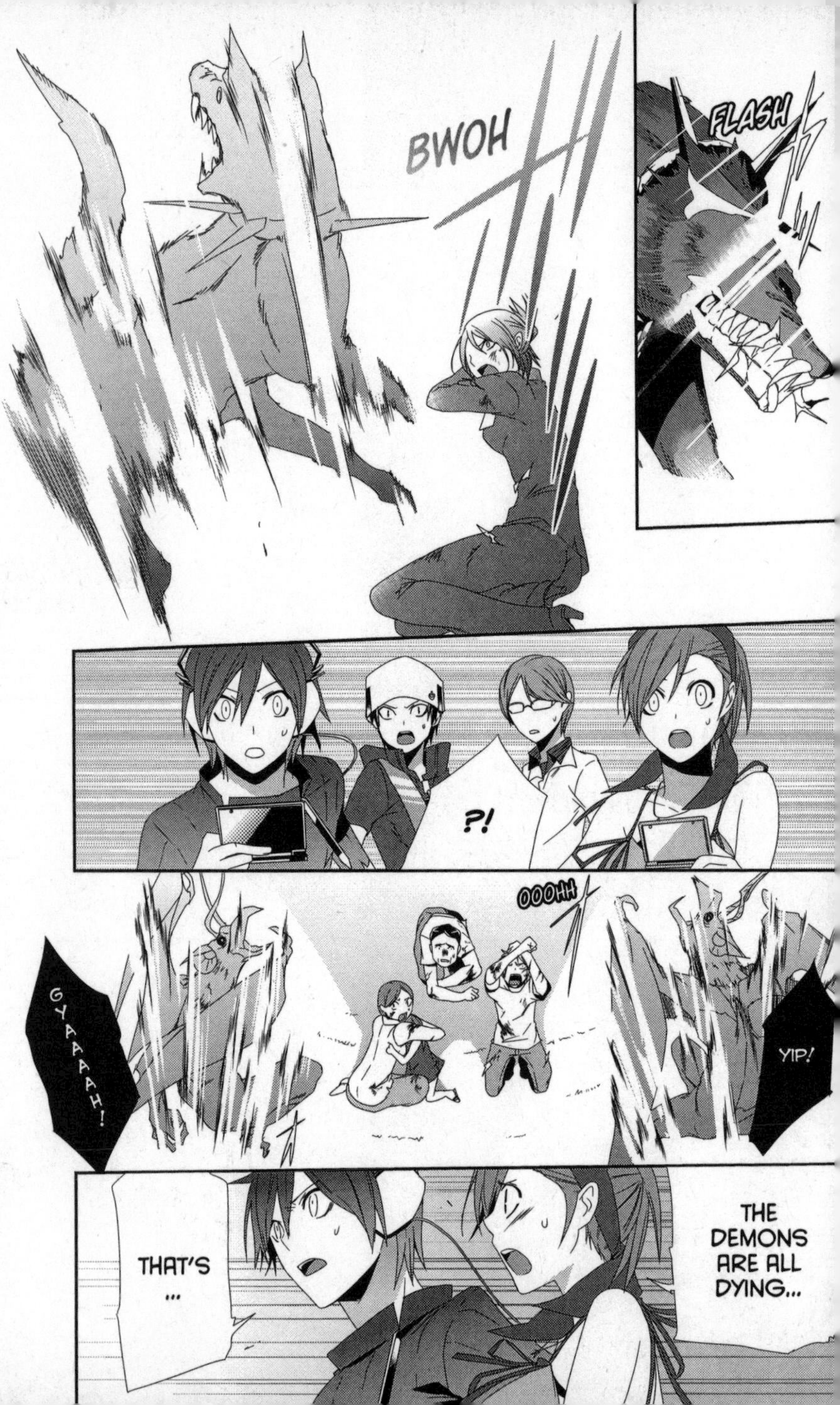
FLASH
BWOH
?!
OOOHH
YIP!
GYAAAAH!
THE DEMONS ARE ALL DYING...
THAT'S ...

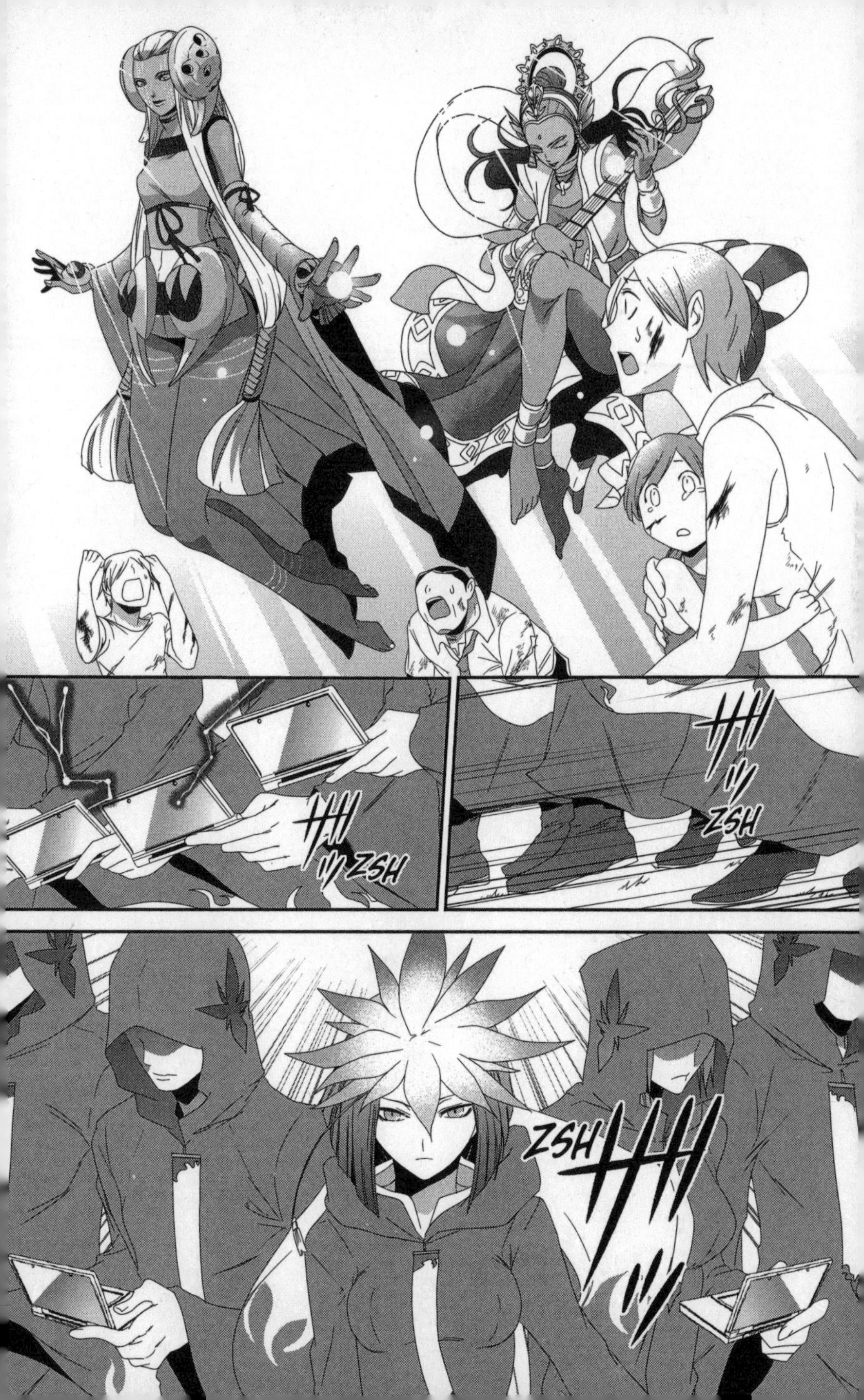
ZSH
ZSH
ZSH

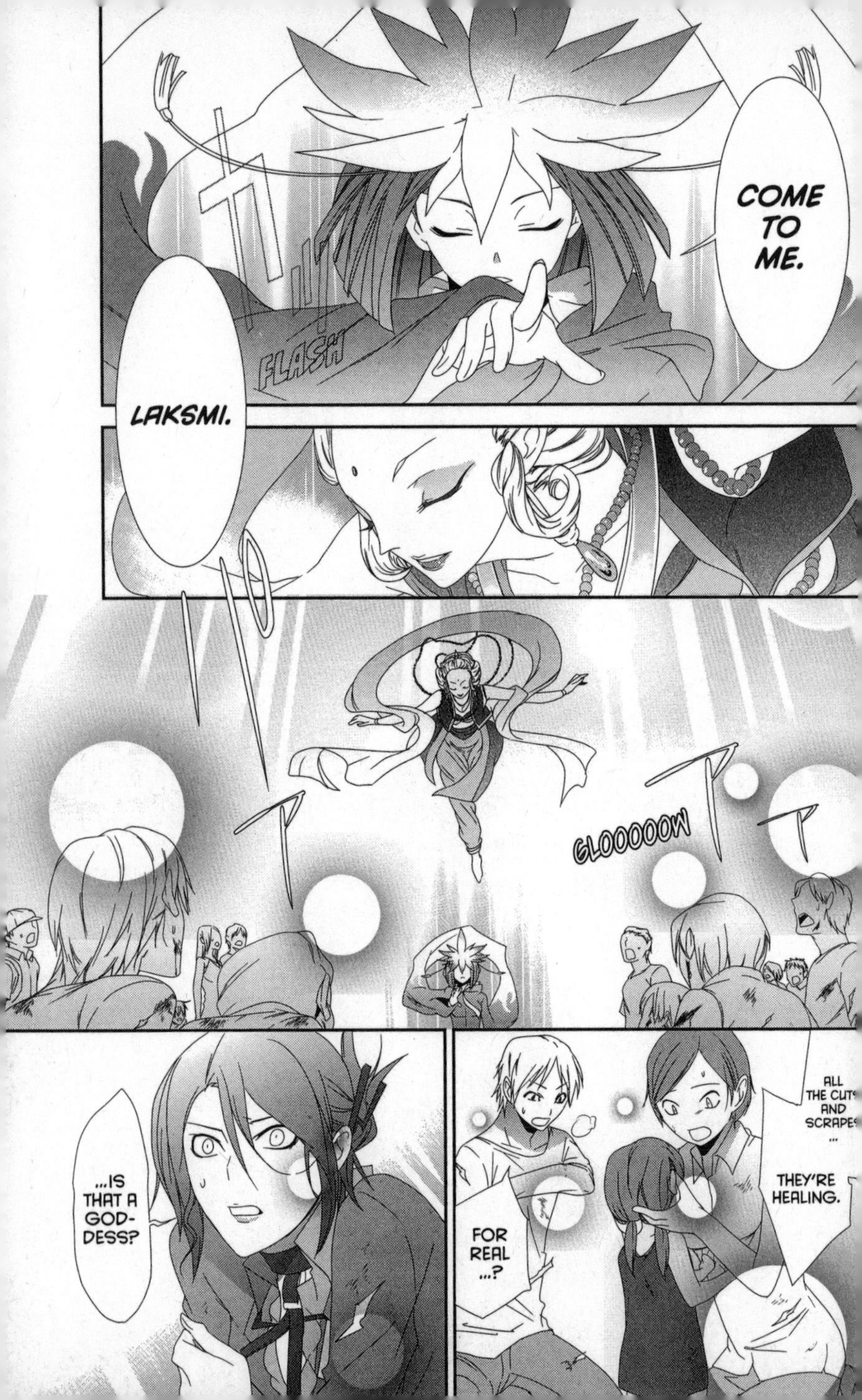
COME TO ME.
FLASH
LAKSMI.
GLOOOOOW
ALL THE CUTS AND SCRAPES...
THEY'RE HEALING.
FOR REAL...?
...IS THAT A GOD-DESS?

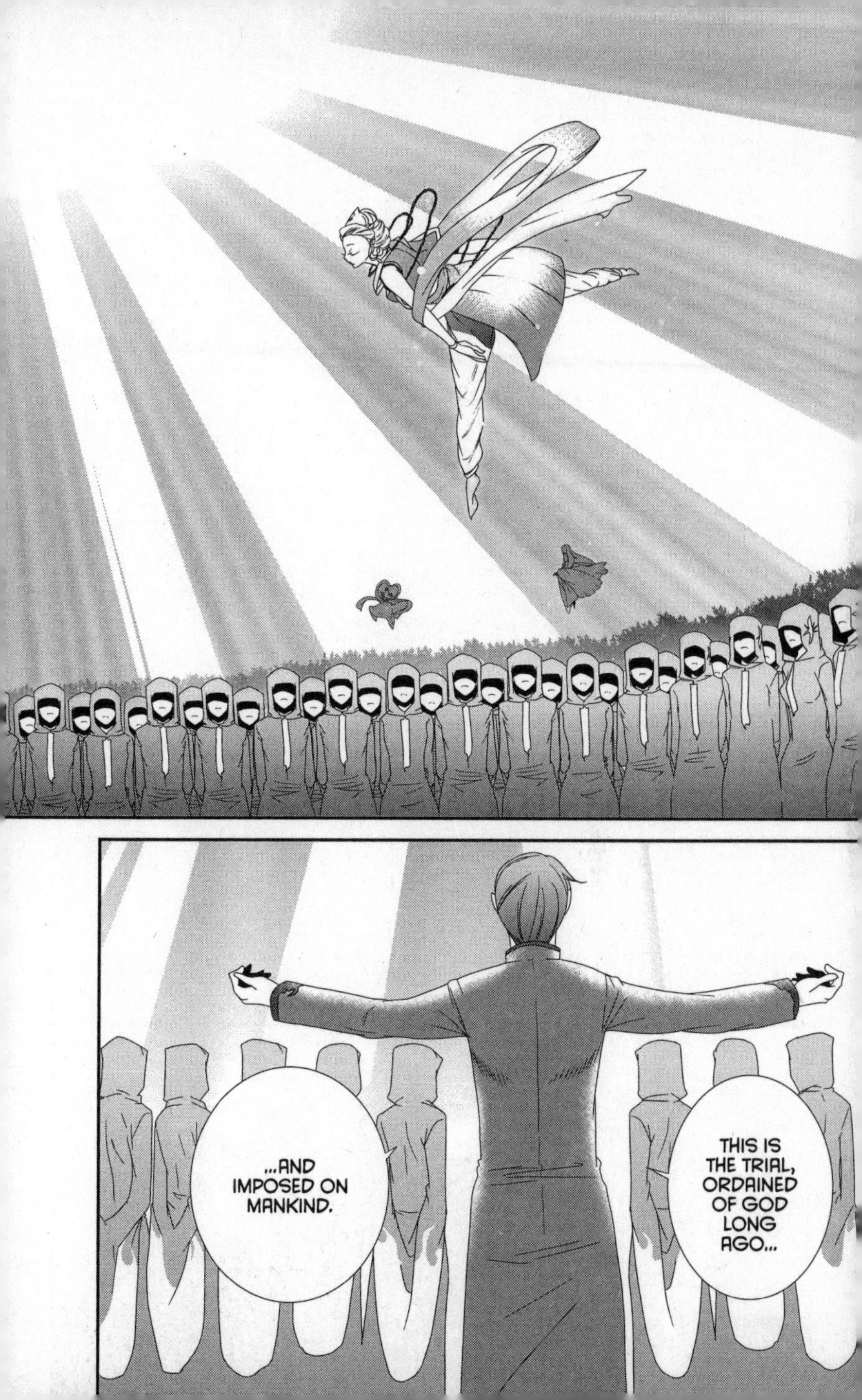
THIS IS THE TRIAL, ORDAINED OF GOD LONG AGO...
...AND IMPOSED ON MANKIND.

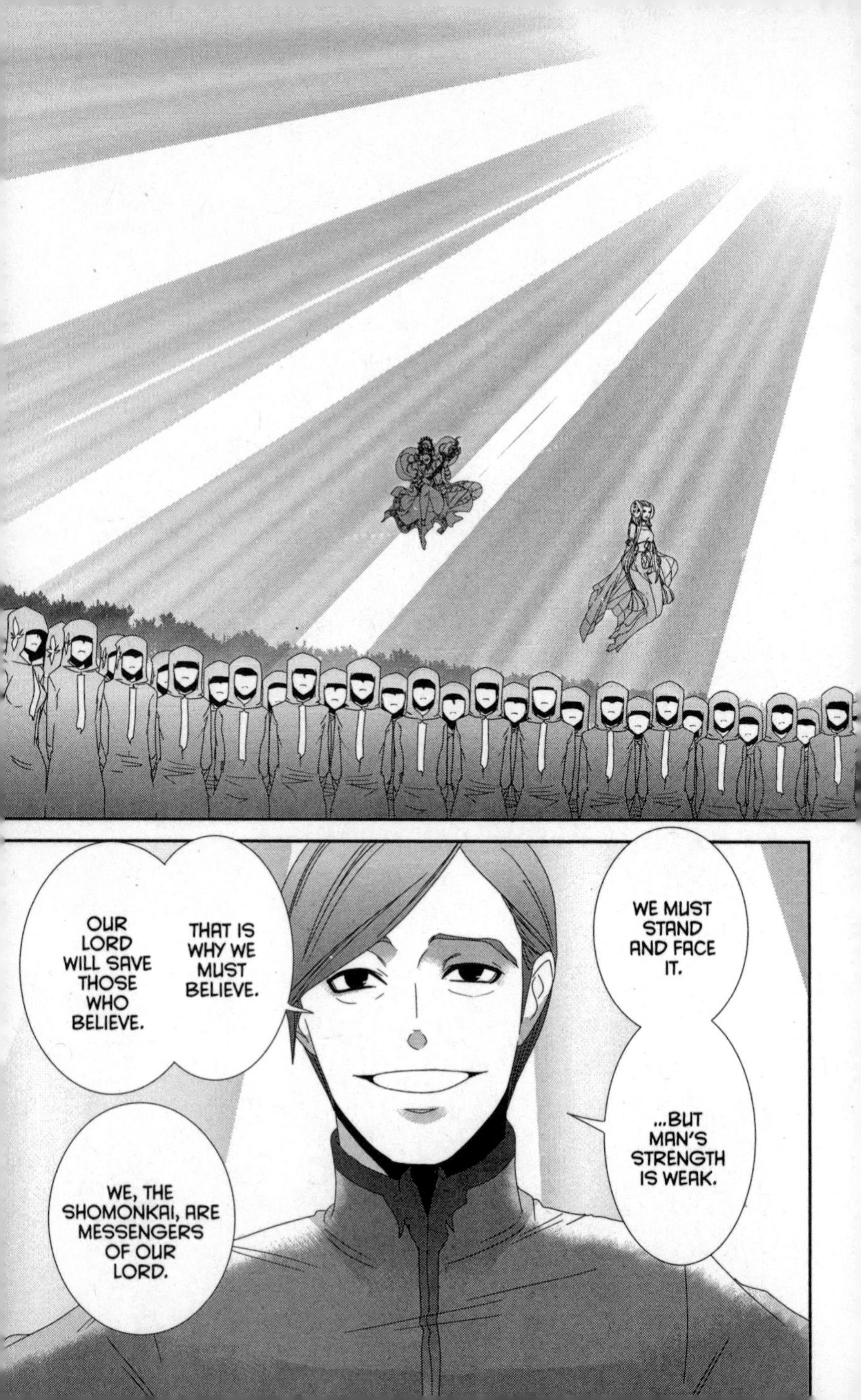
WE MUST STAND AND FACE IT.
...BUT MAN'S STRENGTH IS WEAK.
THAT IS WHY WE MUST BELIEVE.
OUR LORD WILL SAVE THOSE WHO BELIEVE.
WE, THE SHOMONKAI, ARE MESSENGERS OF OUR LORD.

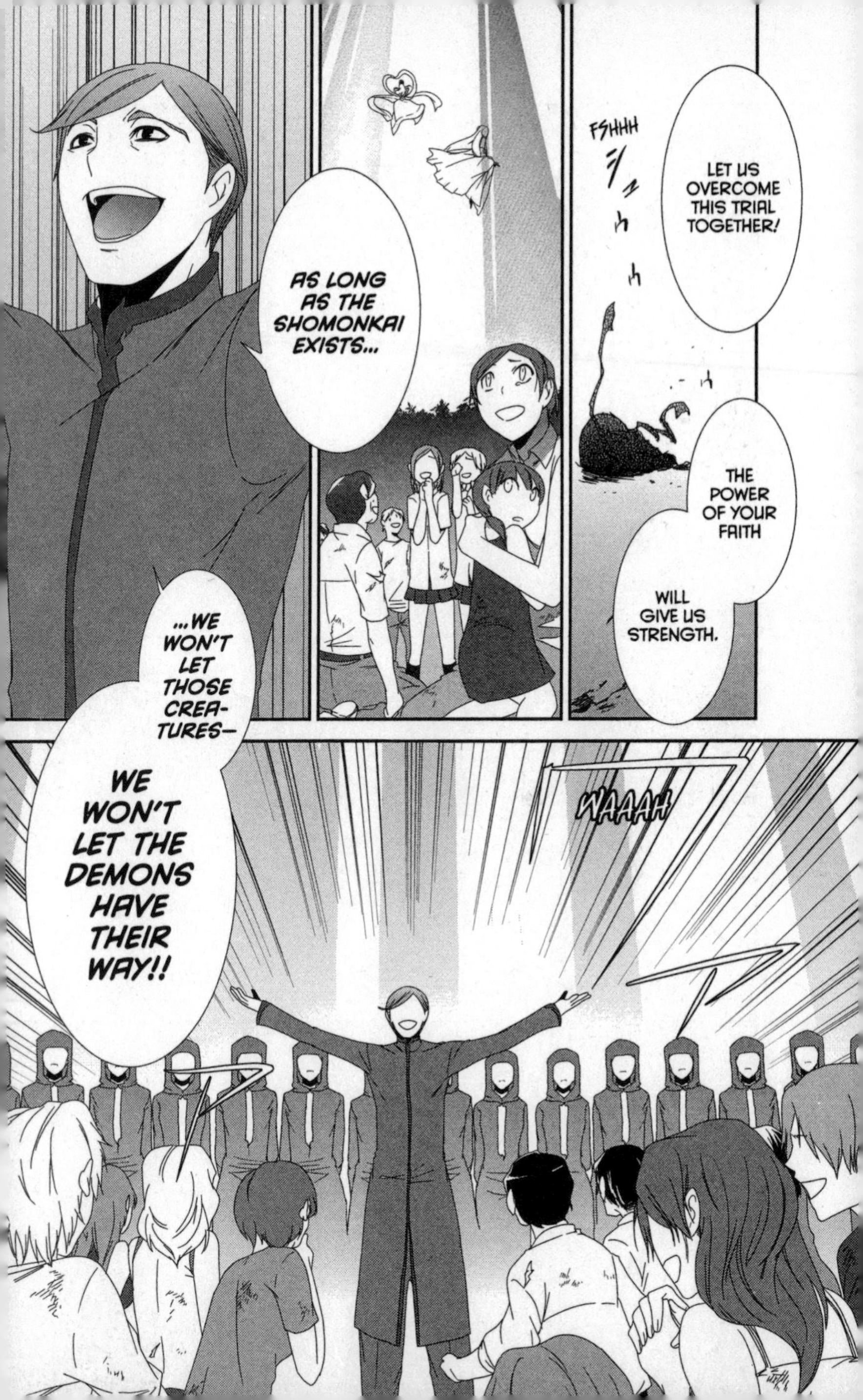
FSHHH
LET US OVERCOME THIS TRIAL TOGETHER!
THE POWER OF YOUR FAITH
WILL GIVE US STRENGTH.
AS LONG AS THE SHOMONKAI EXISTS...
...WE WON'T LET THOSE CREA-TURES—
WE WON'T LET THE DEMONS HAVE THEIR WAY!!
WAAAH

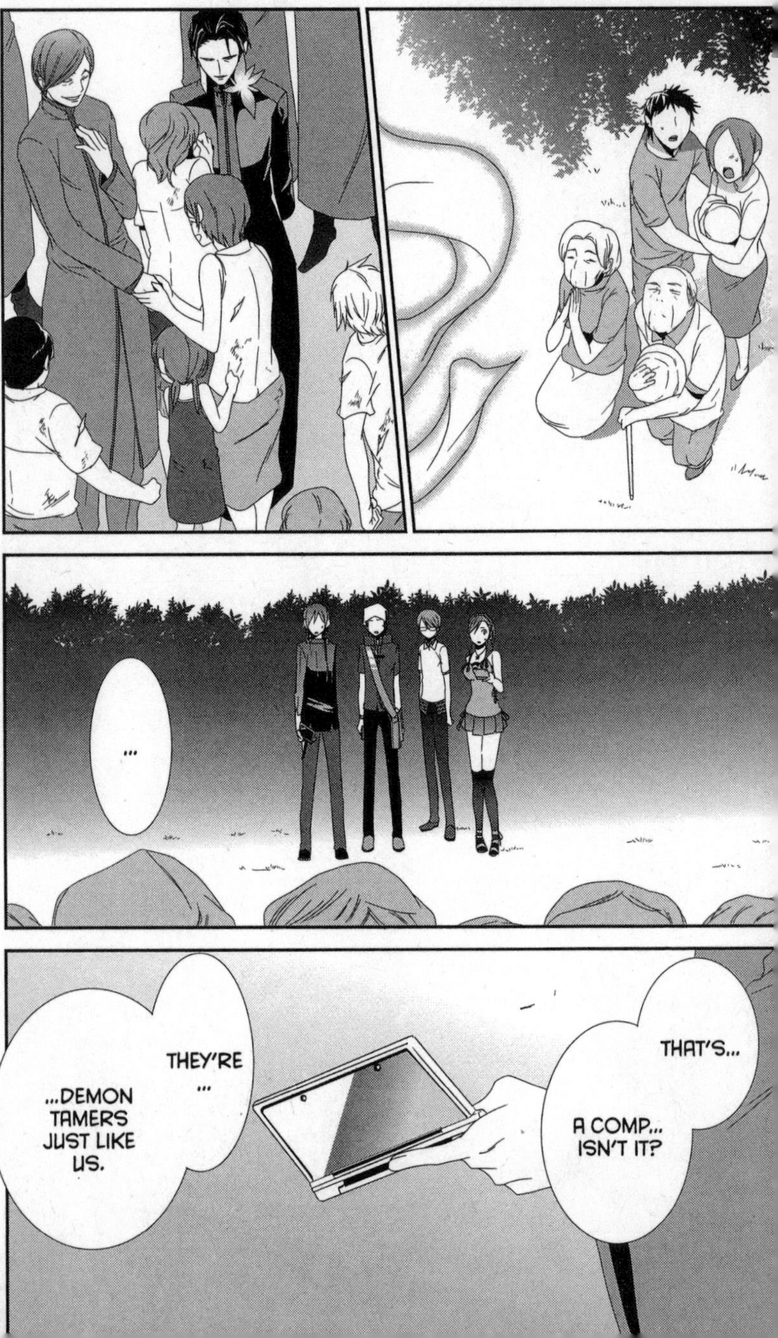
...
THAT'S...
A COMP... ISN'T IT?
THEY'RE...
...DEMON TAMERS JUST LIKE US.

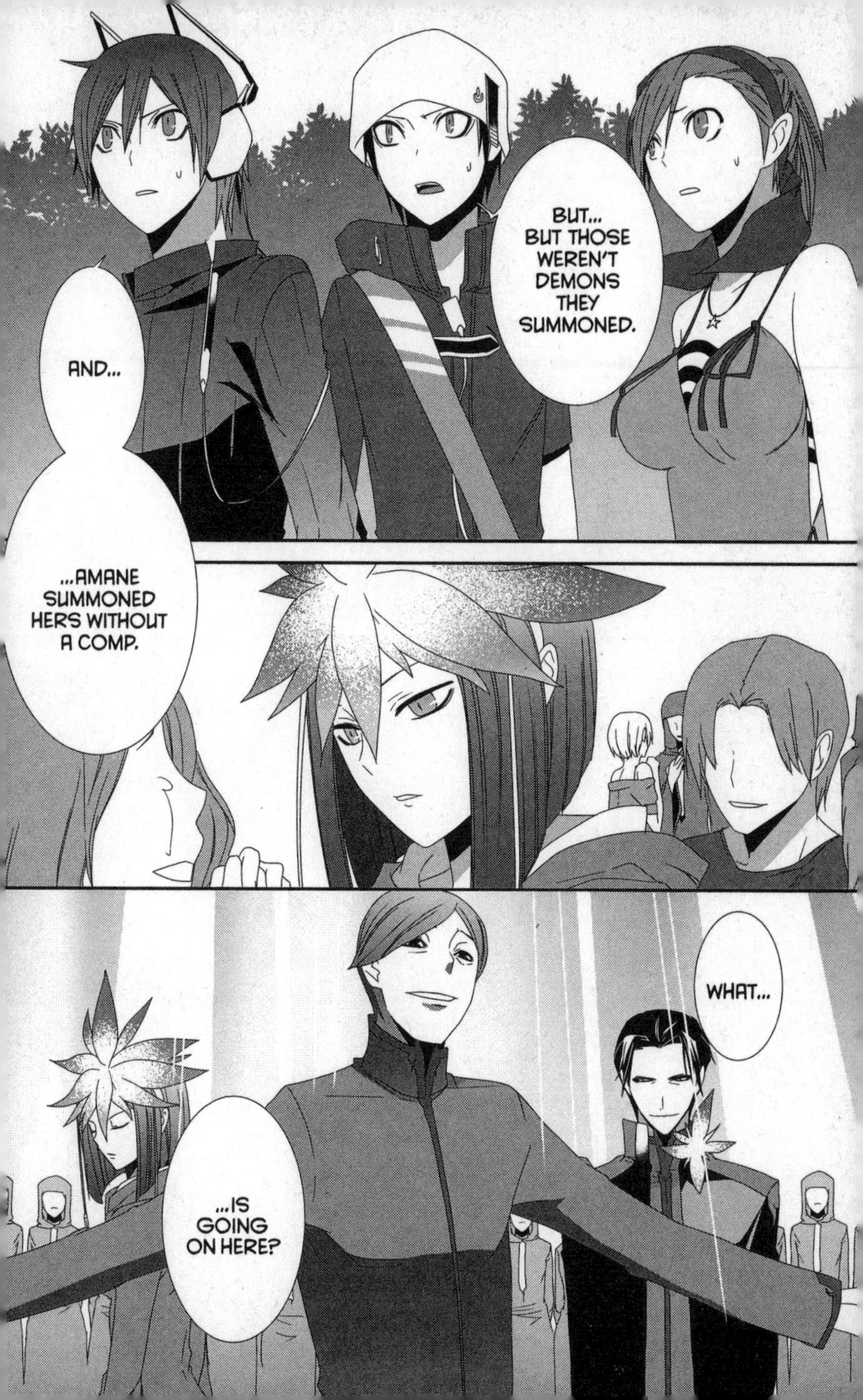
BUT... BUT THOSE WEREN'T DEMONS THEY SUMMONED.
AND...
...AMANE SUMMONED HERS WITHOUT A COMP.
WHAT...
...IS GOING ON HERE?

PROFILE

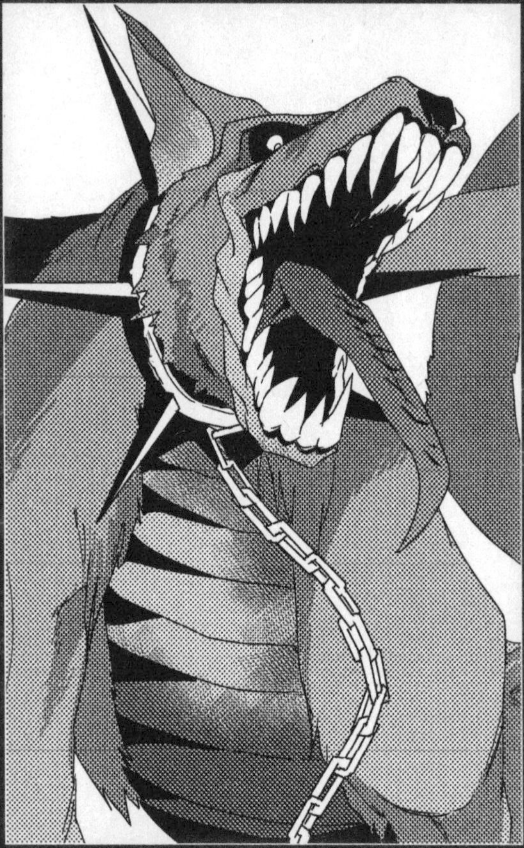

GARM

HUNTING HOUND OF HEL, QUEEN OF THE UNDERWORLD. IT GUARDS THE ENTRANCE TO NIFLHEIM, LAND OF THE DEAD. IT IS SAID THAT THE BLACK FUR ON ITS CHEST WAS DYED CRIMSON WITH THE BLOOD OF THE DEAD, AND THAT ITS FOUR EYES BURN LIKE COAL. IT WATCHES OVER THE DEAD, AND MERCILESSLY ATTACKS AND DEVOURS ANY WHO TRY TO ESCAPE. IT IS BOUND WITH AN UNBREAKABLE CHAIN, BUT ACCORDING TO LEGEND, IT WILL BE SET LOOSE AT RAGNAROK, THE FINAL WAR OF THE GODS. THERE IT WILL FIGHT TYR, GOD OF THE LAW, AND THEY WILL STRIKE EACH OTHER DOWN.

DEVIL SURVIVOR

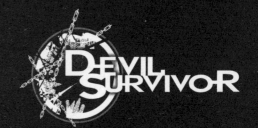

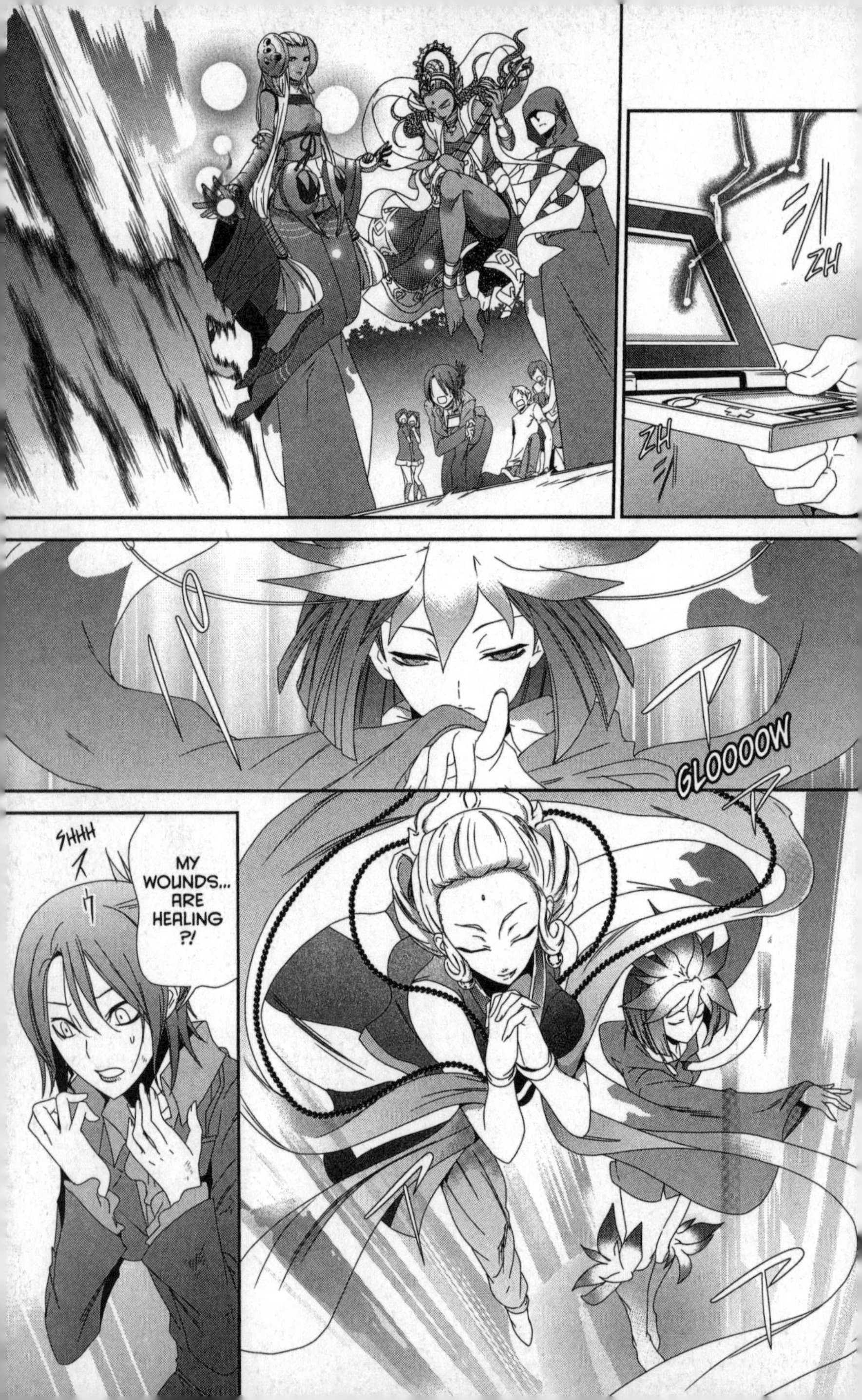
ZH
ZH
GLOOOOW
SHHH
MY WOUNDS... ARE HEALING ?!

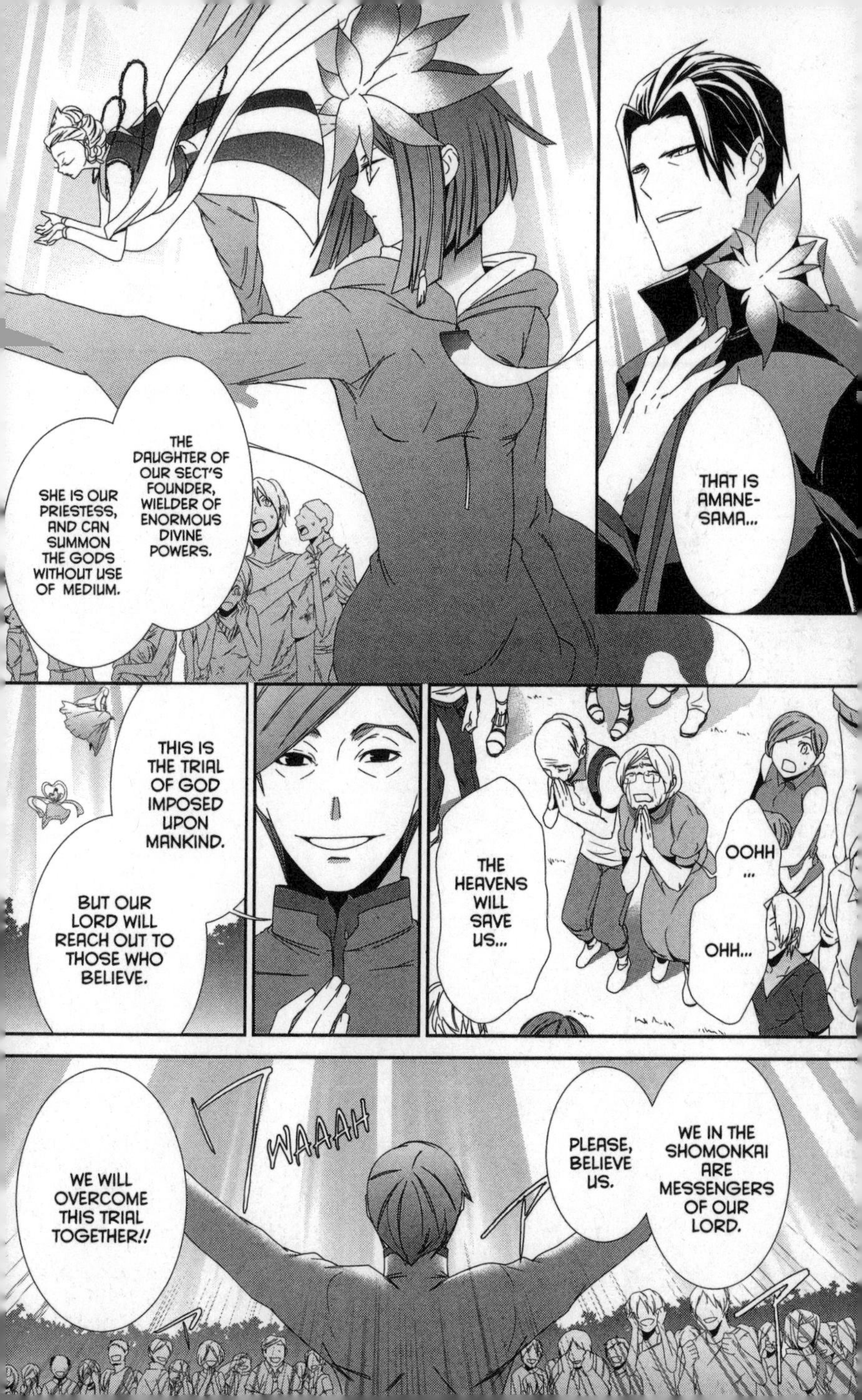
THAT IS AMANE-SAMA...
THE DAUGHTER OF OUR SECT'S FOUNDER, WIELDER OF ENORMOUS DIVINE POWERS.
SHE IS OUR PRIESTESS, AND CAN SUMMON THE GODS WITHOUT USE OF MEDIUM.
OOHH ...
OHH...
THE HEAVENS WILL SAVE US...
THIS IS THE TRIAL OF GOD IMPOSED UPON MANKIND.
BUT OUR LORD WILL REACH OUT TO THOSE WHO BELIEVE.
WE IN THE SHOMONKAI ARE MESSENGERS OF OUR LORD.
PLEASE, BELIEVE US.
WAAAAH
WE WILL OVERCOME THIS TRIAL TOGETHER!!

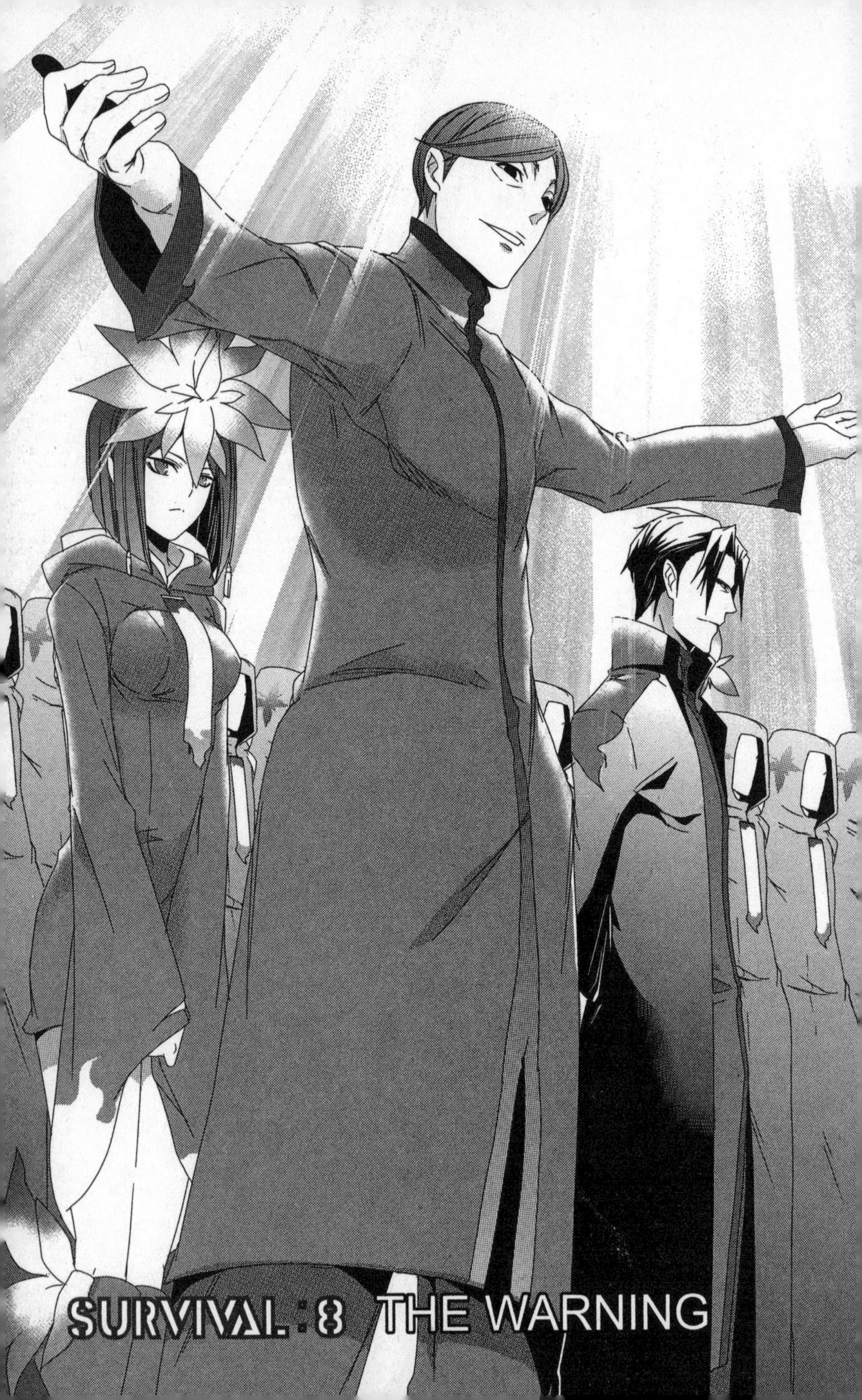
SURVIVAL :8 THE WARNING

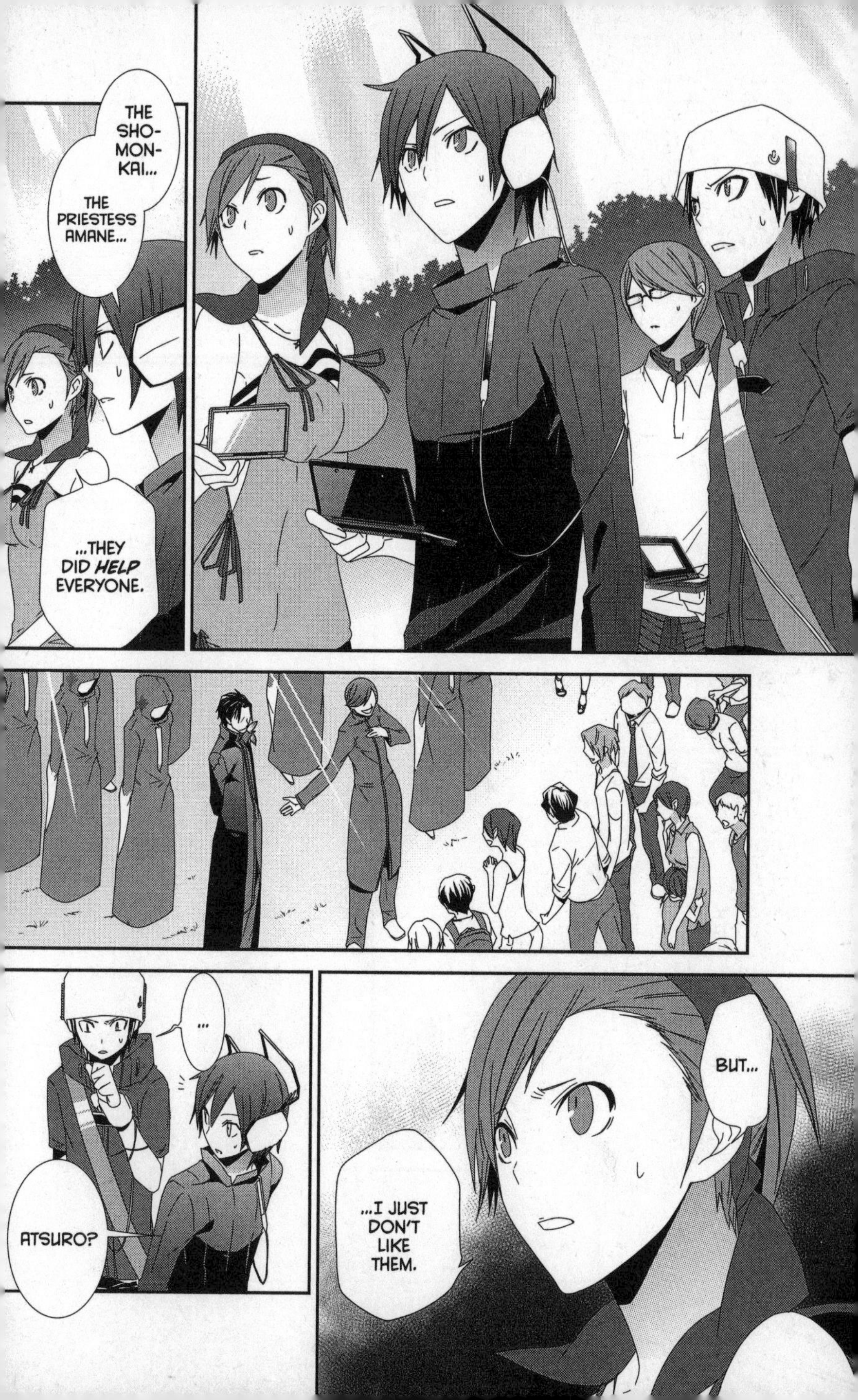
THE SHO-MON-KAI...
THE PRIESTESS AMANE...
...THEY DID *HELP* EVERYONE.
BUT...
...I JUST DON'T LIKE THEM.
...
ATSURO?

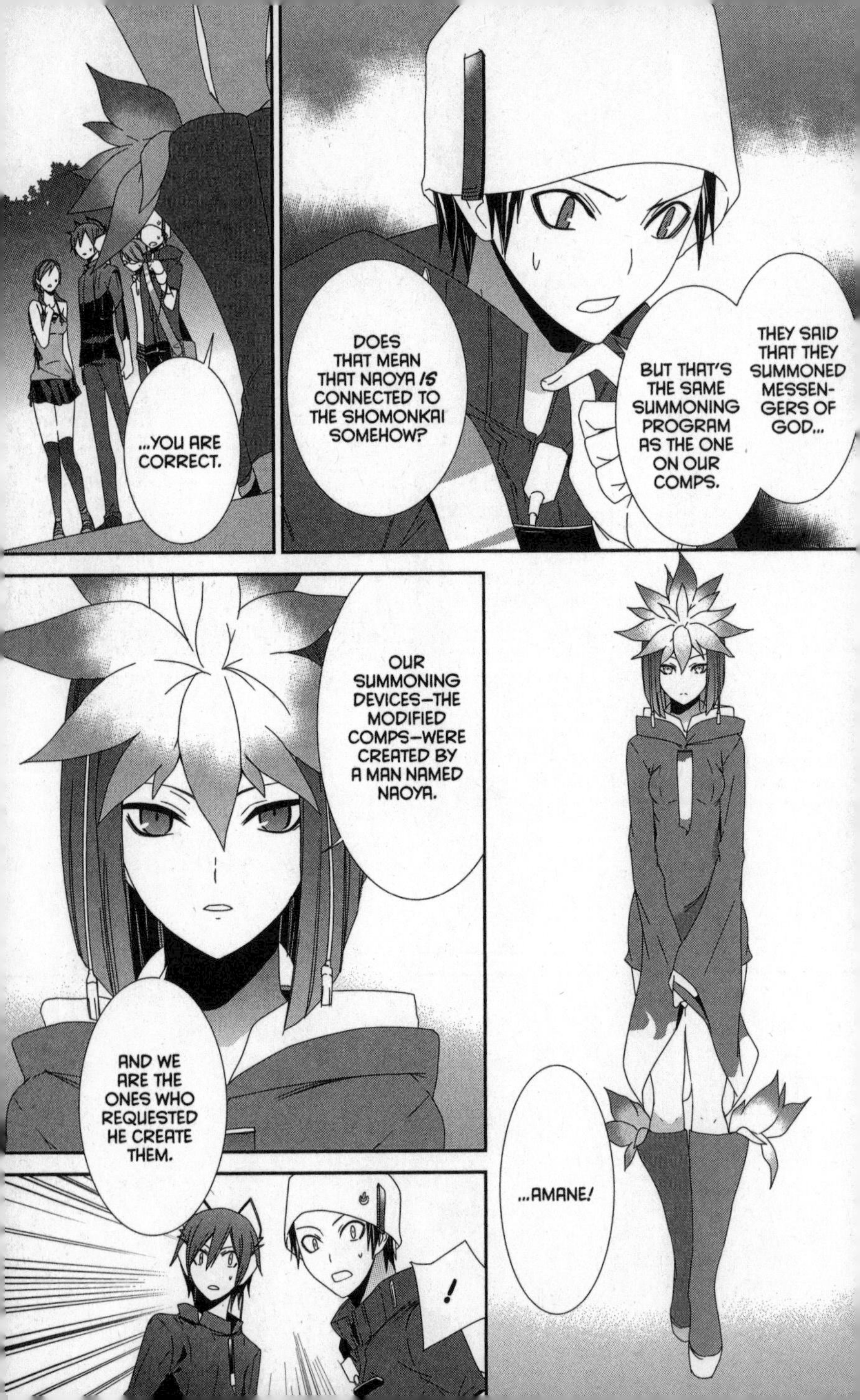
THEY SAID THAT THEY SUMMONED MESSEN-GERS OF GOD...
BUT THAT'S THE SAME SUMMONING PROGRAM AS THE ONE ON OUR COMPS.
DOES THAT MEAN THAT NAOYA *IS* CONNECTED TO THE SHOMONKAI SOMEHOW?
...YOU ARE CORRECT.
...AMANE!
OUR SUMMONING DEVICES—THE MODIFIED COMPS—WERE CREATED BY A MAN NAMED NAOYA.
AND WE ARE THE ONES WHO REQUESTED HE CREATE THEM.
!

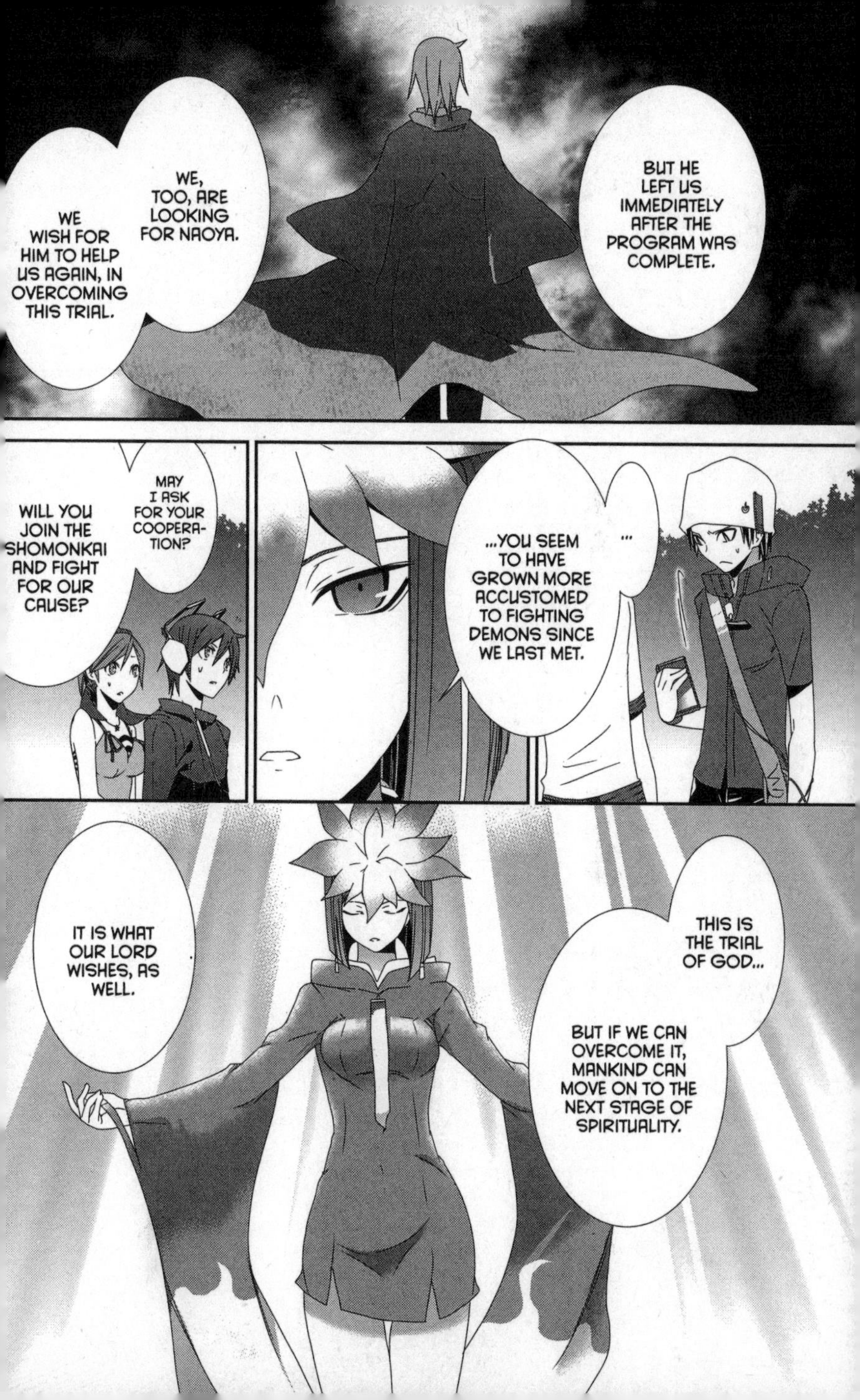
BUT HE LEFT US IMMEDIATELY AFTER THE PROGRAM WAS COMPLETE.
WE, TOO, ARE LOOKING FOR NAOYA.
WE WISH FOR HIM TO HELP US AGAIN, IN OVERCOMING THIS TRIAL.
...
...YOU SEEM TO HAVE GROWN MORE ACCUSTOMED TO FIGHTING DEMONS SINCE WE LAST MET.
MAY I ASK FOR YOUR COOPERA-TION?
WILL YOU JOIN THE SHOMONKAI AND FIGHT FOR OUR CAUSE?
THIS IS THE TRIAL OF GOD...
BUT IF WE CAN OVERCOME IT, MANKIND CAN MOVE ON TO THE NEXT STAGE OF SPIRITUALITY.
IT IS WHAT OUR LORD WISHES, AS WELL.

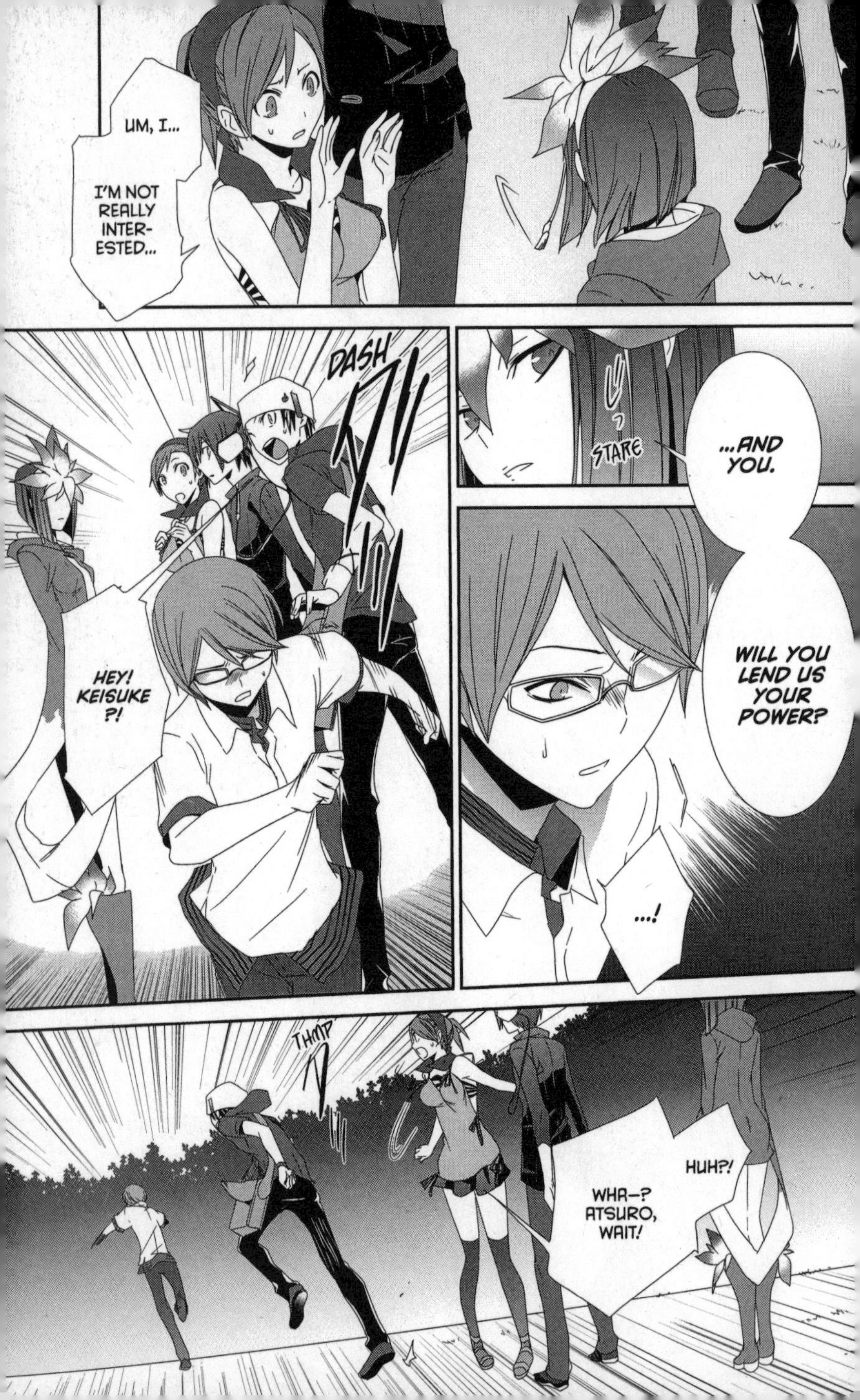
UM, I...
I'M NOT REALLY INTERESTED...
STARE
...AND YOU.
WILL YOU LEND US YOUR POWER?
...!
DASH
HEY! KEISUKE?!
THMP
HUH?!
WHA-? ATSURO, WAIT!

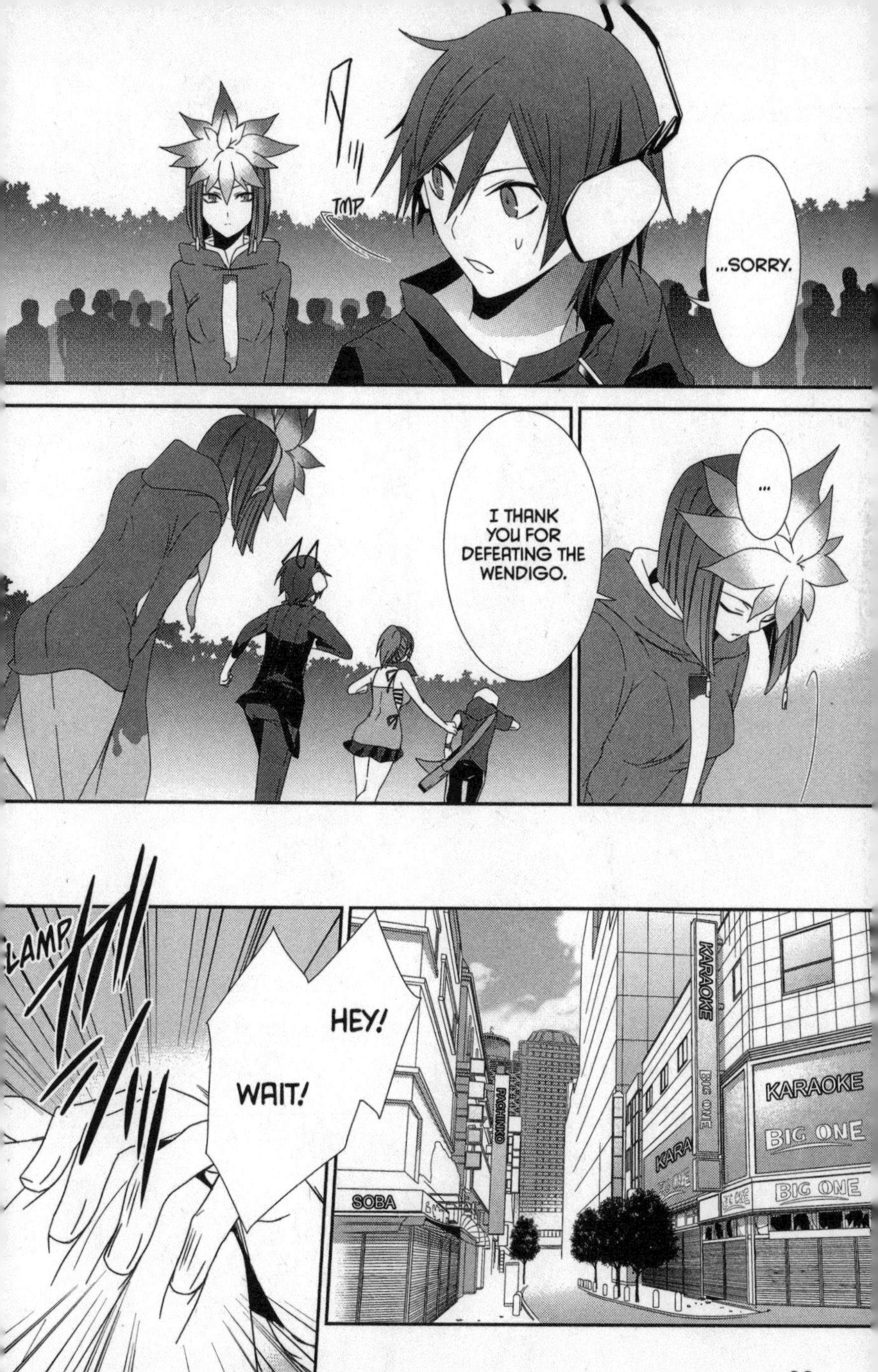
TMP
...SORRY.
...
I THANK YOU FOR DEFEATING THE WENDIGO.
KARAOKE
BIG ONE
KARAOKE
BIG ONE
BIG ONE
PACHINKO
SOBA
HEY!
WAIT!
CLAMP

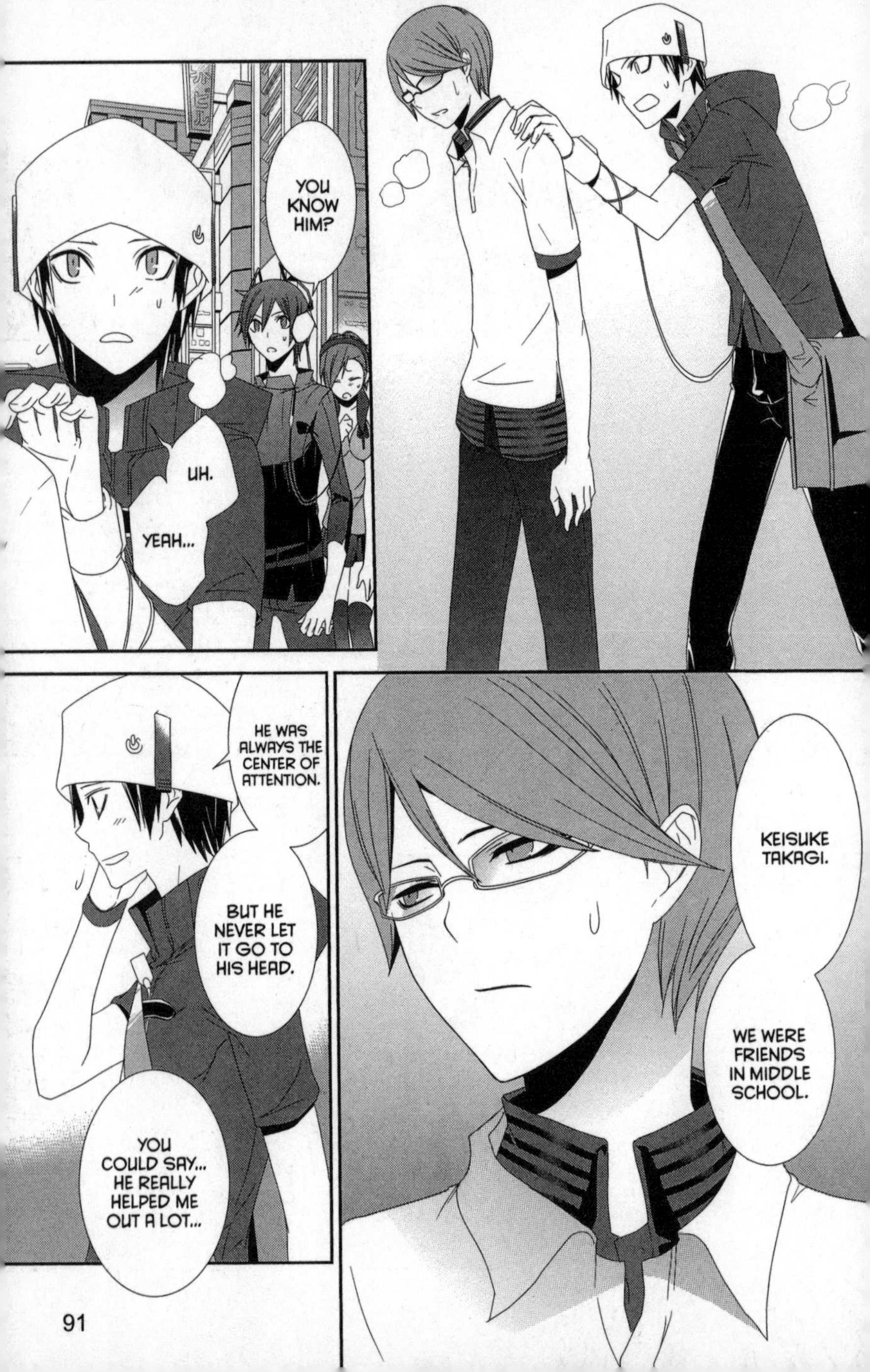
YOU KNOW HIM?
UH.
YEAH...
KEISUKE TAKAGI.
WE WERE FRIENDS IN MIDDLE SCHOOL.
HE WAS ALWAYS THE CENTER OF ATTENTION.
BUT HE NEVER LET IT GO TO HIS HEAD.
YOU COULD SAY... HE REALLY HELPED ME OUT A LOT...

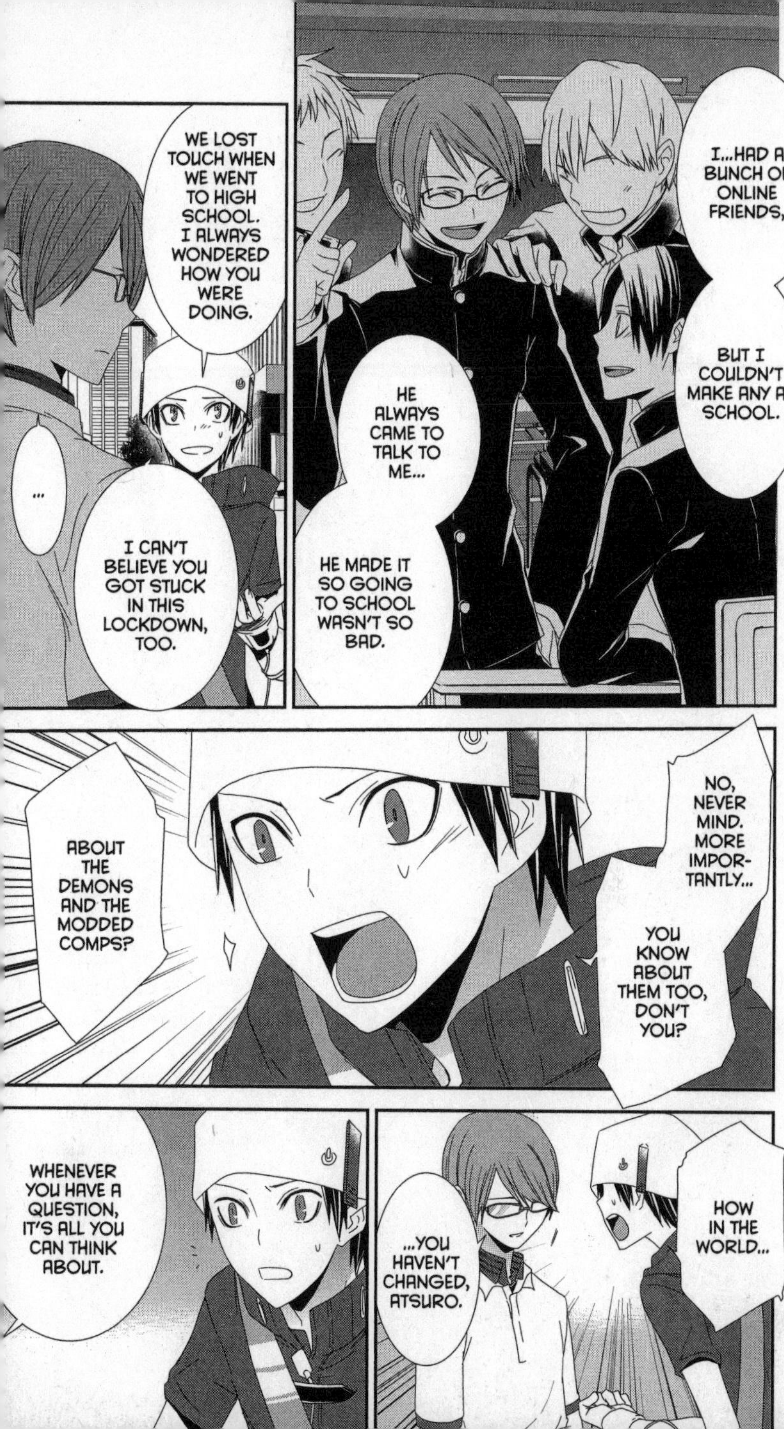
I...HAD A BUNCH OF ONLINE FRIENDS,
BUT I COULDN'T MAKE ANY AT SCHOOL.
HE ALWAYS CAME TO TALK TO ME...
HE MADE IT SO GOING TO SCHOOL WASN'T SO BAD.
WE LOST TOUCH WHEN WE WENT TO HIGH SCHOOL. I ALWAYS WONDERED HOW YOU WERE DOING.
I CAN'T BELIEVE YOU GOT STUCK IN THIS LOCKDOWN, TOO.
...
NO, NEVER MIND. MORE IMPOR-TANTLY...
YOU KNOW ABOUT THEM TOO, DON'T YOU?
ABOUT THE DEMONS AND THE MODDED COMPS?
HOW IN THE WORLD...
...YOU HAVEN'T CHANGED, ATSURO.
WHENEVER YOU HAVE A QUESTION, IT'S ALL YOU CAN THINK ABOUT.

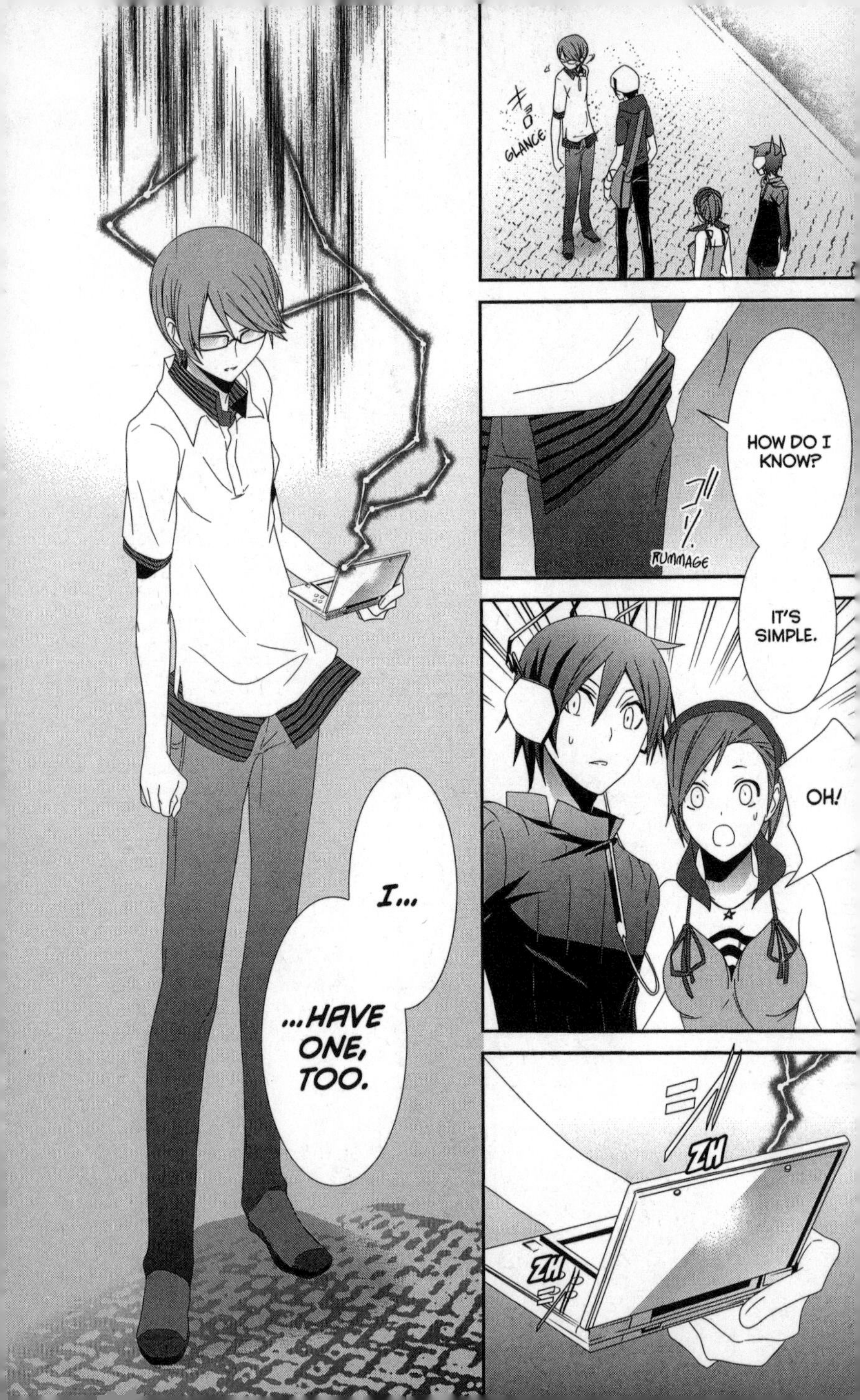
GLANCE
HOW DO I KNOW?
RUMMAGE
IT'S SIMPLE.
OH!
ZH
ZH
I...
...HAVE ONE, TOO.

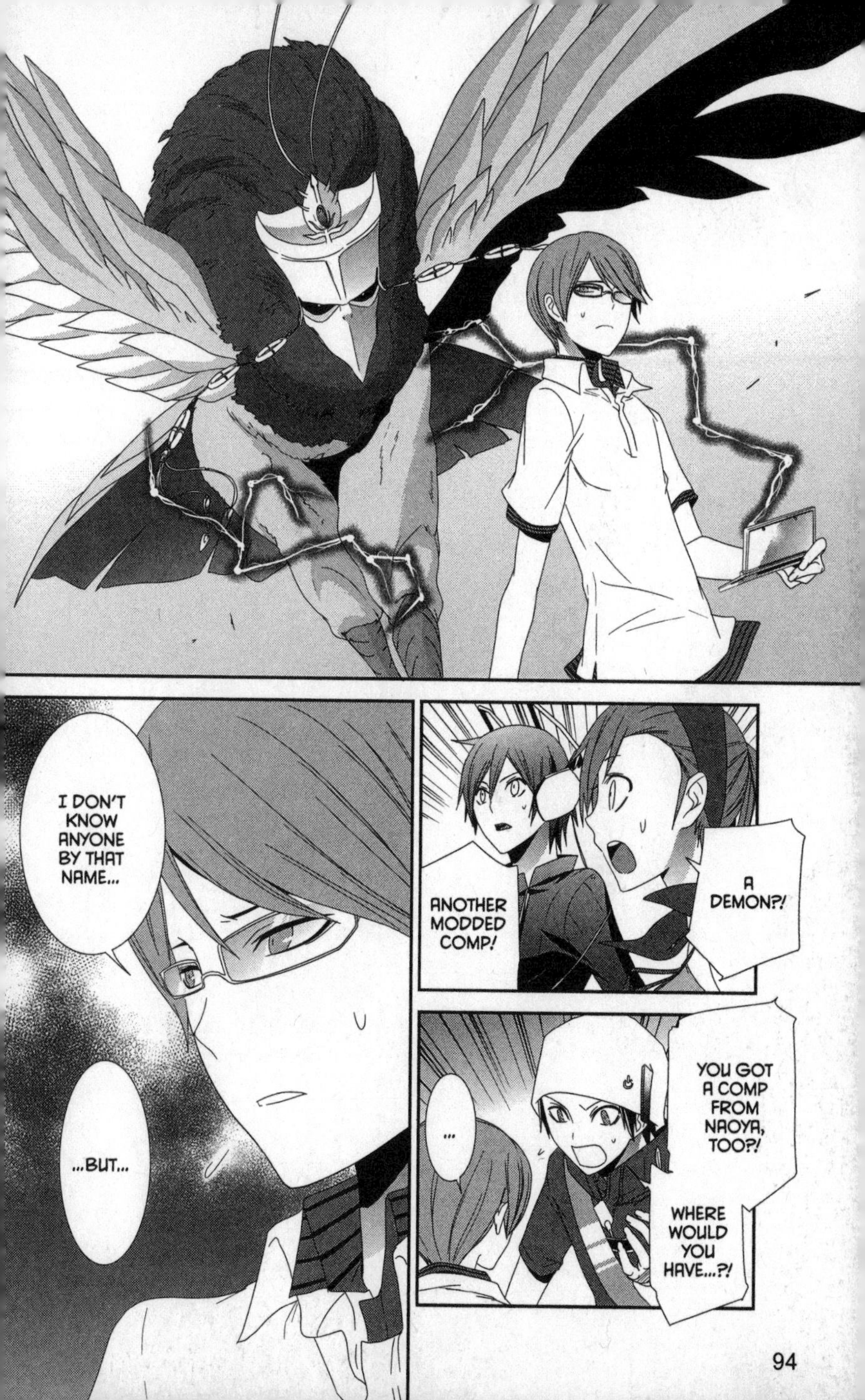
A DEMON?!
ANOTHER MODDED COMP!
YOU GOT A COMP FROM NAOYA, TOO?!
WHERE WOULD YOU HAVE...?!
...
I DON'T KNOW ANYONE BY THAT NAME...
...BUT...

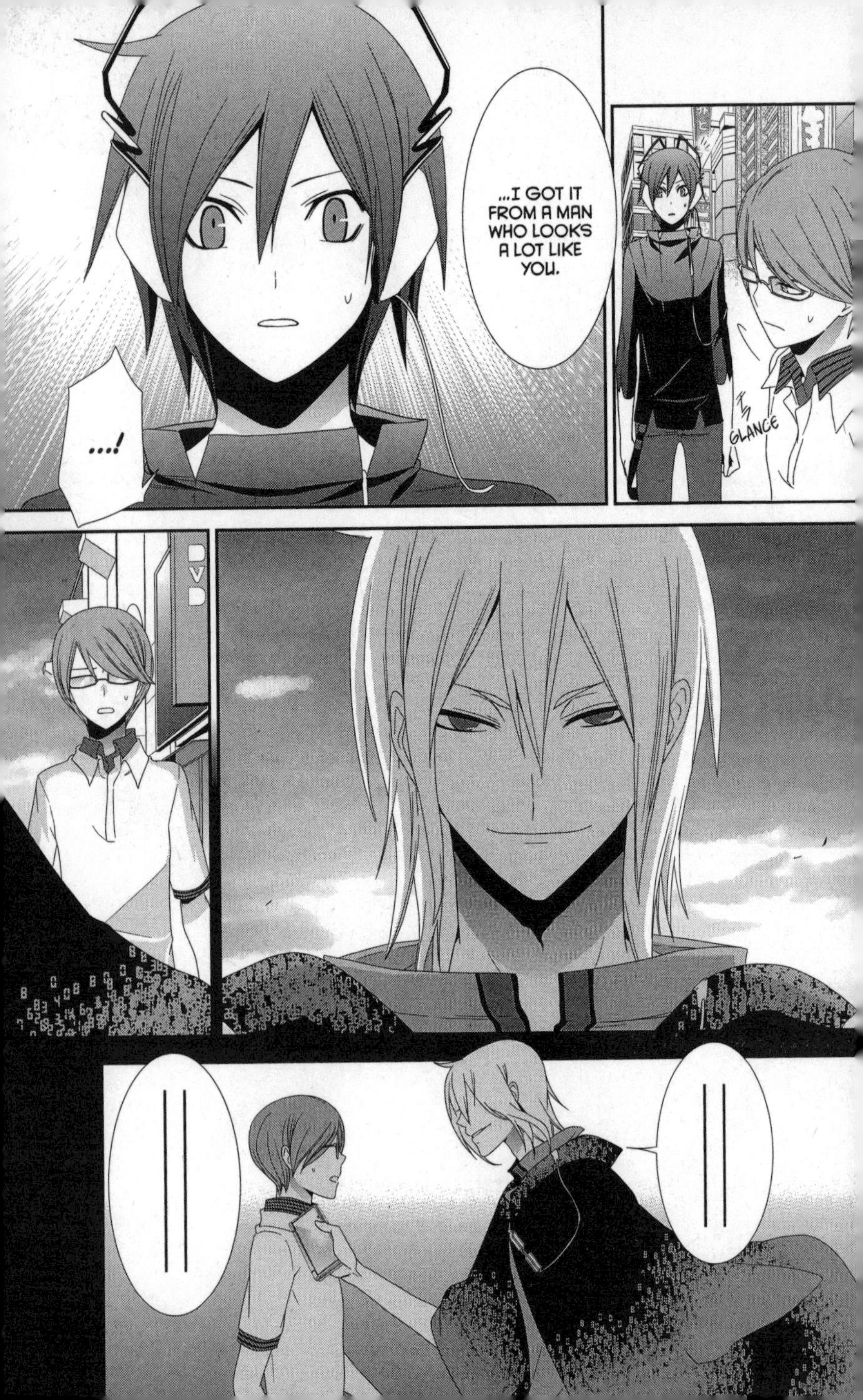
GLANCE
...I GOT IT FROM A MAN WHO LOOKS A LOT LIKE YOU.
...!
DVD

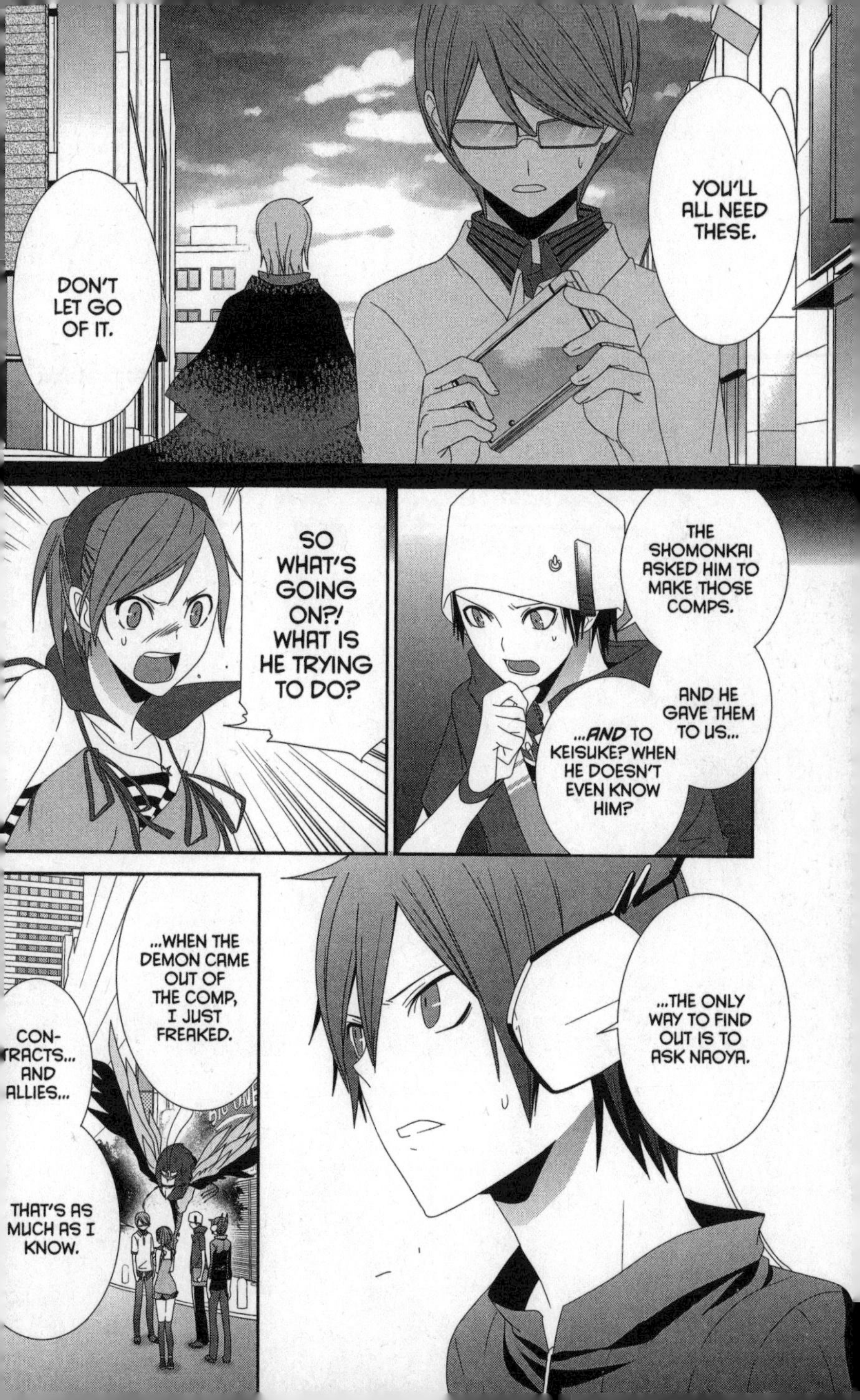

YOU'LL ALL NEED THESE.
DON'T LET GO OF IT.
THE SHOMONKAI ASKED HIM TO MAKE THOSE COMPS.
AND HE GAVE THEM TO US...
...AND TO KEISUKE? WHEN HE DOESN'T EVEN KNOW HIM?
SO WHAT'S GOING ON?! WHAT IS HE TRYING TO DO?
...THE ONLY WAY TO FIND OUT IS TO ASK NAOYA.
...WHEN THE DEMON CAME OUT OF THE COMP, I JUST FREAKED.
CON- RACTS... AND ALLIES...
THAT'S AS MUCH AS I KNOW.

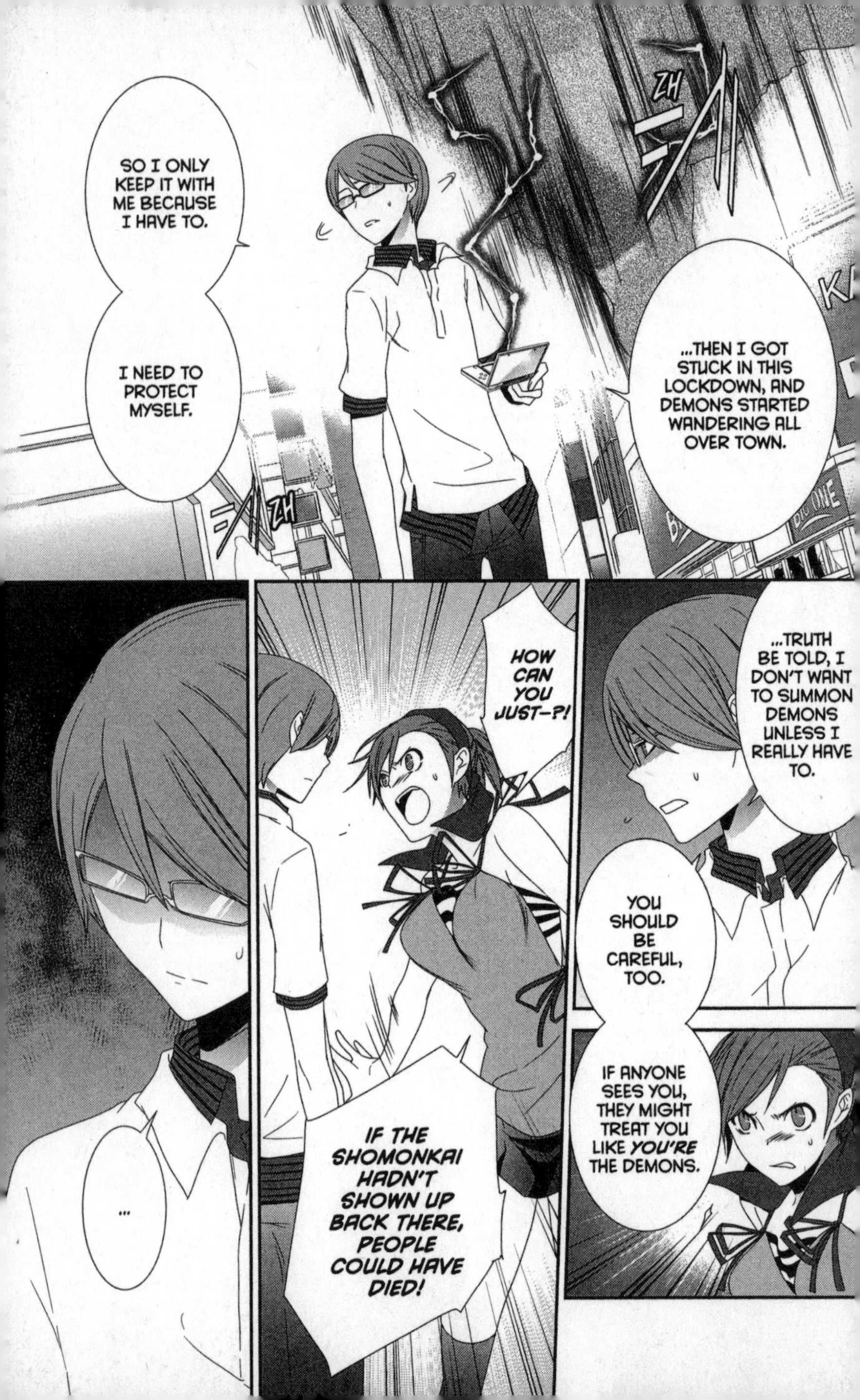
ZH
...THEN I GOT STUCK IN THIS LOCKDOWN, AND DEMONS STARTED WANDERING ALL OVER TOWN.
SO I ONLY KEEP IT WITH ME BECAUSE I HAVE TO.
I NEED TO PROTECT MYSELF.
ZH
...TRUTH BE TOLD, I DON'T WANT TO SUMMON DEMONS UNLESS I REALLY HAVE TO.
YOU SHOULD BE CAREFUL, TOO.
IF ANYONE SEES YOU, THEY MIGHT TREAT YOU LIKE *YOU'RE* THE DEMONS.
HOW CAN YOU JUST-?!
IF THE SHOMONKAI HADN'T SHOWN UP BACK THERE, PEOPLE COULD HAVE DIED!
...

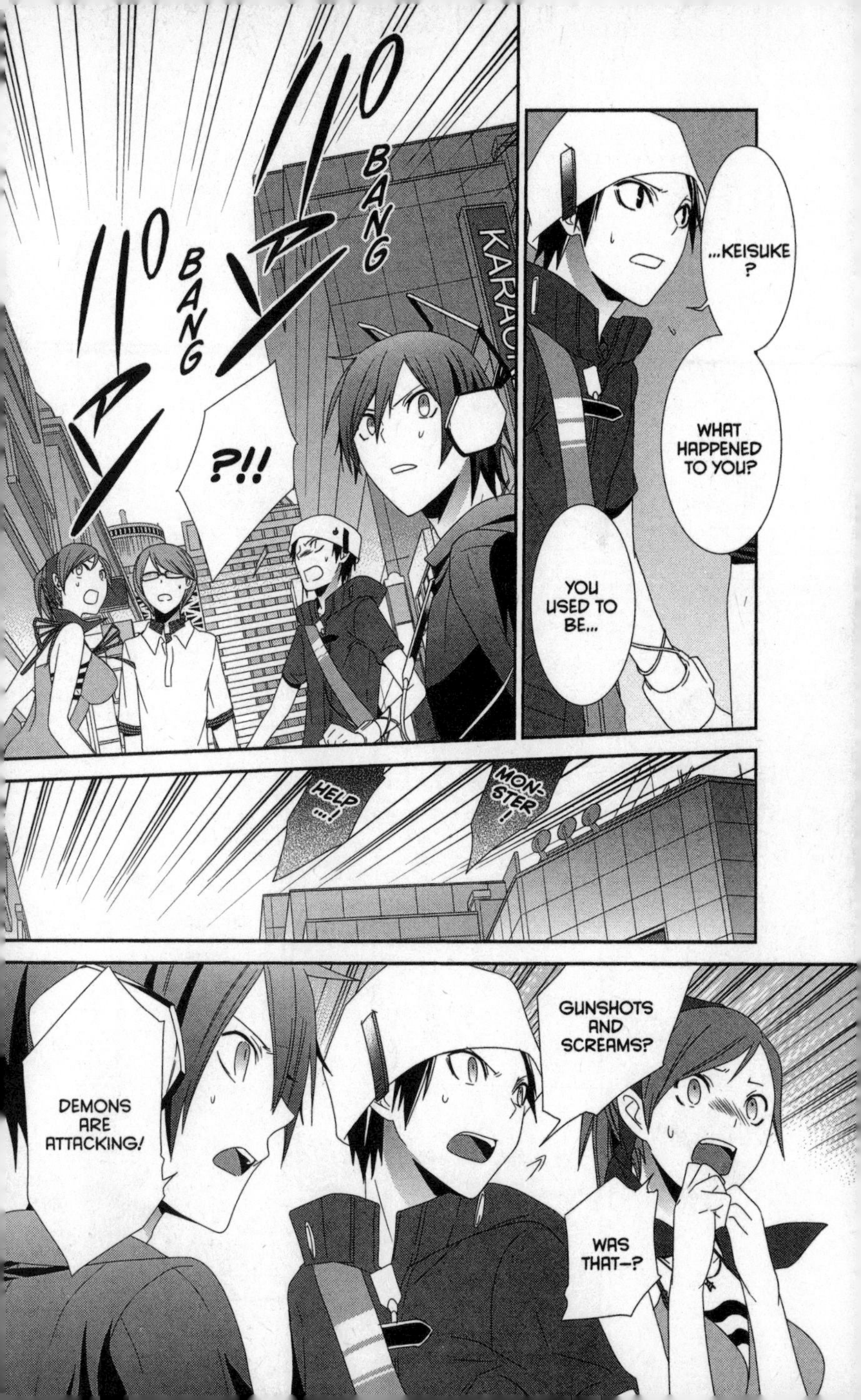
...KEISUKE?
WHAT HAPPENED TO YOU?
YOU USED TO BE...
BANG
BANG
?!!
MON-STER!
HELP...!
GUNSHOTS AND SCREAMS?
WAS THAT—?
DEMONS ARE ATTACKING!

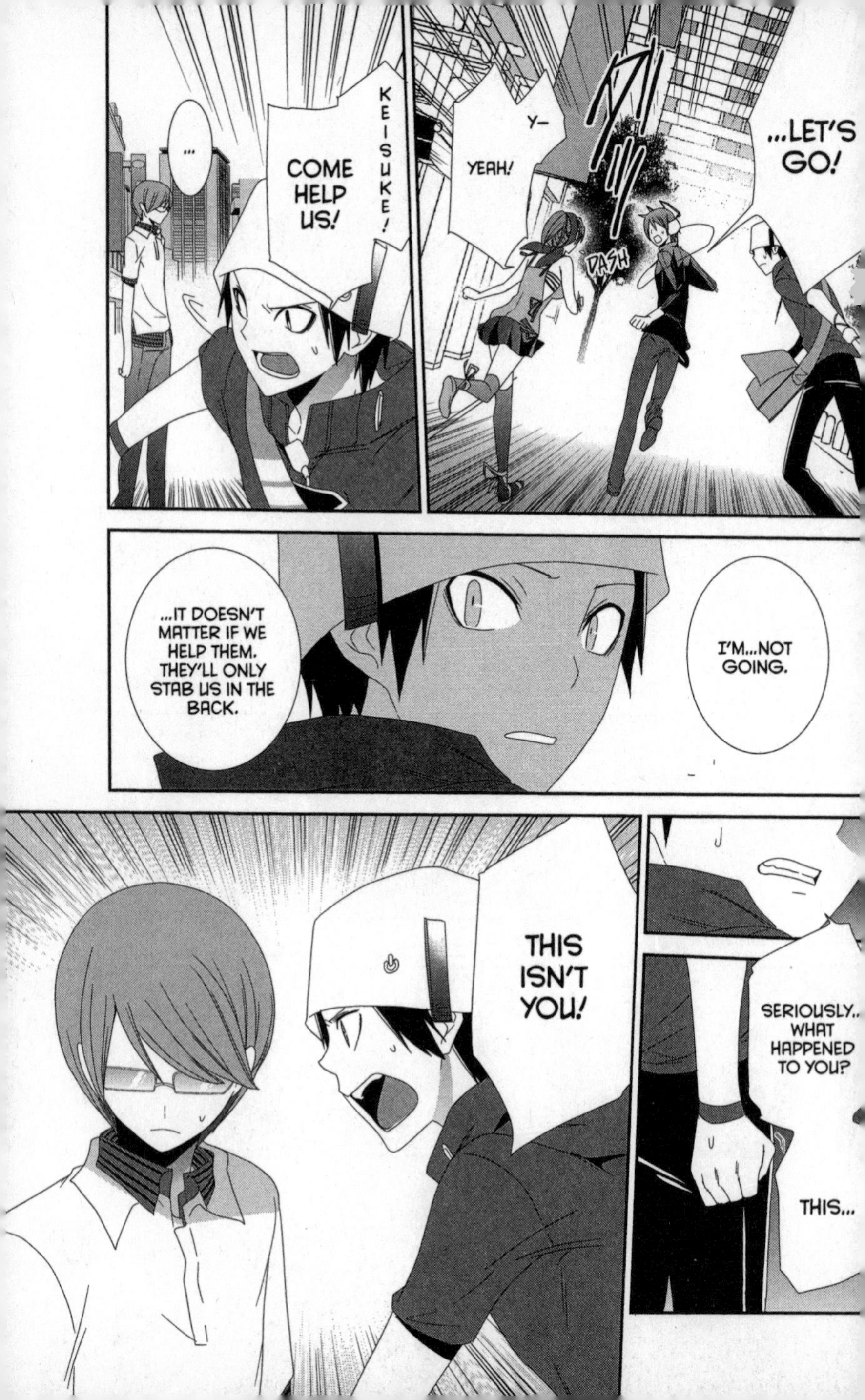
...LET'S GO!
Y— YEAH!
DASH
KEISUKE!
COME HELP US!
...
I'M...NOT GOING.
...IT DOESN'T MATTER IF WE HELP THEM. THEY'LL ONLY STAB US IN THE BACK.
SERIOUSLY.. WHAT HAPPENED TO YOU?
THIS...
THIS ISN'T YOU!

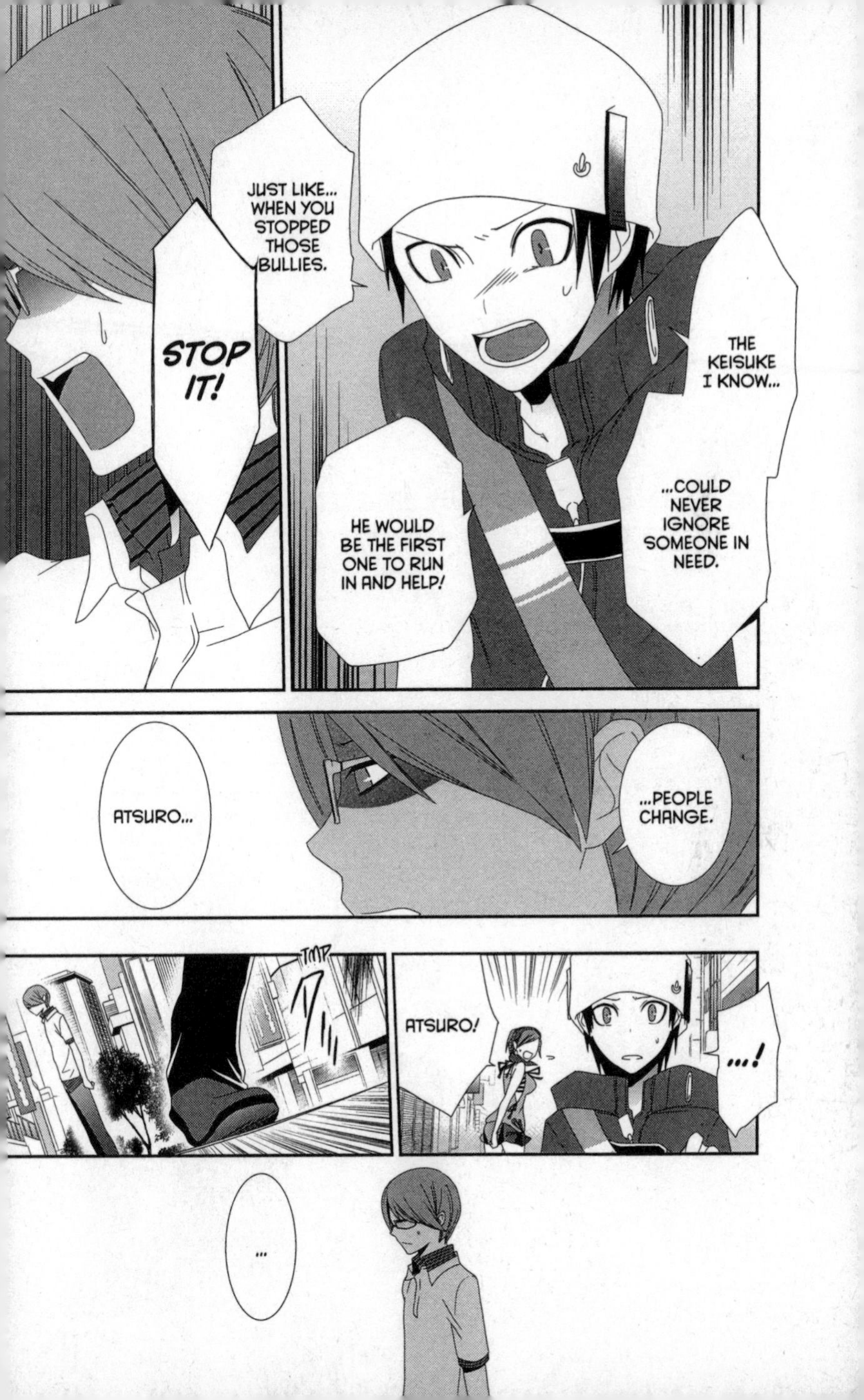
THE KEISUKE I KNOW...
...COULD NEVER IGNORE SOMEONE IN NEED.
HE WOULD BE THE FIRST ONE TO RUN IN AND HELP!
JUST LIKE... WHEN YOU STOPPED THOSE BULLIES.
STOP IT!
...PEOPLE CHANGE.
ATSURO...
ATSURO!
...!
TMP
...

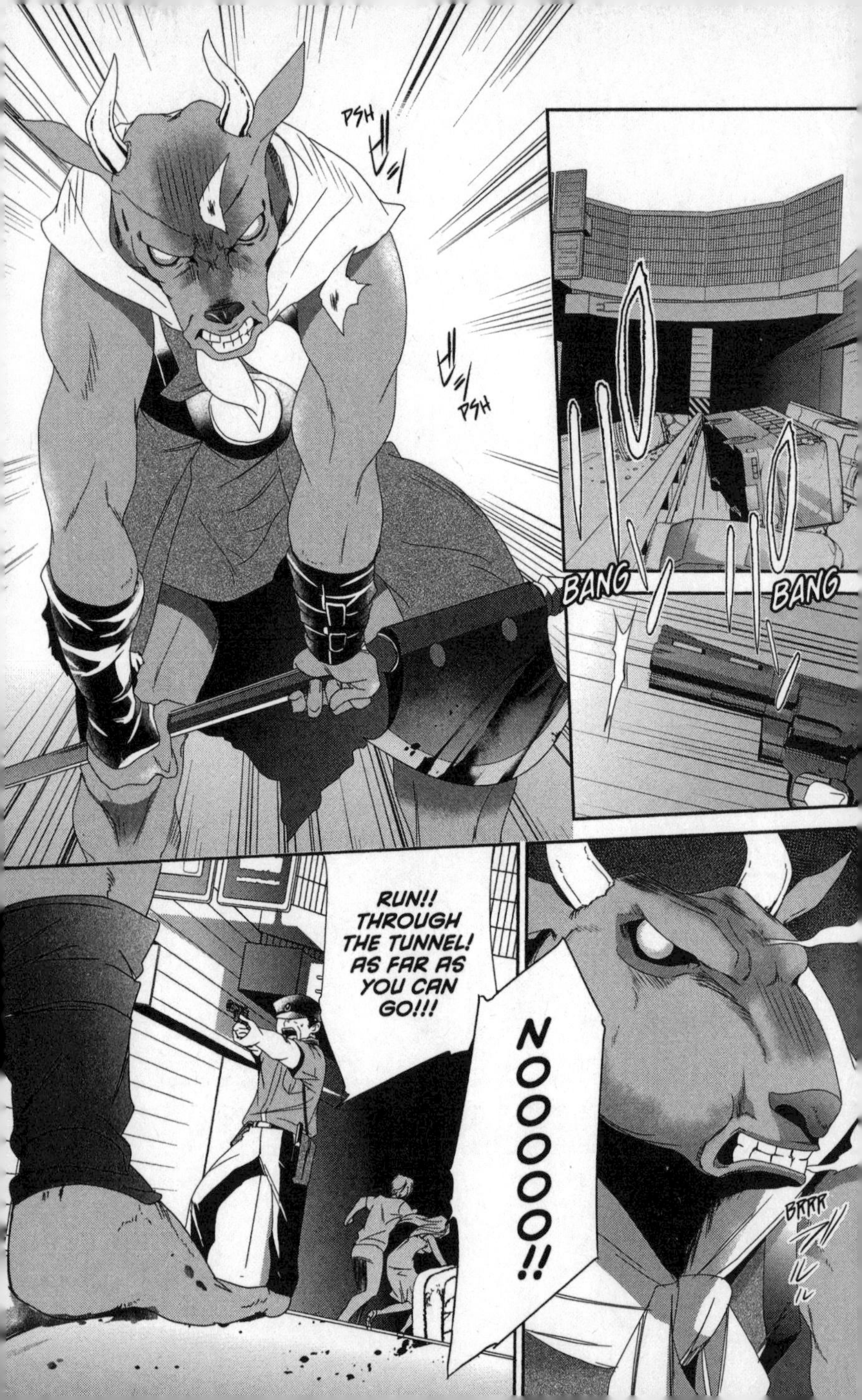
BANG
BANG
PSH
PSH
NOOOOOO!!
BRRR
RUN!! THROUGH THE TUNNEL! AS FAR AS YOU CAN GO!!!

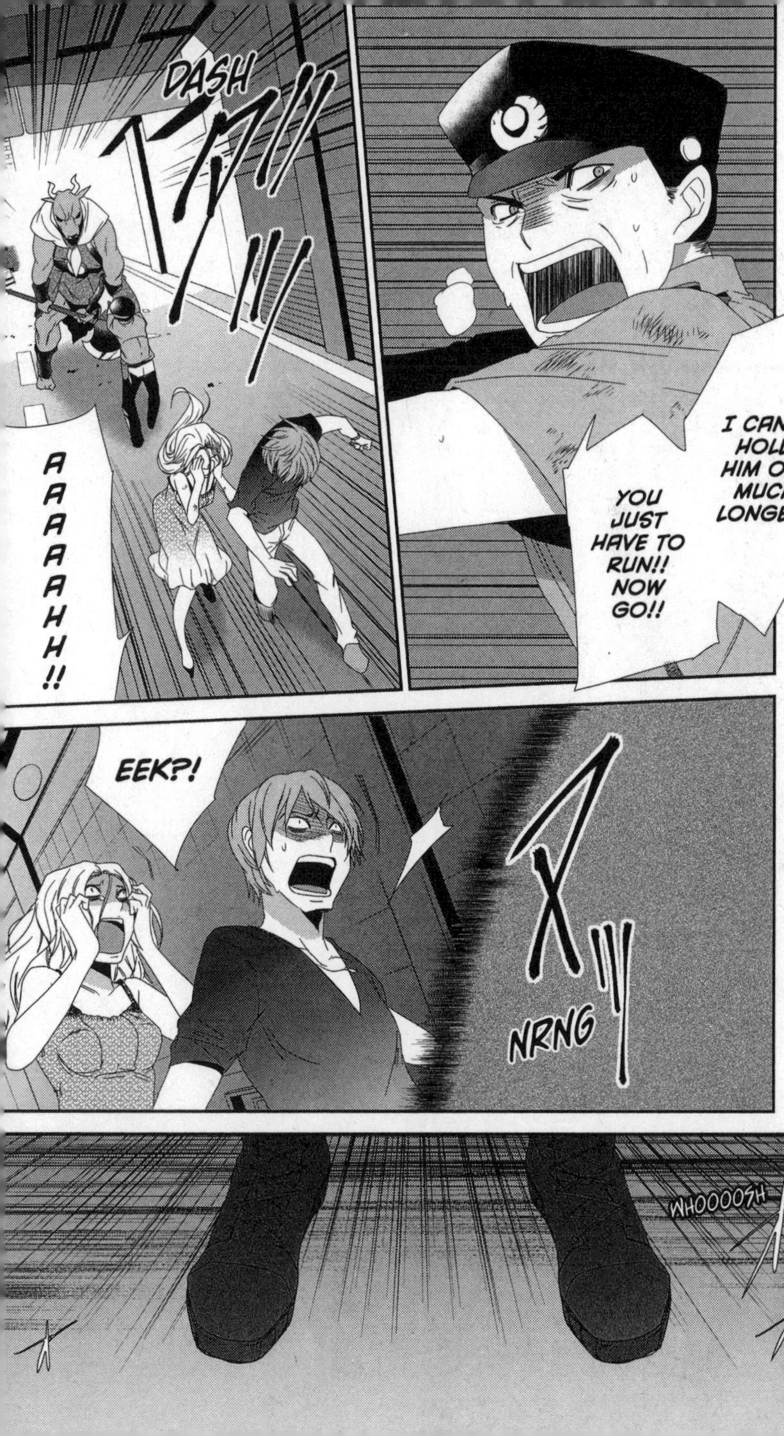
I CAN'T HOLD HIM OFF MUCH LONGER!
YOU JUST HAVE TO RUN!! NOW GO!!
DASH
AAAAAHH!!
EEK?!
NRNG
WHOOOOSH

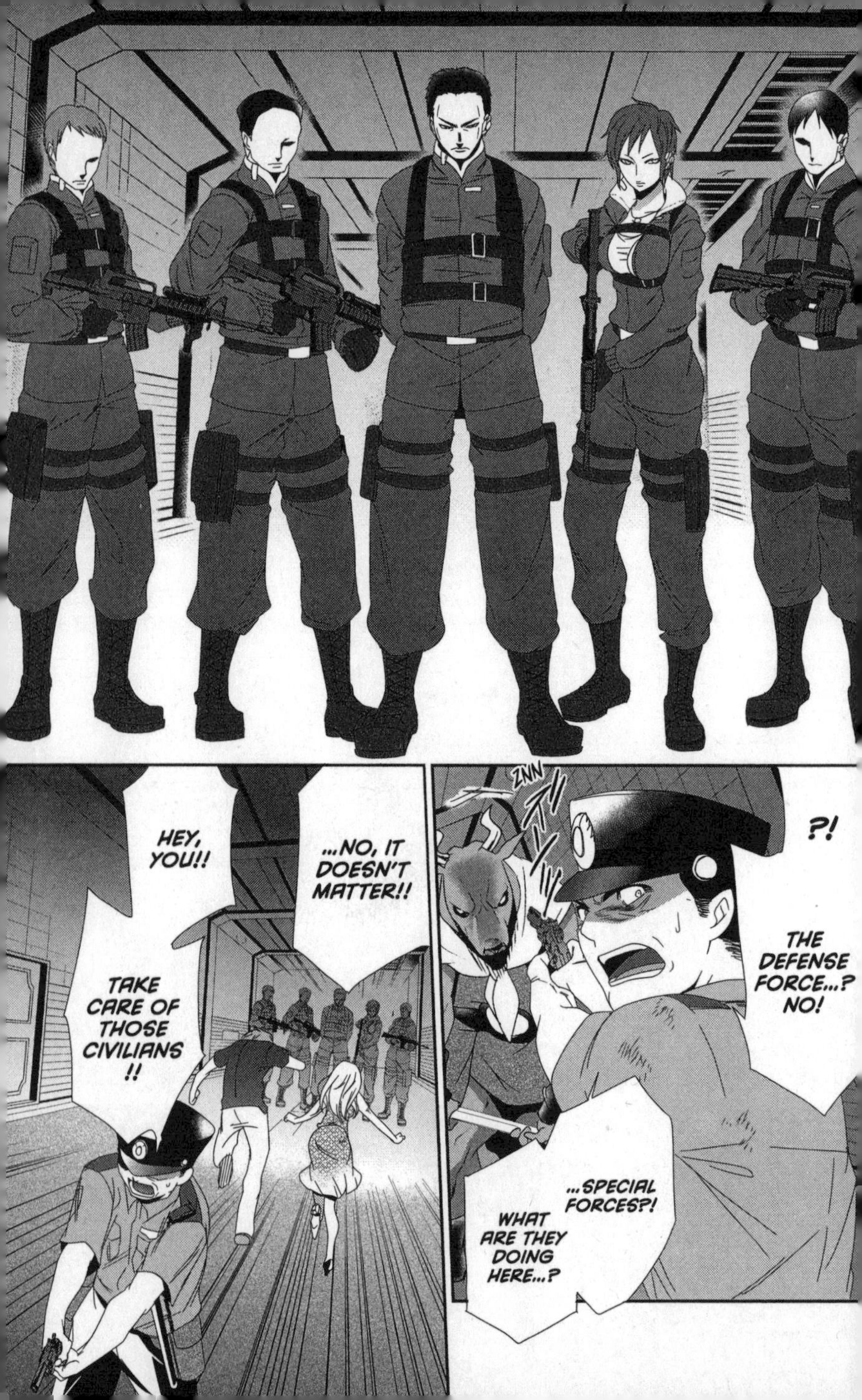
ZNN
?!
THE DEFENSE FORCE...? NO!
...SPECIAL FORCES?!
WHAT ARE THEY DOING HERE...?
HEY, YOU!!
...NO, IT DOESN'T MATTER!!
TAKE CARE OF THOSE CIVILIANS!!

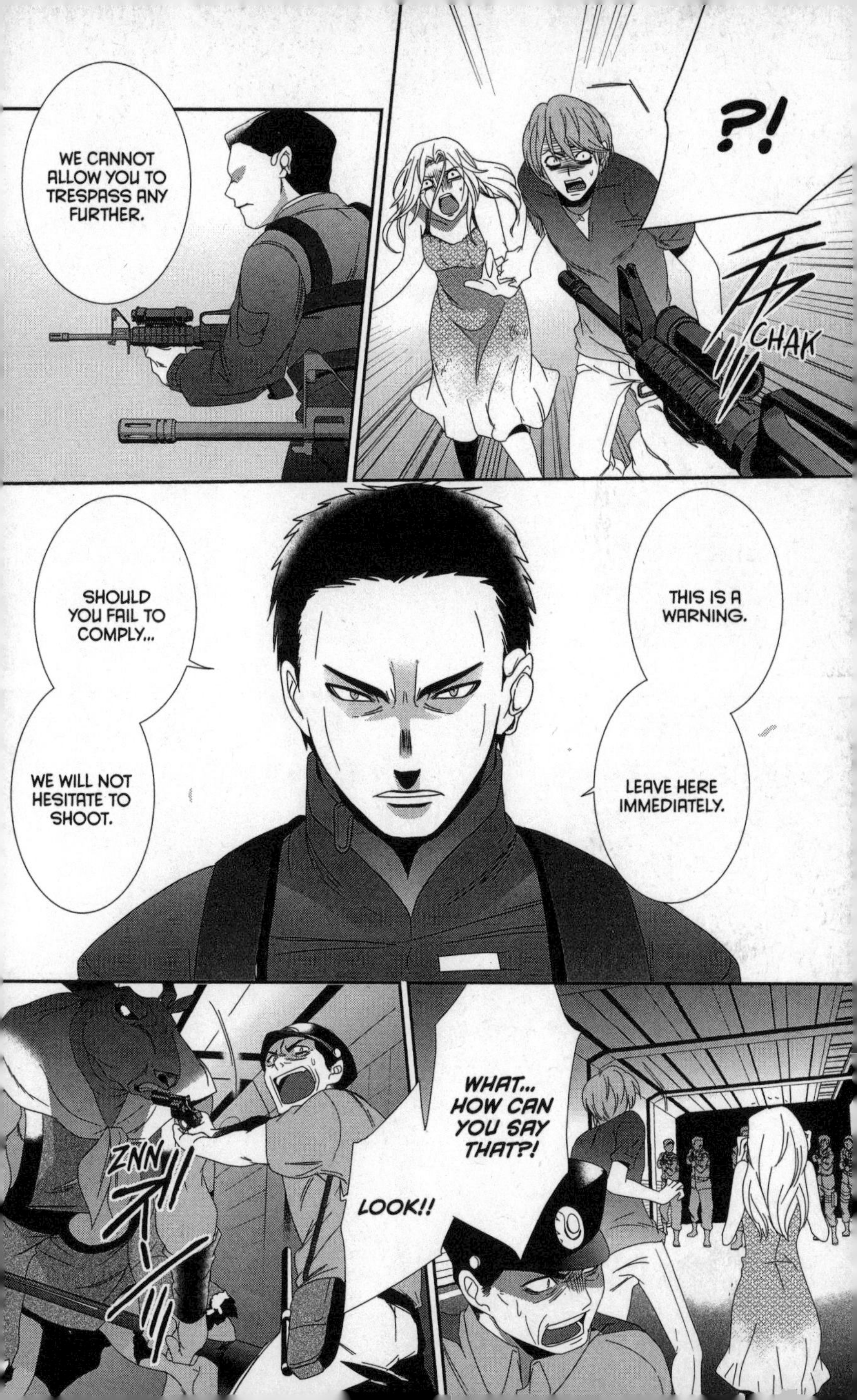
?!
CHAK
WE CANNOT ALLOW YOU TO TRESPASS ANY FURTHER.
THIS IS A WARNING.
LEAVE HERE IMMEDIATELY.
SHOULD YOU FAIL TO COMPLY...
WE WILL NOT HESITATE TO SHOOT.
WHAT... HOW CAN YOU SAY THAT?!
LOOK!!
ZNN

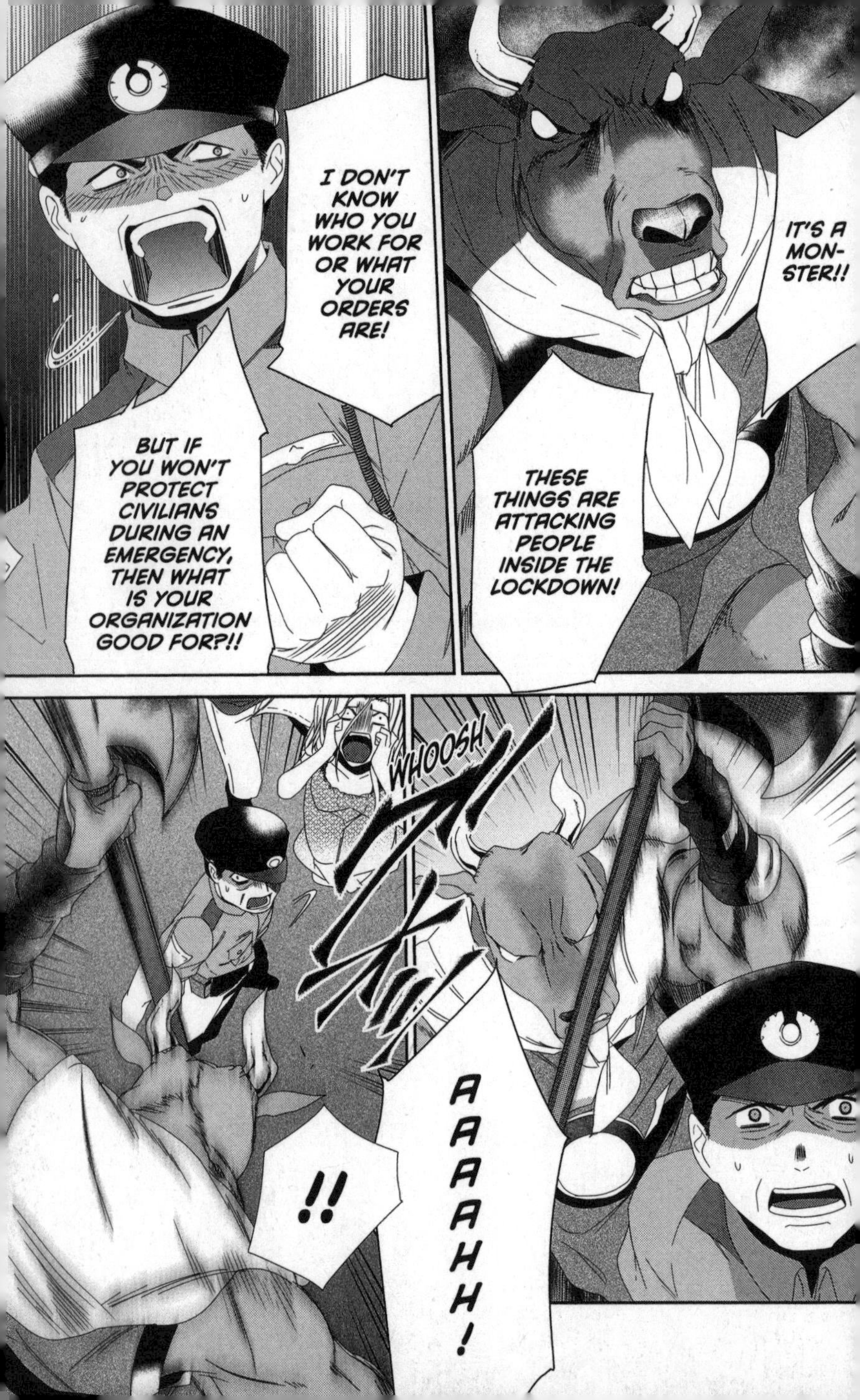
IT'S A MON-STER!!
THESE THINGS ARE ATTACKING PEOPLE INSIDE THE LOCKDOWN!
I DON'T KNOW WHO YOU WORK FOR OR WHAT YOUR ORDERS ARE!
BUT IF YOU WON'T PROTECT CIVILIANS DURING AN EMERGENCY, THEN WHAT IS YOUR ORGANIZATION GOOD FOR?!!
WHOOSH
AAAAAAH!
!!

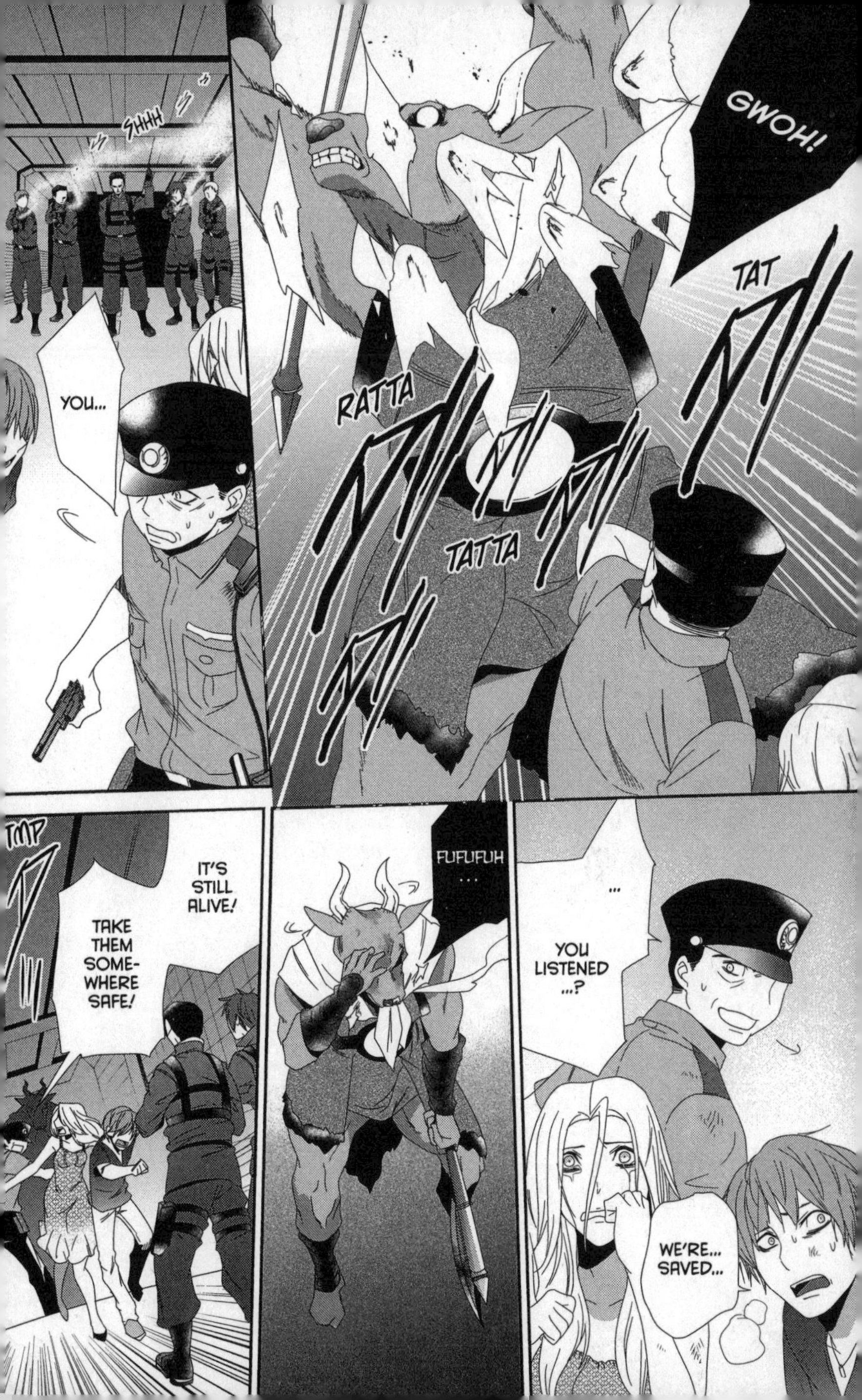

GWOH!
TAT
RATTA
TATTA
SHHH
YOU...
...
YOU LISTENED ...?
WE'RE... SAVED...
FUFUFUH ...
TMP
IT'S STILL ALIVE!
TAKE THEM SOME-WHERE SAFE!

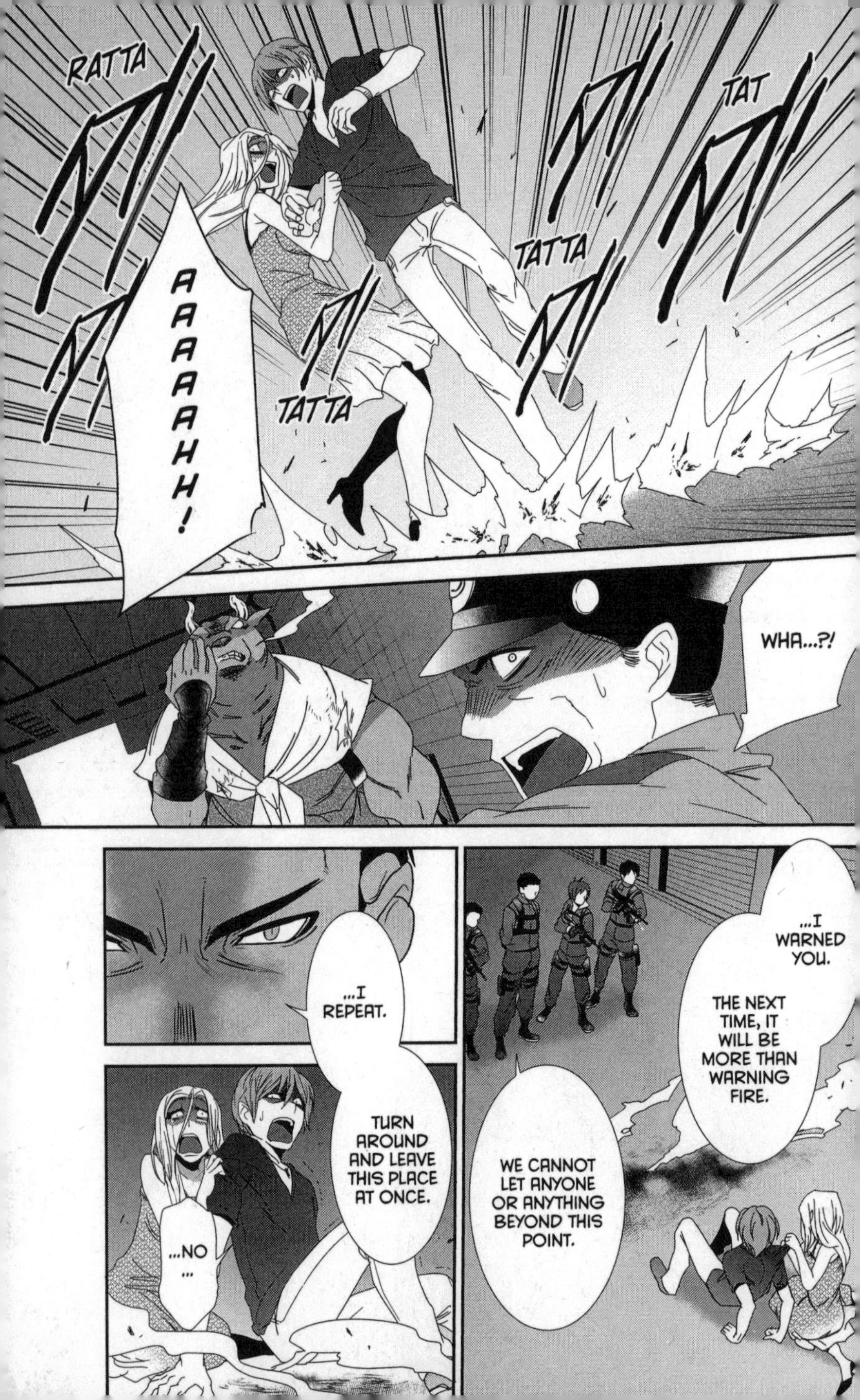
TAT
TATTA
RATTA
AAAAAAHH!
TATTA
WHA...?!
...I WARNED YOU.
THE NEXT TIME, IT WILL BE MORE THAN WARNING FIRE.
WE CANNOT LET ANYONE OR ANYTHING BEYOND THIS POINT.
...I REPEAT.
TURN AROUND AND LEAVE THIS PLACE AT ONCE.
...NO ...

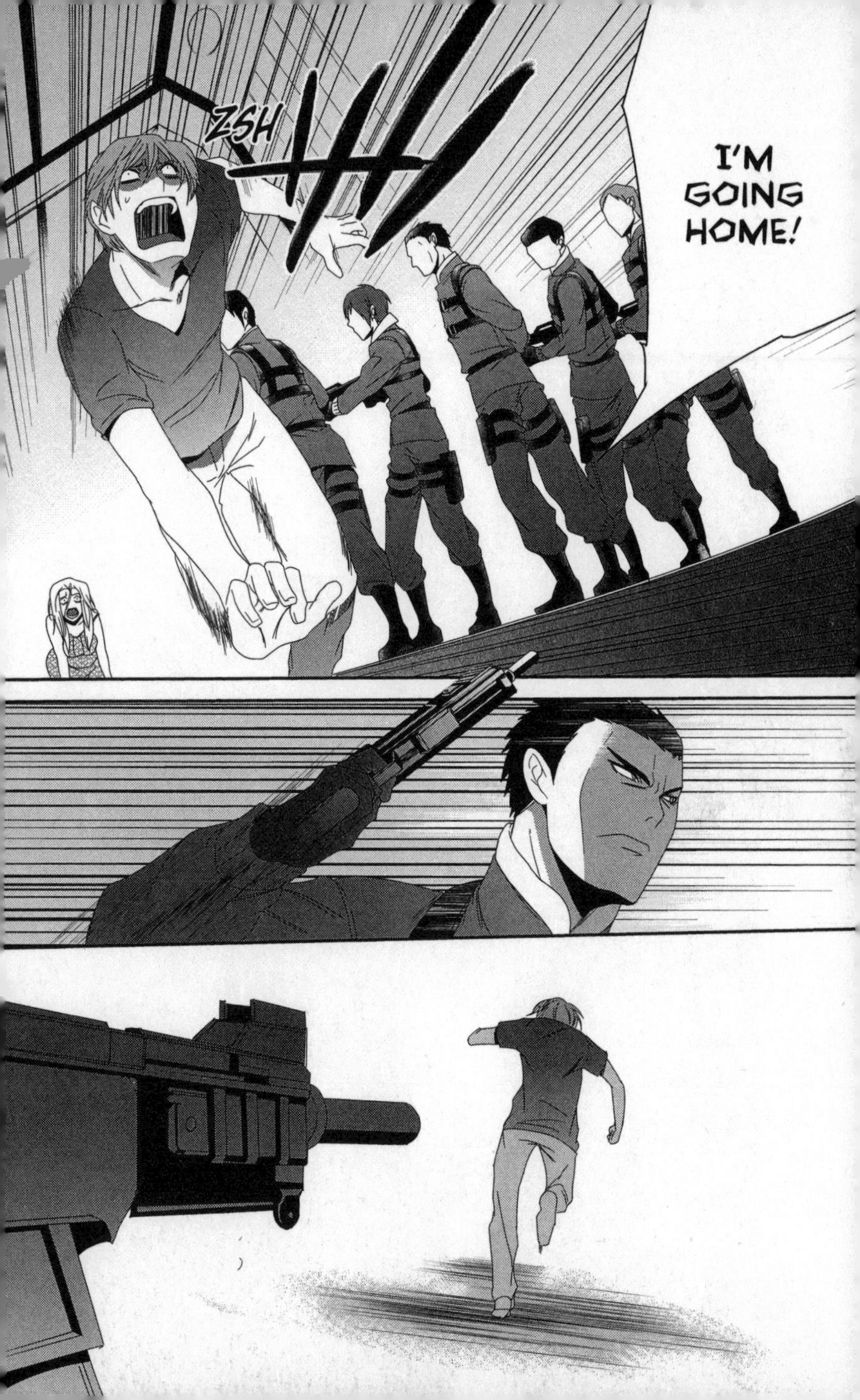
I'M GOING HOME!
ZSH

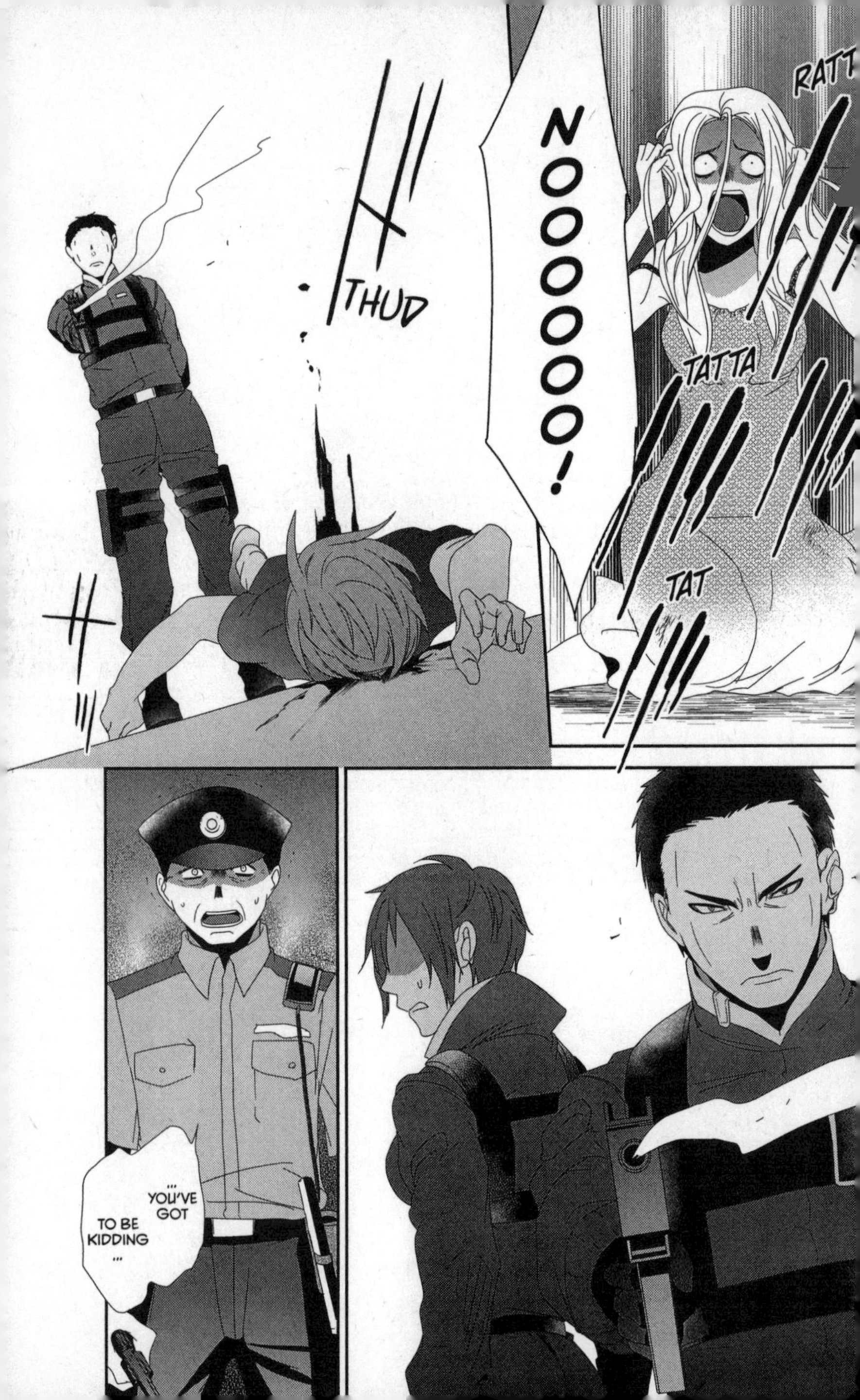
RATT
TATTA
TAT
NOOOOOOO!
THUD
...YOU'VE GOT TO BE KIDDING...

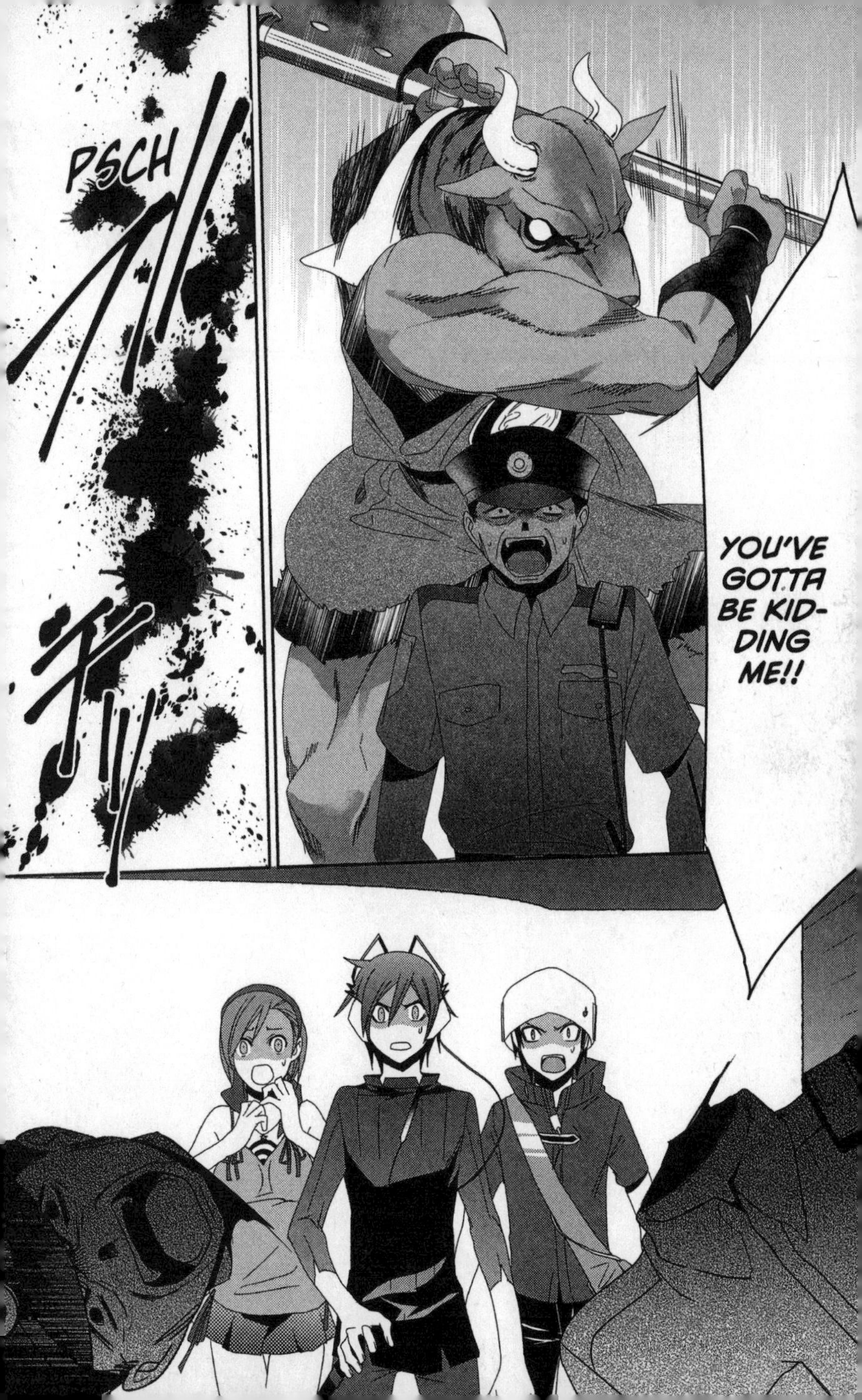
PSCH
YOU'VE GOTTA BE KID-DING ME!!

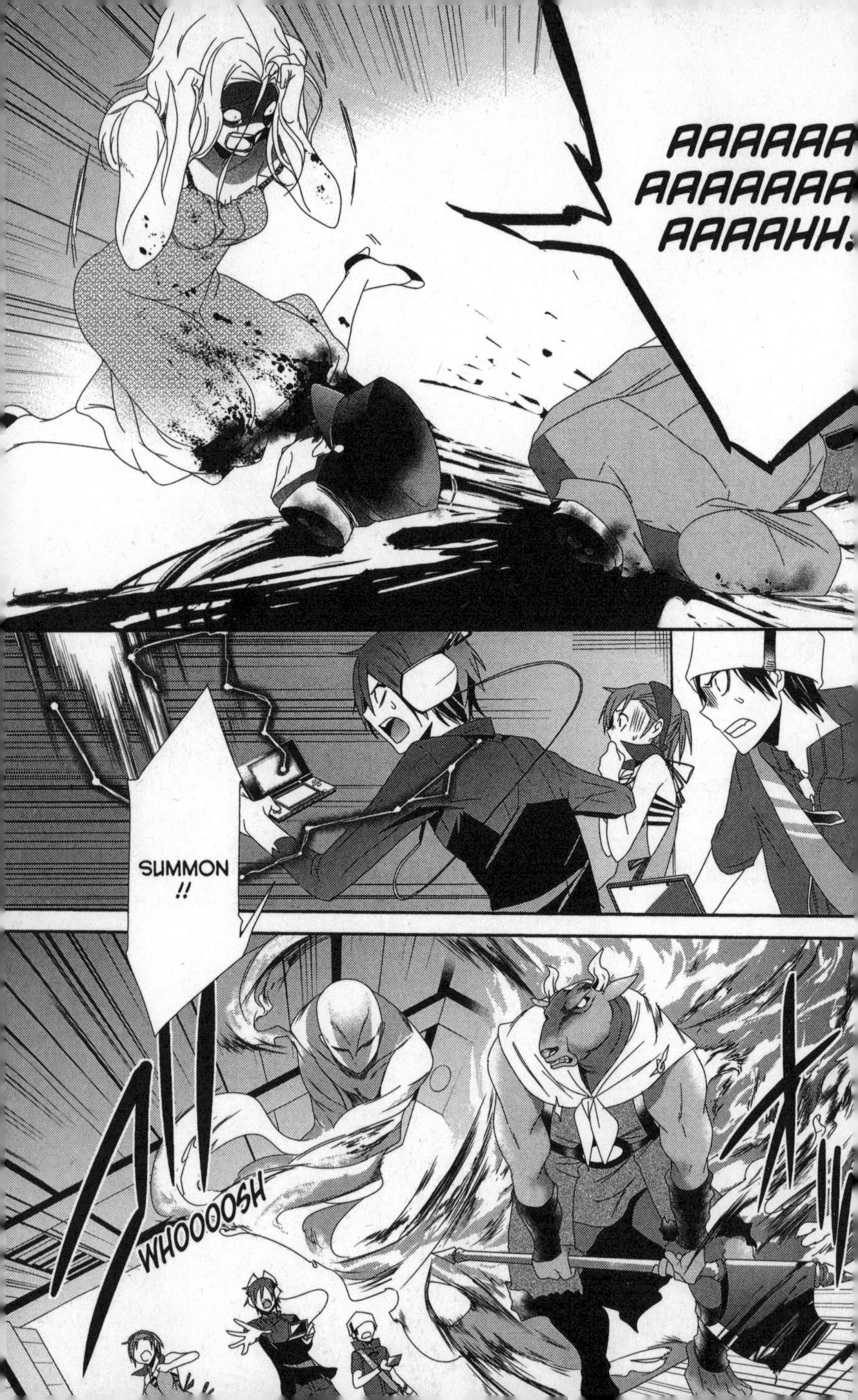
AAAAAA
AAAAAAA
AAAAHH!
SUMMON
!!
WHOOOOSH

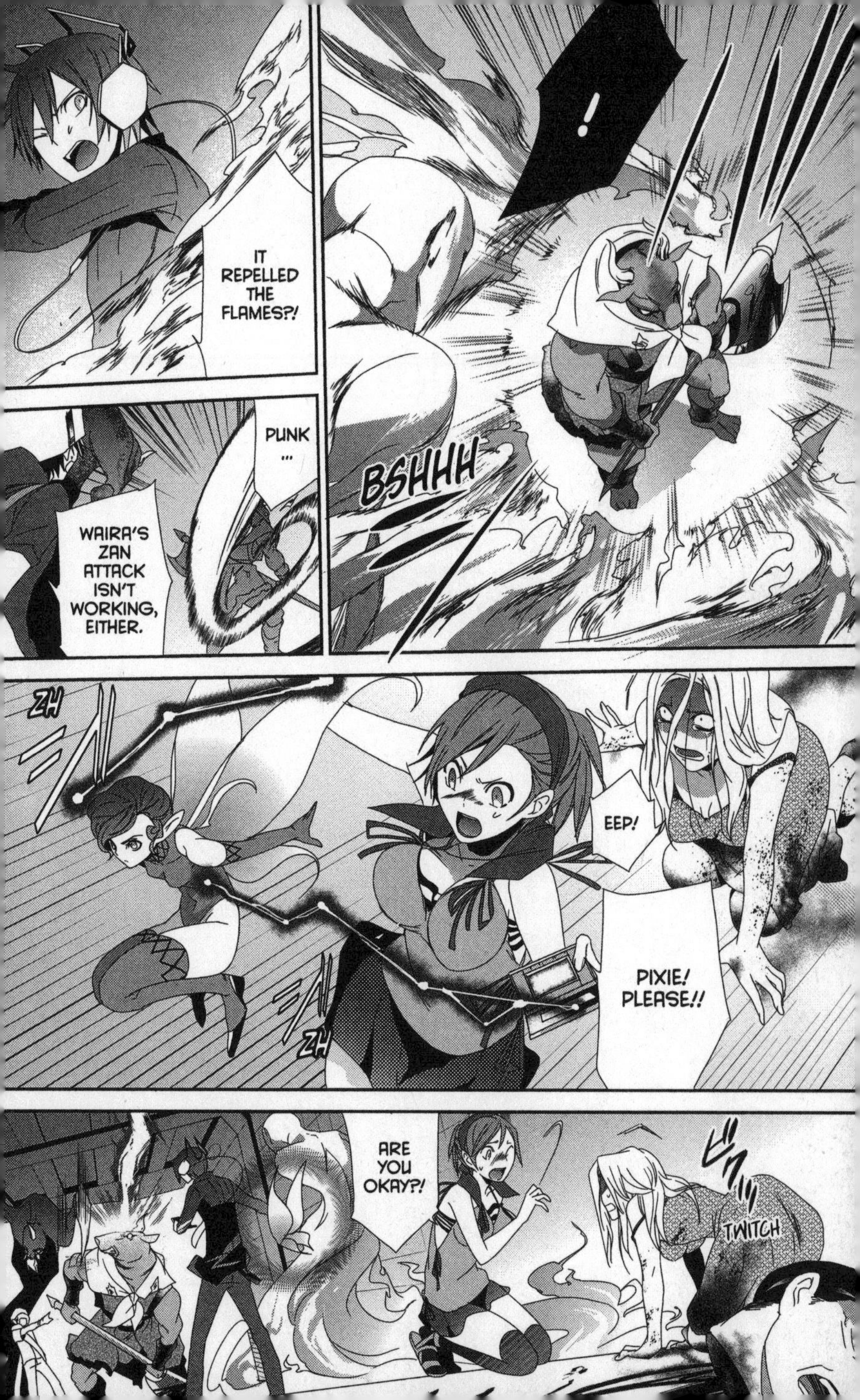
!
BSHHH
IT REPELLED THE FLAMES?!
PUNK ...
WAIRA'S ZAN ATTACK ISN'T WORKING, EITHER.
EEP!
PIXIE! PLEASE!!
ZH
ZH
TWITCH
ARE YOU OKAY?!

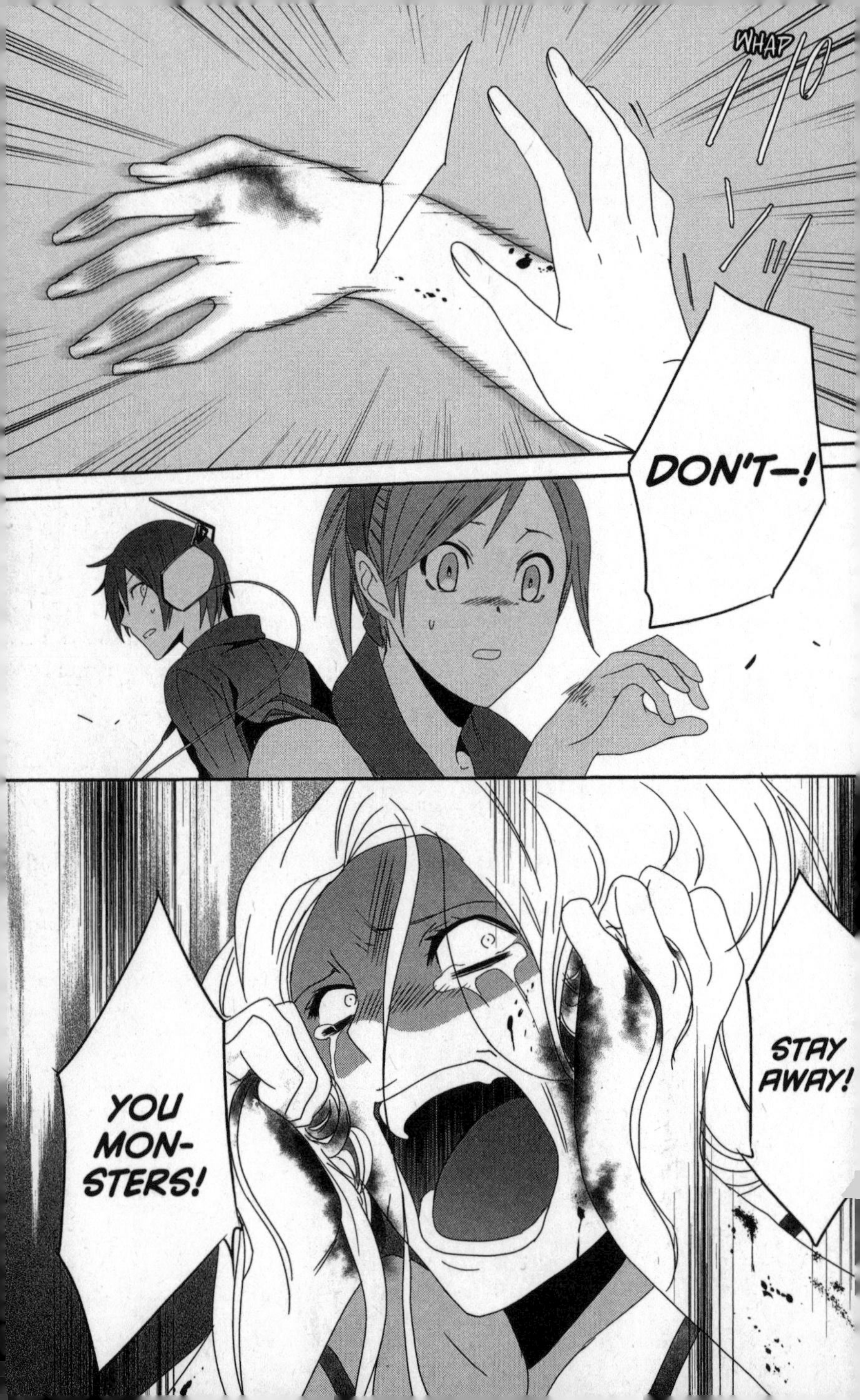
WHAP
DON'T—!
STAY AWAY!
YOU MON-STERS!

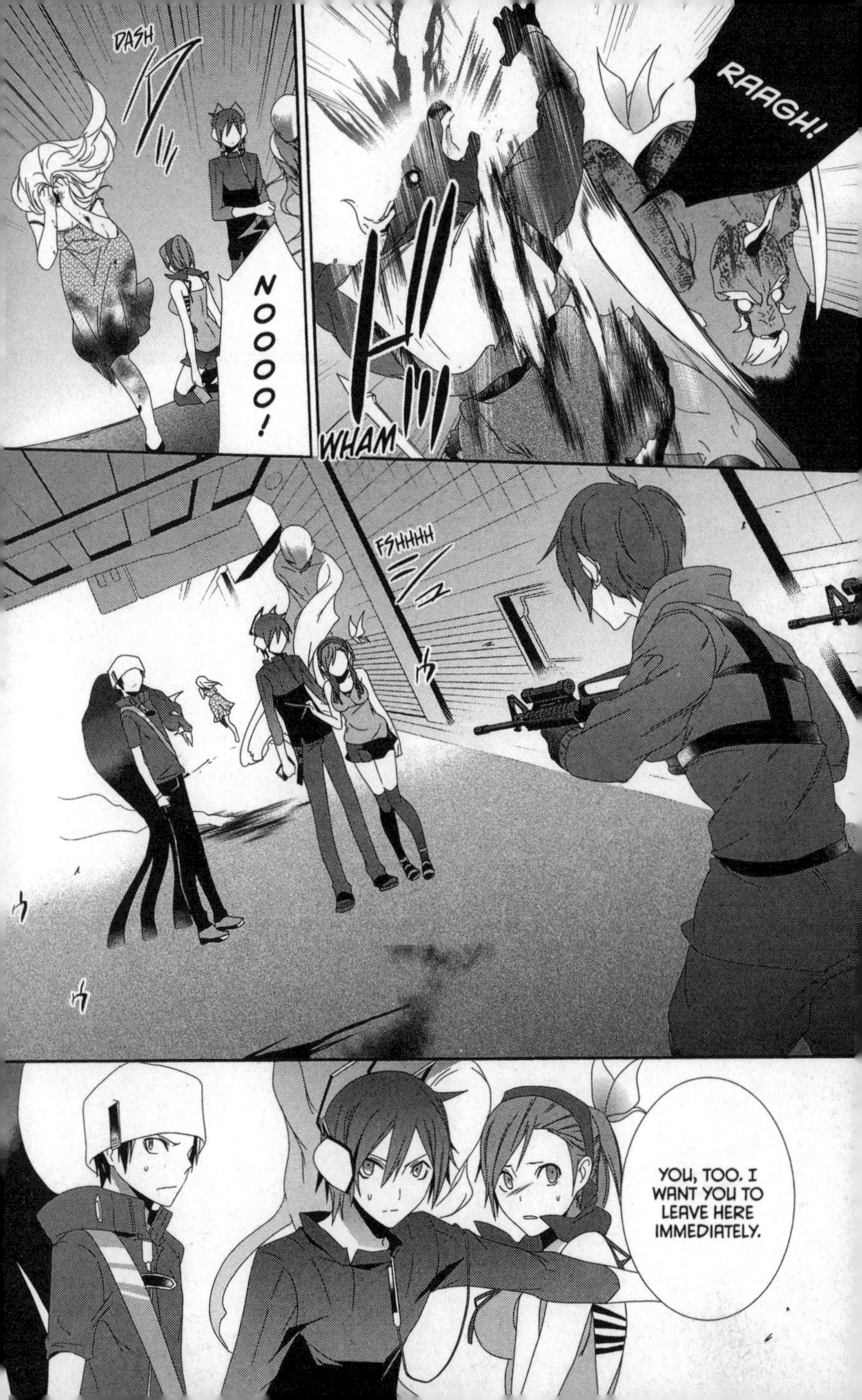
RAAGH!
WHAM
DASH
NOOOOO!
FSHHHH
YOU, TOO. I WANT YOU TO LEAVE HERE IMMEDIATELY.

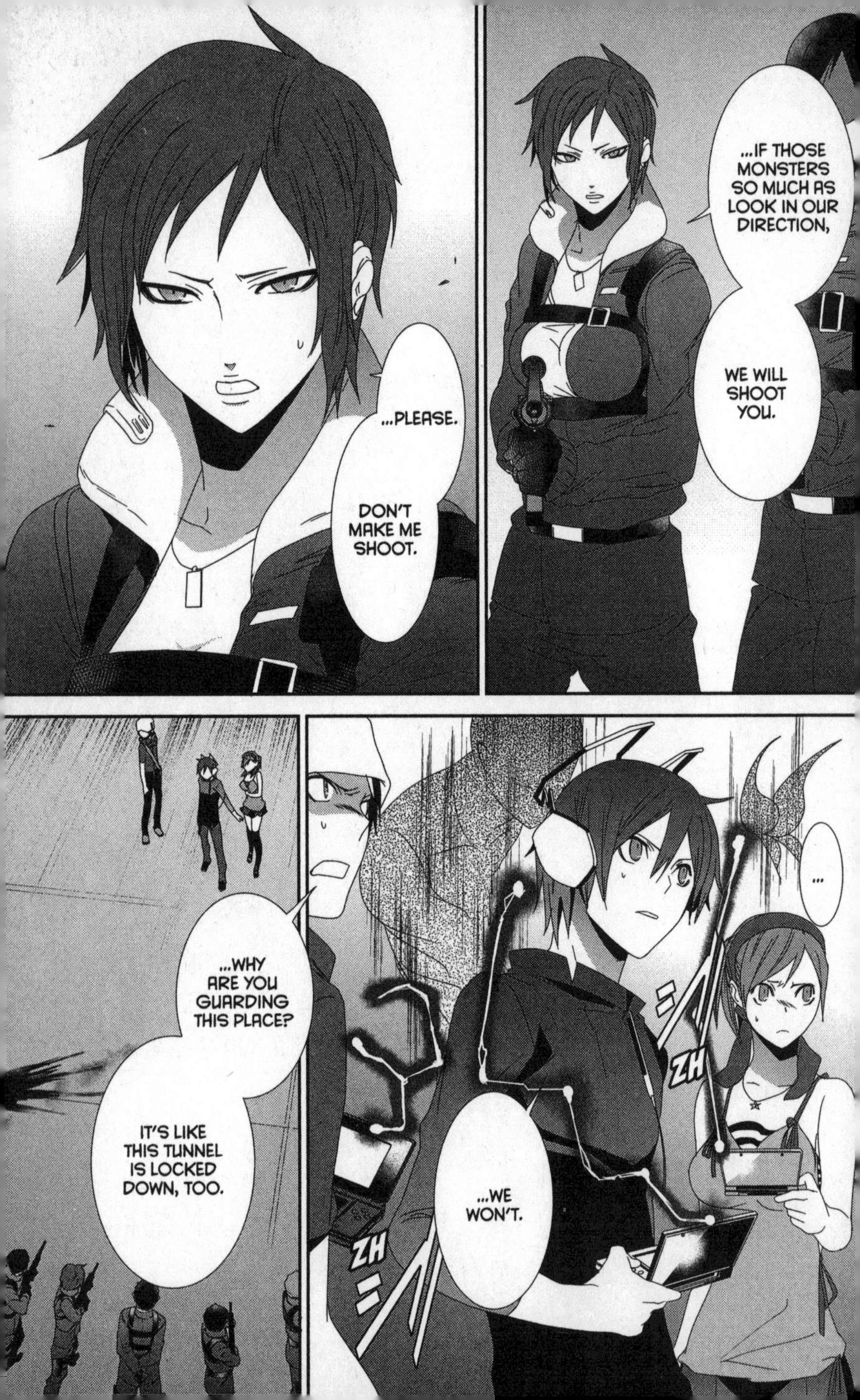
...IF THOSE MONSTERS SO MUCH AS LOOK IN OUR DIRECTION,
WE WILL SHOOT YOU.
...PLEASE.
DON'T MAKE ME SHOOT.
...
ZH
...WE WON'T.
ZH
...WHY ARE YOU GUARDING THIS PLACE?
IT'S LIKE THIS TUNNEL IS LOCKED DOWN, TOO.

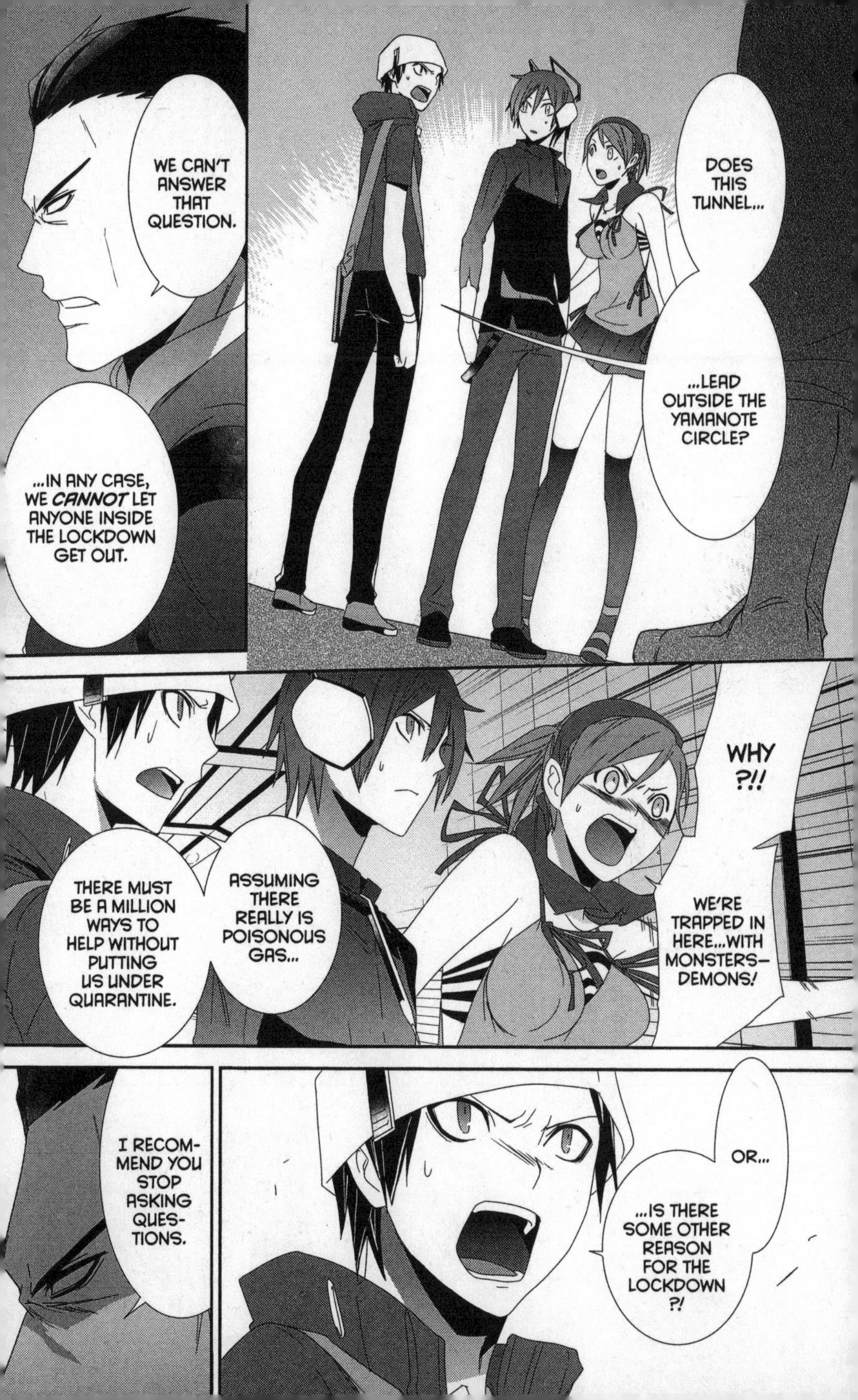
DOES THIS TUNNEL...
...LEAD OUTSIDE THE YAMANOTE CIRCLE?
WE CAN'T ANSWER THAT QUESTION.
...IN ANY CASE, WE *CANNOT* LET ANYONE INSIDE THE LOCKDOWN GET OUT.
WHY?!!
WE'RE TRAPPED IN HERE...WITH MONSTERS—DEMONS!
ASSUMING THERE REALLY IS POISONOUS GAS...
THERE MUST BE A MILLION WAYS TO HELP WITHOUT PUTTING US UNDER QUARANTINE.
OR...
...IS THERE SOME OTHER REASON FOR THE LOCKDOWN?!
I RECOMMEND YOU STOP ASKING QUESTIONS.

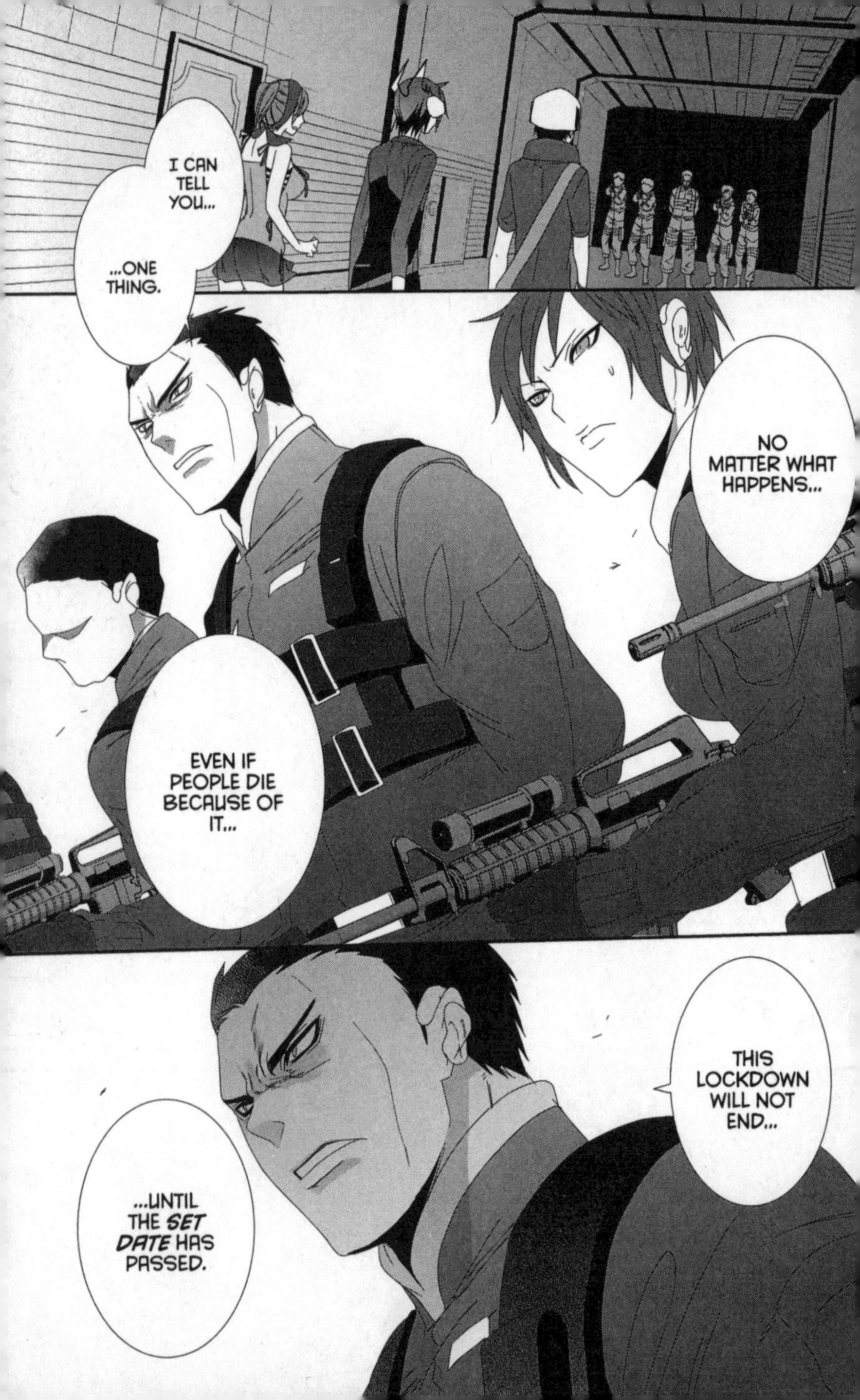
I CAN TELL YOU...
...ONE THING.
NO MATTER WHAT HAPPENS...
EVEN IF PEOPLE DIE BECAUSE OF IT...
THIS LOCKDOWN WILL NOT END...
...UNTIL THE *SET DATE* HAS PASSED.

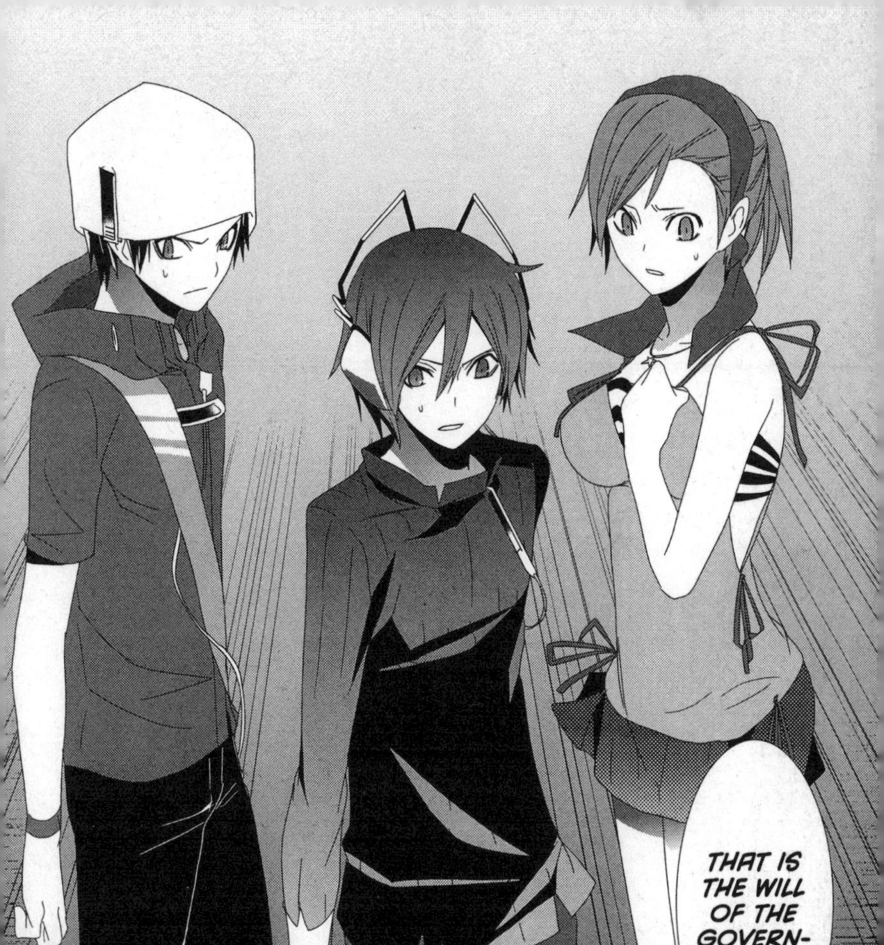
THAT IS THE WILL OF THE GOVERN-MENT...
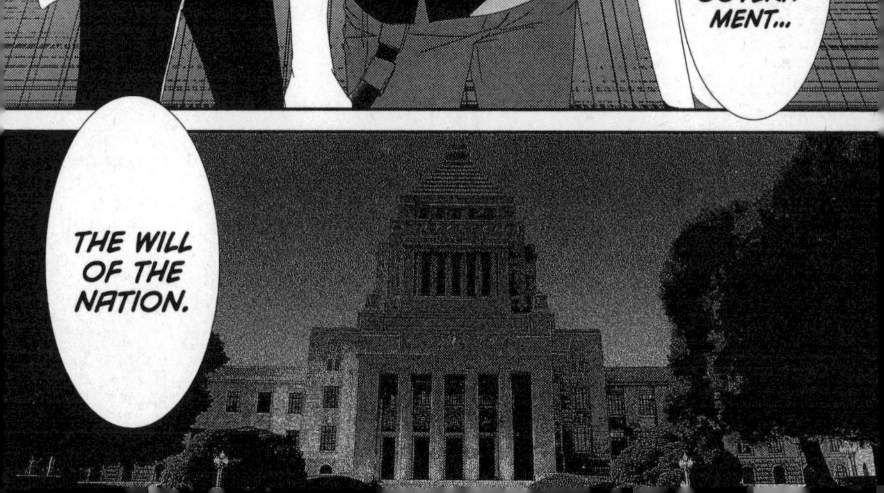
THE WILL OF THE NATION.

OFILE

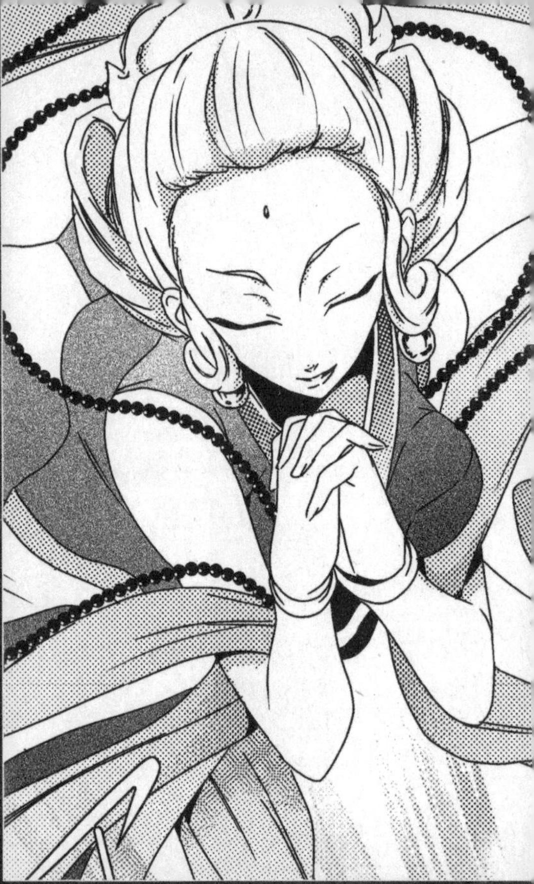

LAKSMI

THE INDIAN GODDESS OF BEAUTY AND PROSPERITY, SHE IS A CONSORT OF VISHNU A THE MOTHER OF KAMA, GOD OF LOVE. SHE IS THE EMBODIMENT OF THE IDEAL WOMAN, AN SHE BOASTS GREAT BEAUTY. SHE IS SAID TO HAVE CHARMED MANY OF THE GODS WITH HE BEWITCHING DANCE.

DEVIL SURVIVOR

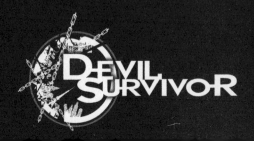

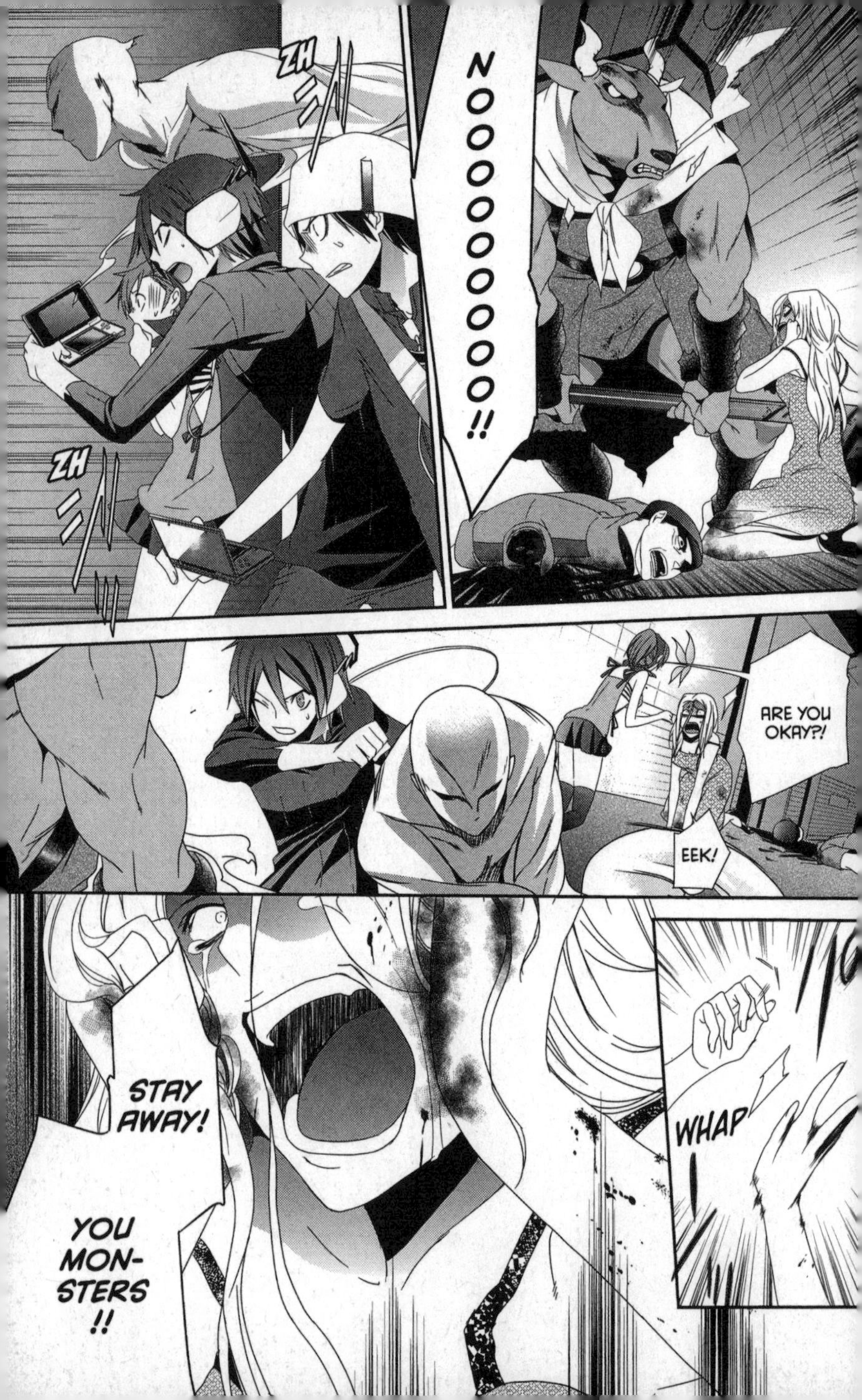
NOOOOOOOOOO!!
ZH
ZH
ARE YOU OKAY?!
EEK!
WHAP
STAY AWAY!
YOU MON-STERS!!

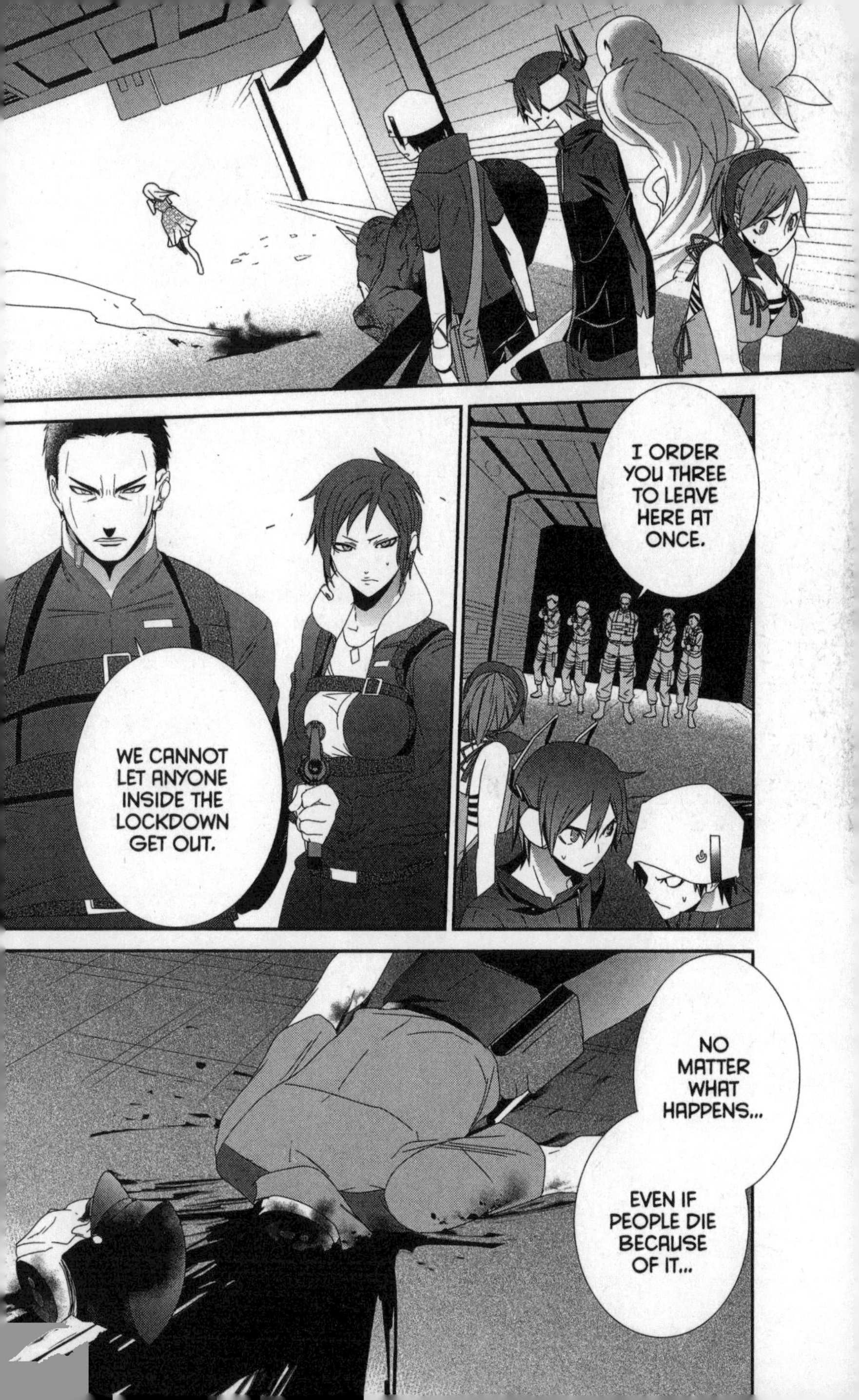
I ORDER YOU THREE TO LEAVE HERE AT ONCE.
WE CANNOT LET ANYONE INSIDE THE LOCKDOWN GET OUT.
NO MATTER WHAT HAPPENS...
EVEN IF PEOPLE DIE BECAUSE OF IT...

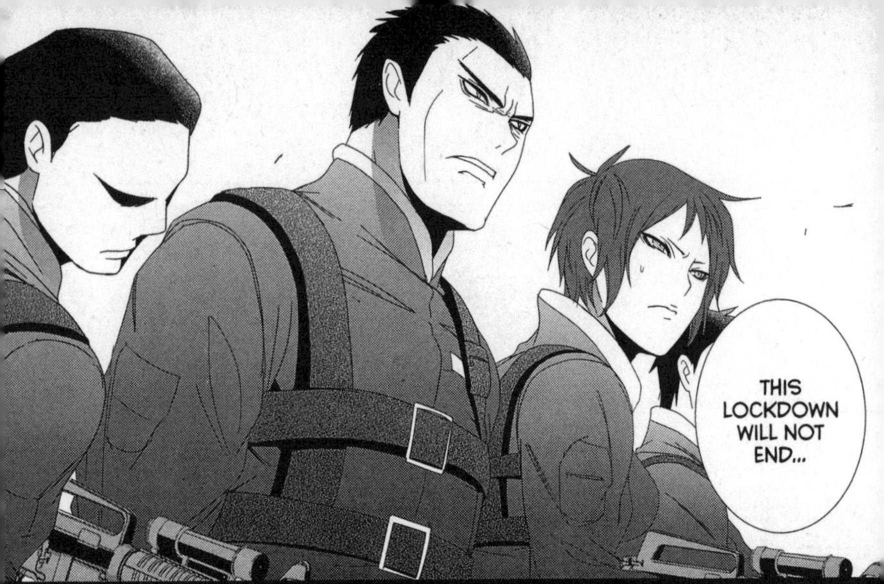
THIS LOCKDOWN WILL NOT END...

SURVIVAL 9 FRIENDSHIP

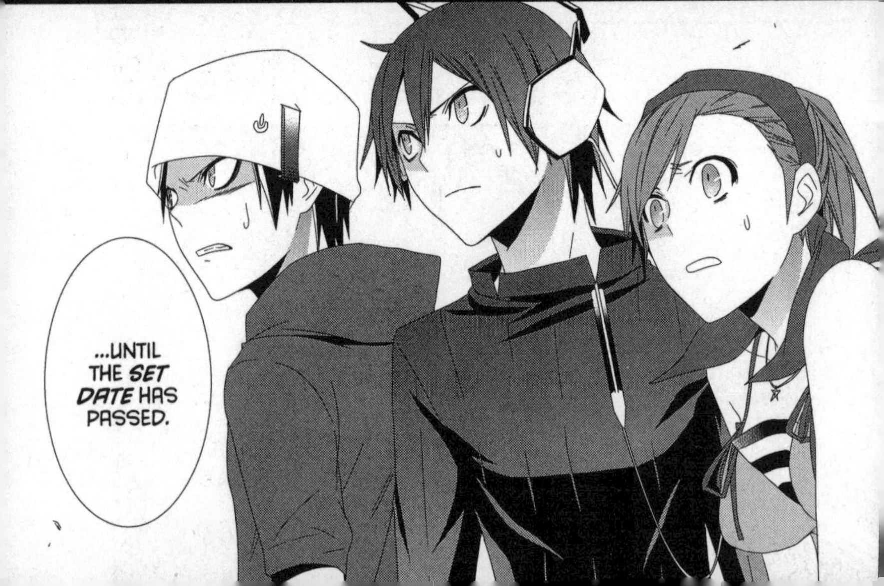
...UNTIL THE SET DATE HAS PASSED.

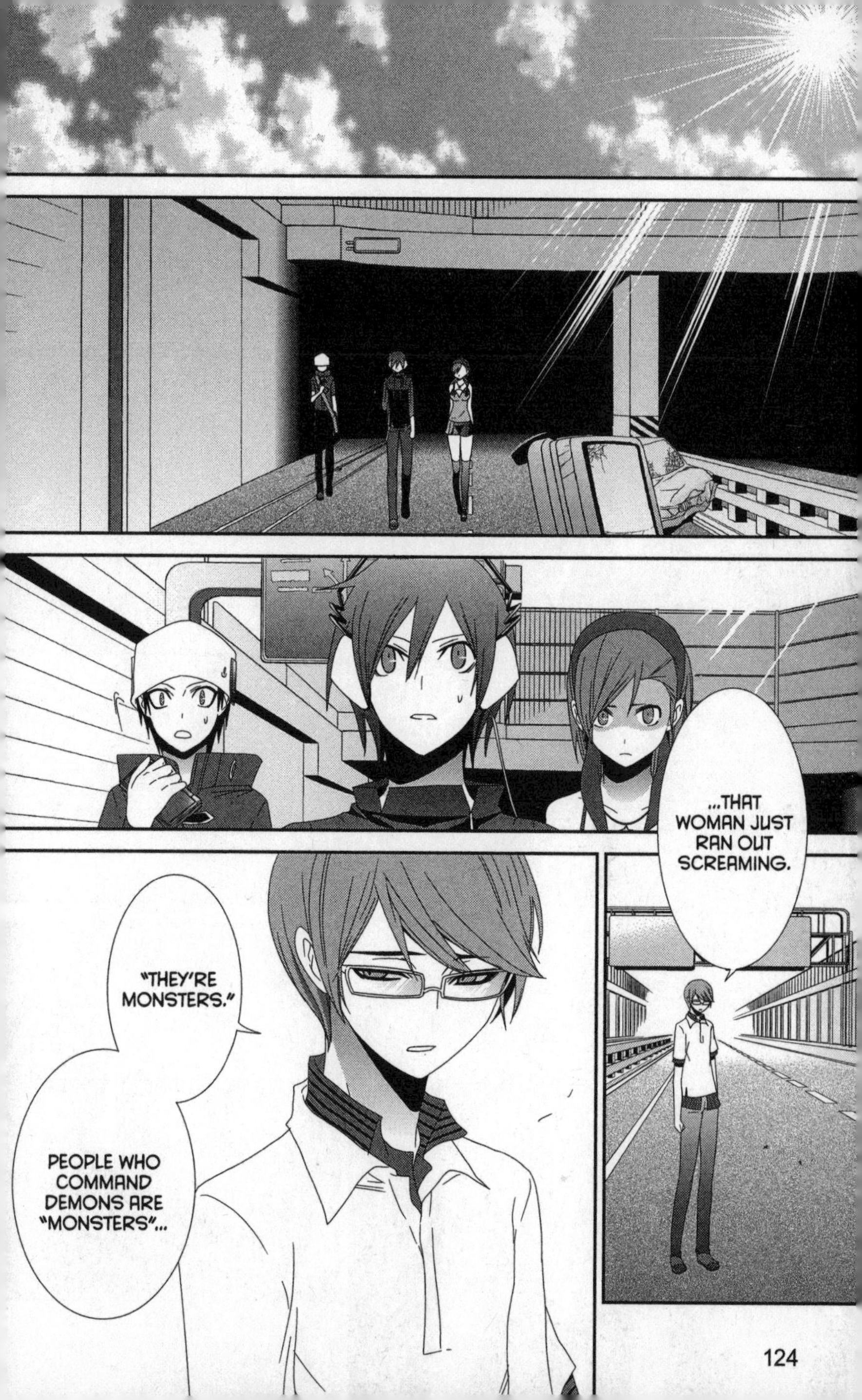
...THAT WOMAN JUST RAN OUT SCREAMING.
"THEY'RE MONSTERS."
PEOPLE WHO COMMAND DEMONS ARE "MONSTERS"...

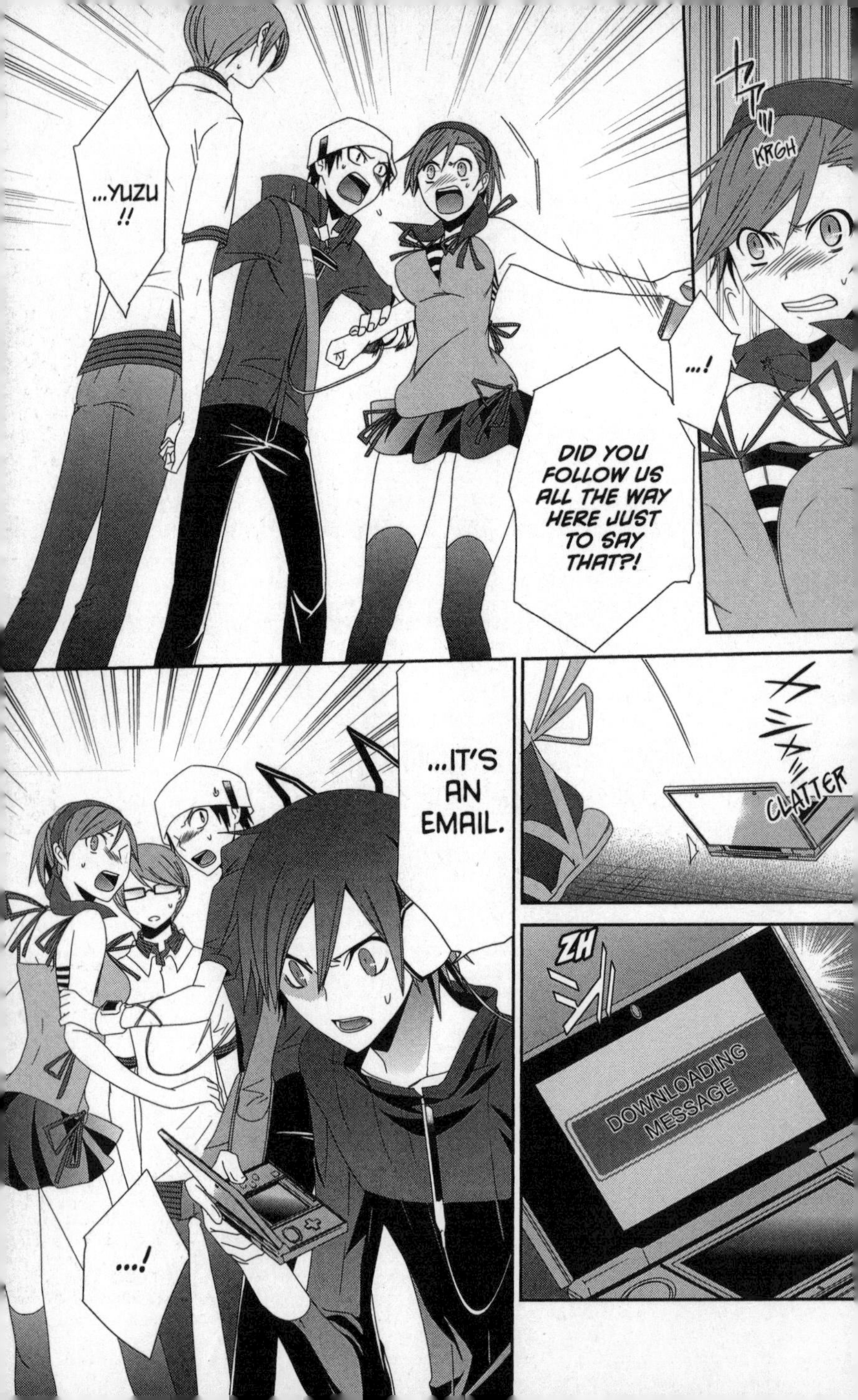
KRGH
...!
...YUZU!!
DID YOU FOLLOW US ALL THE WAY HERE JUST TO SAY THAT?!
CLATTER
ZH
DOWNLOADING MESSAGE
...IT'S AN EMAIL.
...!

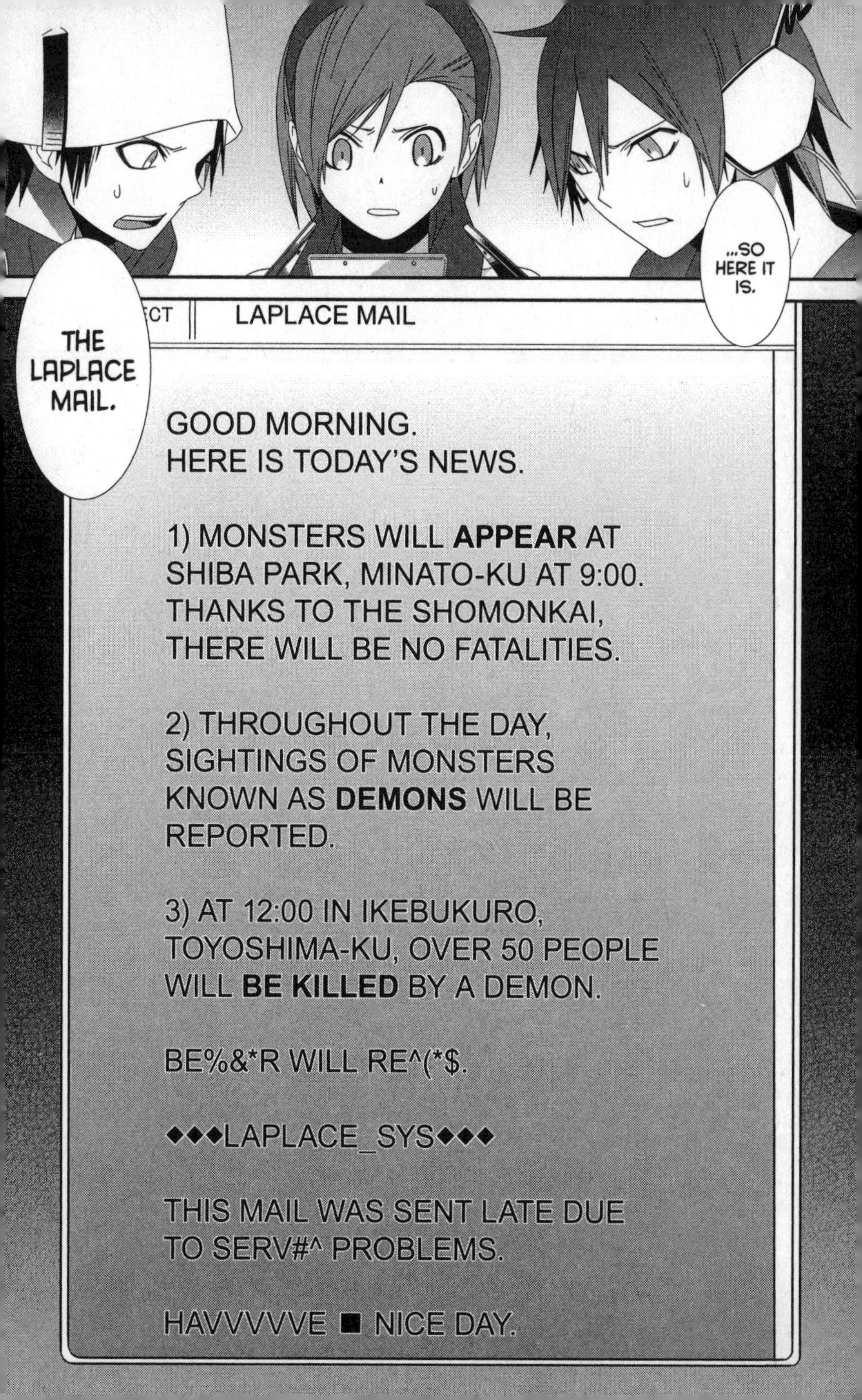
...SO HERE IT IS.
THE LAPLACE MAIL.
LAPLACE MAIL
GOOD MORNING.
HERE IS TODAY'S NEWS.
1) MONSTERS WILL **APPEAR** AT SHIBA PARK, MINATO-KU AT 9:00. THANKS TO THE SHOMONKAI, THERE WILL BE NO FATALITIES.
2) THROUGHOUT THE DAY, SIGHTINGS OF MONSTERS KNOWN AS **DEMONS** WILL BE REPORTED.
3) AT 12:00 IN IKEBUKURO, TOYOSHIMA-KU, OVER 50 PEOPLE WILL **BE KILLED** BY A DEMON.
BE%&*R WILL RE^(*$.
◆◆◆LAPLACE_SYS◆◆◆
THIS MAIL WAS SENT LATE DUE TO SERV#^ PROBLEMS.
HAVVVVVE ■ NICE DAY.

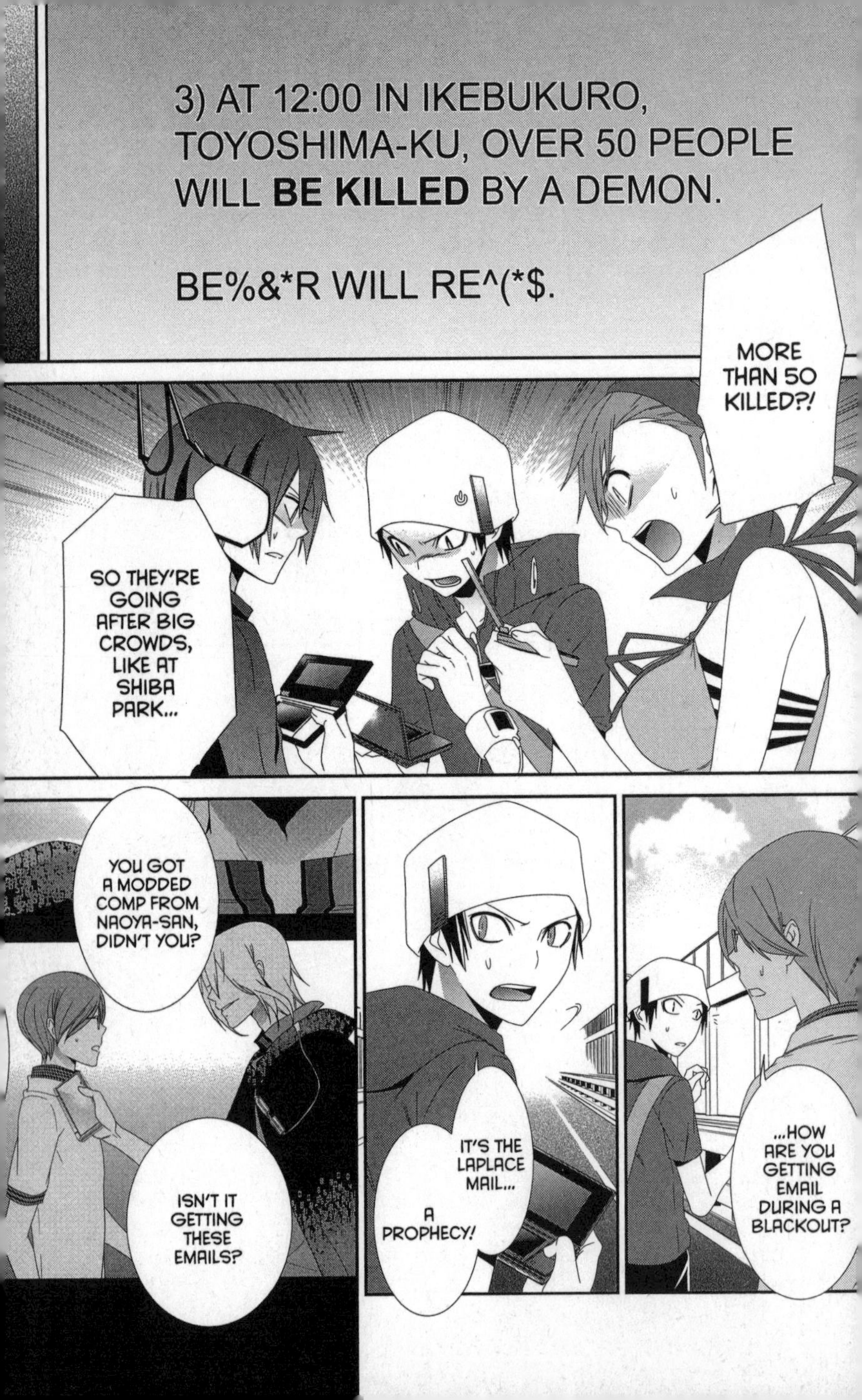
3) AT 12:00 IN IKEBUKURO, TOYOSHIMA-KU, OVER 50 PEOPLE WILL **BE KILLED** BY A DEMON.
BE%&*R WILL RE^(*$.
MORE THAN 50 KILLED?!
SO THEY'RE GOING AFTER BIG CROWDS, LIKE AT SHIBA PARK...
...HOW ARE YOU GETTING EMAIL DURING A BLACKOUT?
IT'S THE LAPLACE MAIL...
A PROPHECY!
YOU GOT A MODDED COMP FROM NAOYA-SAN, DIDN'T YOU?
ISN'T IT GETTING THESE EMAILS?

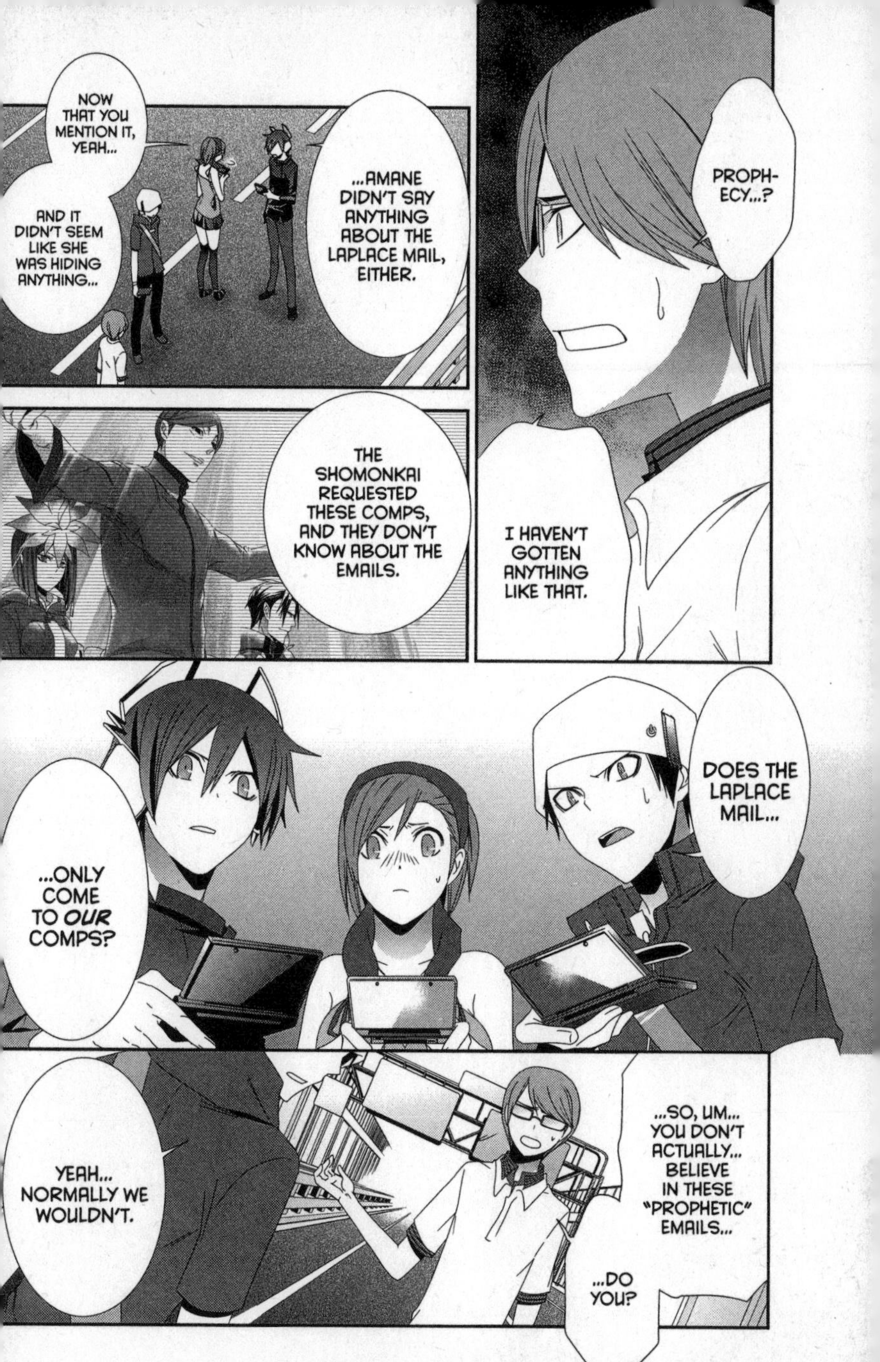
PROPHECY...?
I HAVEN'T GOTTEN ANYTHING LIKE THAT.
...AMANE DIDN'T SAY ANYTHING ABOUT THE LAPLACE MAIL, EITHER.
NOW THAT YOU MENTION IT, YEAH...
AND IT DIDN'T SEEM LIKE SHE WAS HIDING ANYTHING...
THE SHOMONKAI REQUESTED THESE COMPS, AND THEY DON'T KNOW ABOUT THE EMAILS.
DOES THE LAPLACE MAIL...
...ONLY COME TO *OUR* COMPS?
...SO, UM... YOU DON'T ACTUALLY... BELIEVE IN THESE "PROPHETIC" EMAILS...
...DO YOU?
YEAH... NORMALLY WE WOULDN'T.

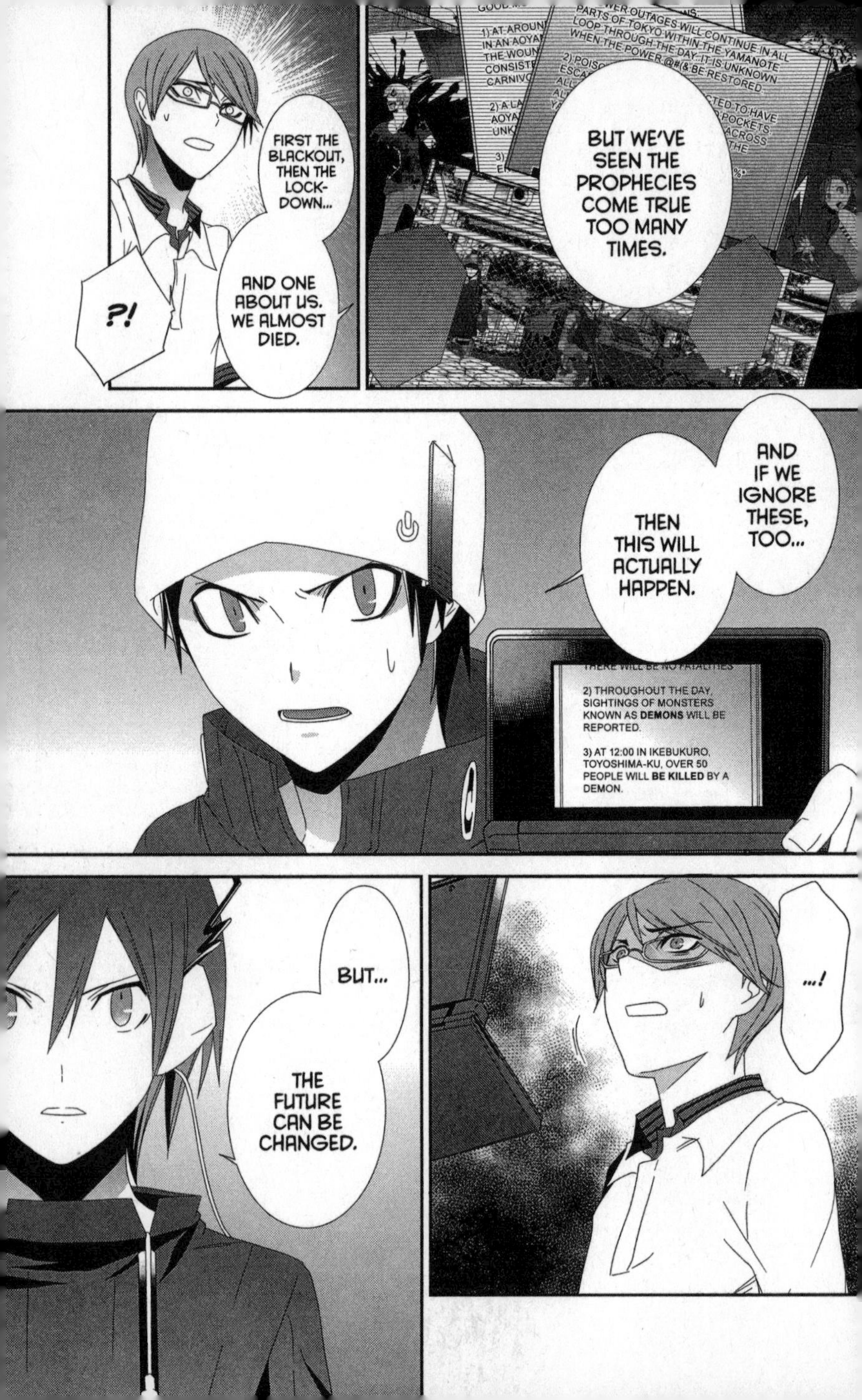

POWER OUTAGES WILL CONTINUE IN ALL PARTS OF TOKYO WITHIN THE YAMANOTE LOOP THROUGH THE DAY. IT IS UNKNOWN WHEN THE POWER @#(& BE RESTORED.
BUT WE'VE SEEN THE PROPHECIES COME TRUE TOO MANY TIMES.
FIRST THE BLACKOUT, THEN THE LOCK-DOWN...
AND ONE ABOUT US. WE ALMOST DIED.
?!
AND IF WE IGNORE THESE, TOO...
THEN THIS WILL ACTUALLY HAPPEN.
2) THROUGHOUT THE DAY, SIGHTINGS OF MONSTERS KNOWN AS DEMONS WILL BE REPORTED.
3) AT 12:00 IN IKEBUKURO, TOYOSHIMA-KU, OVER 50 PEOPLE WILL BE KILLED BY A DEMON.
...!
BUT...
THE FUTURE CAN BE CHANGED.

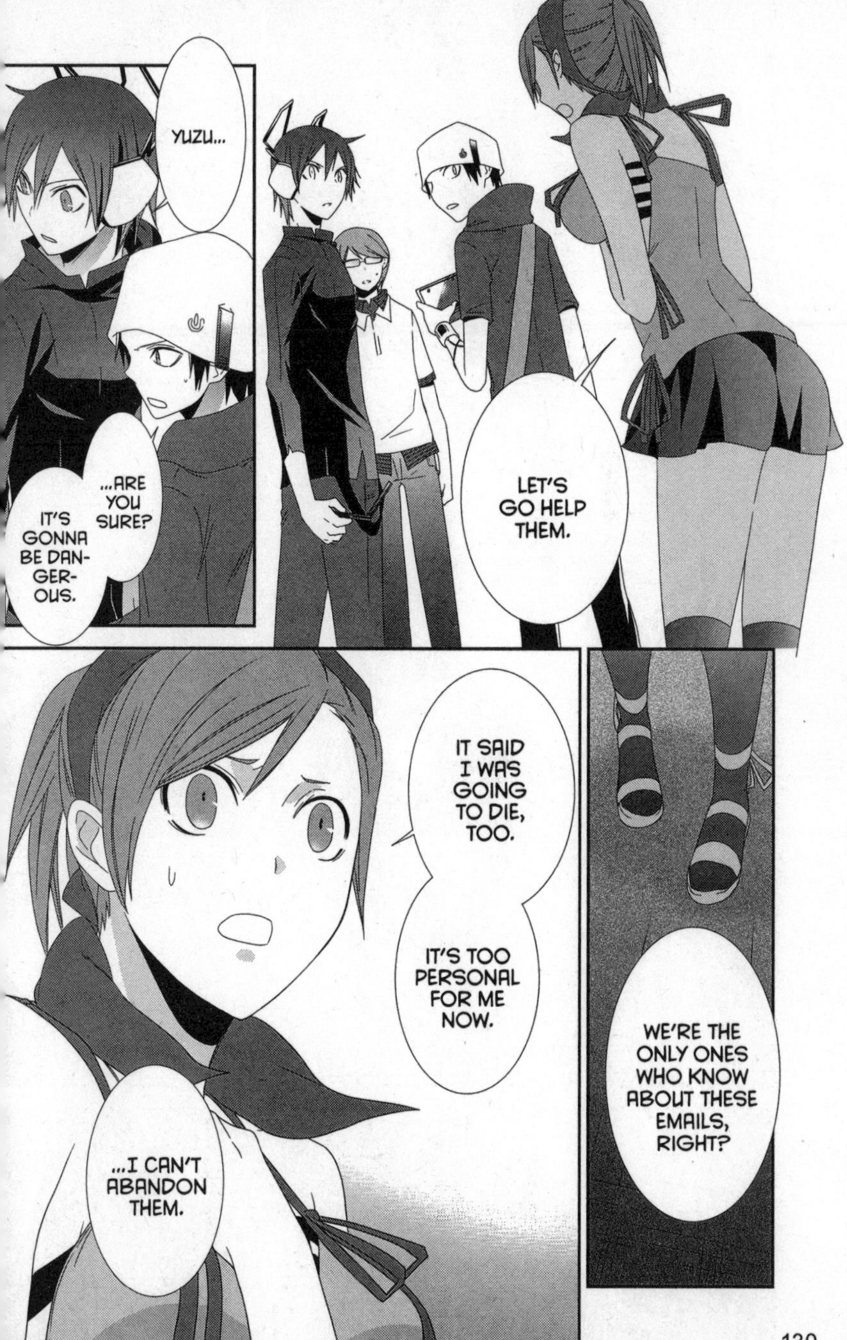
LET'S GO HELP THEM.
YUZU...
...ARE YOU SURE?
IT'S GONNA BE DAN-GER-OUS.
WE'RE THE ONLY ONES WHO KNOW ABOUT THESE EMAILS, RIGHT?
IT SAID I WAS GOING TO DIE, TOO.
IT'S TOO PERSONAL FOR ME NOW.
...I CAN'T ABANDON THEM.

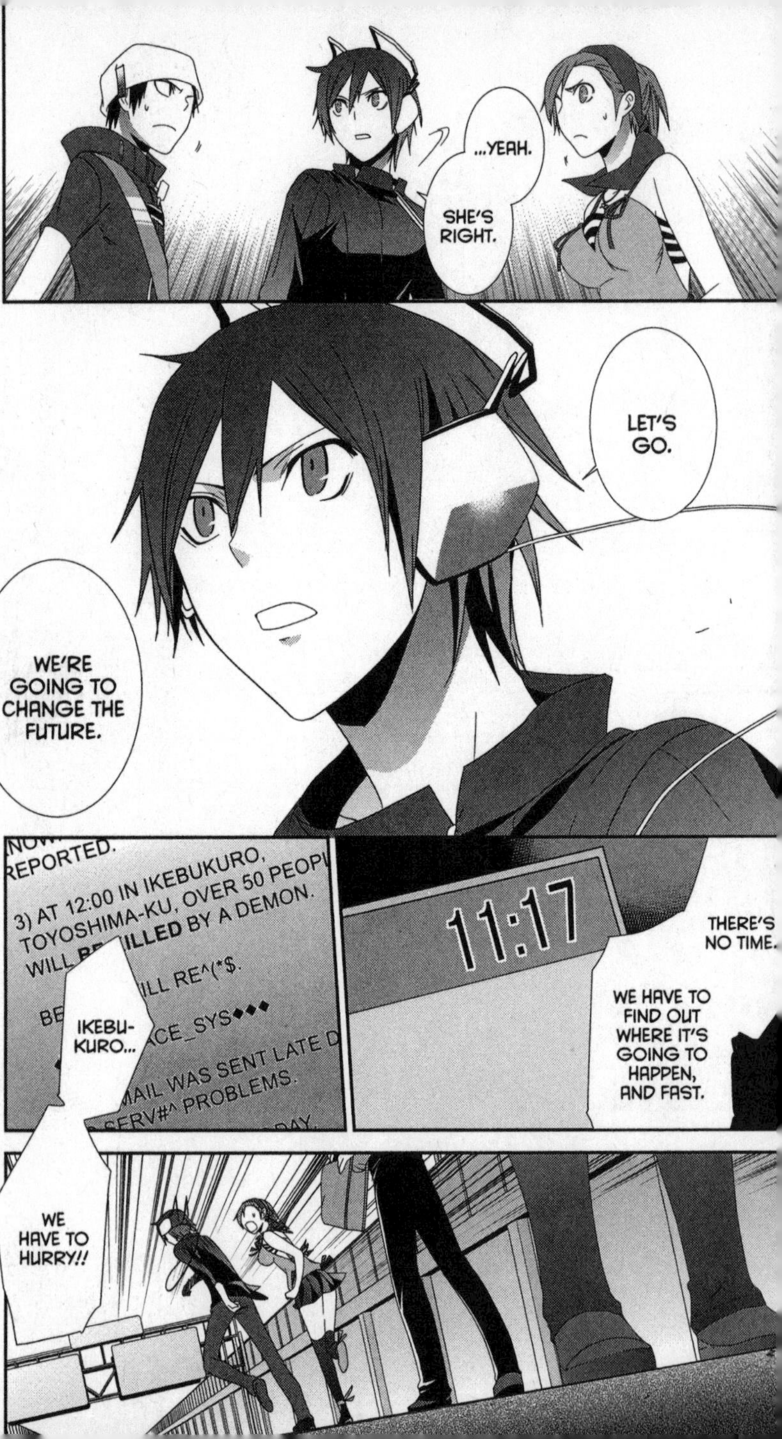

...YEAH.
SHE'S RIGHT.
LET'S GO.
WE'RE GOING TO CHANGE THE FUTURE.
THERE'S NO TIME.
WE HAVE TO FIND OUT WHERE IT'S GOING TO HAPPEN, AND FAST.
REPORTED.
3) AT 12:00 IN IKEBUKURO, TOYOSHIMA-KU, OVER 50 PEOPL
WILL BE ILLED BY A DEMON.
ILL RE^(*$.
ACE_SYS◆◆◆
MAIL WAS SENT LATE D
SERV#^ PROBLEMS.
IKEBU-KURO...
11:17
WE HAVE TO HURRY!!

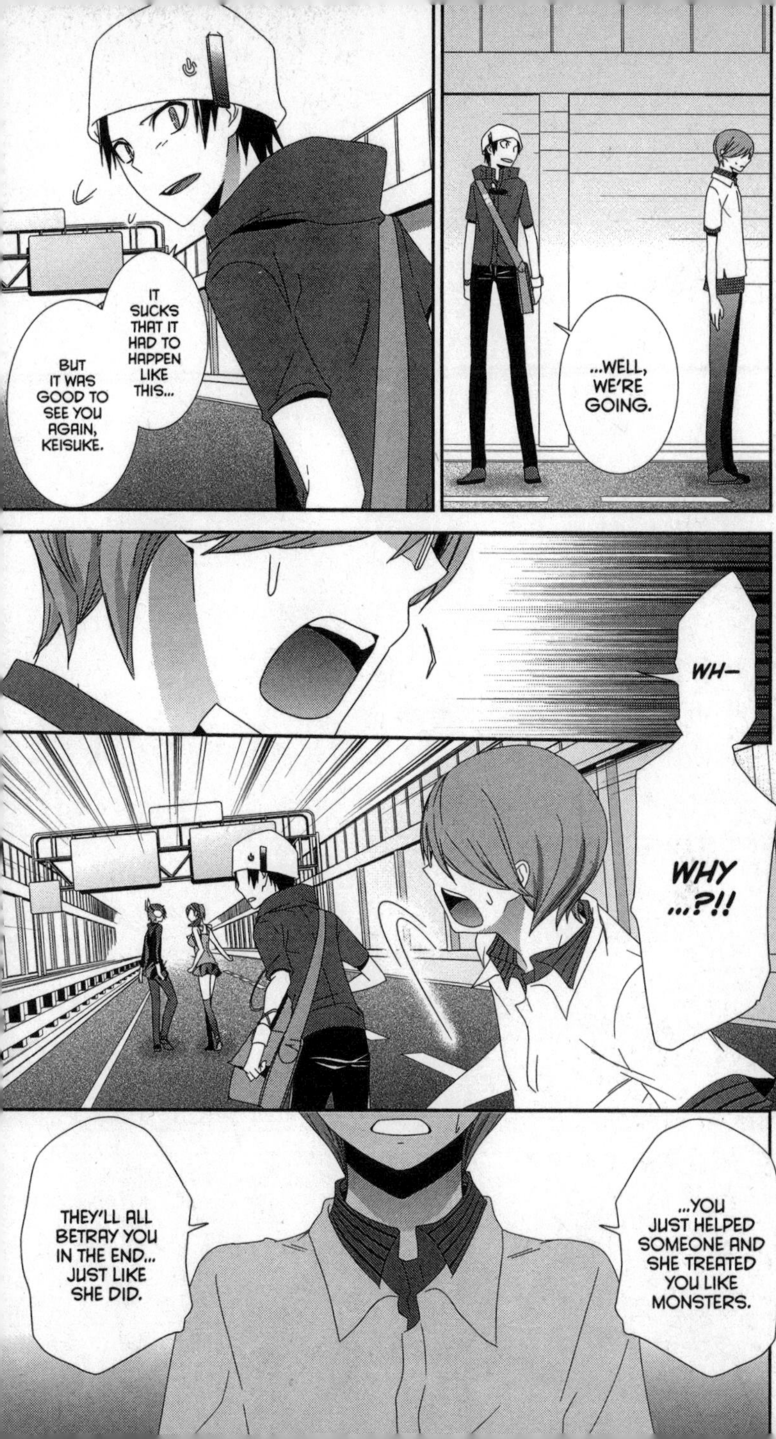
...WELL, WE'RE GOING.
IT SUCKS THAT IT HAD TO HAPPEN LIKE THIS...
BUT IT WAS GOOD TO SEE YOU AGAIN, KEISUKE.
WH–
WHY ...?!!
...YOU JUST HELPED SOMEONE AND SHE TREATED YOU LIKE MONSTERS.
THEY'LL ALL BETRAY YOU IN THE END... JUST LIKE SHE DID.

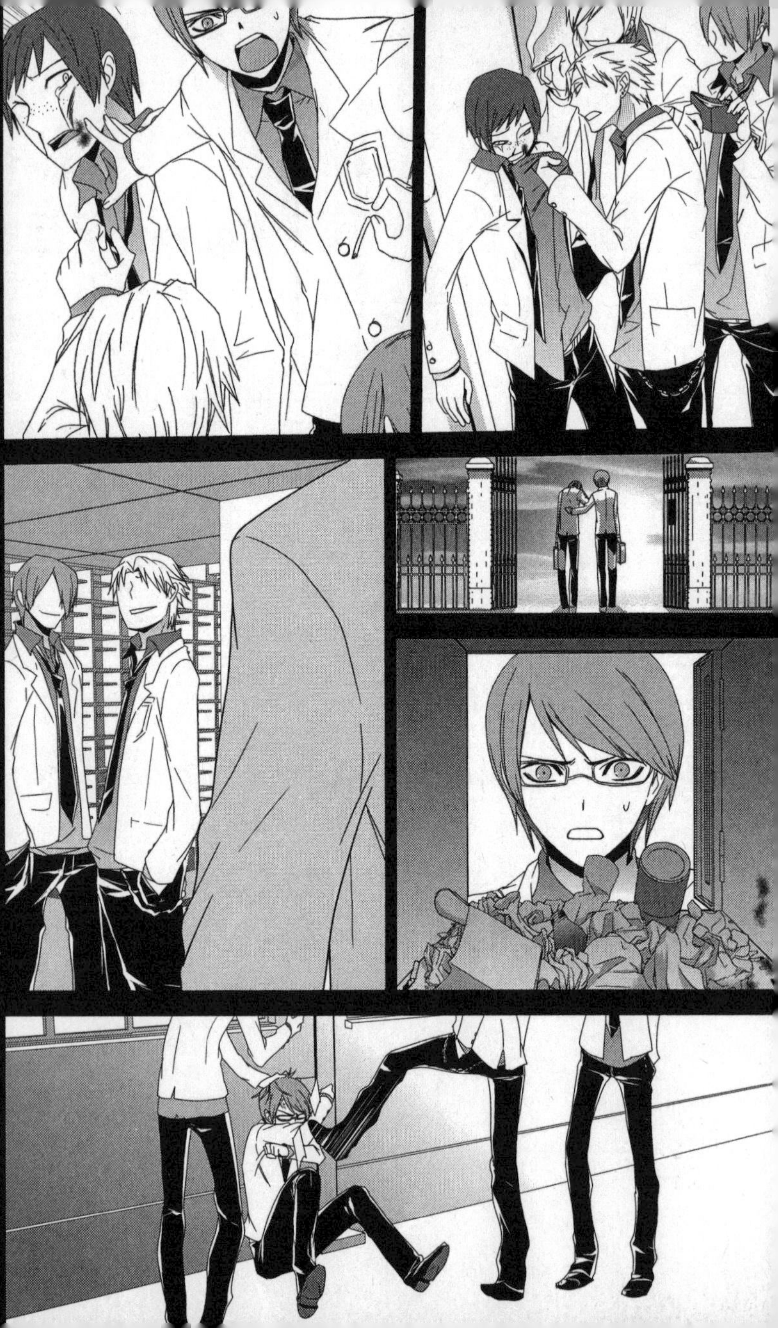

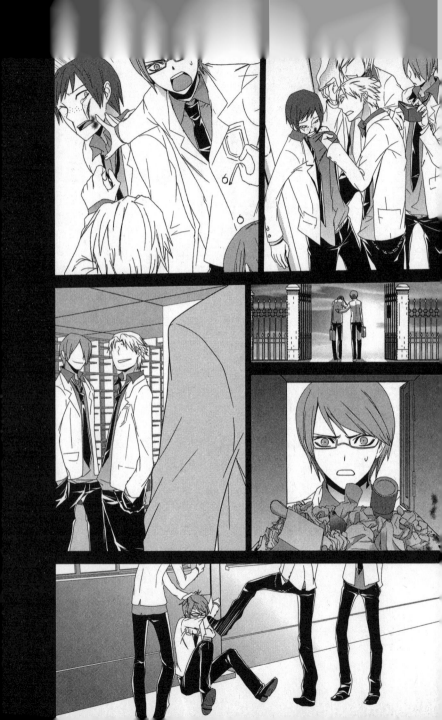

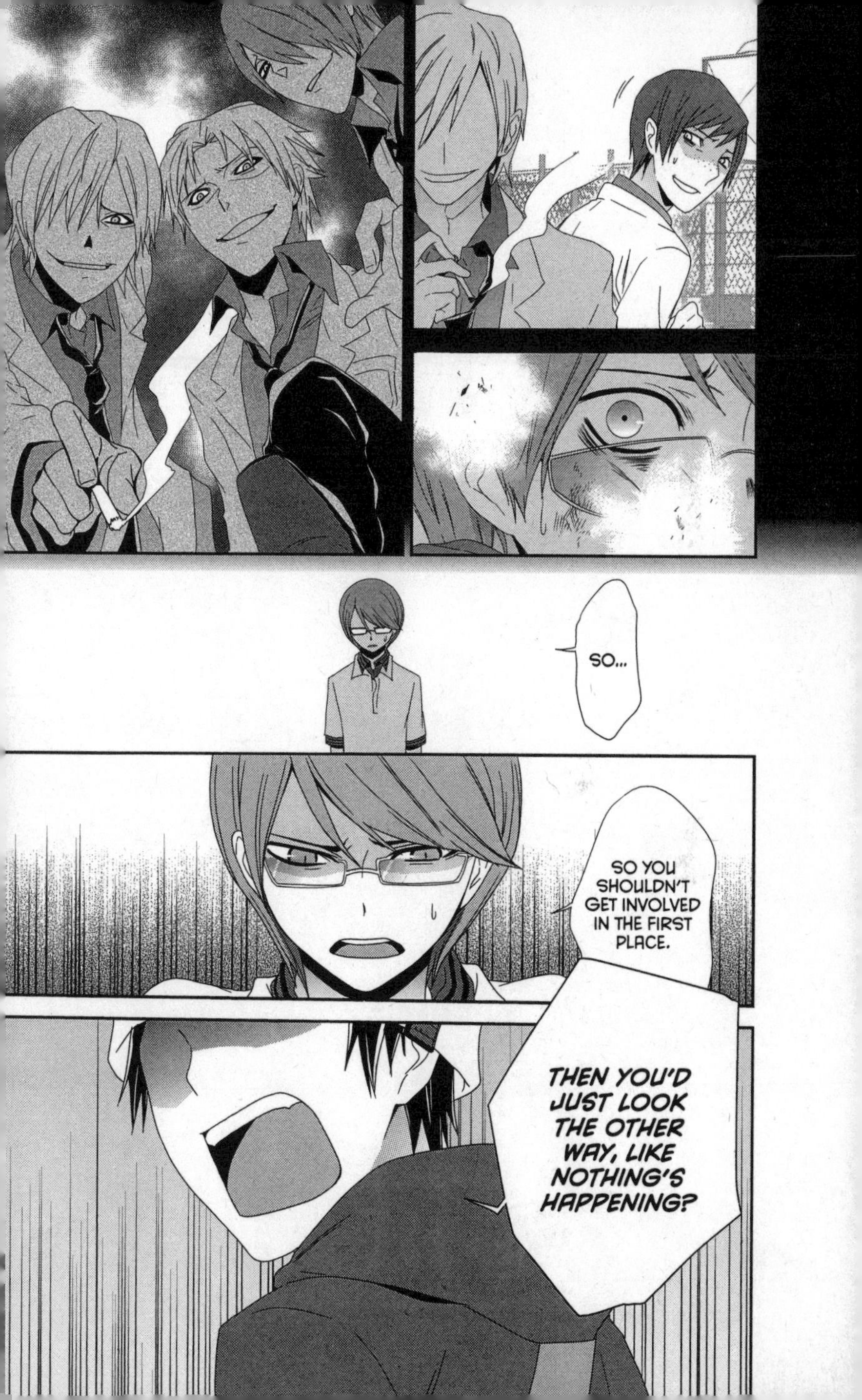
SO...
SO YOU SHOULDN'T GET INVOLVED IN THE FIRST PLACE.
THEN YOU'D JUST LOOK THE OTHER WAY, LIKE NOTHING'S HAPPENING?

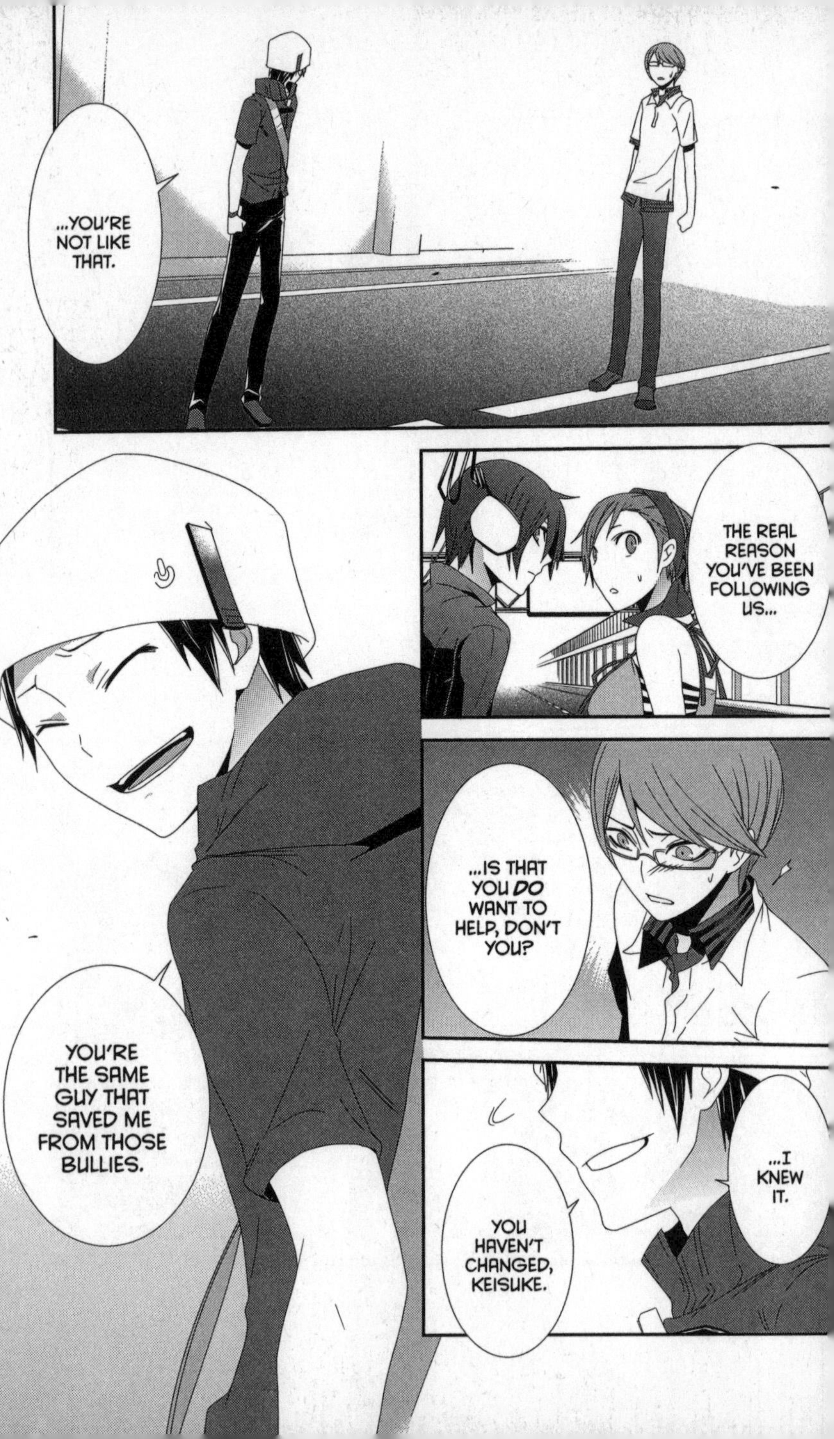
...YOU'RE NOT LIKE THAT.
THE REAL REASON YOU'VE BEEN FOLLOWING US...
...IS THAT YOU *DO* WANT TO HELP, DON'T YOU?
...I KNEW IT.
YOU HAVEN'T CHANGED, KEISUKE.
YOU'RE THE SAME GUY THAT SAVED ME FROM THOSE BULLIES.

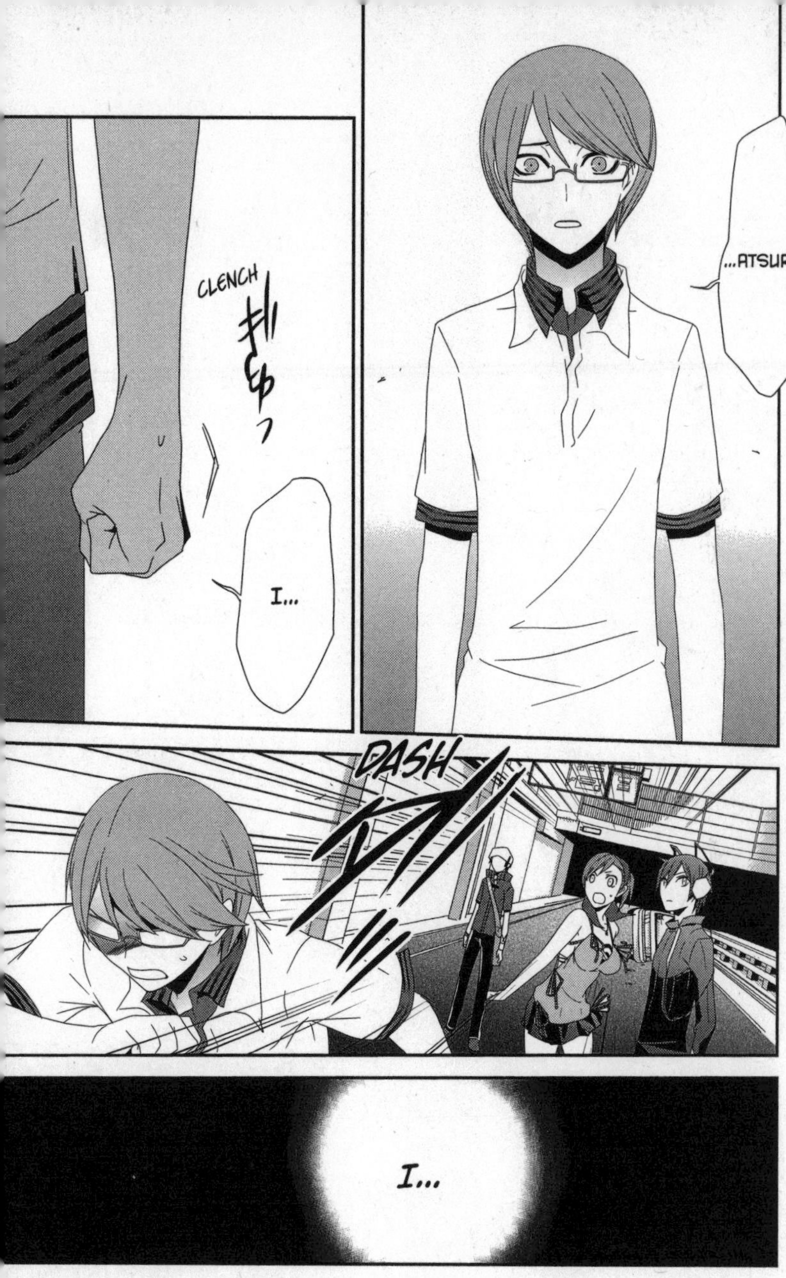
...ATSURO.
CLENCH
I...
DASH
I...

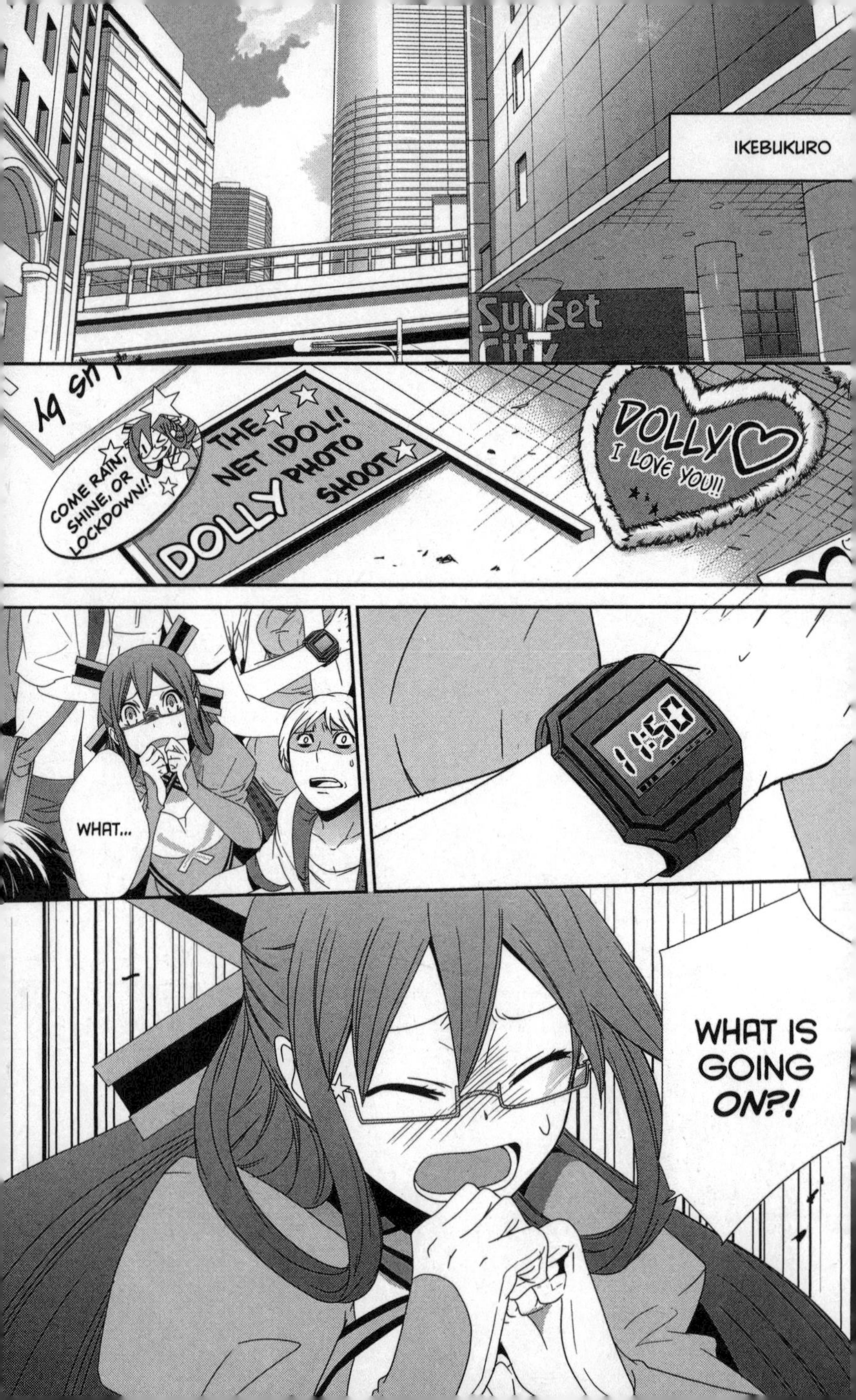
IKEBUKURO
Sunset City
DOLLY I LOVE YOU!!
THE NET IDOL!! DOLLY PHOTO SHOOT
COME RAIN, SHINE, OR LOCKDOWN!!
1:50
WHAT...
WHAT IS GOING ON?!

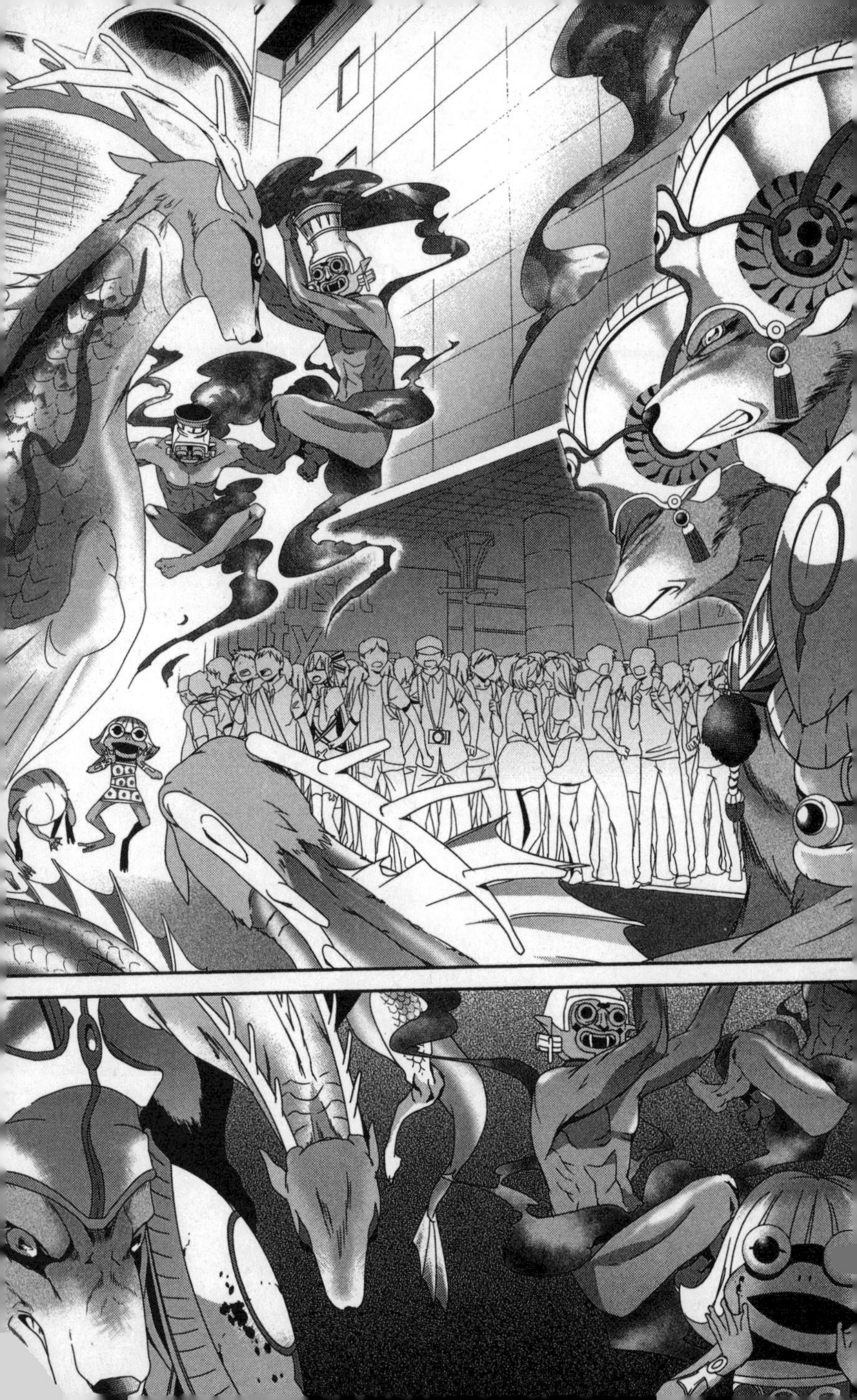

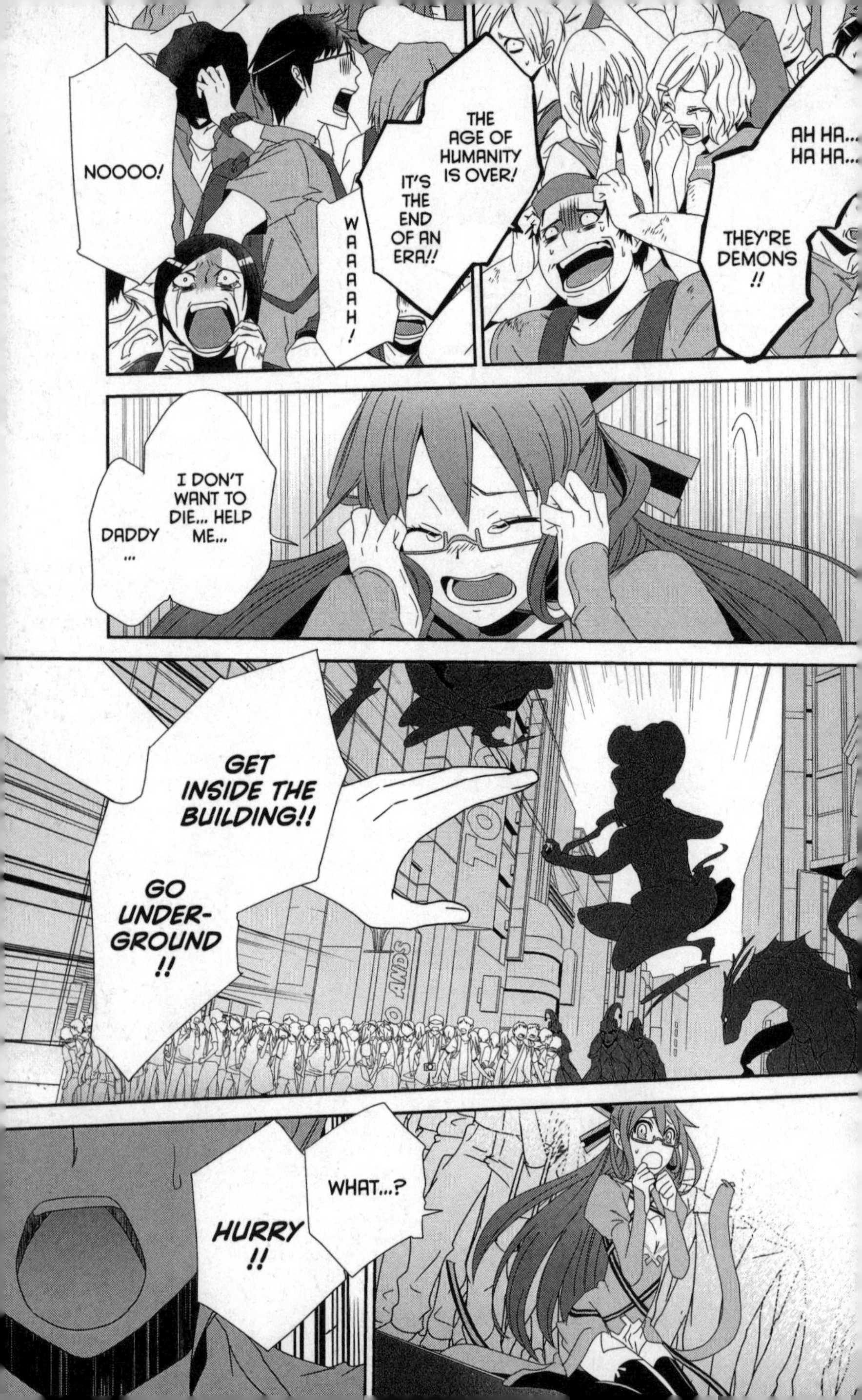
AH HA... HA HA...
THEY'RE DEMONS !!
THE AGE OF HUMANITY IS OVER!
IT'S THE END OF AN ERA!!
WAAAAAH!
NOOOO!
I DON'T WANT TO DIE... HELP ME...
DADDY ...
GET INSIDE THE BUILDING!!
GO UNDER-GROUND !!
WHAT...?
HURRY !!

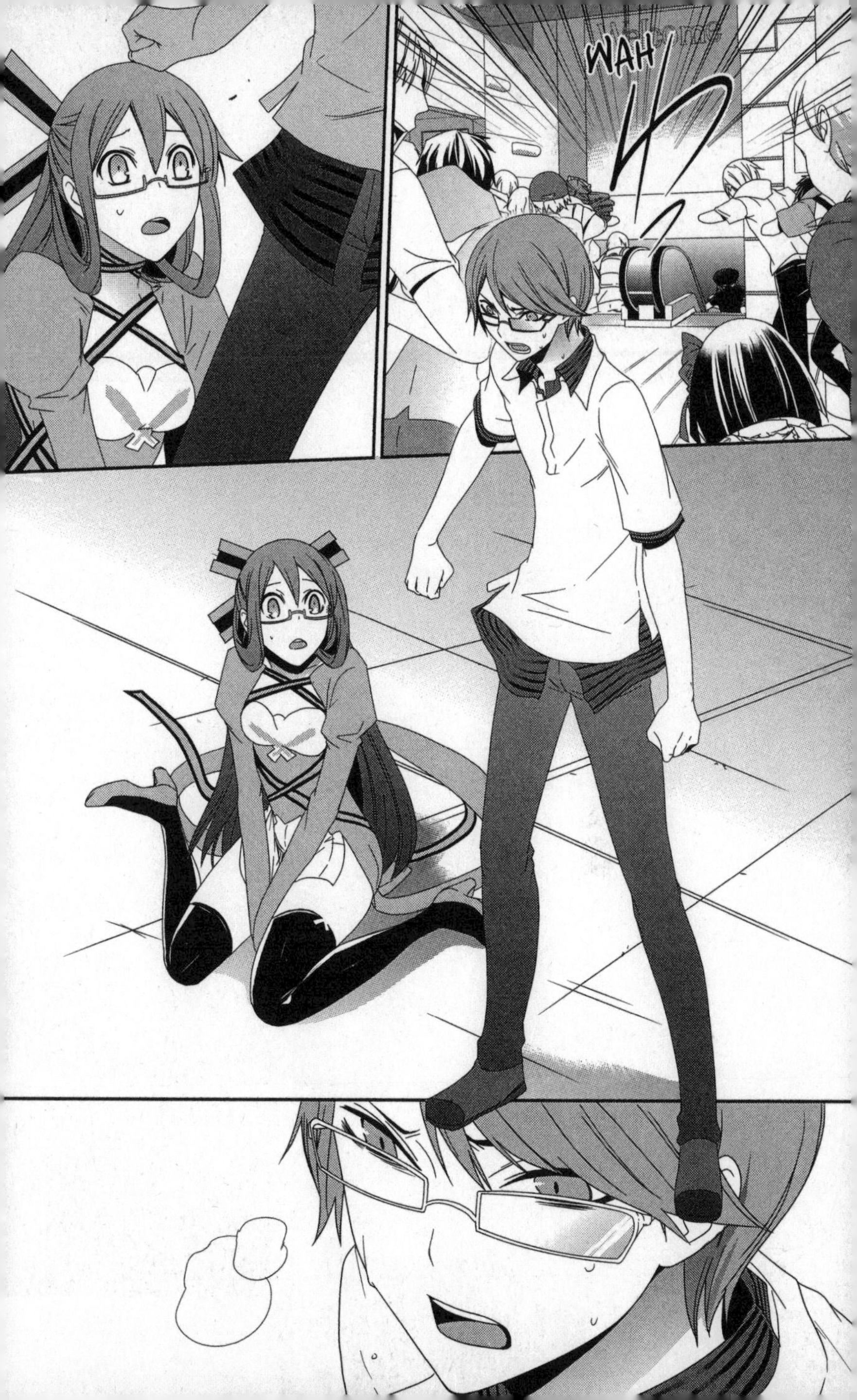
WAH

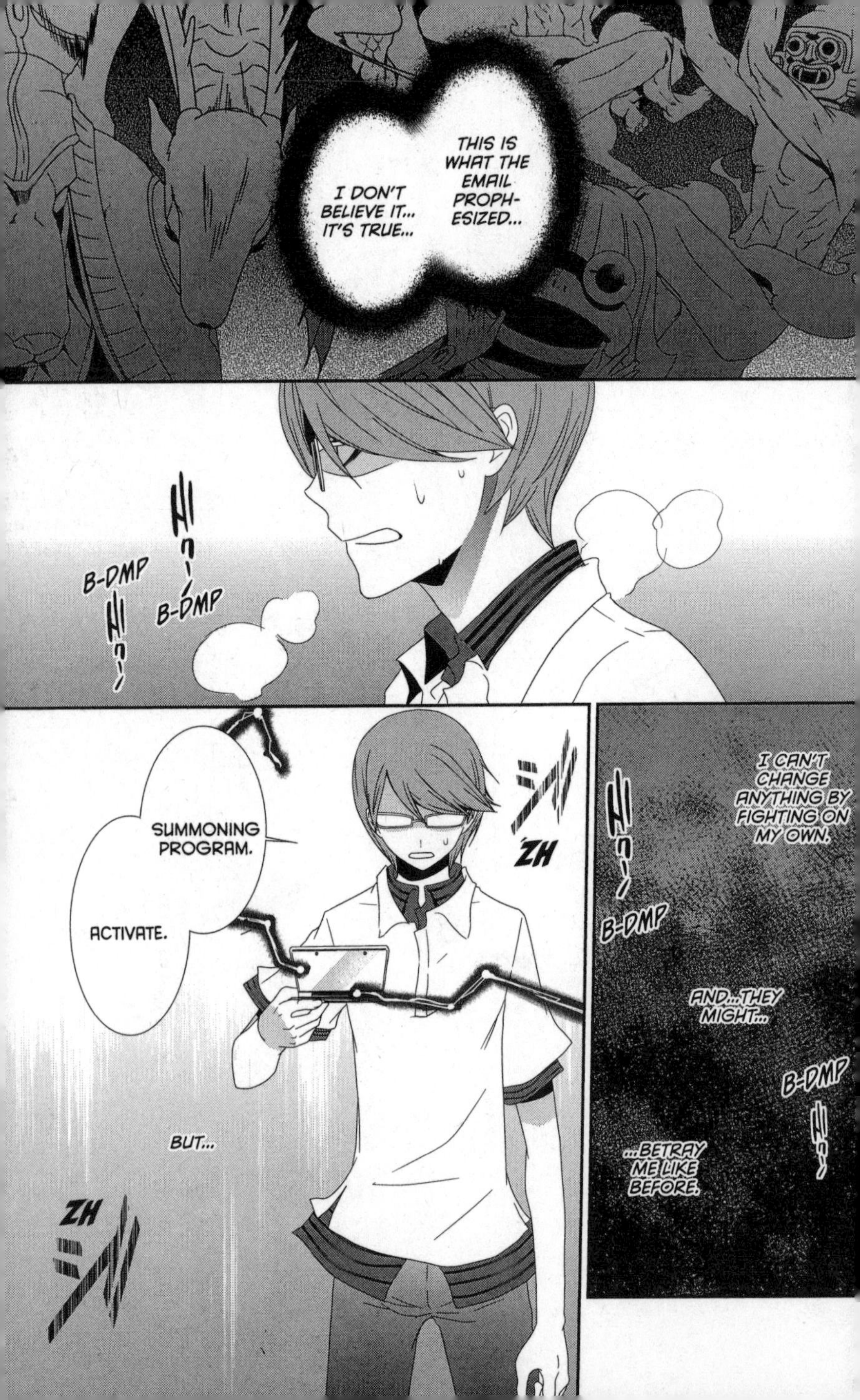
THIS IS WHAT THE EMAIL PROPHESIZED...
I DON'T BELIEVE IT... IT'S TRUE...
B-DMP
B-DMP
I CAN'T CHANGE ANYTHING BY FIGHTING ON MY OWN.
B-DMP
AND...THEY MIGHT...
B-DMP
...BETRAY ME LIKE BEFORE.
ZH
SUMMONING PROGRAM.
ACTIVATE.
BUT...
ZH

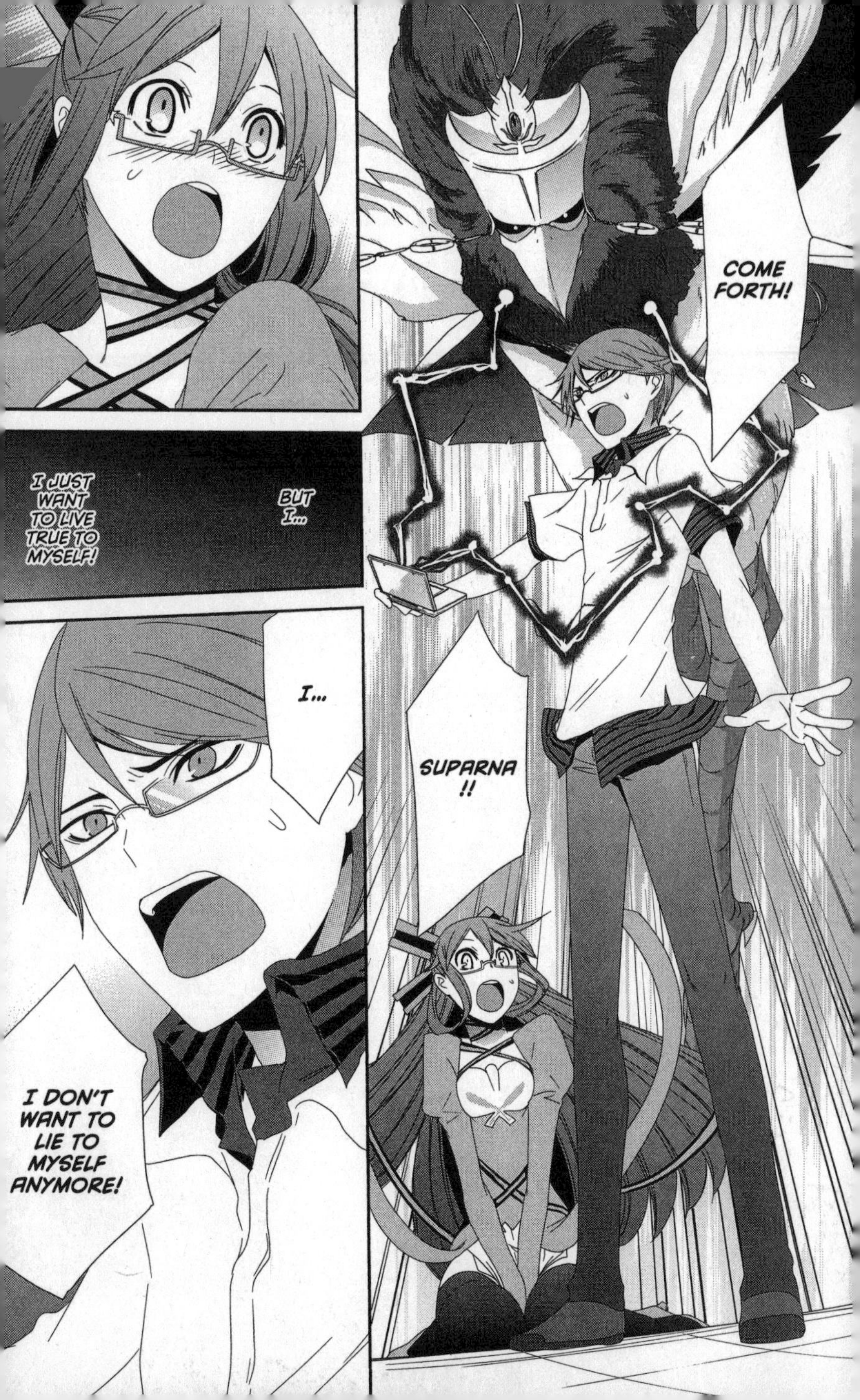
COME FORTH!
SUPARNA !!
BUT I...
I JUST WANT TO LIVE TRUE TO MYSELF!
I...
I DON'T WANT TO LIE TO MYSELF ANYMORE!

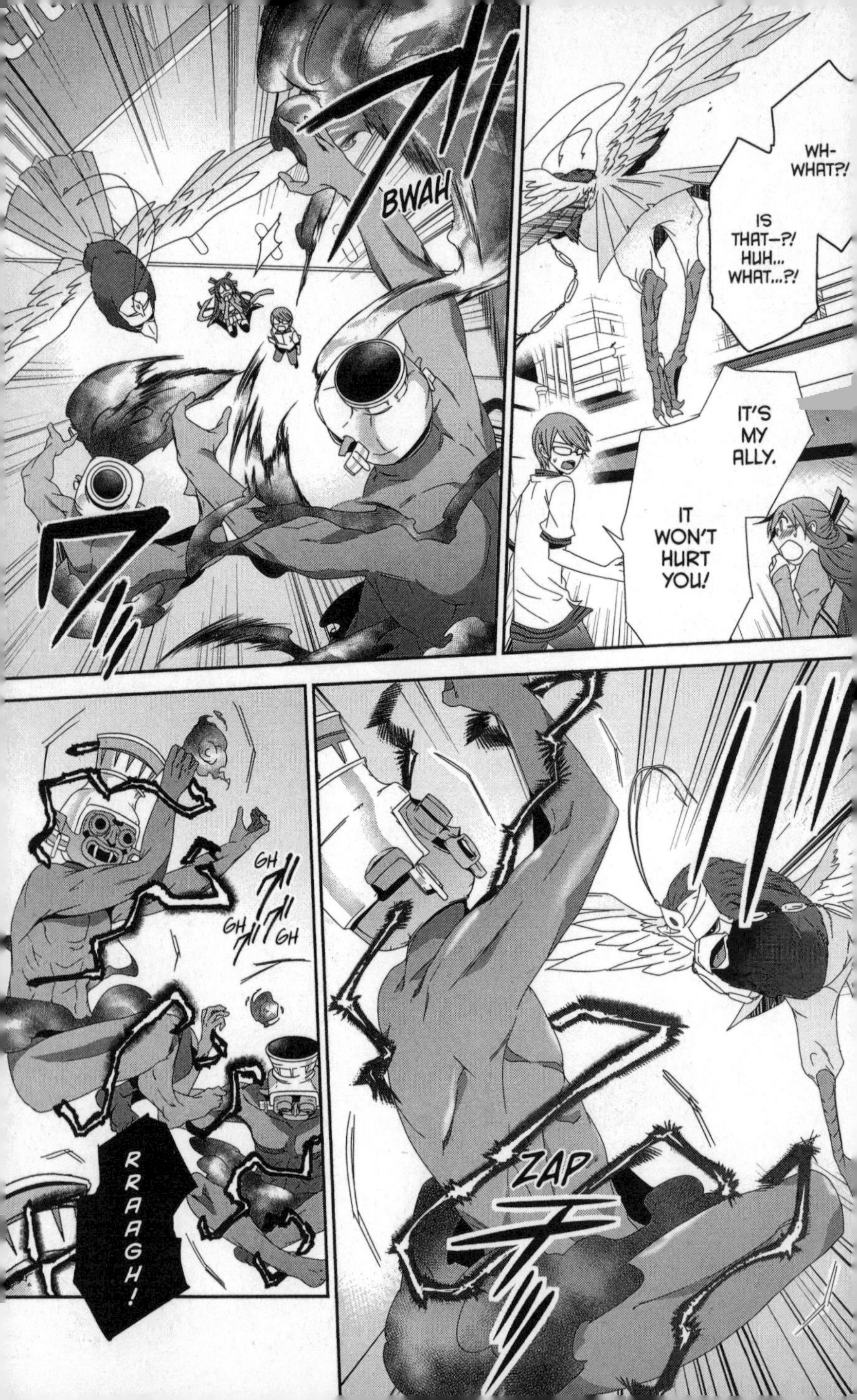
WH-WHAT?! IS THAT—?! HUH... WHAT...?!
IT'S MY ALLY. IT WON'T HURT YOU!
BWAH
ZAP
GH GH GH
RRAAGH!

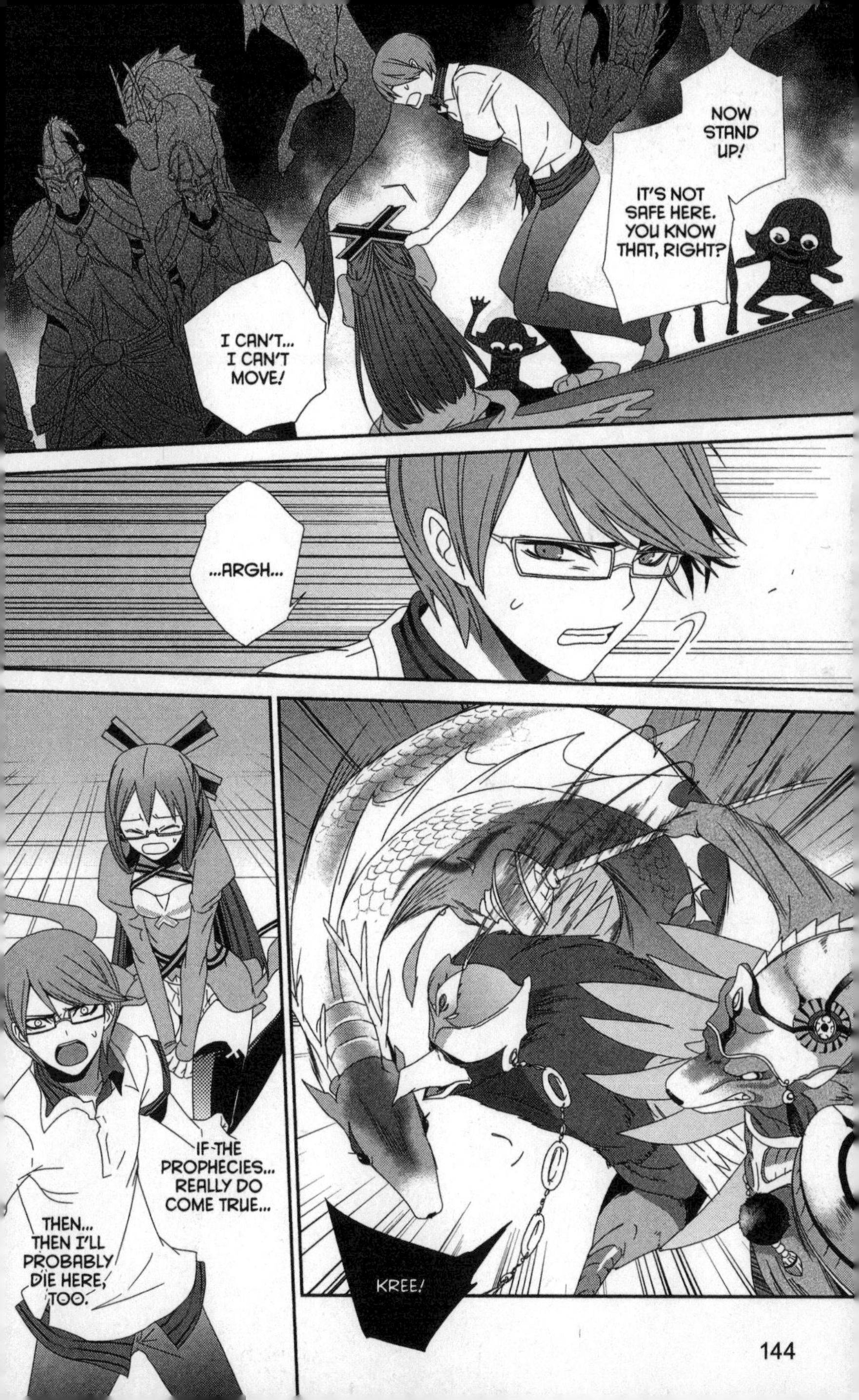
NOW STAND UP!
IT'S NOT SAFE HERE. YOU KNOW THAT, RIGHT?
I CAN'T... I CAN'T MOVE!
...ARGH...
KREE!
IF THE PROPHECIES... REALLY DO COME TRUE...
THEN... THEN I'LL PROBABLY DIE HERE, TOO.

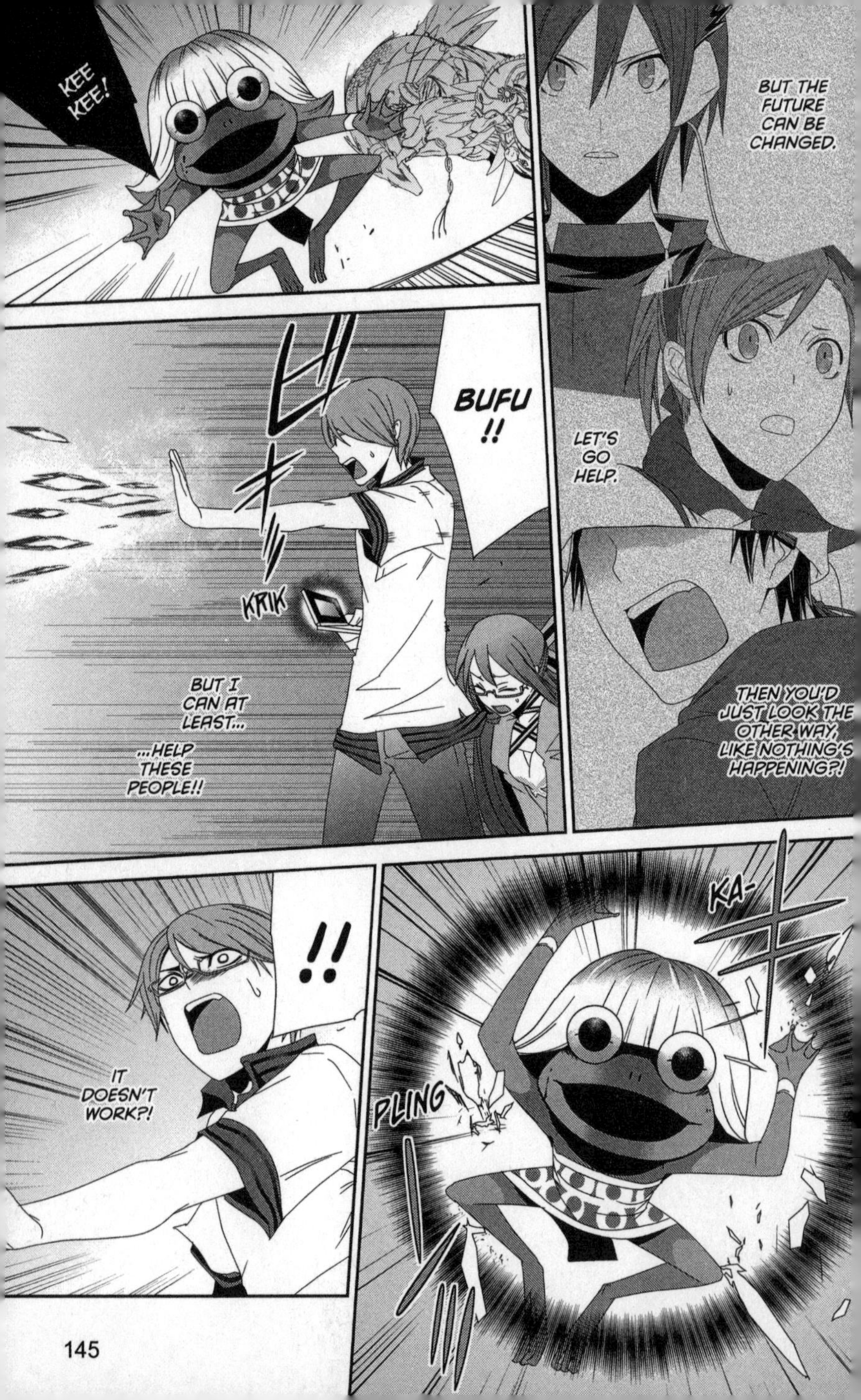
BUT THE FUTURE CAN BE CHANGED.
LET'S GO HELP.
THEN YOU'D JUST LOOK THE OTHER WAY, LIKE NOTHING'S HAPPENING?!
KEE KEE!
BUFU !!
KRIK
BUT I CAN AT LEAST...
...HELP THESE PEOPLE!!
KA-
PLING
!!
IT DOESN'T WORK?!

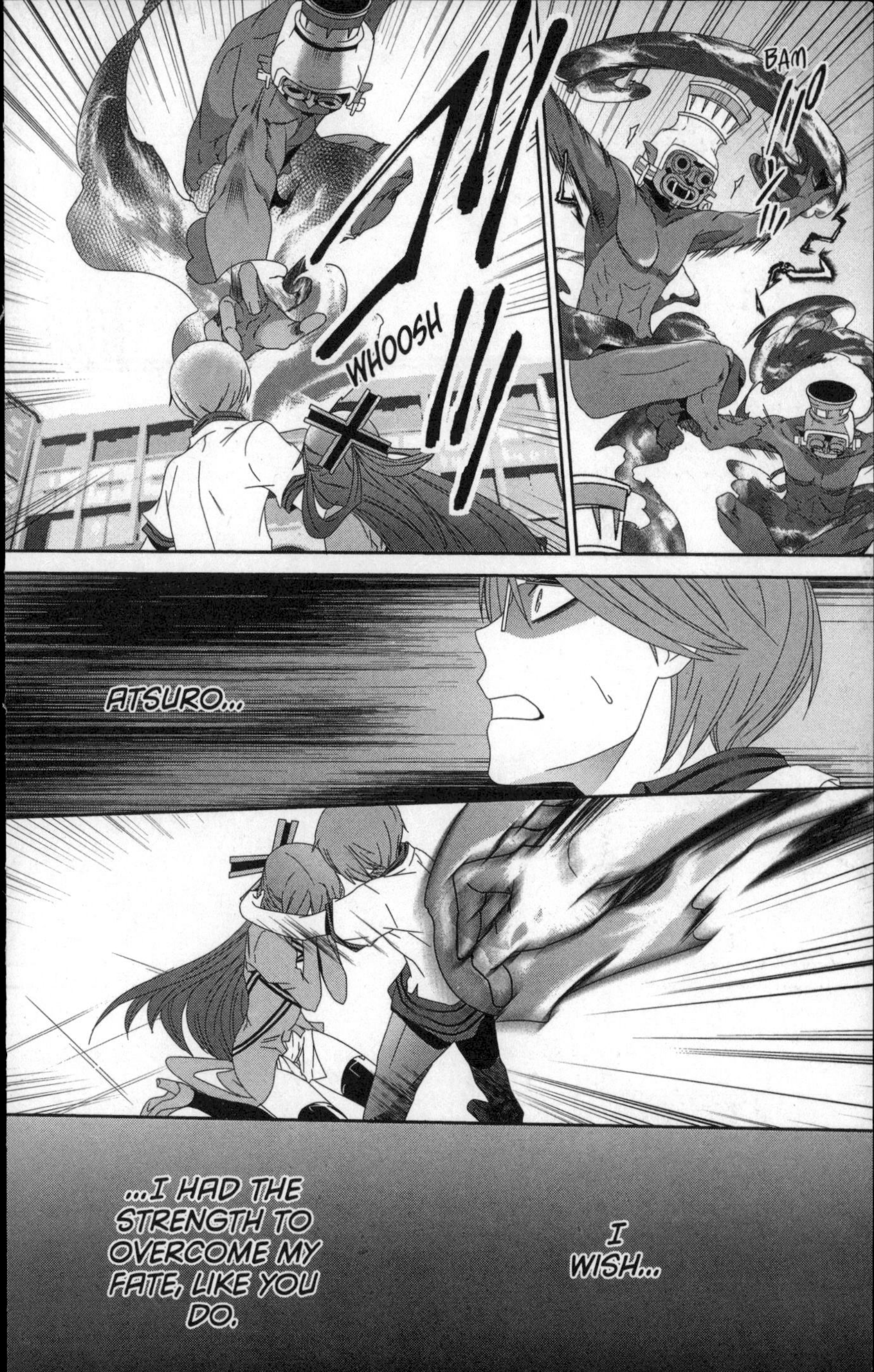
BAM
WHOOSH
ATSURO...
I WISH...
...I HAD THE STRENGTH TO OVERCOME MY FATE, LIKE YOU DO.

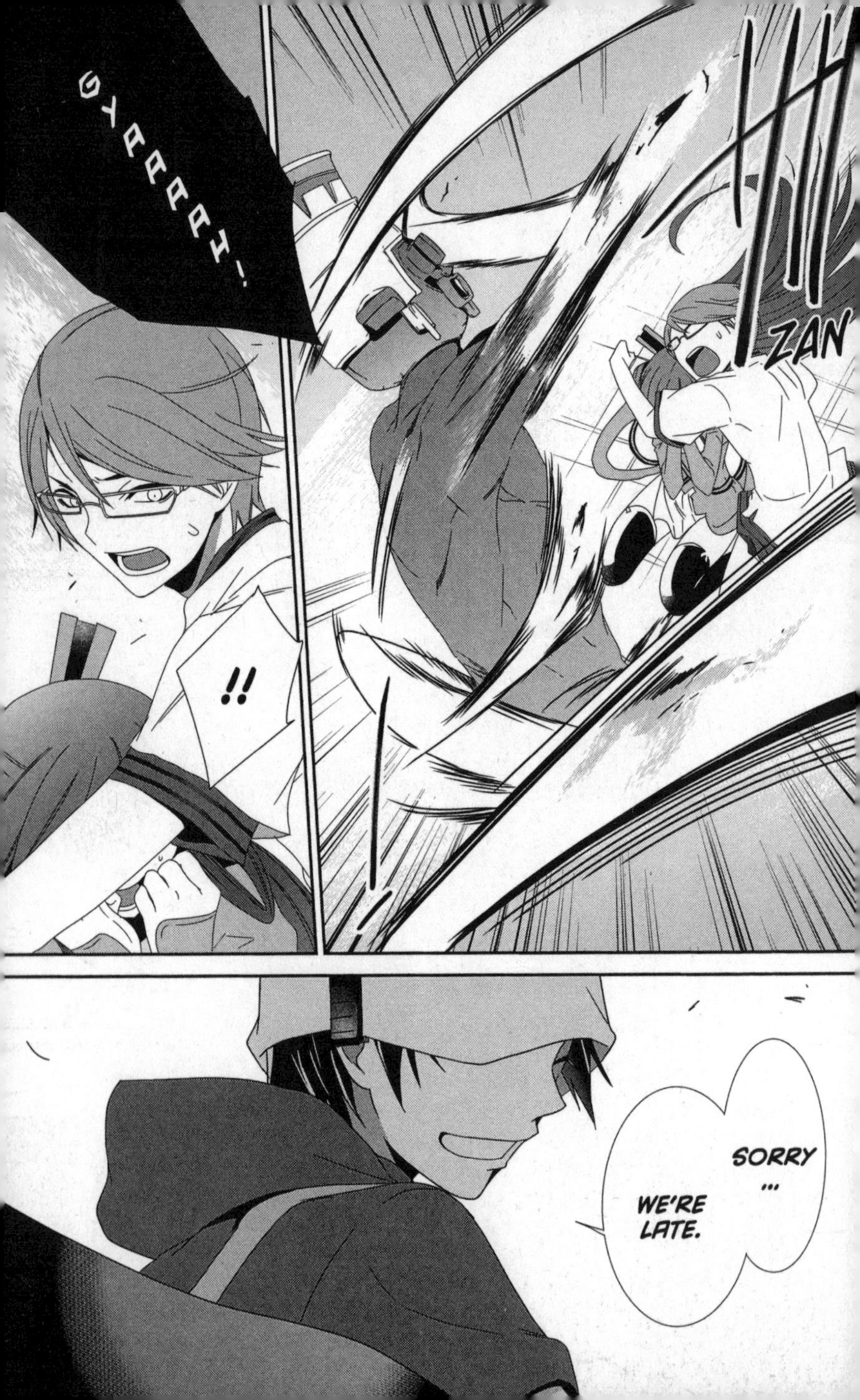
ZAN
GYAAAAH!
!!
SORRY... WE'RE LATE.

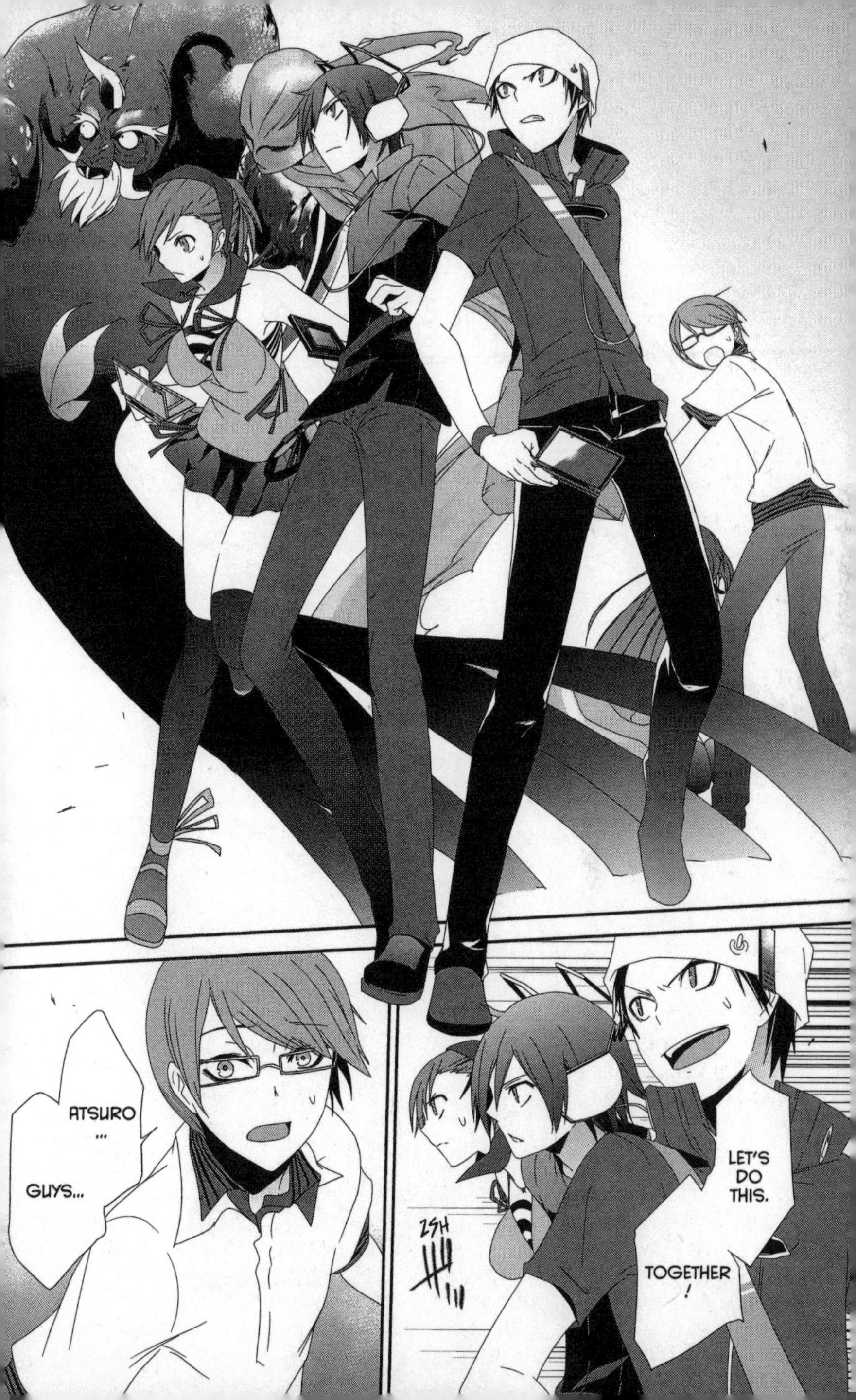
LET'S DO THIS.
TOGETHER!
ZSH
ATSURO...
GUYS...

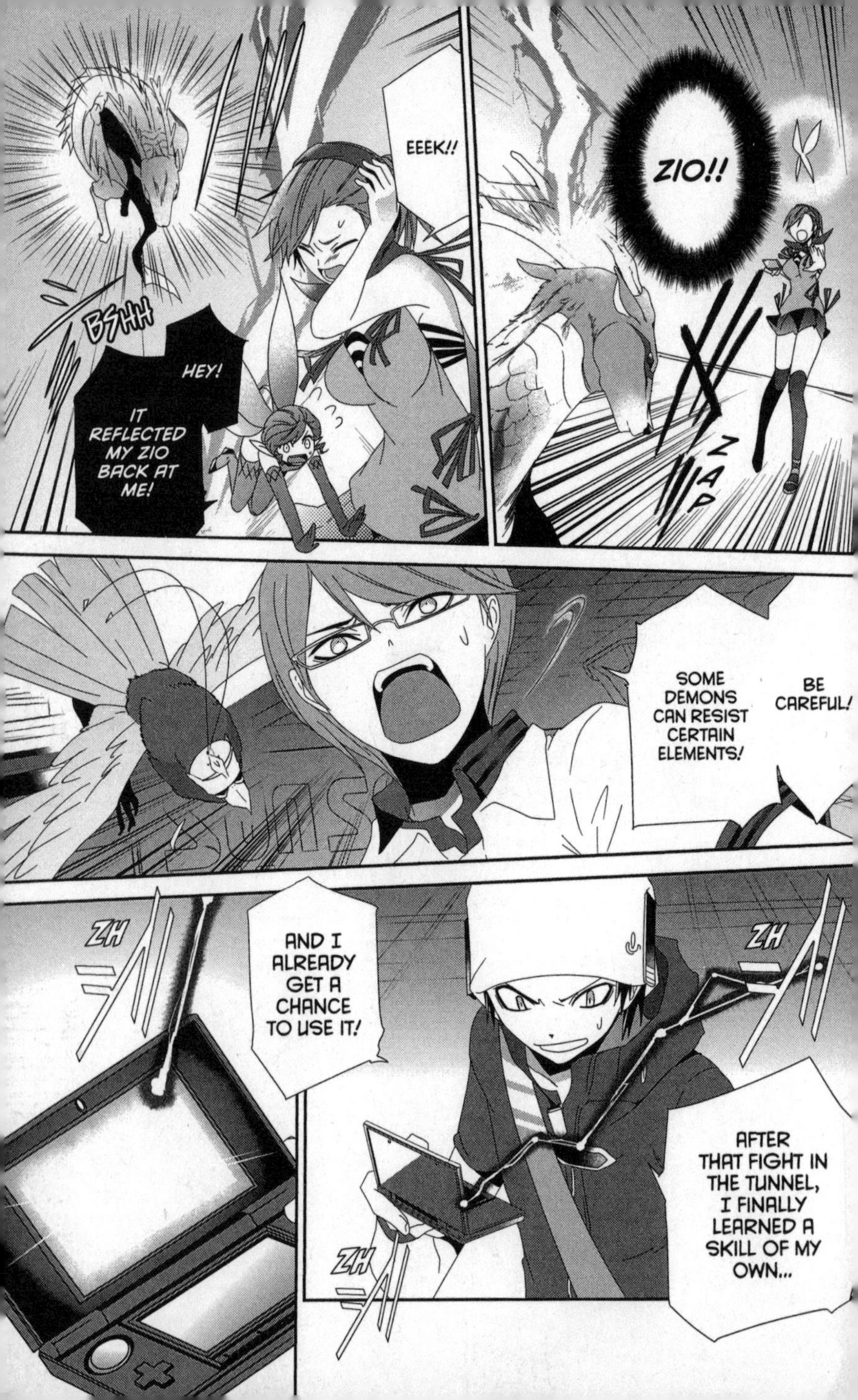

ZIO!!
ZAP
EEEK!!
BSHH
HEY!
IT REFLECTED MY ZIO BACK AT ME!
BE CAREFUL!
SOME DEMONS CAN RESIST CERTAIN ELEMENTS!
ZH
AFTER THAT FIGHT IN THE TUNNEL, I FINALLY LEARNED A SKILL OF MY OWN...
ZH
AND I ALREADY GET A CHANCE TO USE IT!
ZH

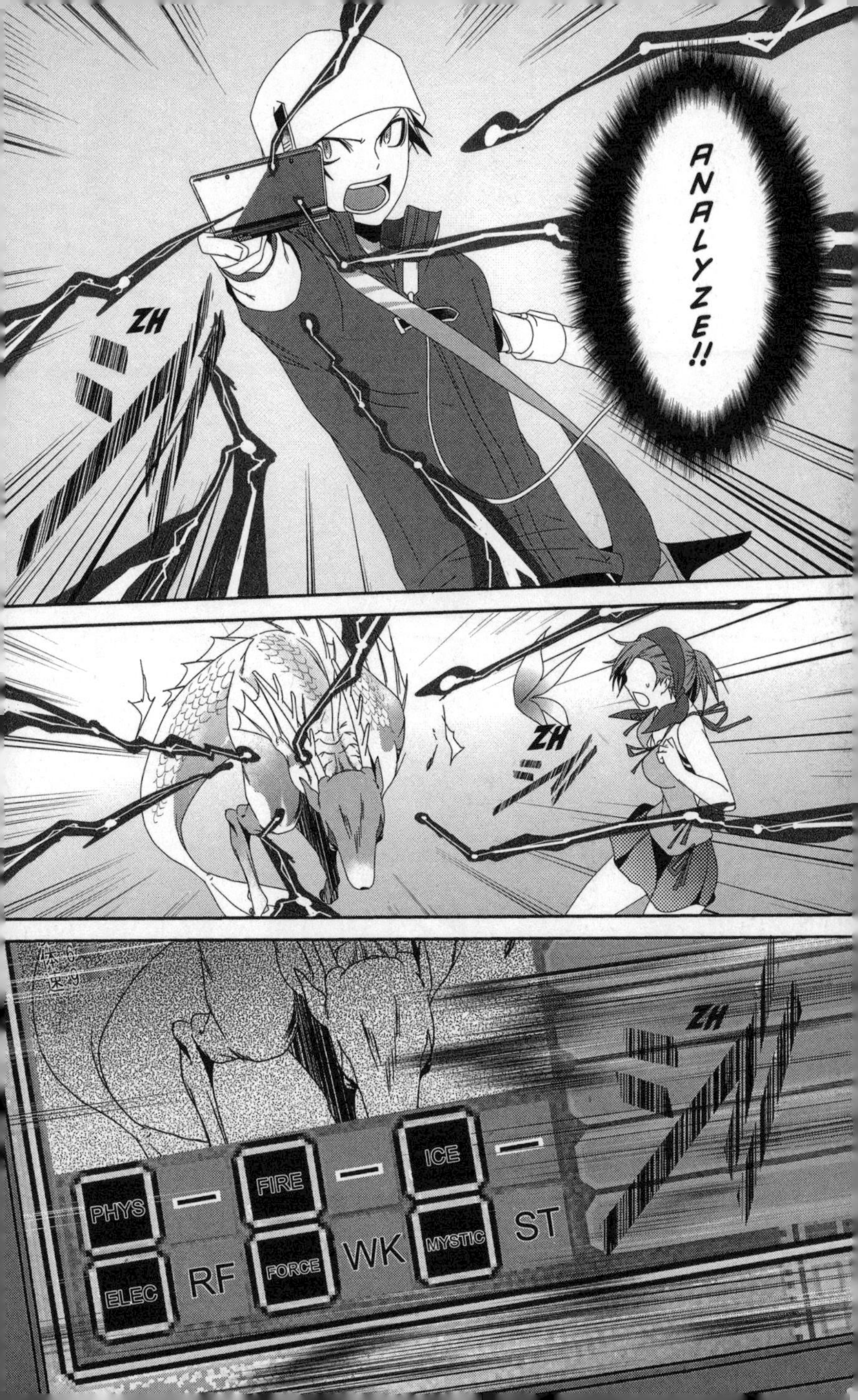
ANALYZE!!
ZH
ZH
ZH
体 6
速 9
ICE
—
FIRE
—
PHYS
—
ST
MYSTIC
WK
FORCE
RF
ELEC

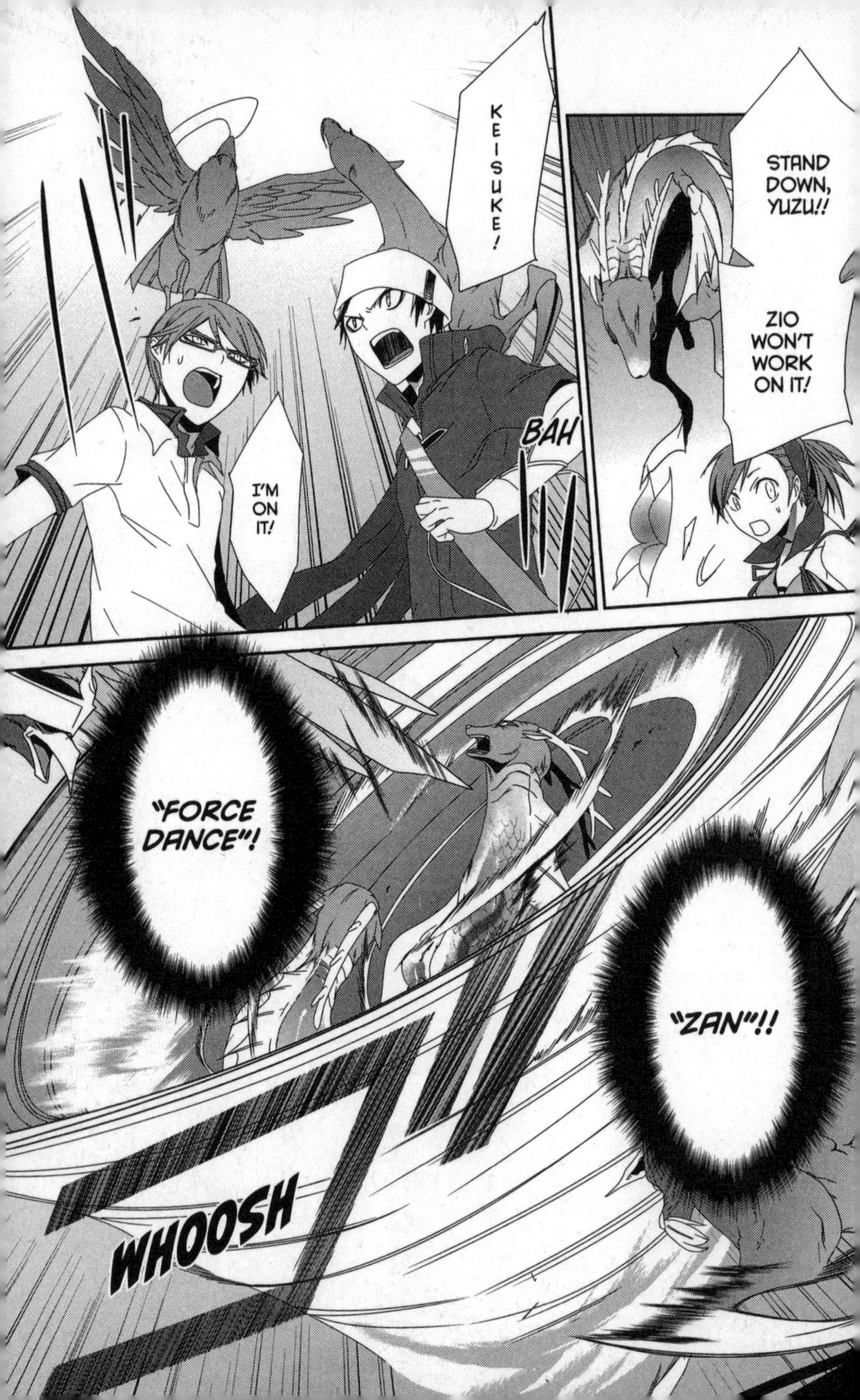
STAND DOWN, YUZU!!
ZIO WON'T WORK ON IT!
KEISUKE!
BAH
I'M ON IT!
"FORCE DANCE"!
"ZAN"!!
WHOOSH

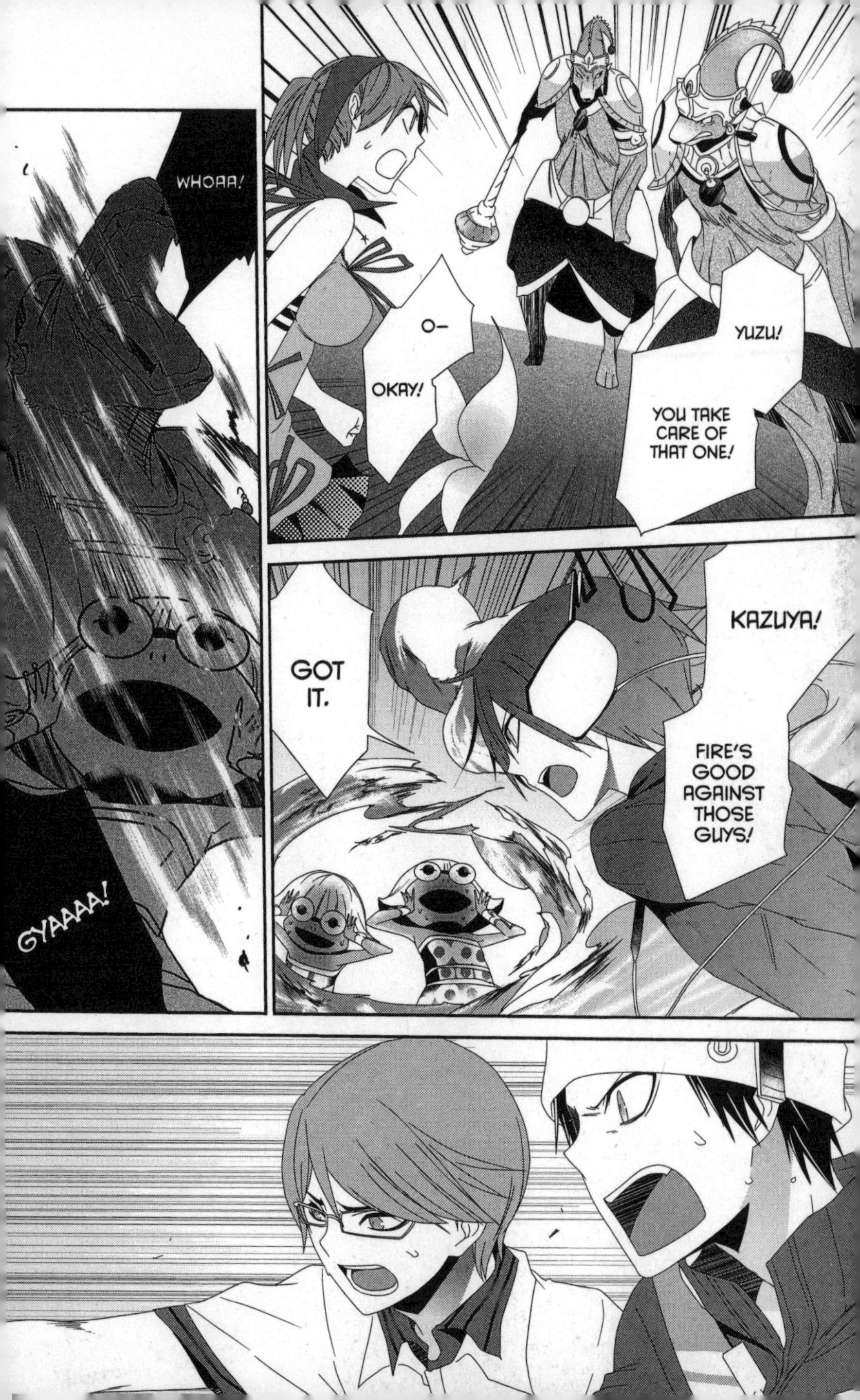
YUZU!
YOU TAKE CARE OF THAT ONE!
O–
OKAY!
KAZUYA!
FIRE'S GOOD AGAINST THOSE GUYS!
GOT IT.
WHOAA!
GYAAAA!

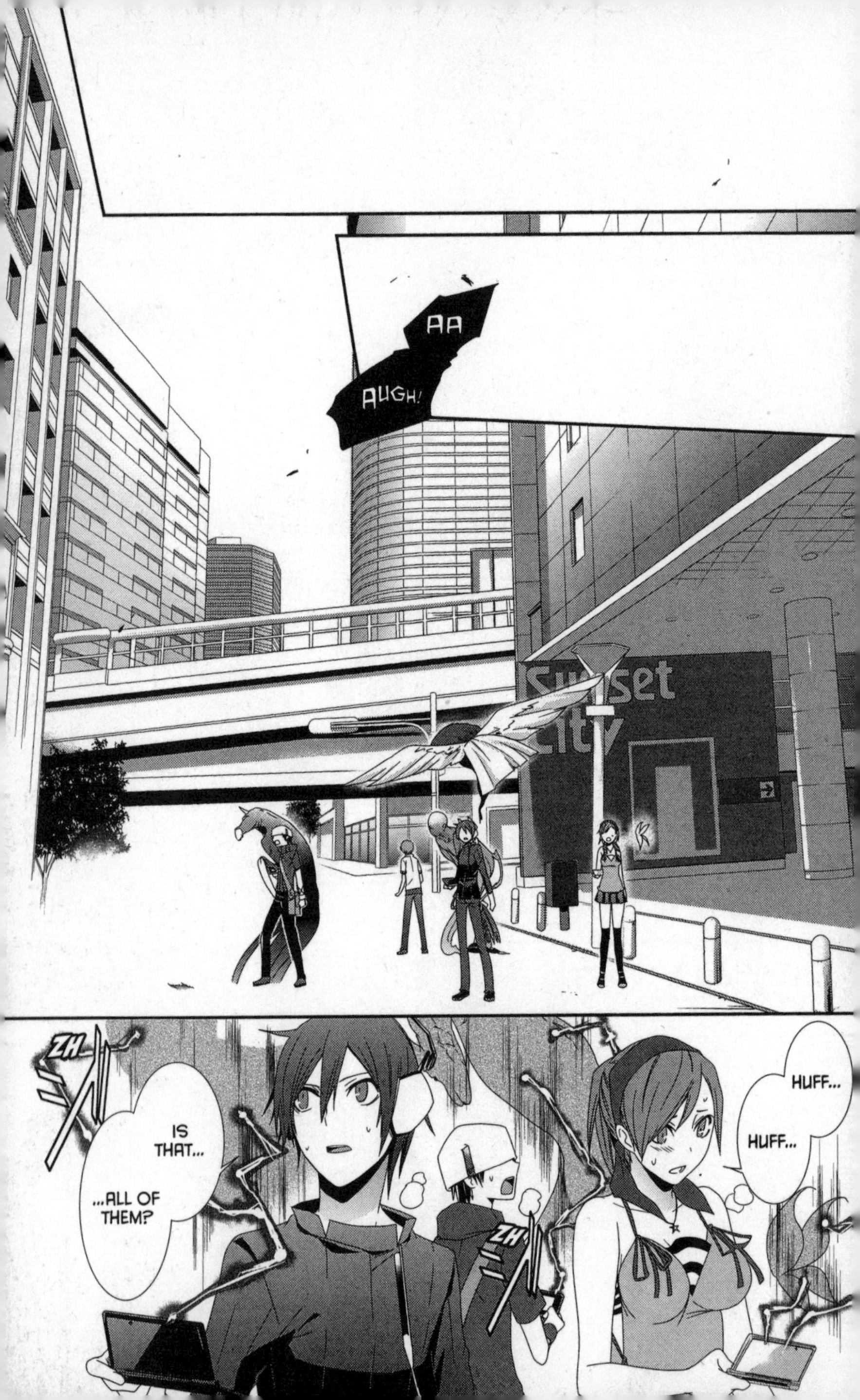
AA
AUGH!
HUFF...
HUFF...
ZH
IS THAT...
...ALL OF THEM?
ZH

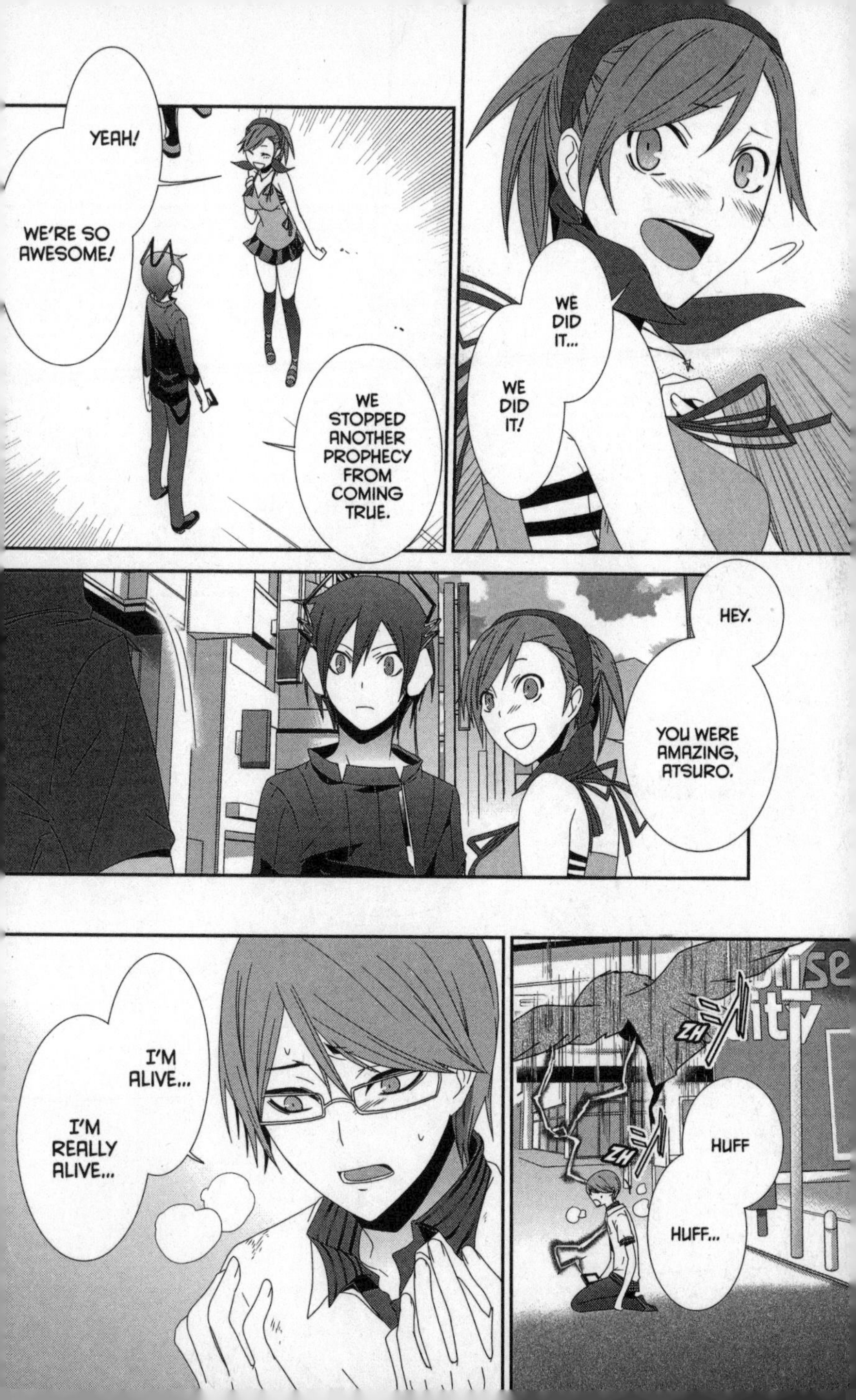
WE DID IT...
WE DID IT!
WE STOPPED ANOTHER PROPHECY FROM COMING TRUE.
YEAH!
WE'RE SO AWESOME!
HEY.
YOU WERE AMAZING, ATSURO.
ZH
ZH
HUFF
HUFF...
I'M ALIVE...
I'M REALLY ALIVE...

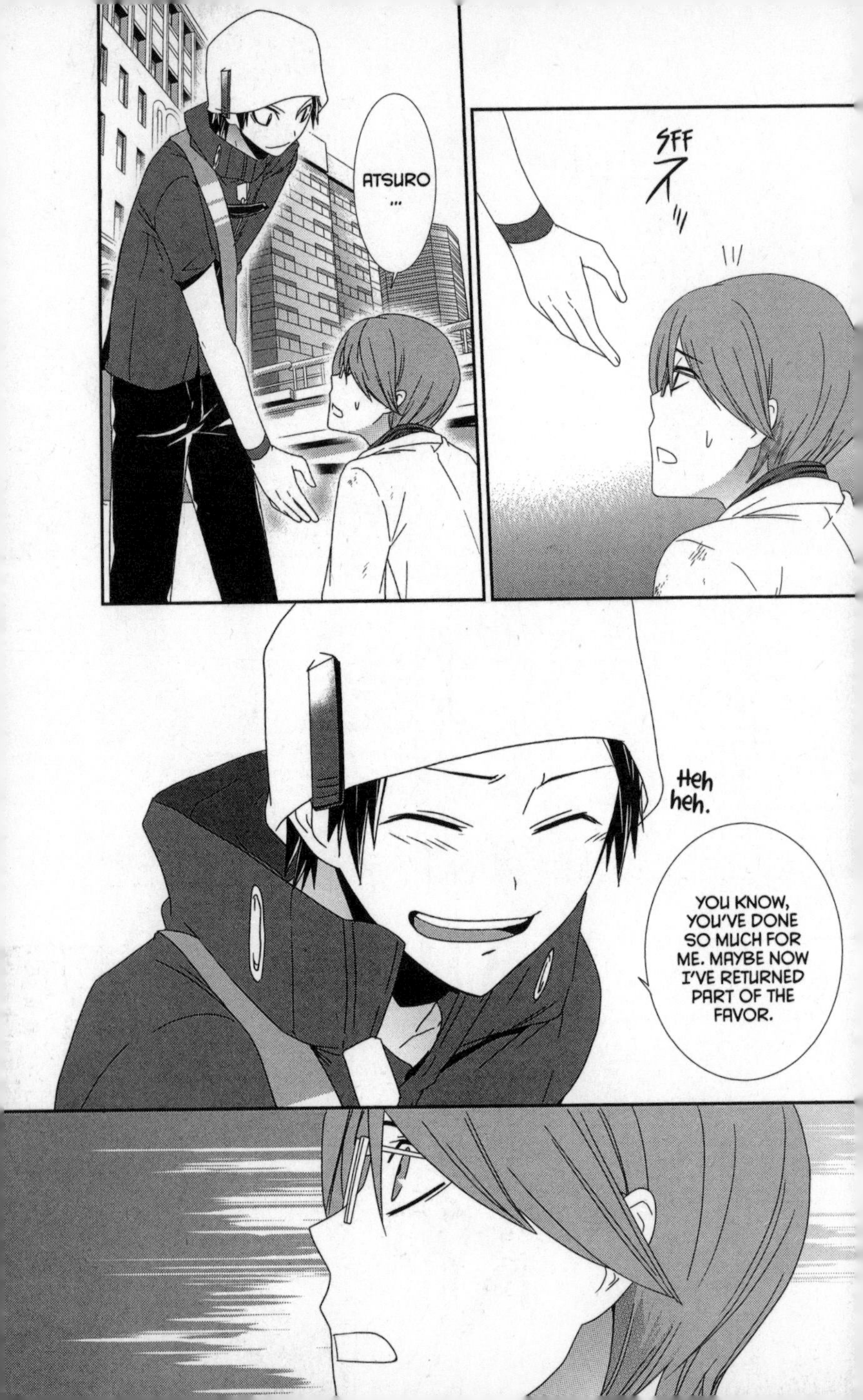
SFF
ATSURO
...
Heh
heh.
YOU KNOW, YOU'VE DONE SO MUCH FOR ME. MAYBE NOW I'VE RETURNED PART OF THE FAVOR.

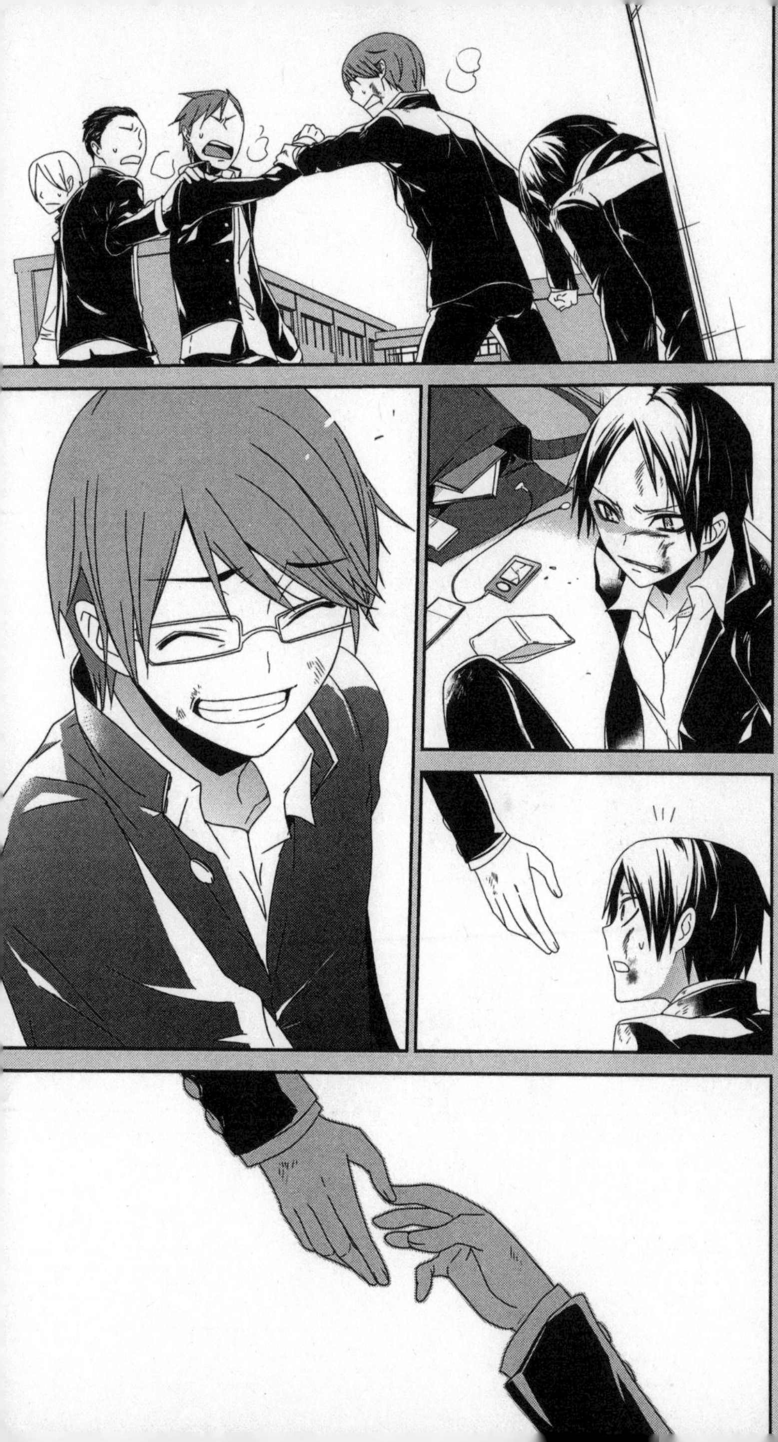

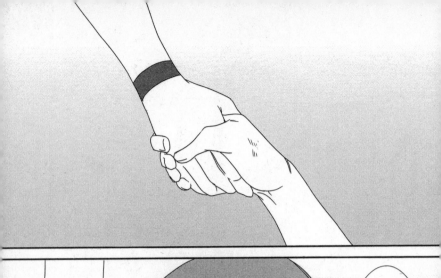

THANKS.

ATSURO
...

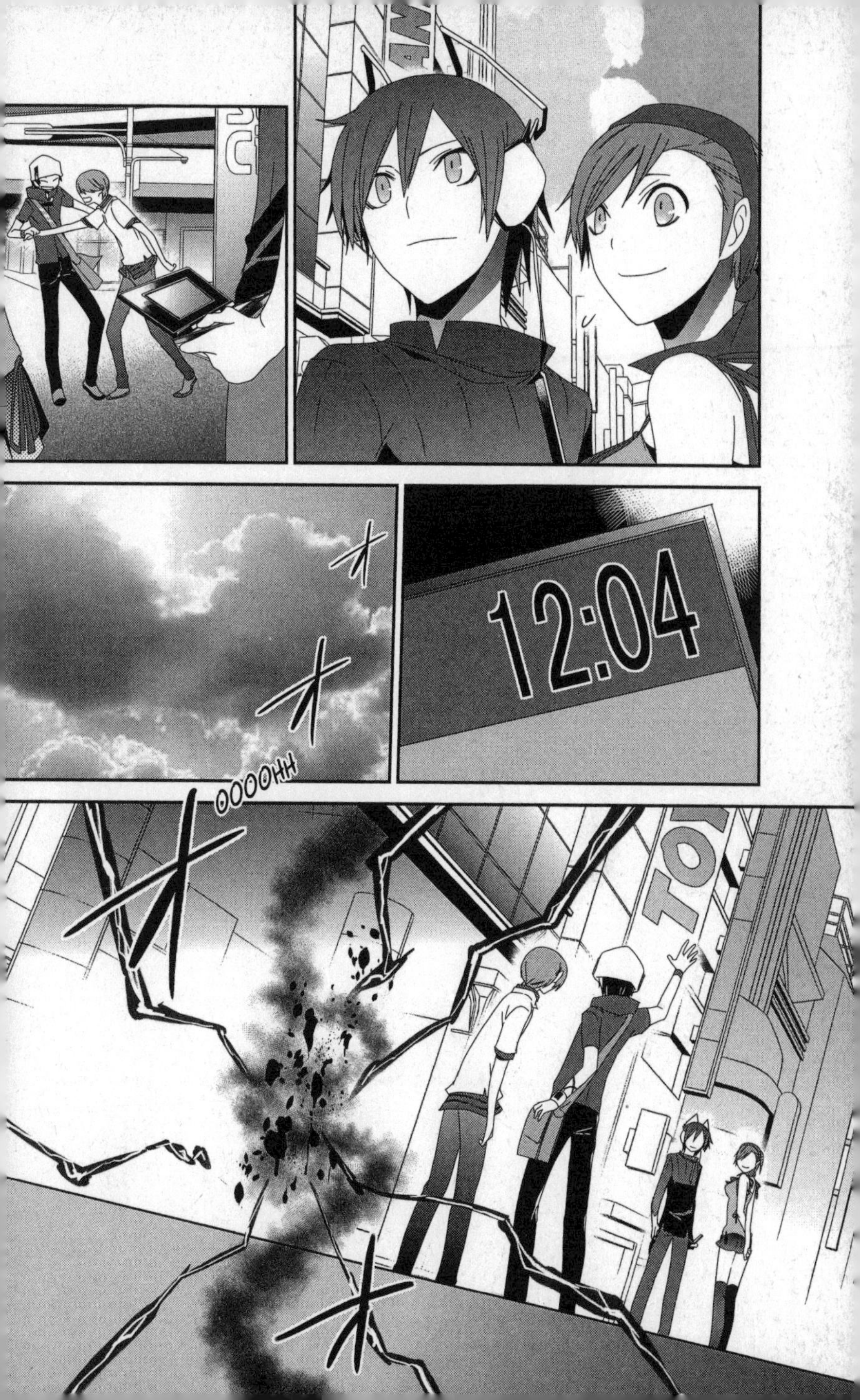
12:04
OOOOHH

PROFILE

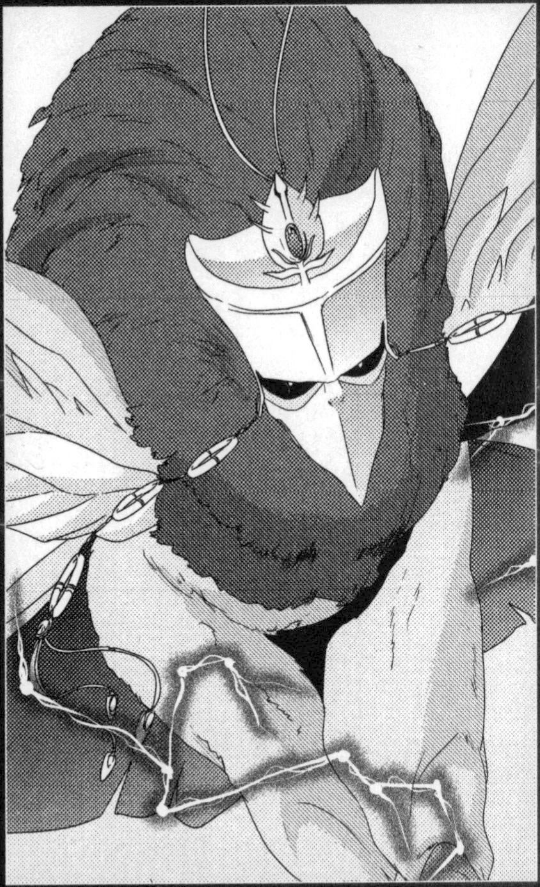

SUPARNA

A LEGENDARY BIRD FROM HINDU MYTHOLOGY. ITS NAME MEANS "ONE WITH BEAUTIFUL WINGS." IT CAN CONTROL THE WIND WITH THE FLAPPING OF ITS WINGS, AND CHANGE THE SIZE OF ITS BODY AT WILL.

DEVIL SURVIVOR

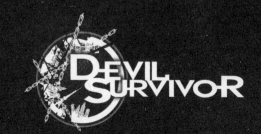

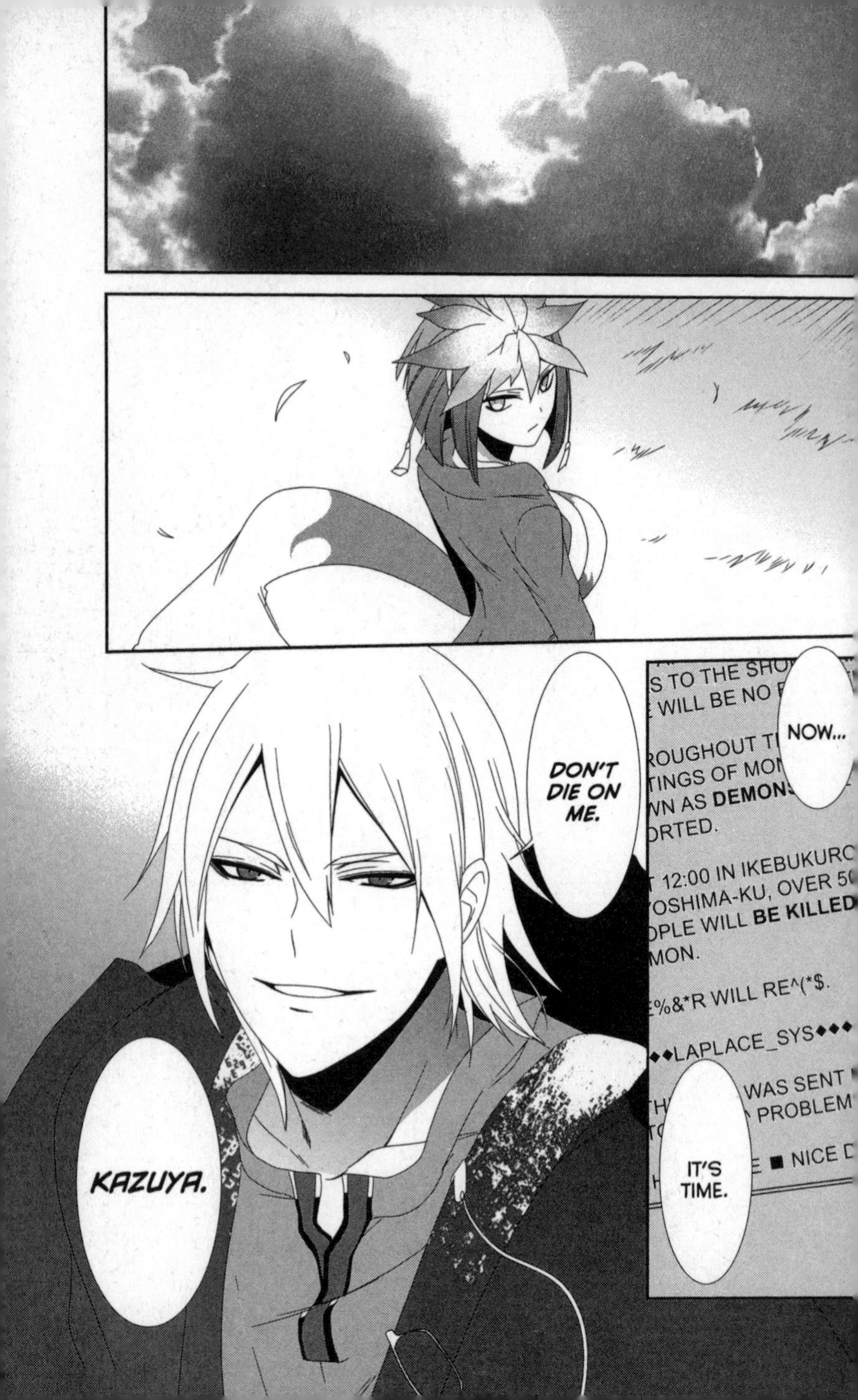
NOW...
DON'T DIE ON ME.
S TO THE SHO
WILL BE NO
ROUGHOUT T
TINGS OF MON
WN AS DEMONS
ORTED.
T 12:00 IN IKEBUKURO
OSHIMA-KU, OVER 50
OPLE WILL BE KILLED
MON.
E%&*R WILL RE^(*$.
LAPLACE_SYS
WAS SENT
PROBLEM
NICE D
IT'S TIME.
KAZUYA.

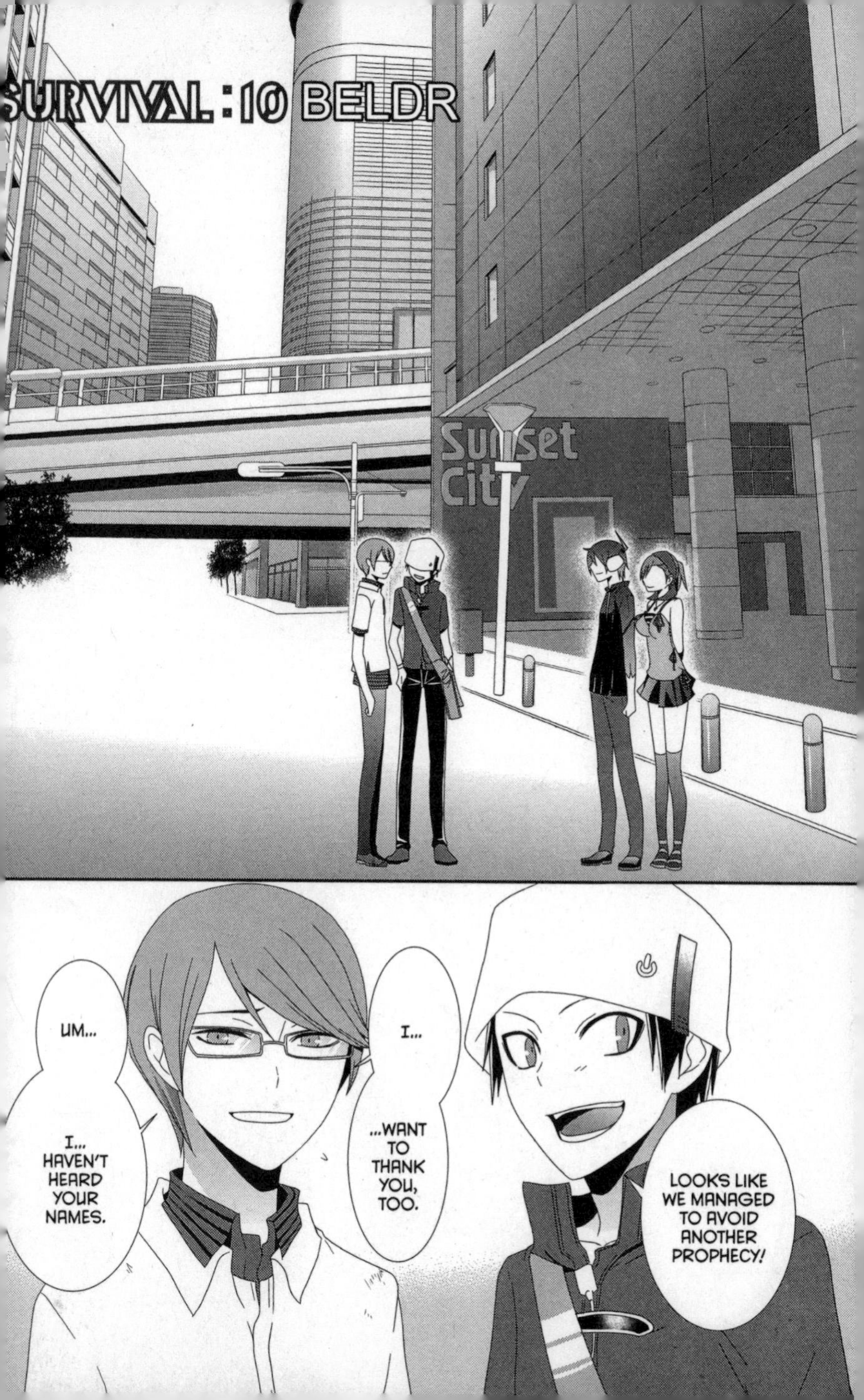
SURVIVAL : 10 BELDR
Sunset City
LOOKS LIKE WE MANAGED TO AVOID ANOTHER PROPHECY!
I...
...WANT TO THANK YOU, TOO.
UM...
I... HAVEN'T HEARD YOUR NAMES.

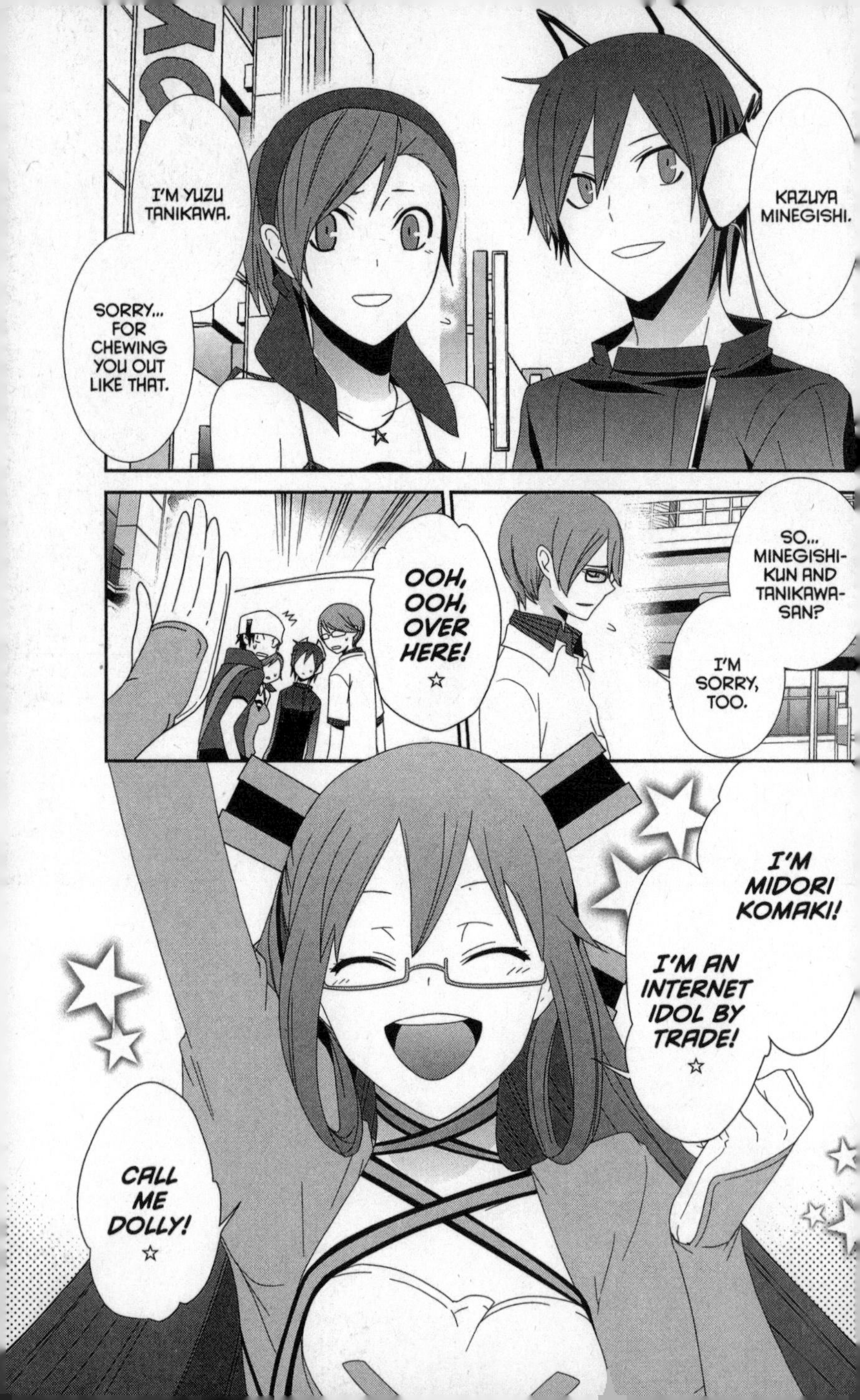
KAZUYA MINEGISHI.
I'M YUZU TANIKAWA.
SORRY... FOR CHEWING YOU OUT LIKE THAT.
SO... MINEGISHI-KUN AND TANIKAWA-SAN?
I'M SORRY, TOO.
OOH, OOH, OVER HERE! ☆
I'M MIDORI KOMAKI!
I'M AN INTERNET IDOL BY TRADE! ☆
CALL ME DOLLY! ☆

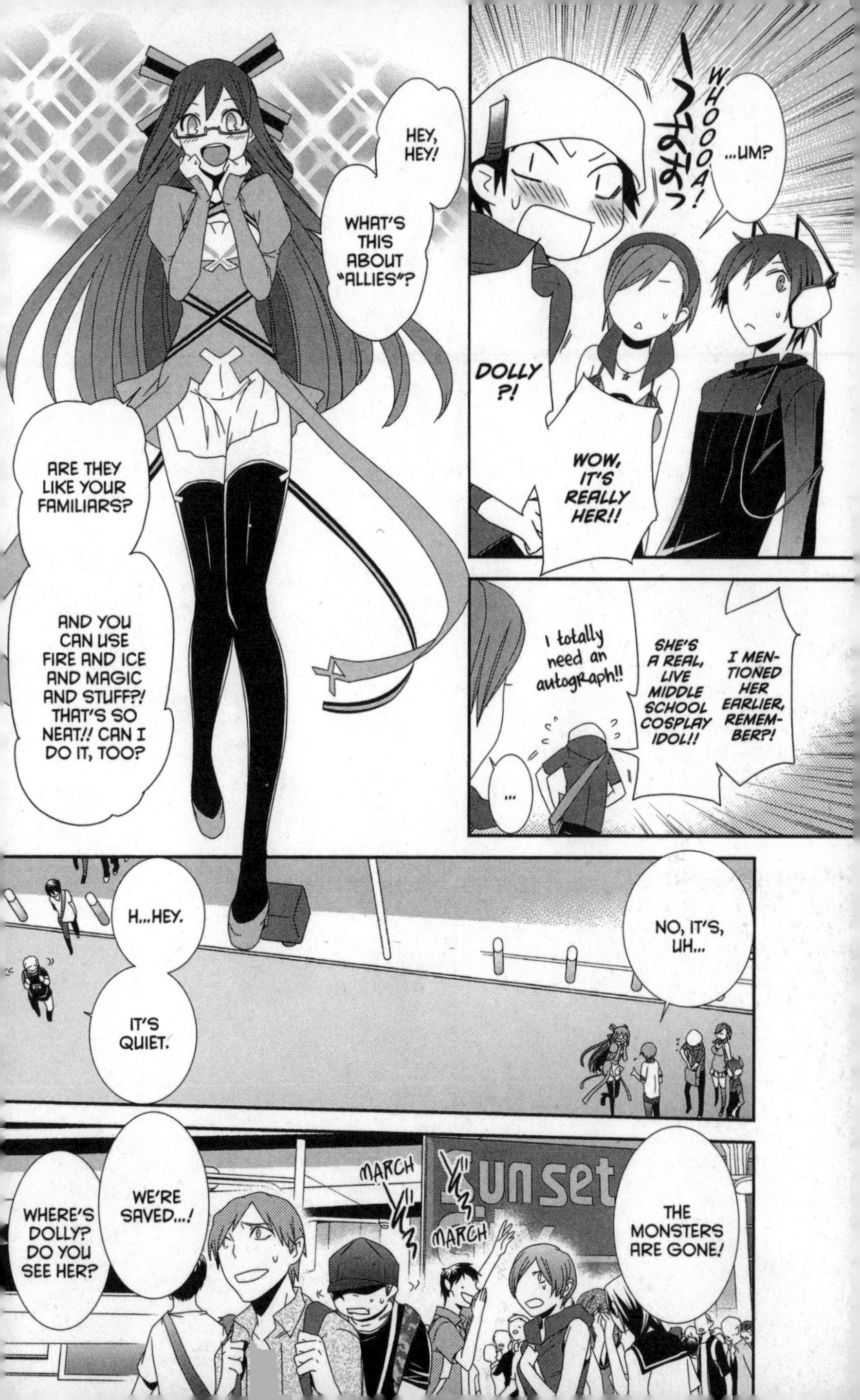
...UM?
WHOOOOA!
DOLLY ?!
WOW, IT'S REALLY HER!!
I MENTIONED HER EARLIER, REMEMBER?!
SHE'S A REAL, LIVE MIDDLE SCHOOL COSPLAY IDOL!!
I totally need an autograph!!
...
HEY, HEY!
WHAT'S THIS ABOUT "ALLIES"?
ARE THEY LIKE YOUR FAMILIARS?
AND YOU CAN USE FIRE AND ICE AND MAGIC AND STUFF?! THAT'S SO NEAT!! CAN I DO IT, TOO?
NO, IT'S, UH...
H...HEY.
IT'S QUIET.
THE MONSTERS ARE GONE!
MARCH
MARCH
WE'RE SAVED...!
WHERE'S DOLLY? DO YOU SEE HER?

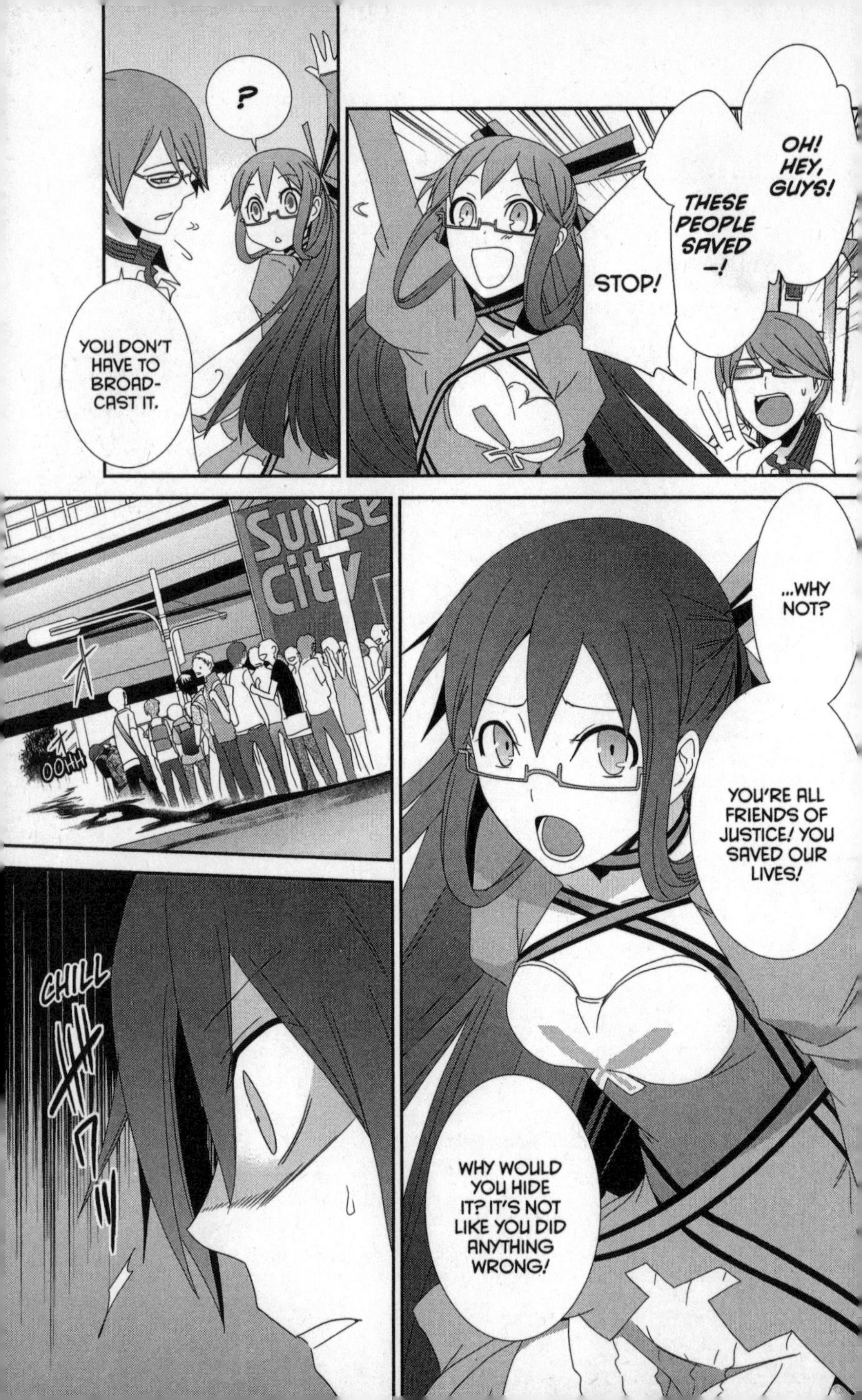
OH! HEY, GUYS!
THESE PEOPLE SAVED —!
STOP!
?
YOU DON'T HAVE TO BROAD-CAST IT.
...WHY NOT?
YOU'RE ALL FRIENDS OF JUSTICE! YOU SAVED OUR LIVES!
WHY WOULD YOU HIDE IT? IT'S NOT LIKE YOU DID ANYTHING WRONG!
OOHH
CHILL

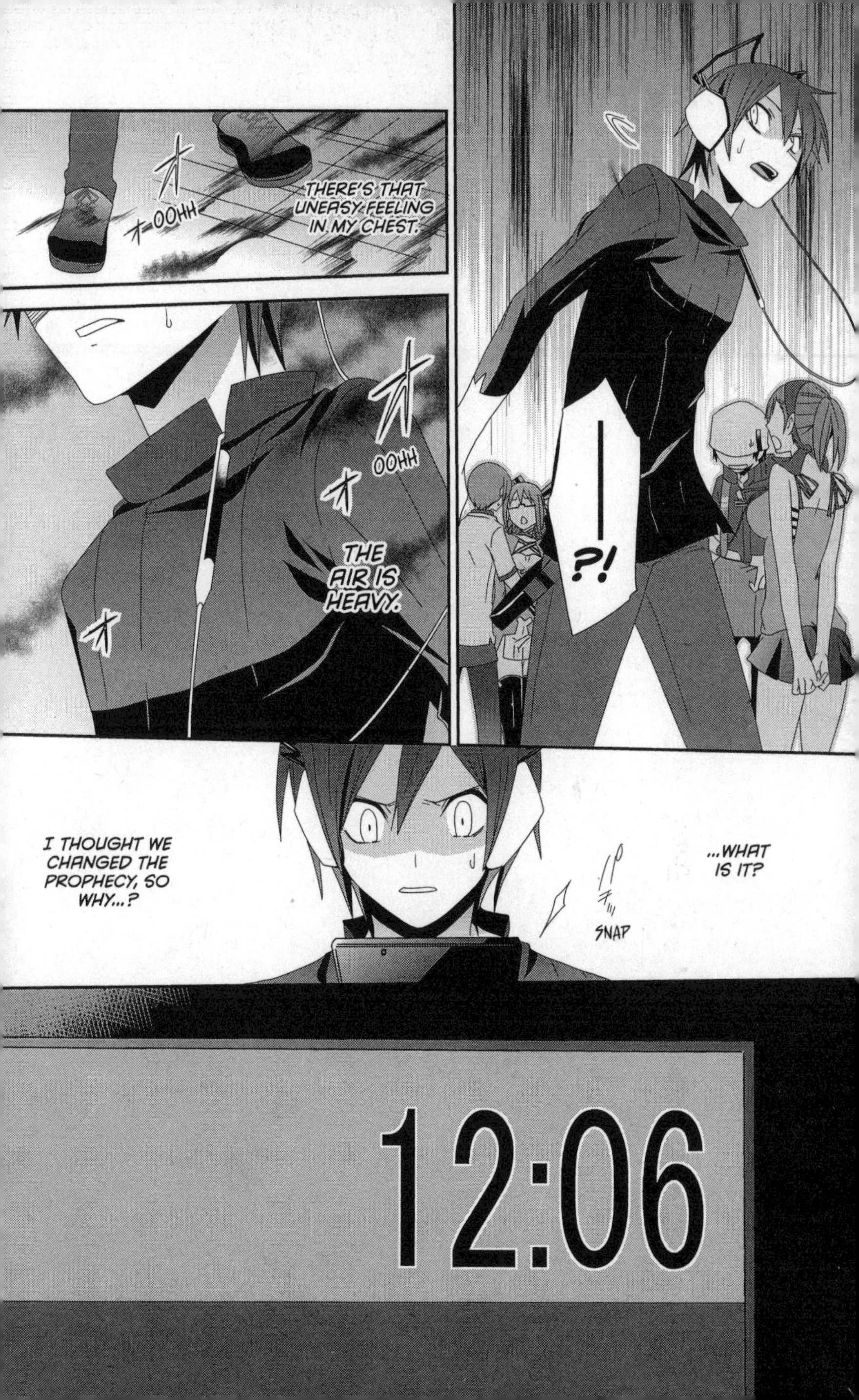
?!
OOHH
THERE'S THAT UNEASY FEELING IN MY CHEST.
OOHH
THE AIR IS HEAVY.
...WHAT IS IT?
SNAP
I THOUGHT WE CHANGED THE PROPHECY, SO WHY...?
12:06

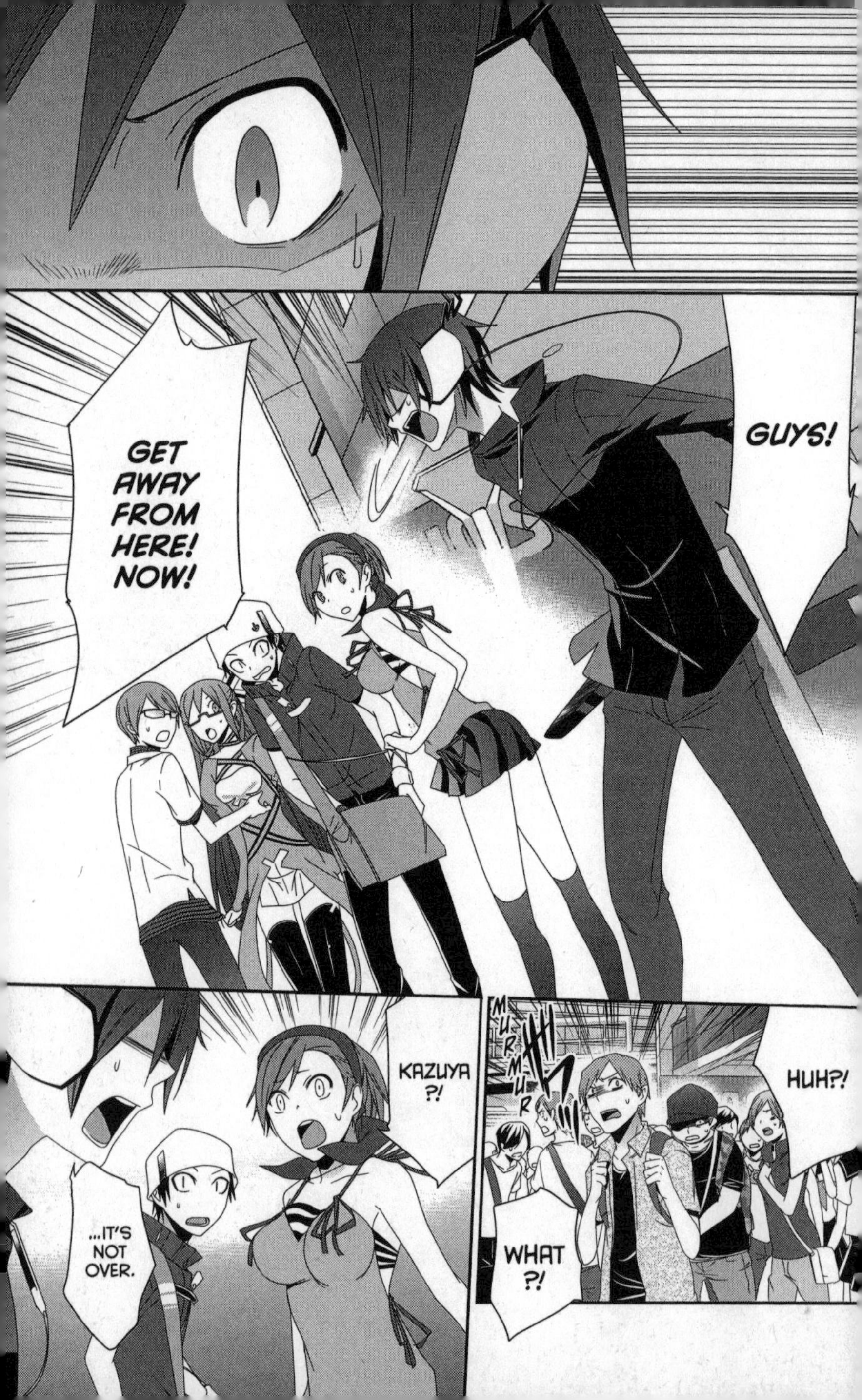
GUYS!
GET AWAY FROM HERE! NOW!
HUH?!
MURMUR
WHAT ?!
KAZUYA ?!
...IT'S NOT OVER.

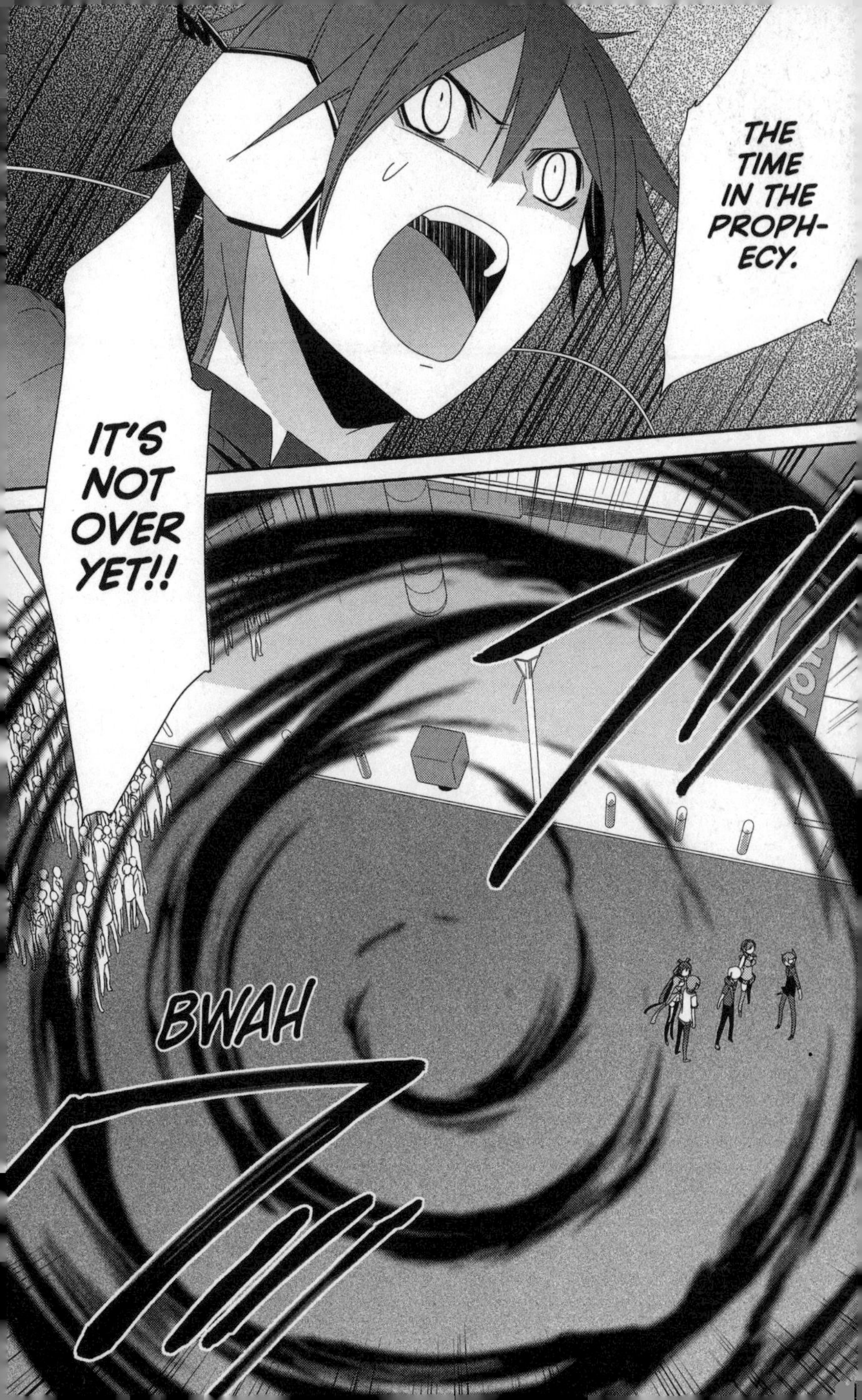
THE TIME IN THE PROPH-ECY.
IT'S NOT OVER YET!!
BWAH

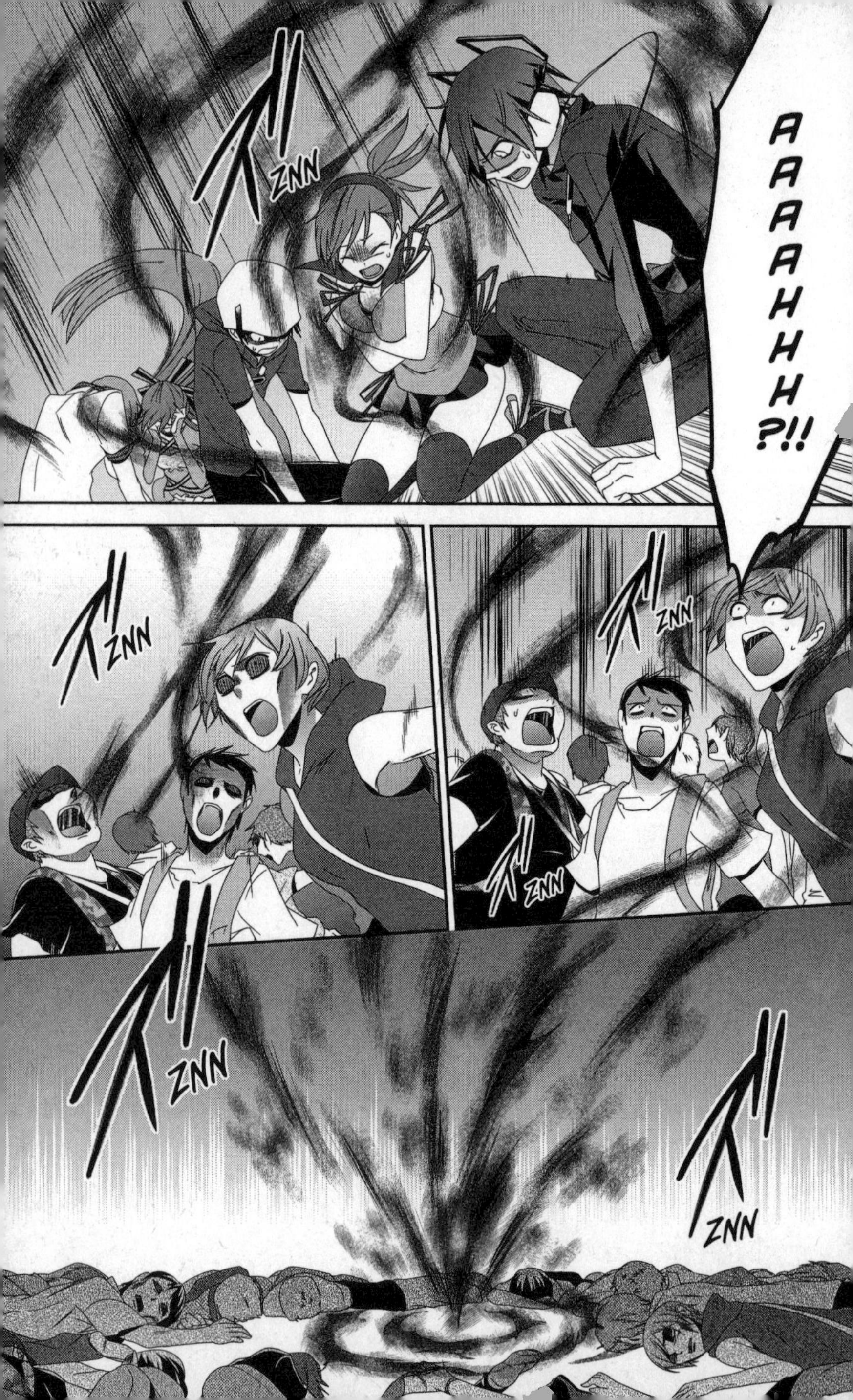
AAAAHHH?!!
ZNN
ZNN
ZNN
ZNN
ZNN
ZNN

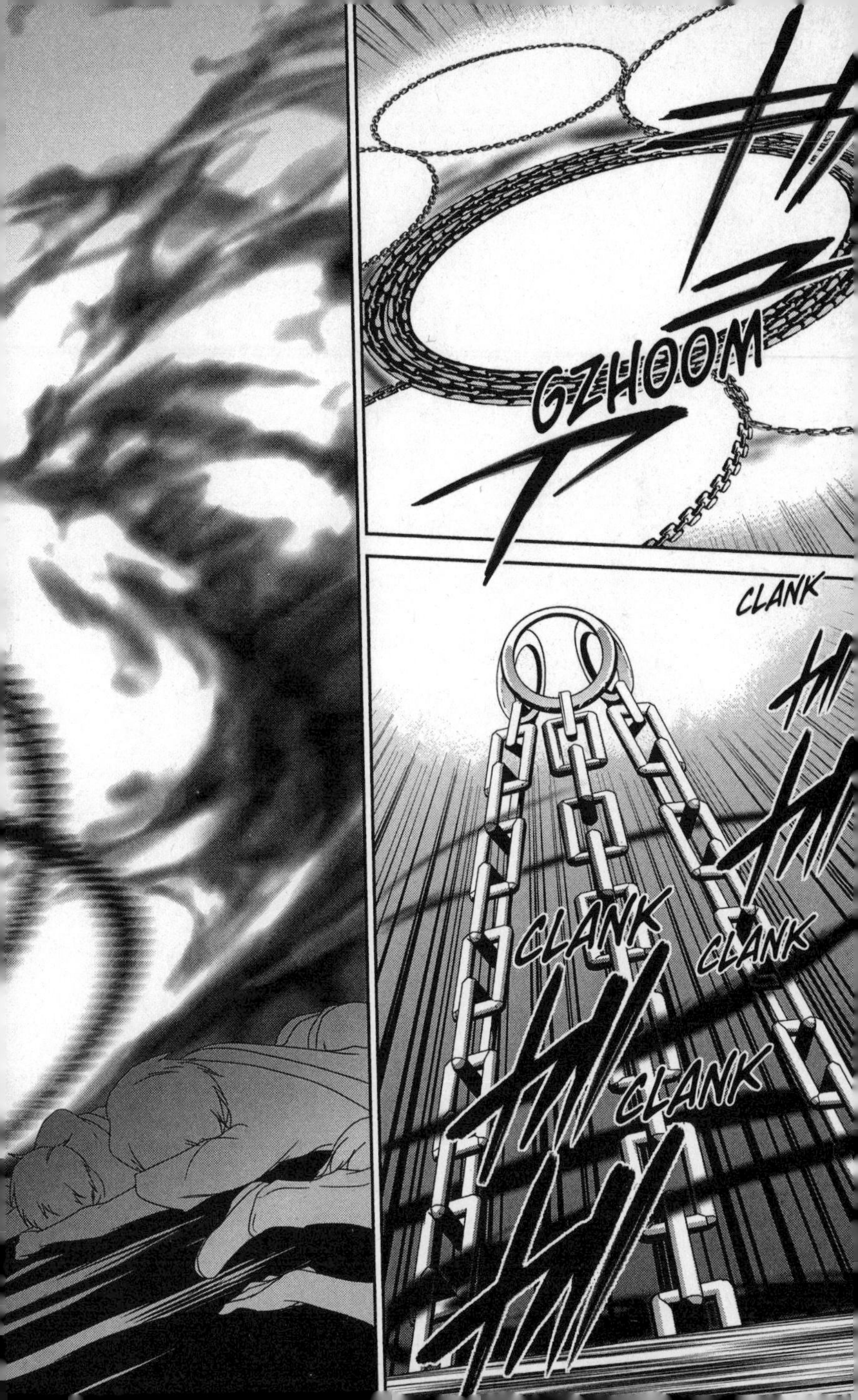
GZHOOM
CLANK
CLANK
CLANK
CLANK

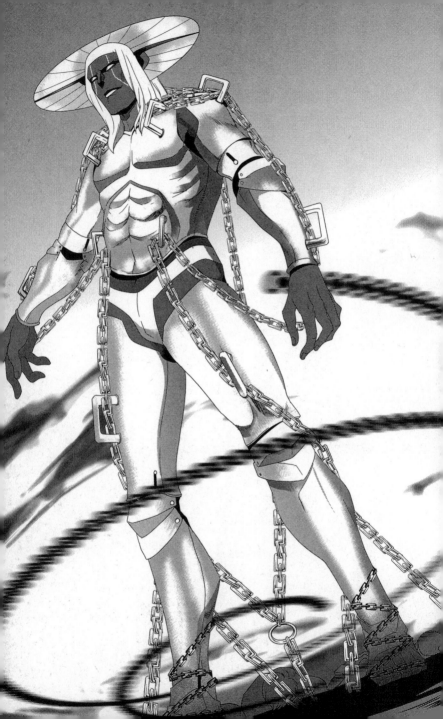

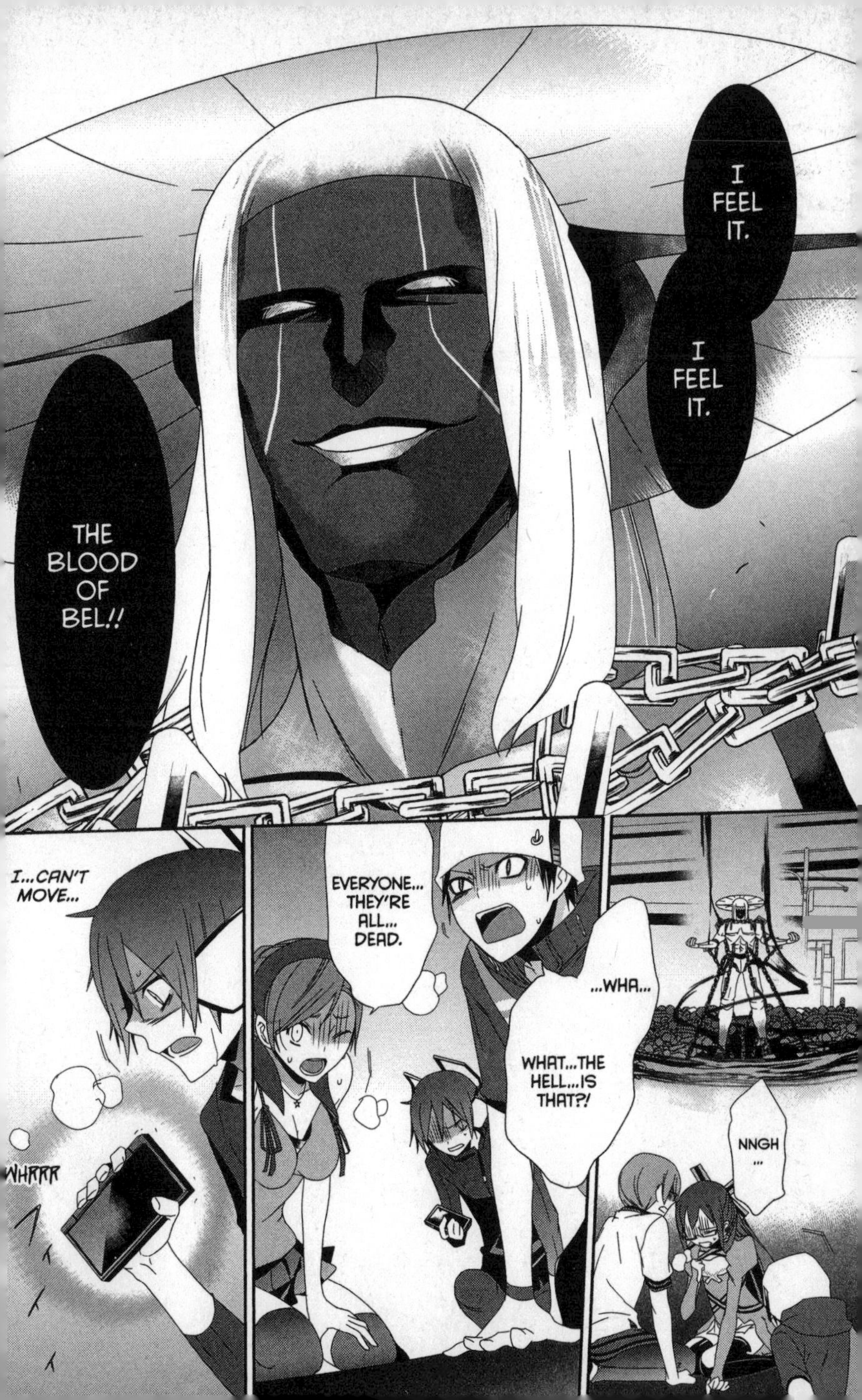
I FEEL IT.
I FEEL IT.
THE BLOOD OF BEL!!
...WHA...
WHAT...THE HELL...IS THAT?!
NNGH ...
EVERYONE... THEY'RE ALL... DEAD.
I...CAN'T MOVE...
WHRRR

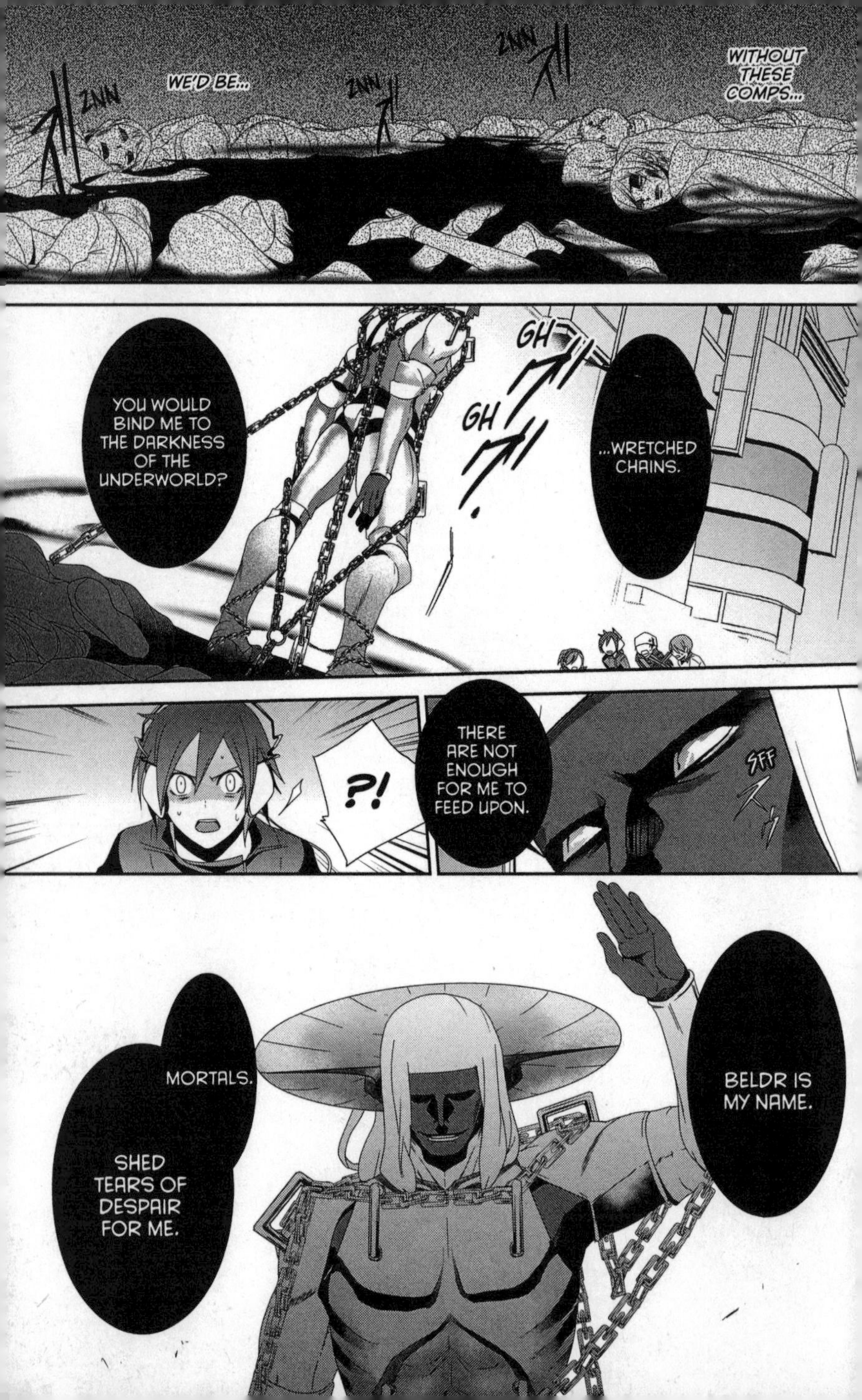
WITHOUT THESE COMPS...
ZNN
ZNN
WE'D BE...
ZNN
...WRETCHED CHAINS.
GH
GH
YOU WOULD BIND ME TO THE DARKNESS OF THE UNDERWORLD?
SFF
THERE ARE NOT ENOUGH FOR ME TO FEED UPON.
?!
BELDR IS MY NAME.
MORTALS.
SHED TEARS OF DESPAIR FOR ME.

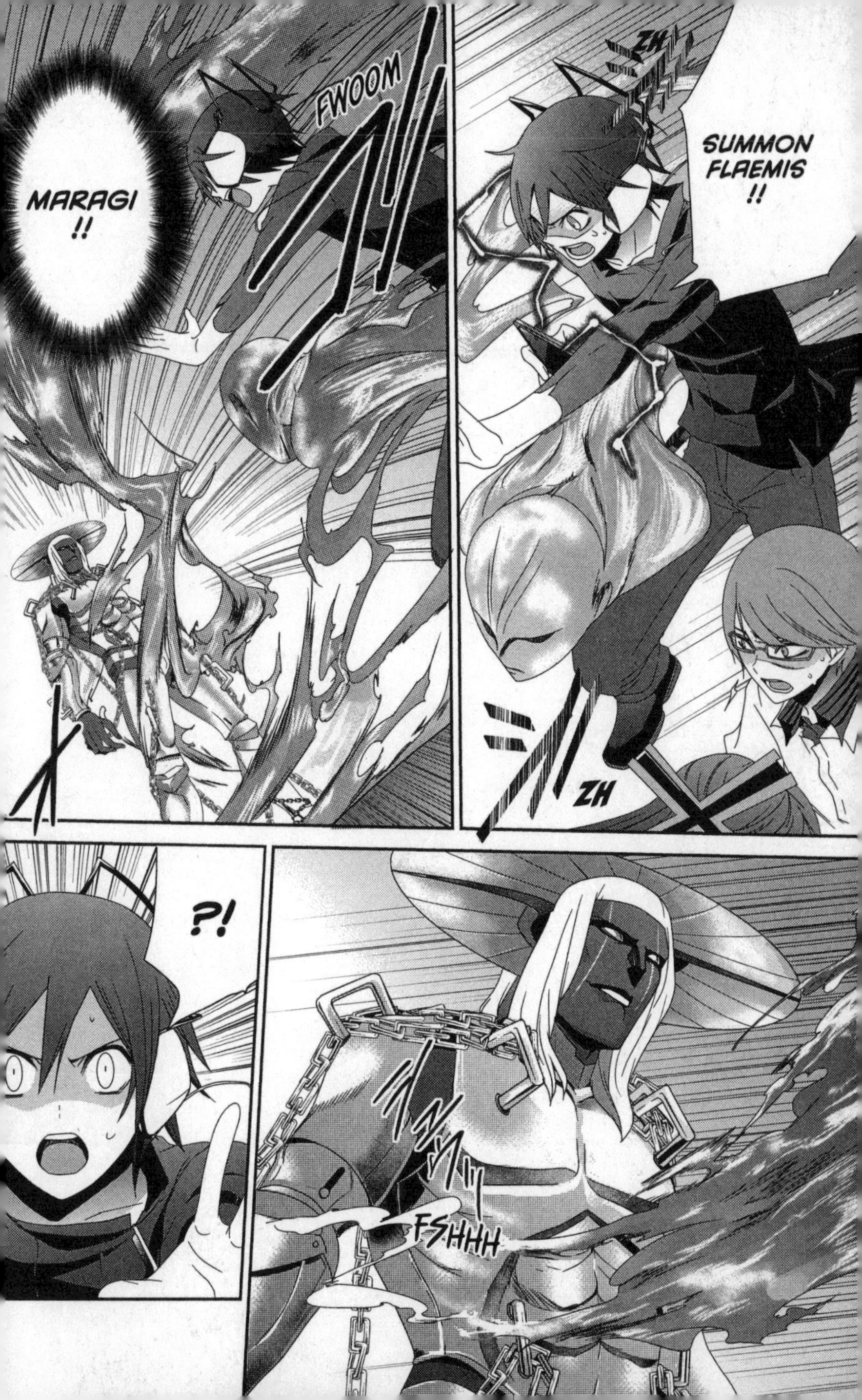
SUMMON FLAEMIS !!
ZH
ZH
MARAGI !!
FWOOM
FSHHH
?!

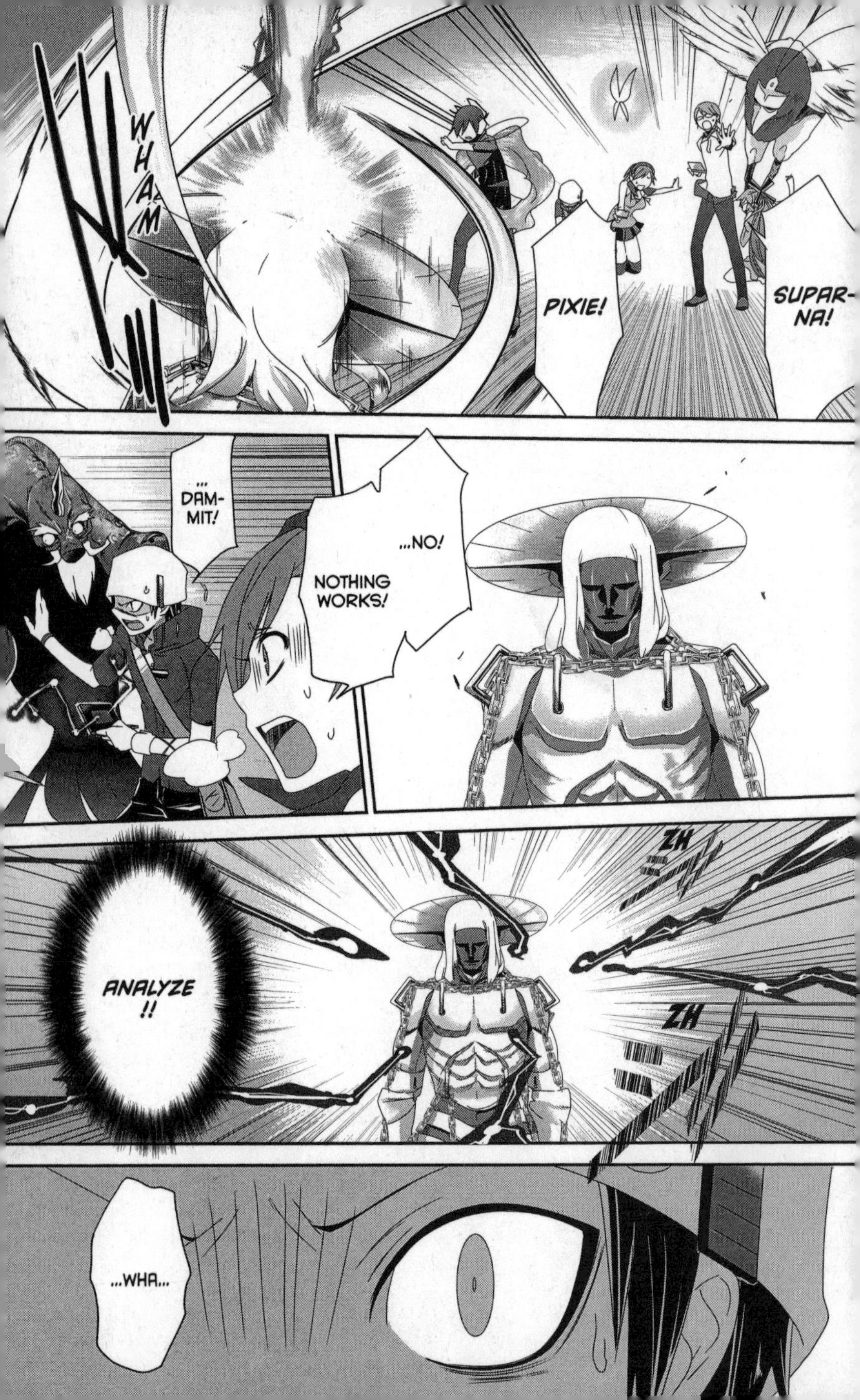
SUPAR-
NA!
PIXIE!
WHAM
...NO!
NOTHING WORKS!
... DAM-
MIT!
ZH
ZH
ANALYZE
!!
...WHA...

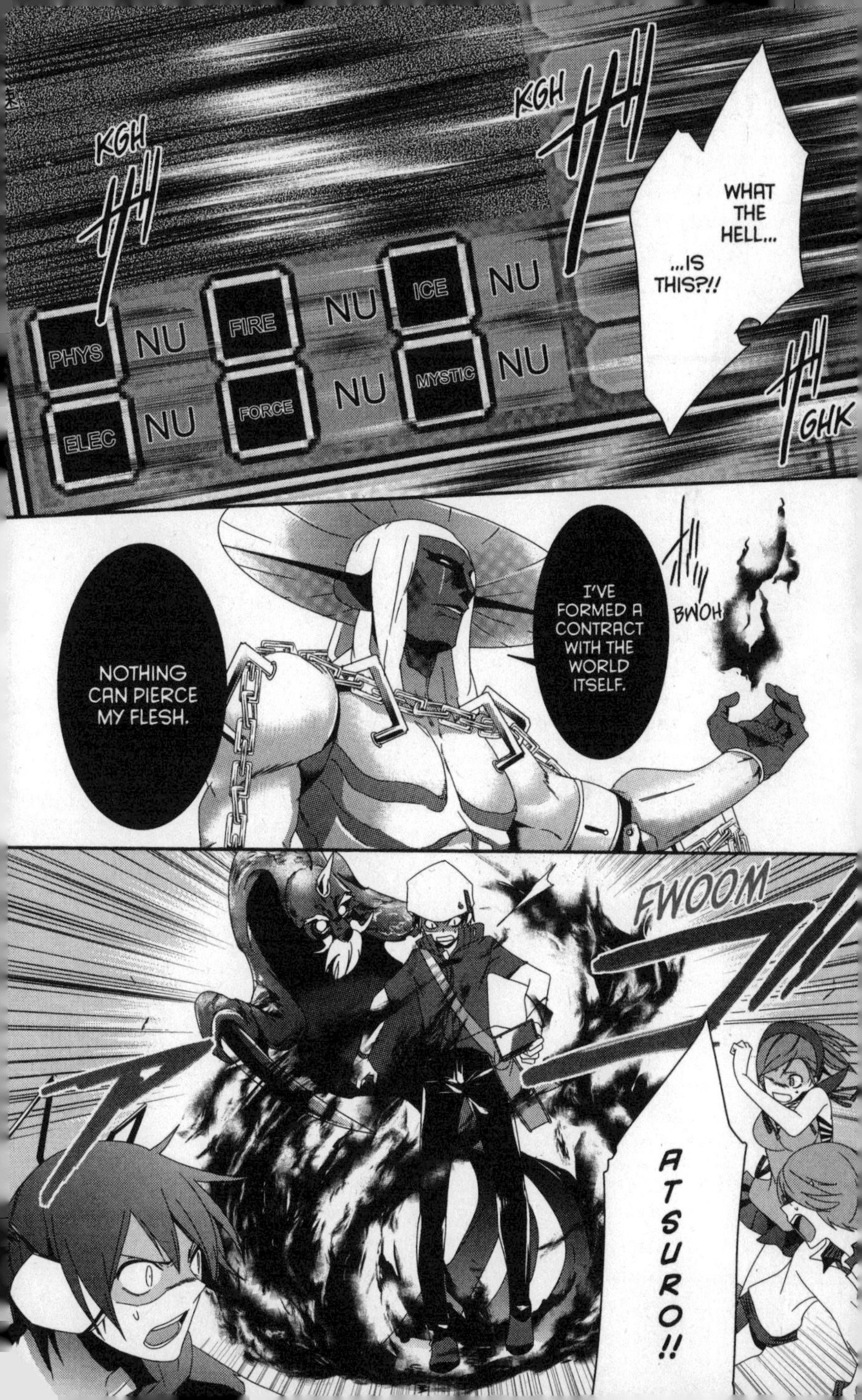
WHAT THE HELL...
...IS THIS?!!
KGH
GHK
KGH
ICE NU
MYSTIC NU
FIRE NU
FORCE NU
PHYS NU
ELEC NU
BWOH
I'VE FORMED A CONTRACT WITH THE WORLD ITSELF.
NOTHING CAN PIERCE MY FLESH.
FWOOM
ATSURO!!

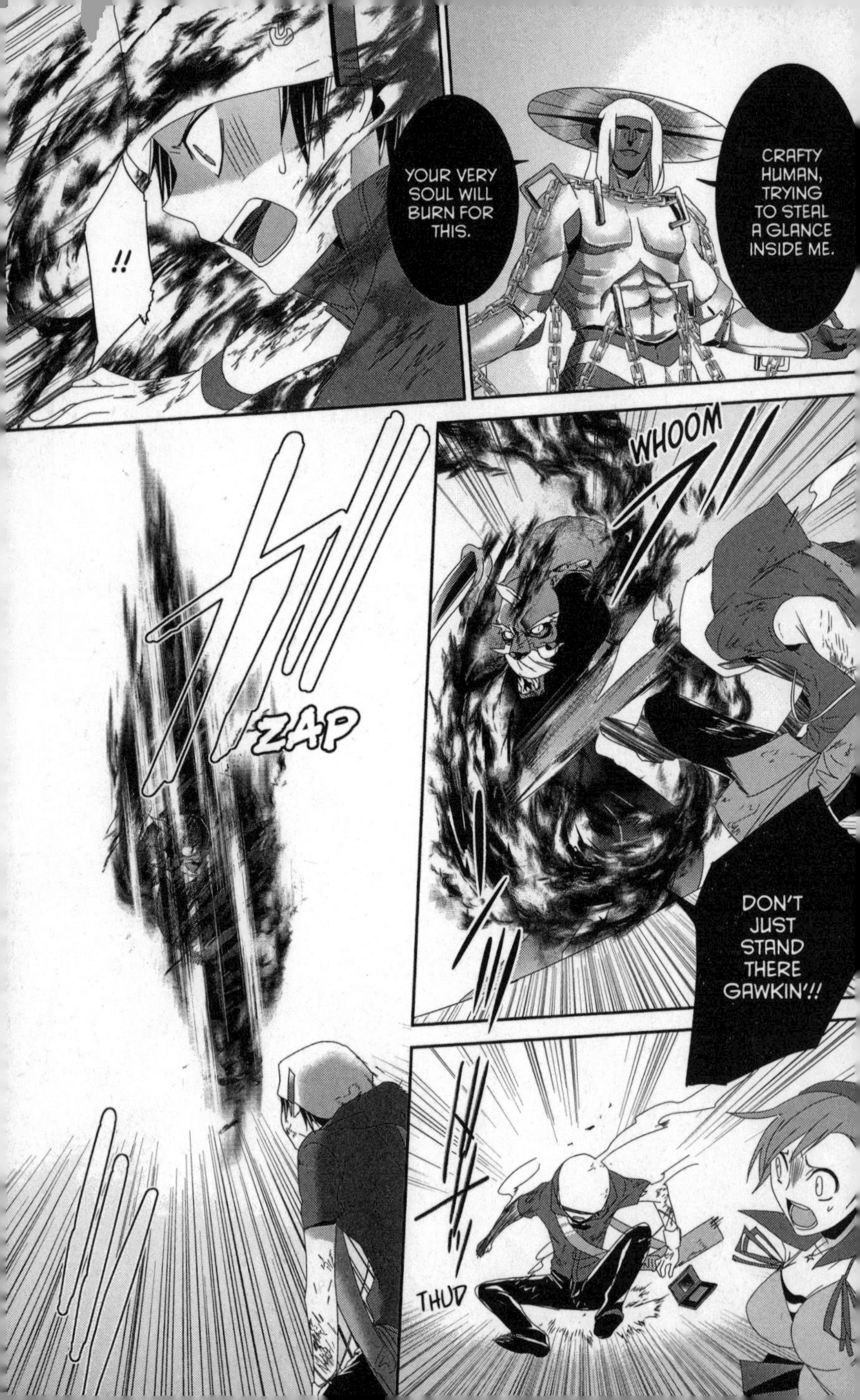
CRAFTY HUMAN, TRYING TO STEAL A GLANCE INSIDE ME.
YOUR VERY SOUL WILL BURN FOR THIS.
!!
WHOOM
DON'T JUST STAND THERE GAWKIN'!!
THUD
ZAP

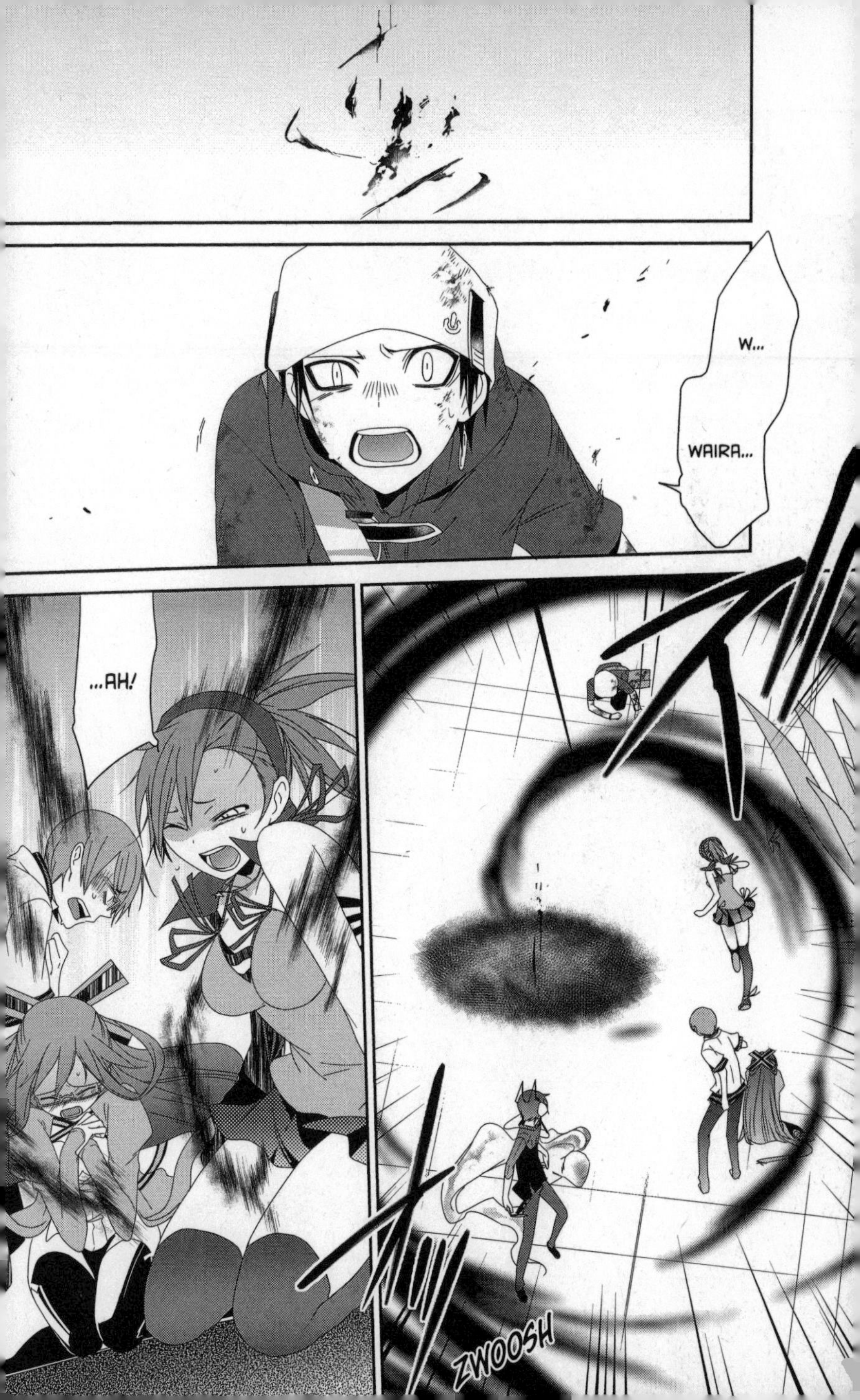
W...
WAIRA...
ZWOOSH
...AH!

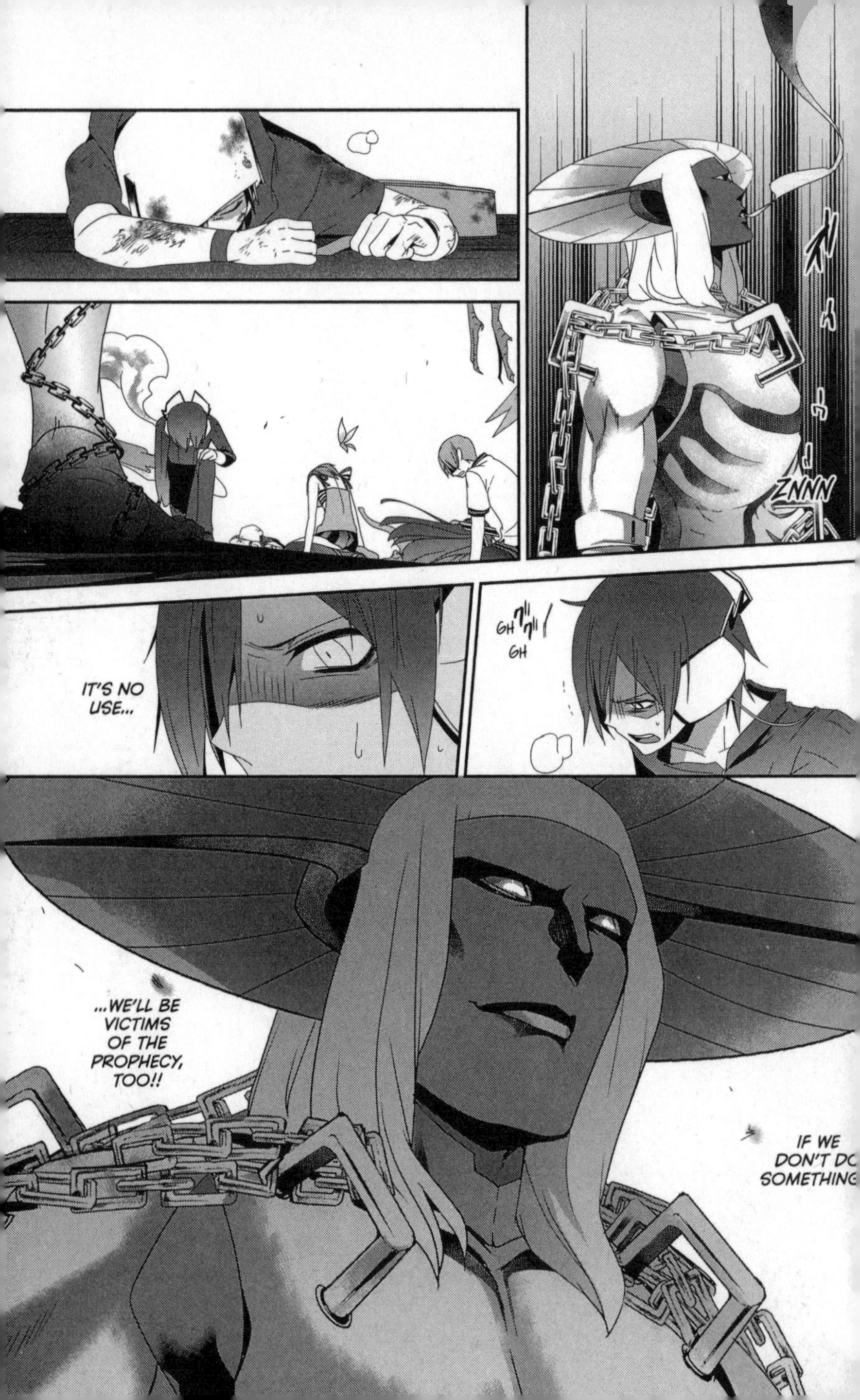
ZNNN
GH
GH
IT'S NO USE...
IF WE DON'T DO SOMETHING
...WE'LL BE VICTIMS OF THE PROPHECY, TOO!!

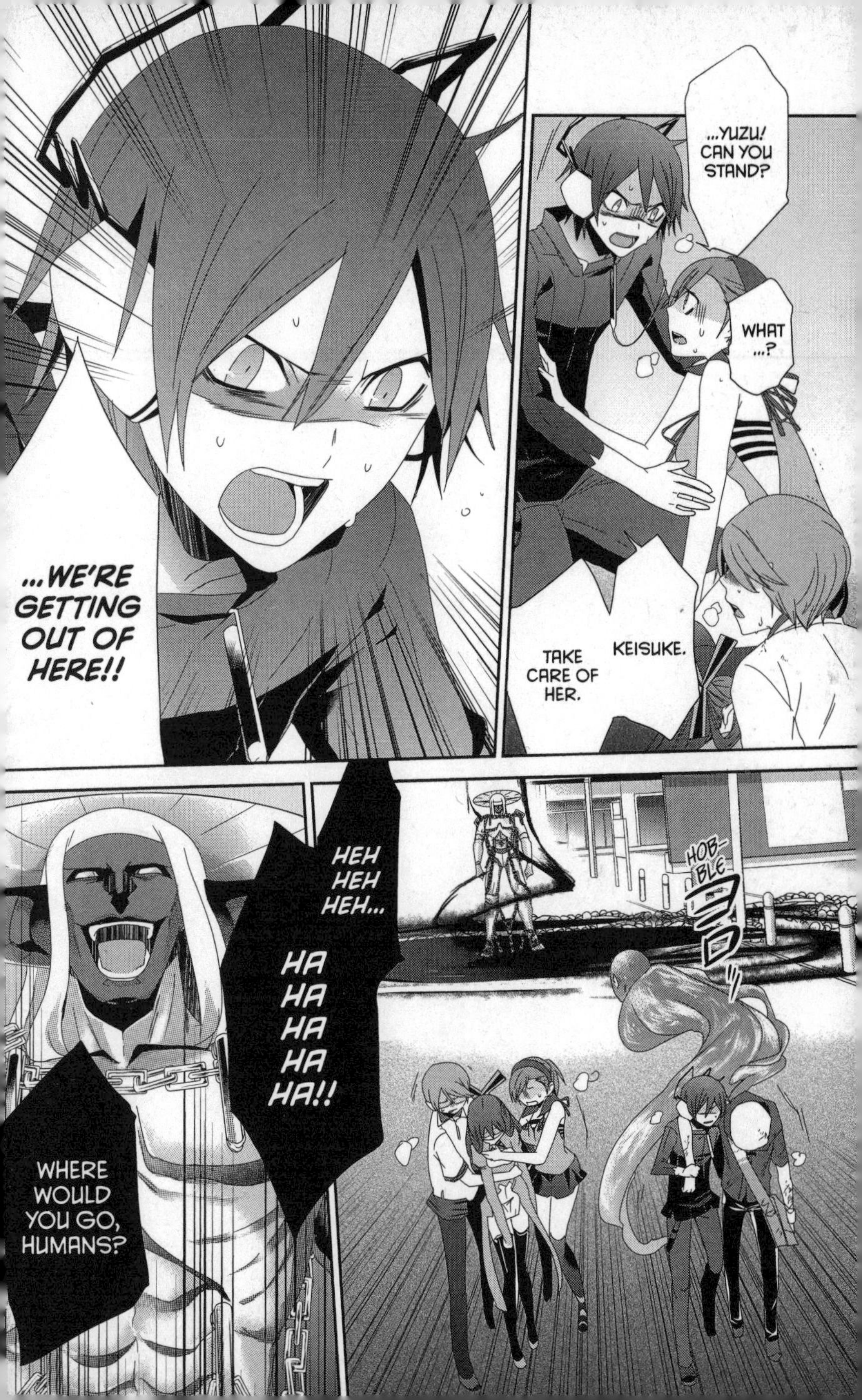
...YUZU! CAN YOU STAND?
WHAT ...?
KEISUKE.
TAKE CARE OF HER.
...WE'RE GETTING OUT OF HERE!!
HOB-BLE
HEH HEH HEH...
HA HA HA HA HA!!
WHERE WOULD YOU GO, HUMANS?

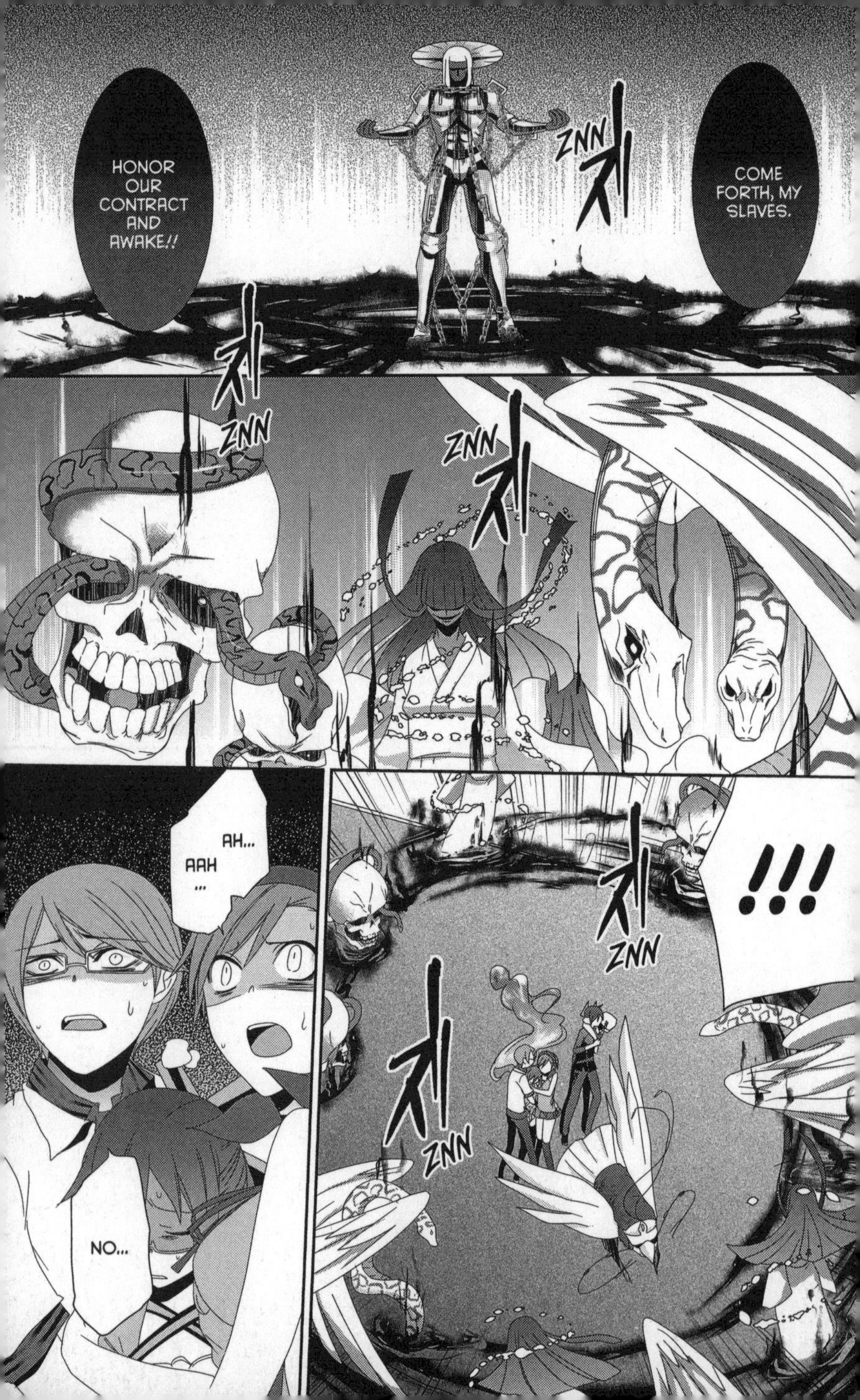
COME FORTH, MY SLAVES.
ZNN
HONOR OUR CONTRACT AND AWAKE!!
ZNN
ZNN
!!!
ZNN
ZNN
AH... AAH ...
NO...

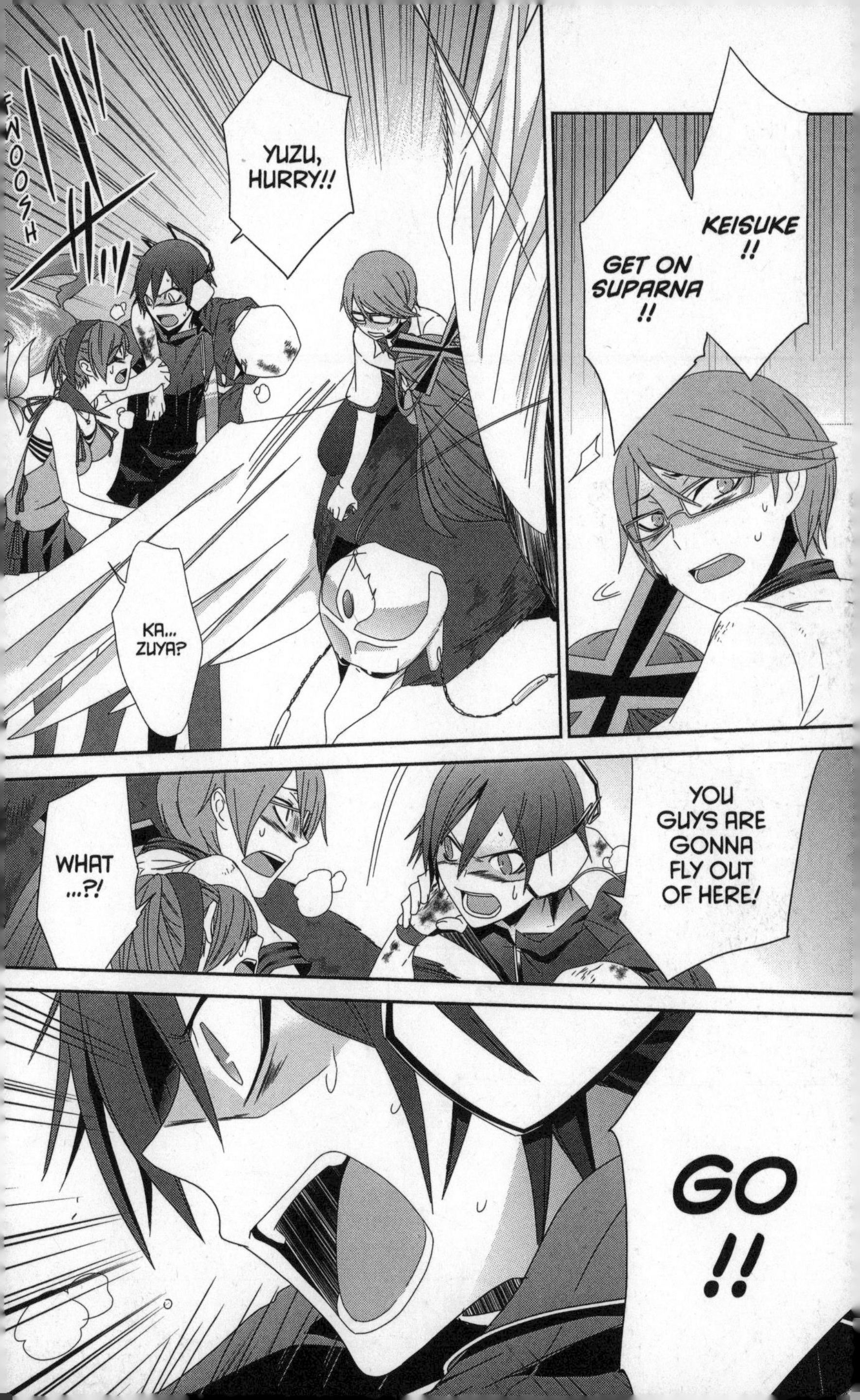
KEISUKE!!
GET ON SUPARNA!!
YUZU, HURRY!!
FWOOSH
KA... ZUYA?
YOU GUYS ARE GONNA FLY OUT OF HERE!
WHAT ...?!
GO!!

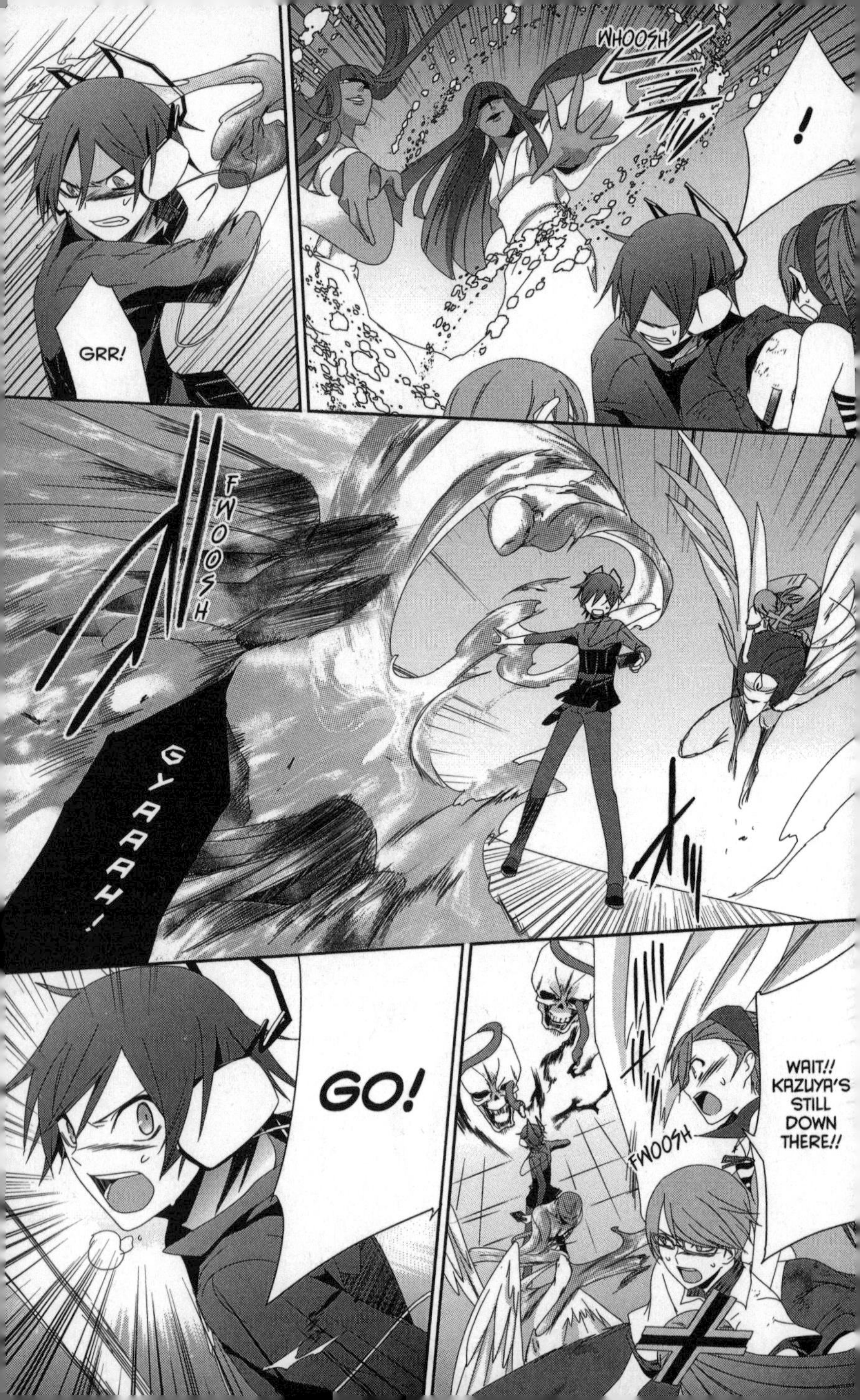
WHOOSH
!
GRR!
FWOOSH
GYAAAAH!
WAIT!! KAZUYA'S STILL DOWN THERE!!
FWOOSH
GO!

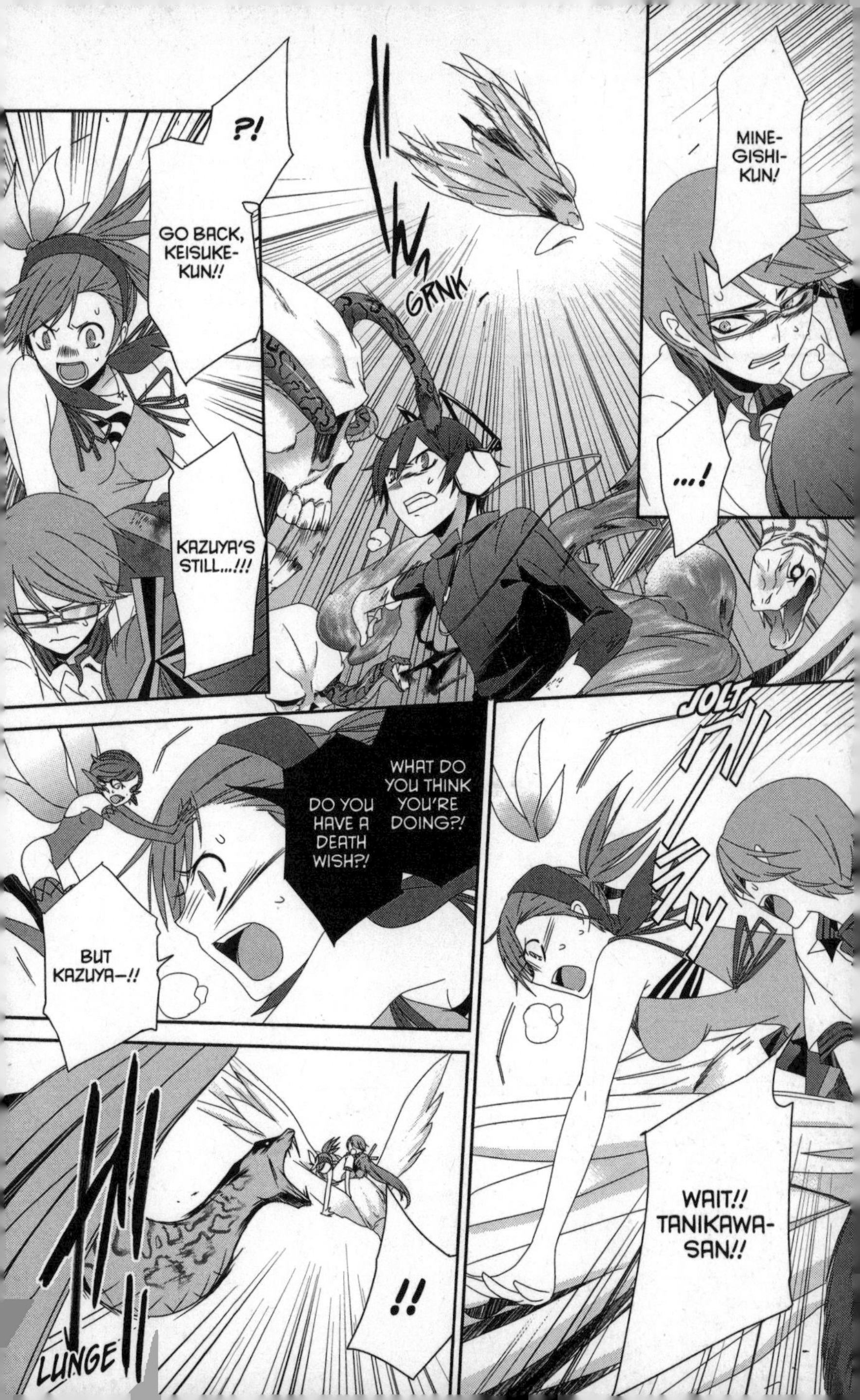
MINE-GISHI-KUN!
...!
GRNK
?!
GO BACK, KEISUKE-KUN!!
KAZUYA'S STILL...!!!
JOLT
WAIT!! TANIKAWA-SAN!!
WHAT DO YOU THINK YOU'RE DOING?!
DO YOU HAVE A DEATH WISH?!
BUT KAZUYA—!!
!!
LUNGE

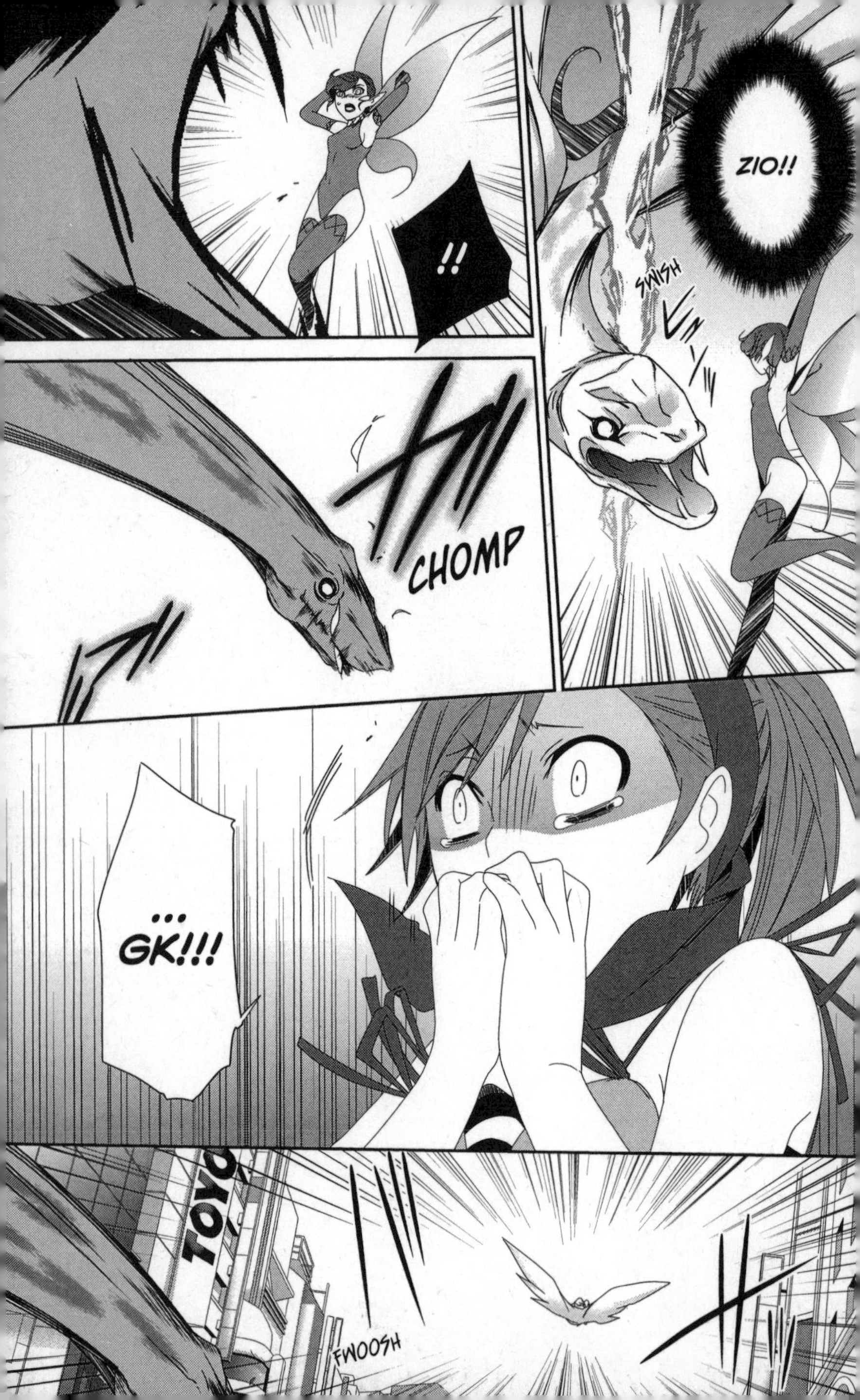
ZIO!!
SWISH
!!
CHOMP
...GK!!!
TOYO
FWOOSH

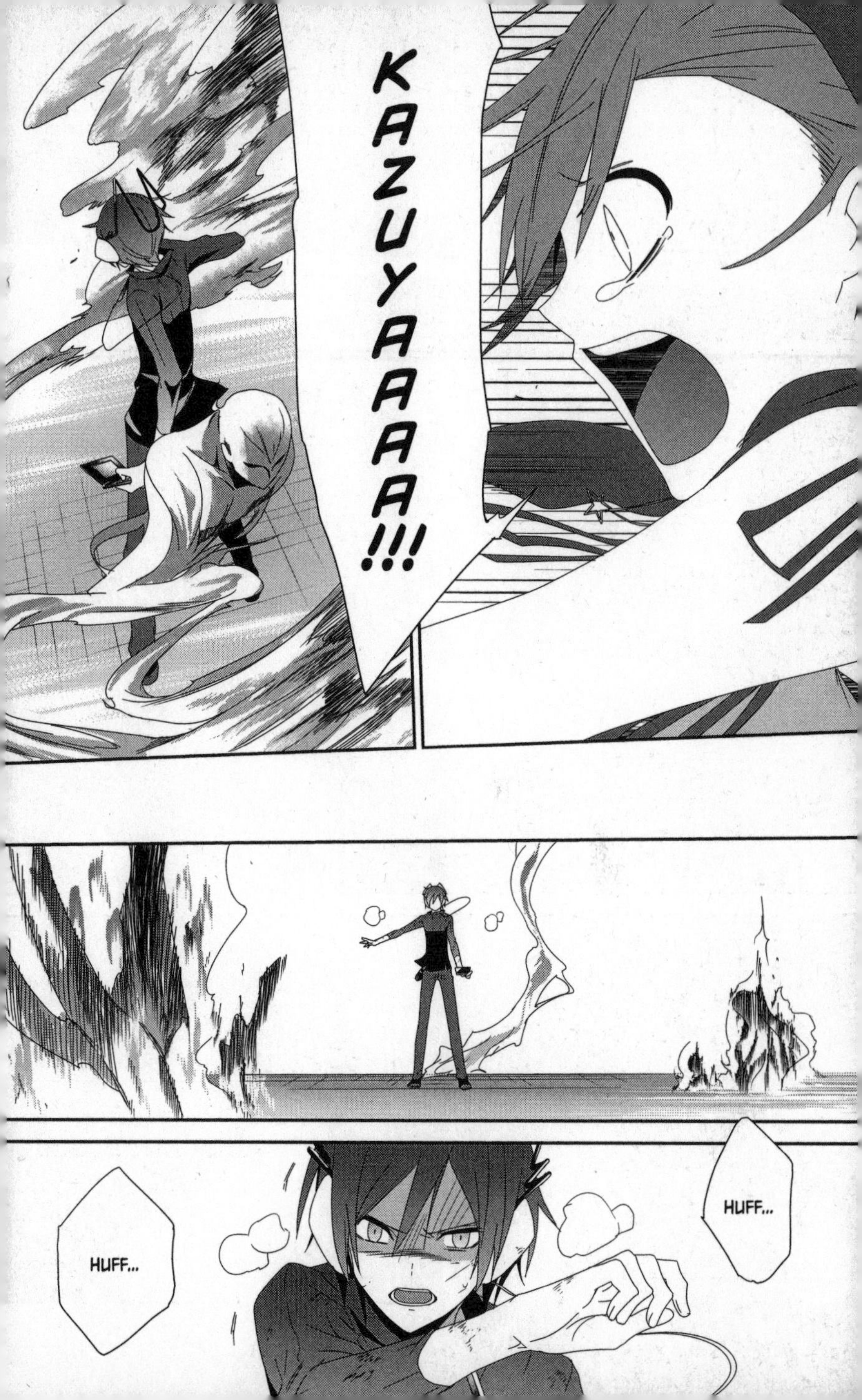
KAZUYAAAAAA!!!
HUFF...
HUFF...

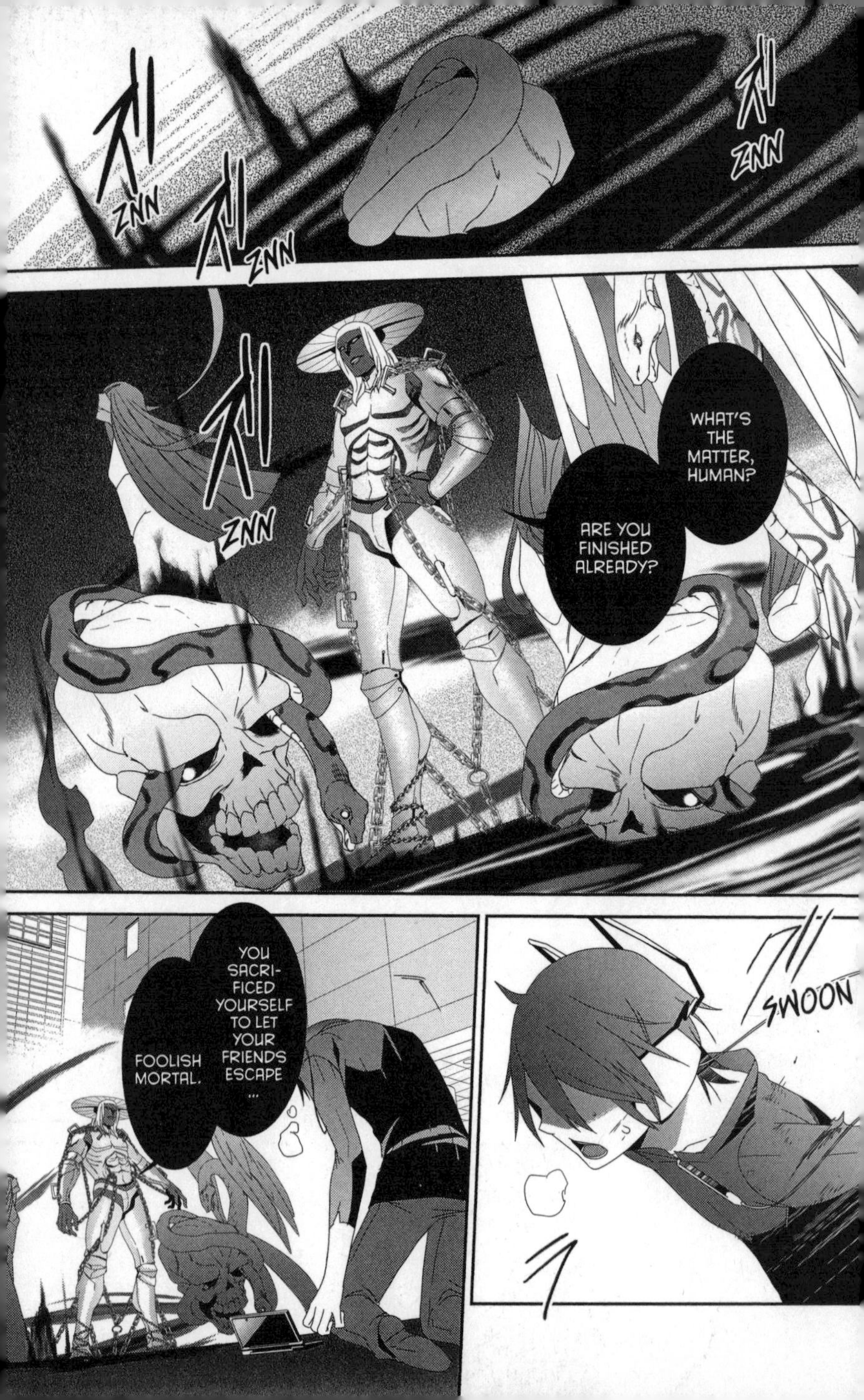
ZNN
ZNN
ZNN
WHAT'S THE MATTER, HUMAN?
ARE YOU FINISHED ALREADY?
ZNN
SWOON
YOU SACRI-FICED YOURSELF TO LET YOUR FRIENDS ESCAPE ...
FOOLISH MORTAL.

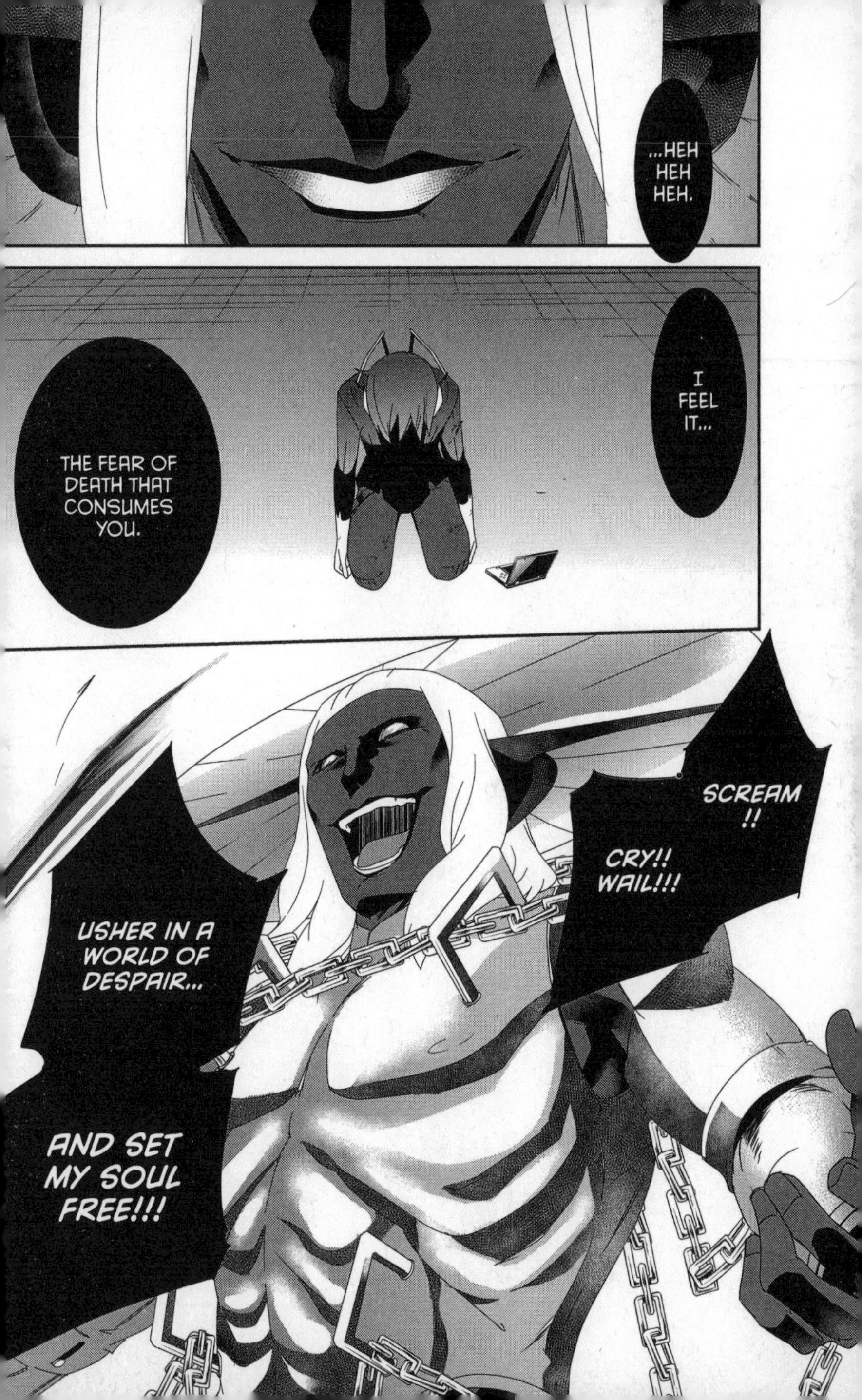
...HEH HEH HEH.
I FEEL IT...
THE FEAR OF DEATH THAT CONSUMES YOU.
SCREAM!!
CRY!! WAIL!!!
USHER IN A WORLD OF DESPAIR...
AND SET MY SOUL FREE!!!

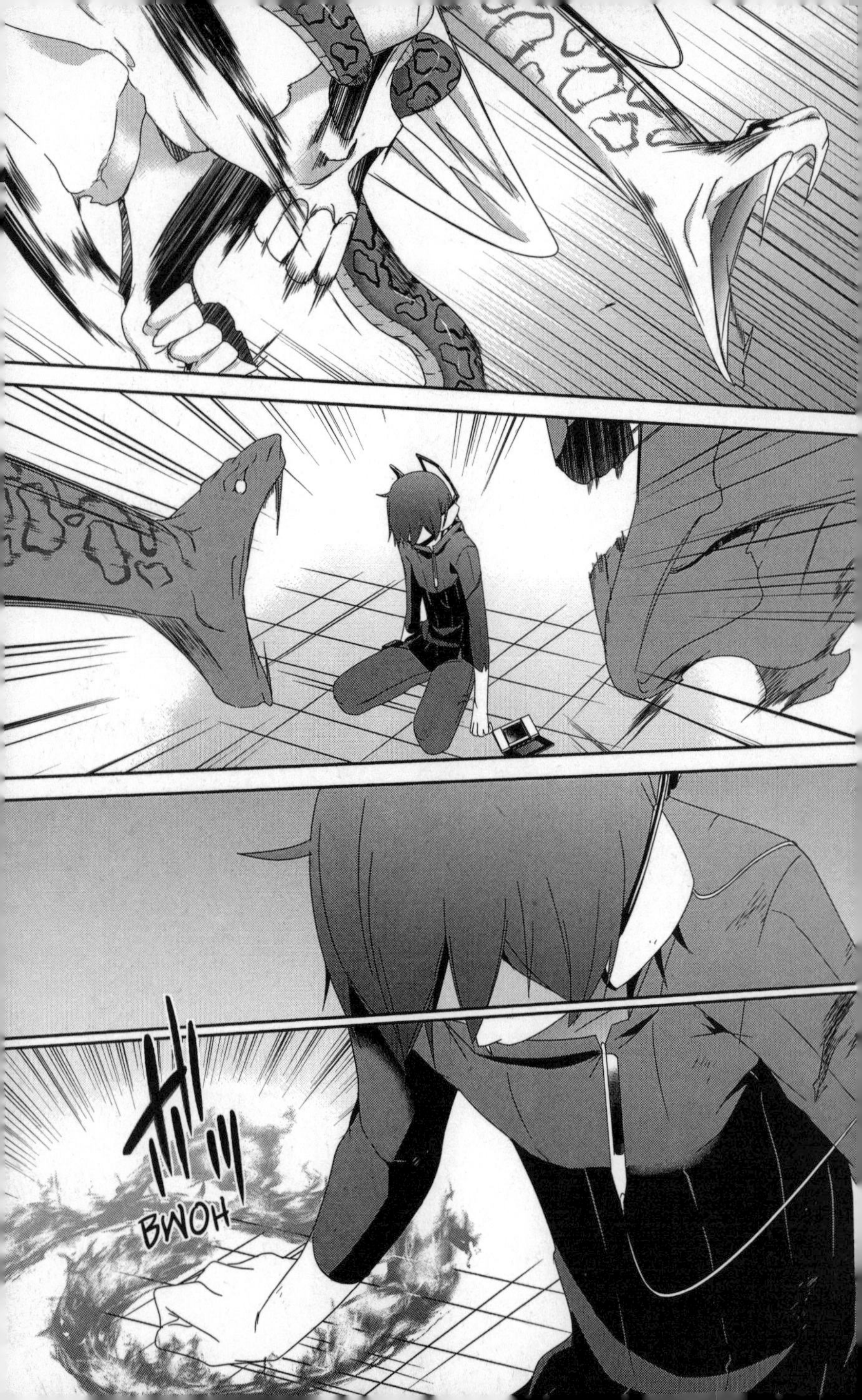
BWOH

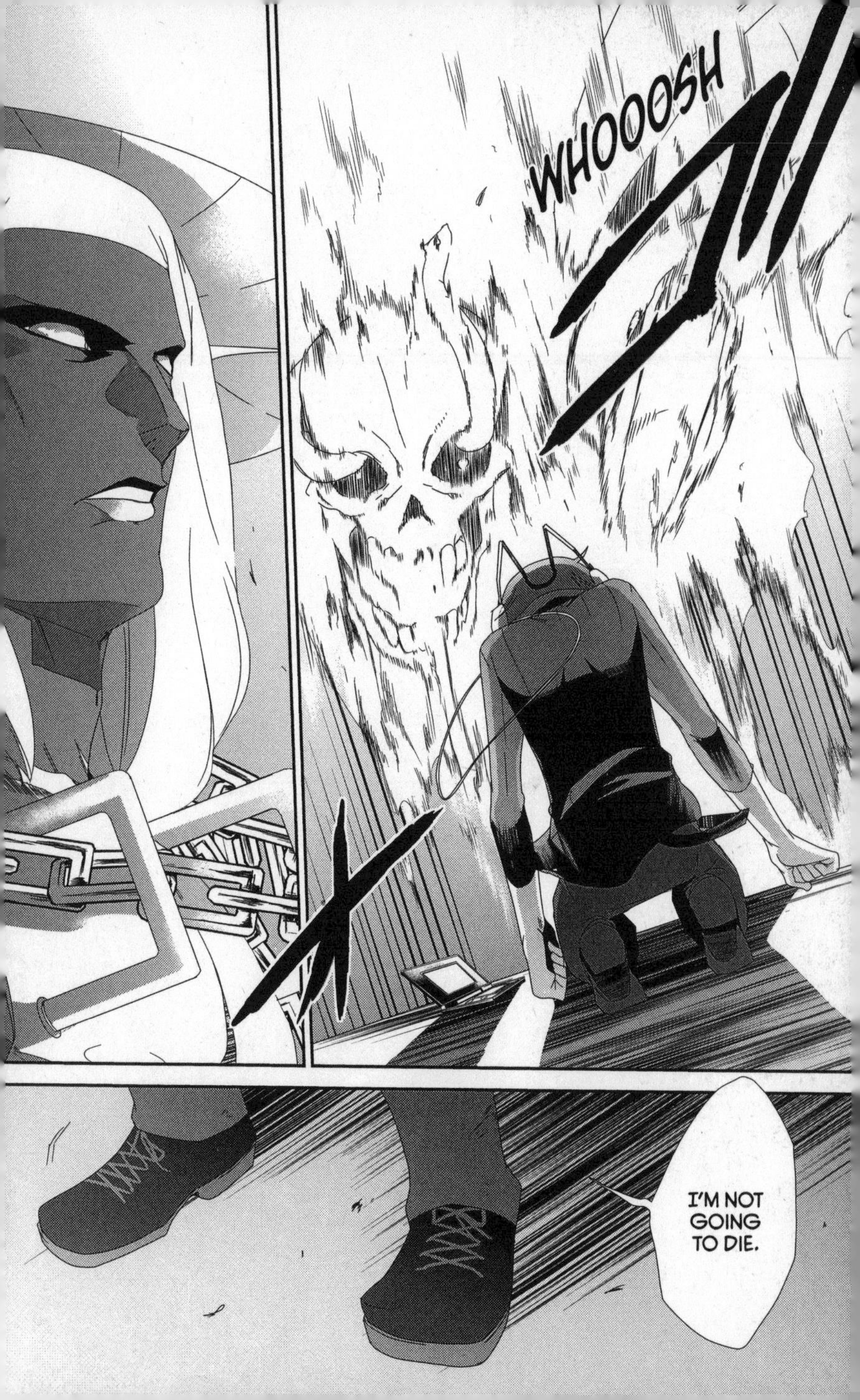
WHOOOSH
I'M NOT GOING TO DIE.

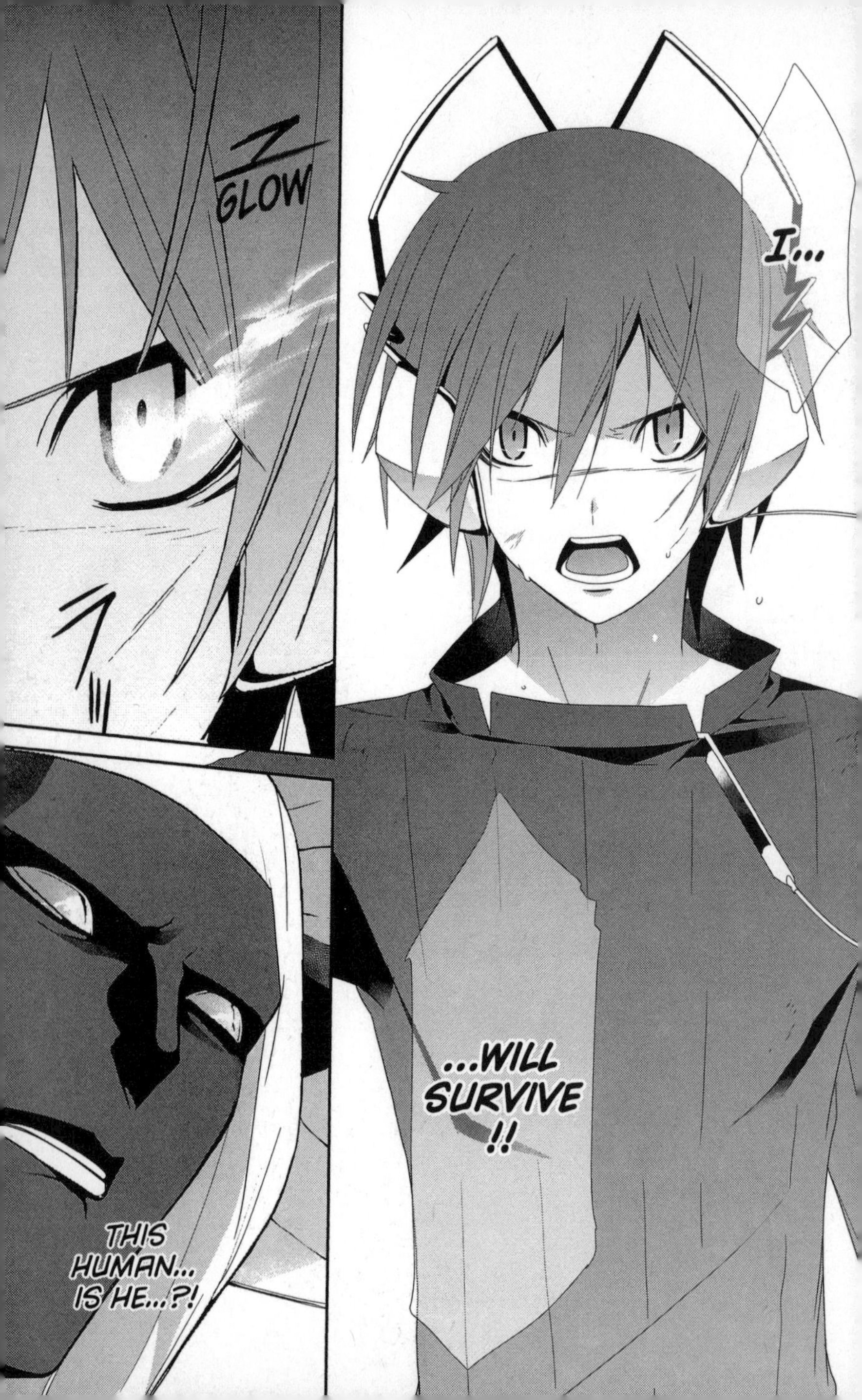
I...
...WILL SURVIVE !!
GLOW
THIS HUMAN... IS HE...?!

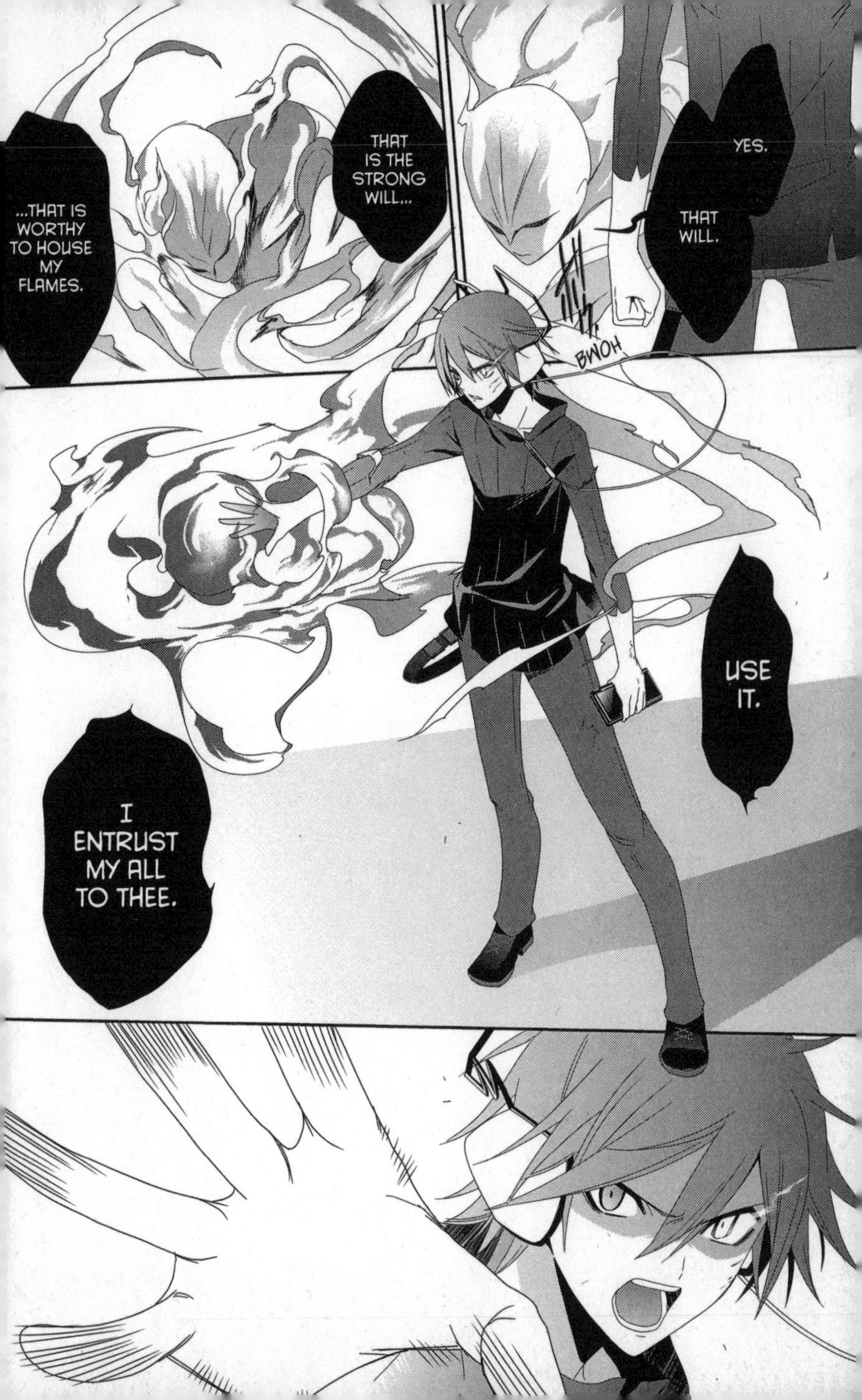
YES.
THAT WILL.
BWOH
THAT IS THE STRONG WILL...
...THAT IS WORTHY TO HOUSE MY FLAMES.
USE IT.
I ENTRUST MY ALL TO THEE.

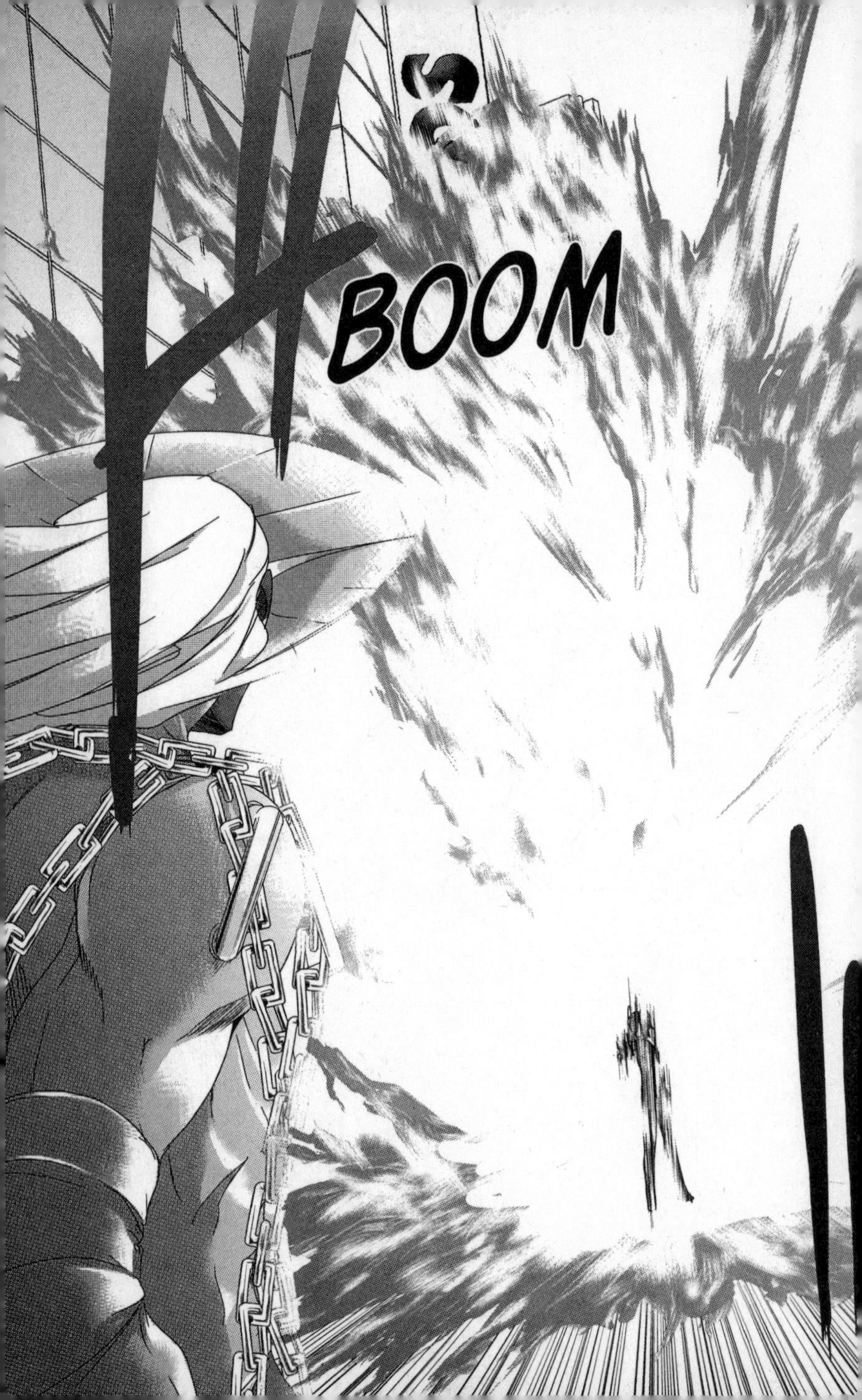
BOOM

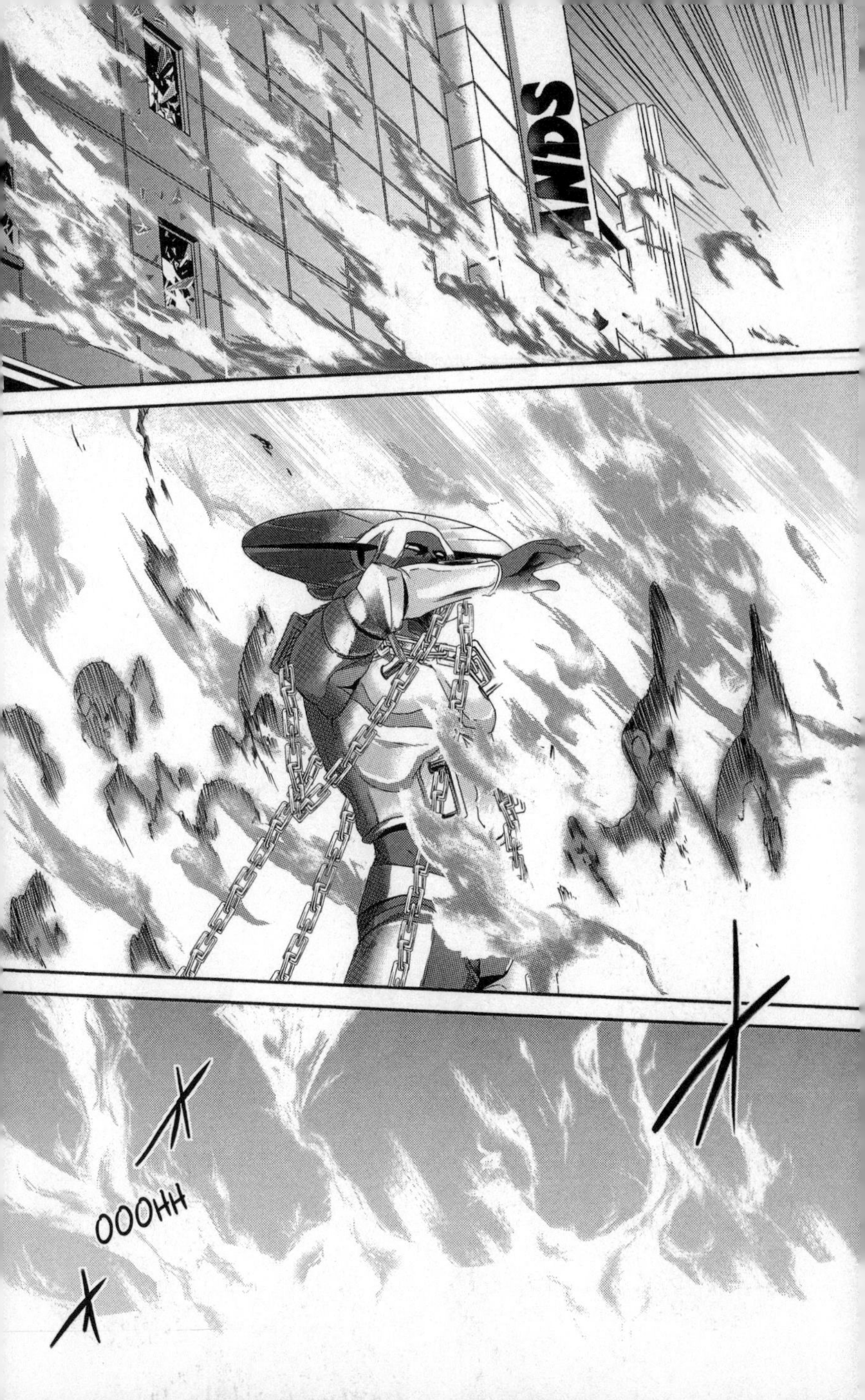
OOOHH

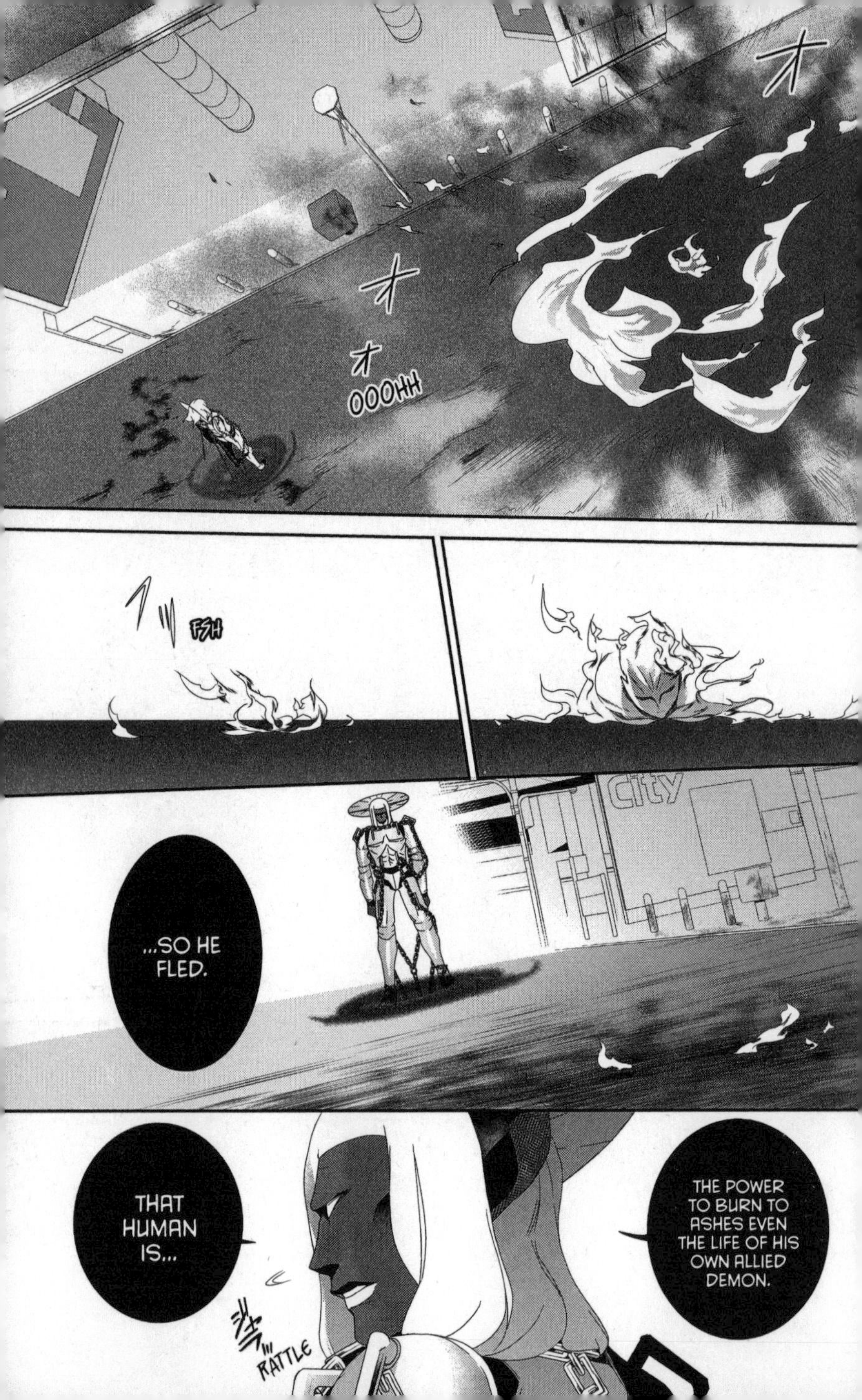

OOOHH
FSH
...SO HE FLED.
THAT HUMAN IS...
THE POWER TO BURN TO ASHES EVEN THE LIFE OF HIS OWN ALLIED DEMON.
RATTLE

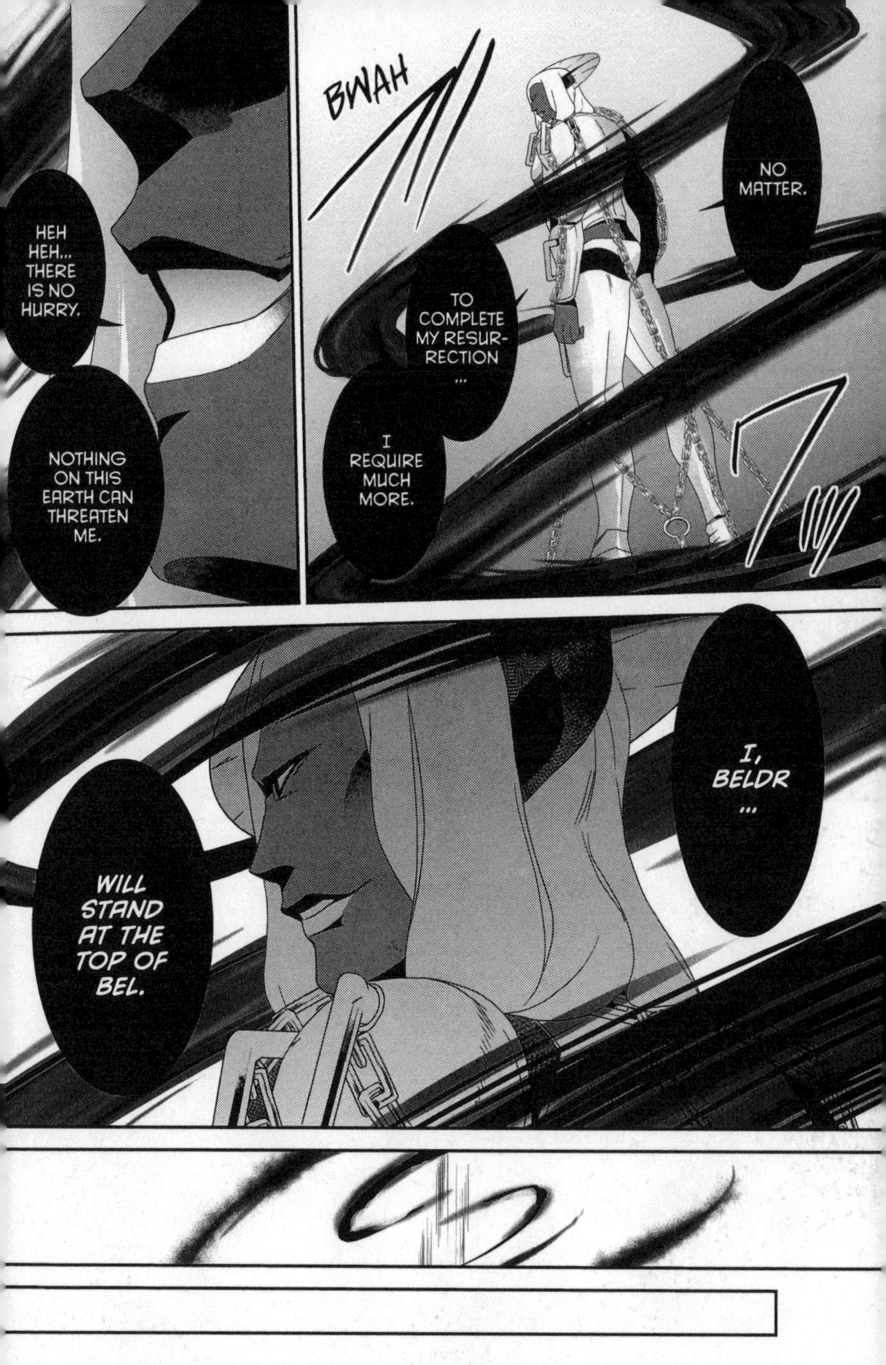
NO MATTER.
BWAH
TO COMPLETE MY RESURRECTION...
I REQUIRE MUCH MORE.
HEH HEH... THERE IS NO HURRY.
NOTHING ON THIS EARTH CAN THREATEN ME.
I, BELDR...
WILL STAND AT THE TOP OF BEL.

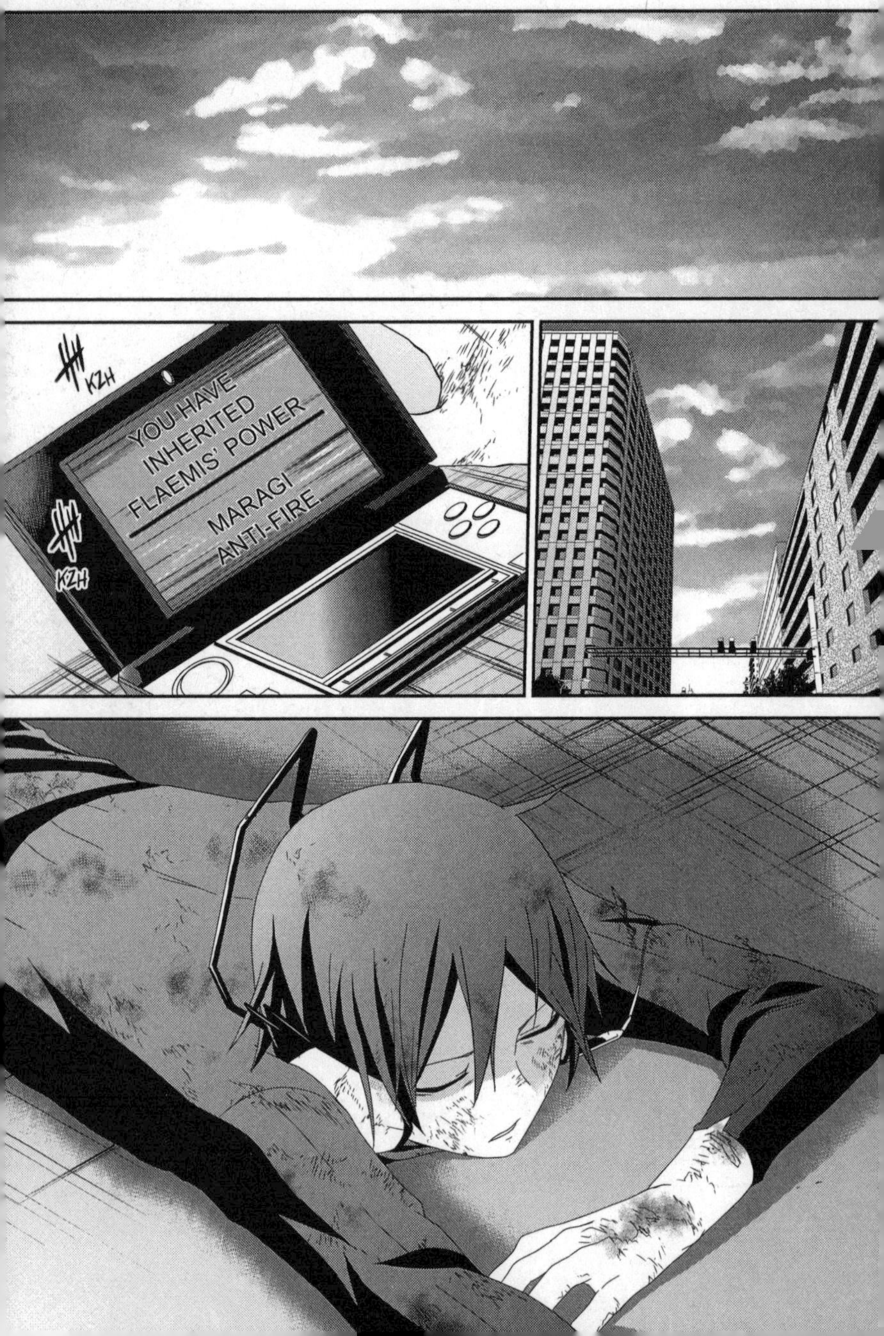
KZH
YOU HAVE INHERITED FLAEMIS' POWER
MARAGI
ANTI-FIRE
KZH

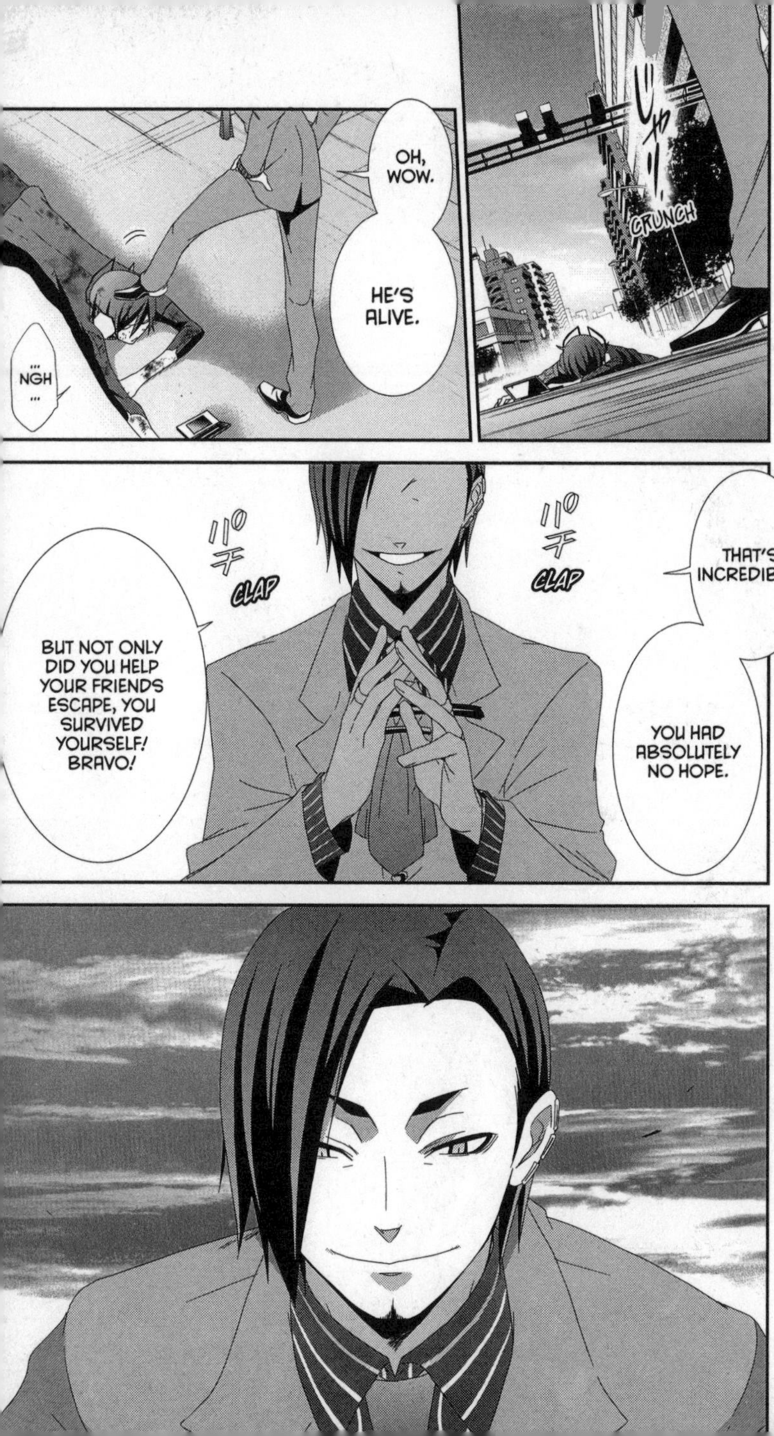
CRUNCH
OH, WOW.
HE'S ALIVE.
... NGH ...
THAT'S INCREDIBLE!
YOU HAD ABSOLUTELY NO HOPE.
パチ
CLAP
パチ
CLAP
BUT NOT ONLY DID YOU HELP YOUR FRIENDS ESCAPE, YOU SURVIVED YOURSELF! BRAVO!

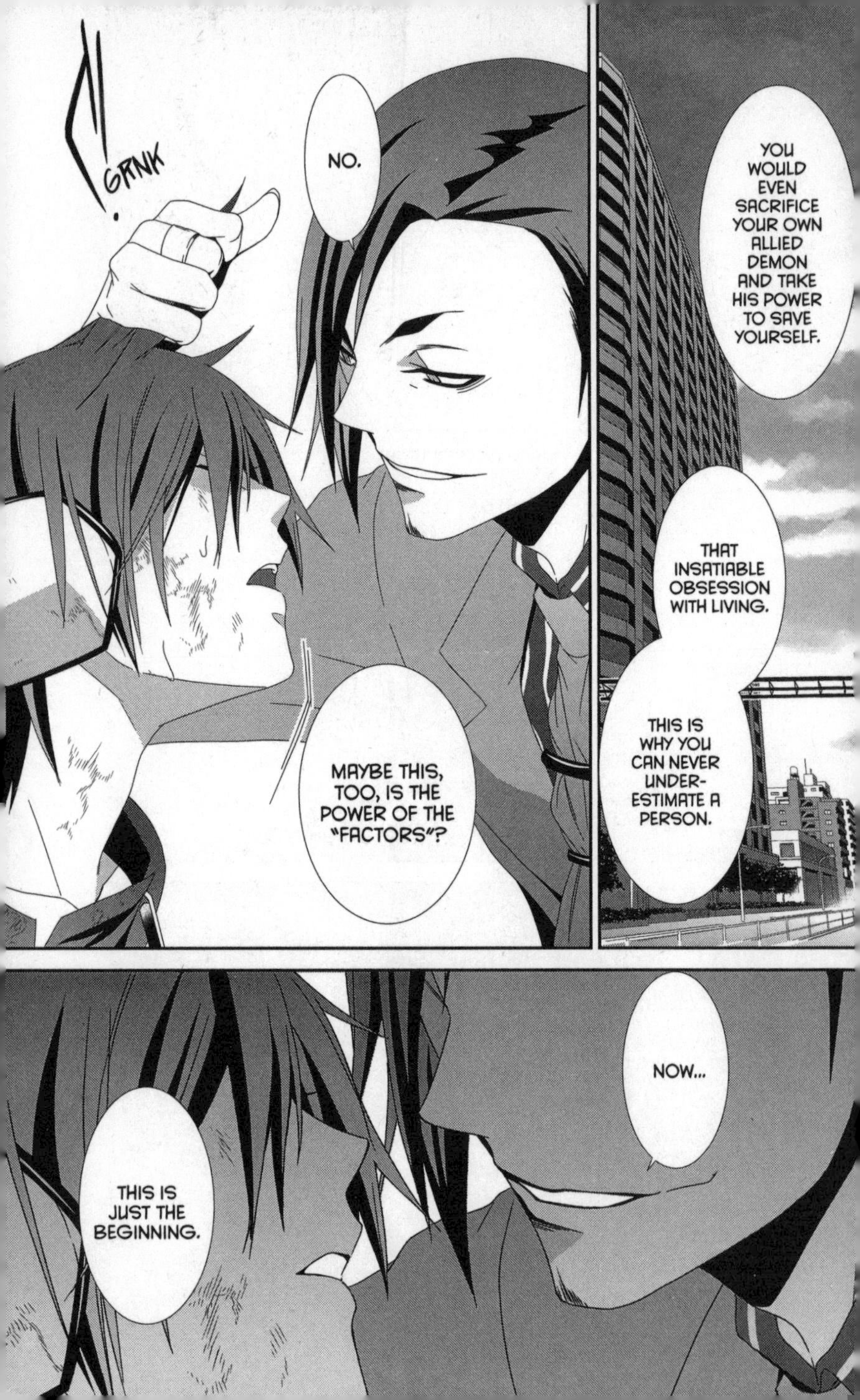
YOU WOULD EVEN SACRIFICE YOUR OWN ALLIED DEMON AND TAKE HIS POWER TO SAVE YOURSELF.
THAT INSATIABLE OBSESSION WITH LIVING.
THIS IS WHY YOU CAN NEVER UNDER-ESTIMATE A PERSON.
NO.
GRNK
MAYBE THIS, TOO, IS THE POWER OF THE "FACTORS"?
NOW...
THIS IS JUST THE BEGINNING.

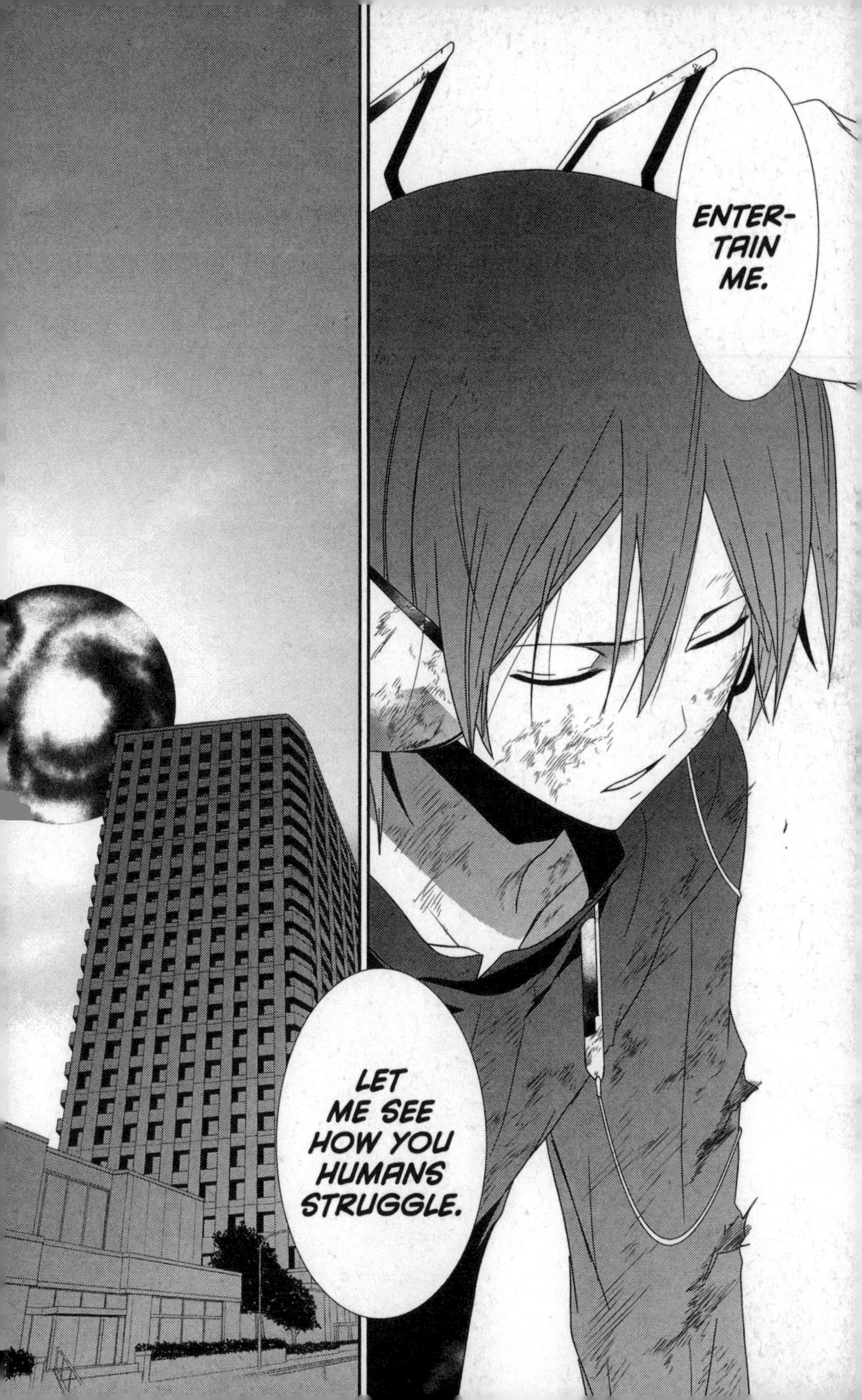
ENTER-TAIN ME.
LET ME SEE HOW YOU HUMANS STRUGGLE.

To be continued......
Comics Volume.3

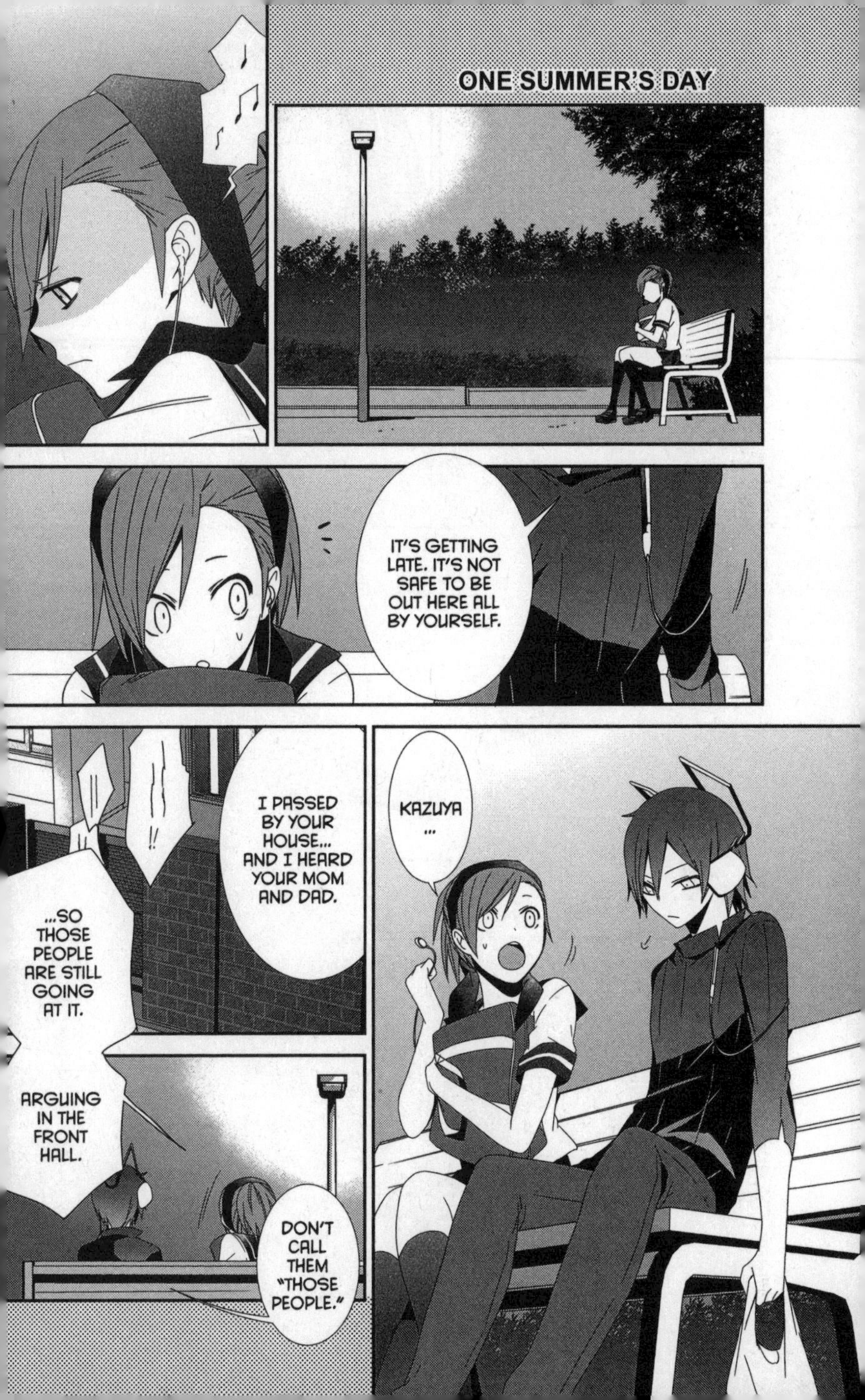
ONE SUMMER'S DAY
IT'S GETTING LATE. IT'S NOT SAFE TO BE OUT HERE ALL BY YOURSELF.
KAZUYA ...
I PASSED BY YOUR HOUSE... AND I HEARD YOUR MOM AND DAD.
...SO THOSE PEOPLE ARE STILL GOING AT IT.
ARGUING IN THE FRONT HALL.
DON'T CALL THEM "THOSE PEOPLE."

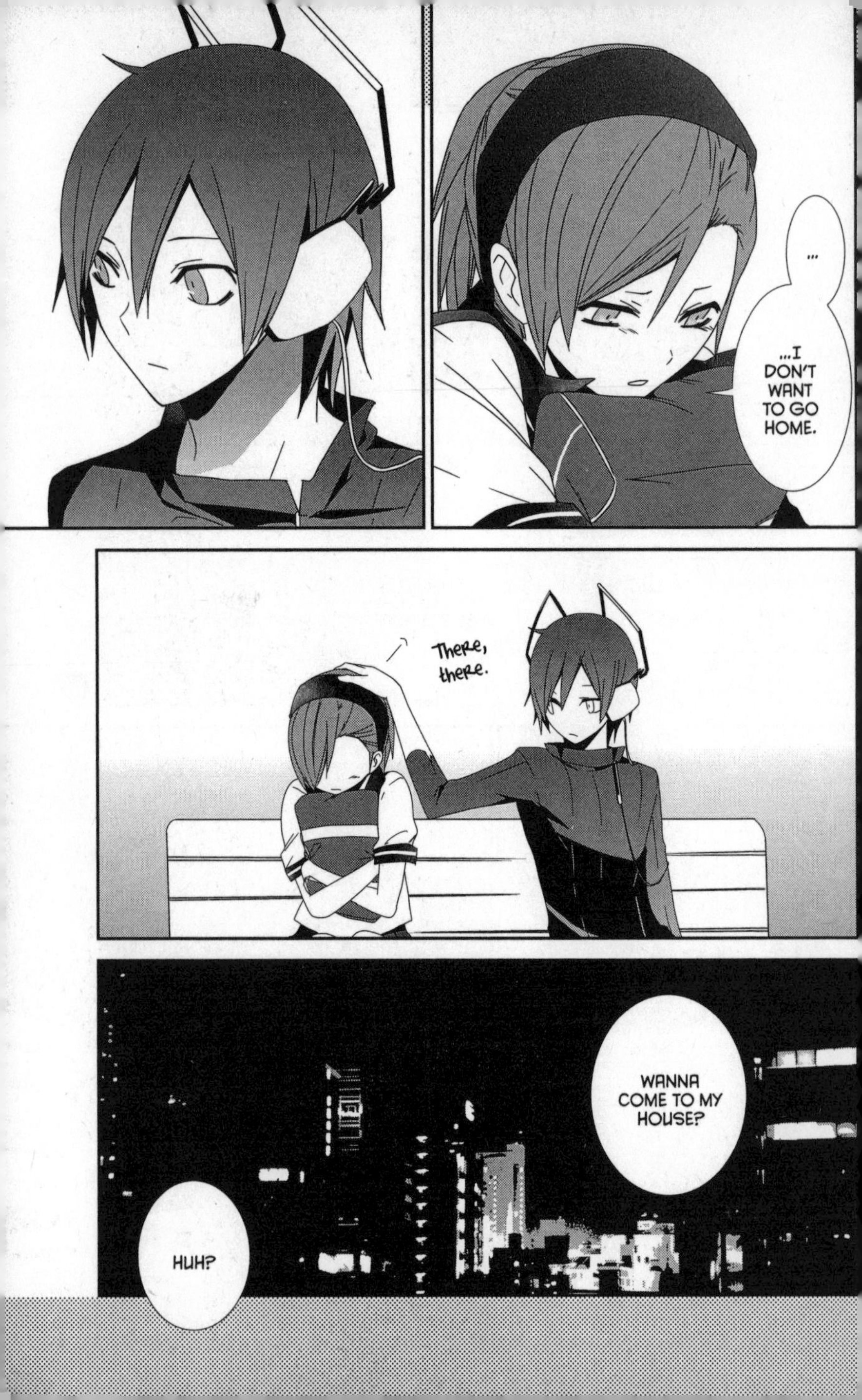
...
...I DON'T WANT TO GO HOME.
There, there.
WANNA COME TO MY HOUSE?
HUH?

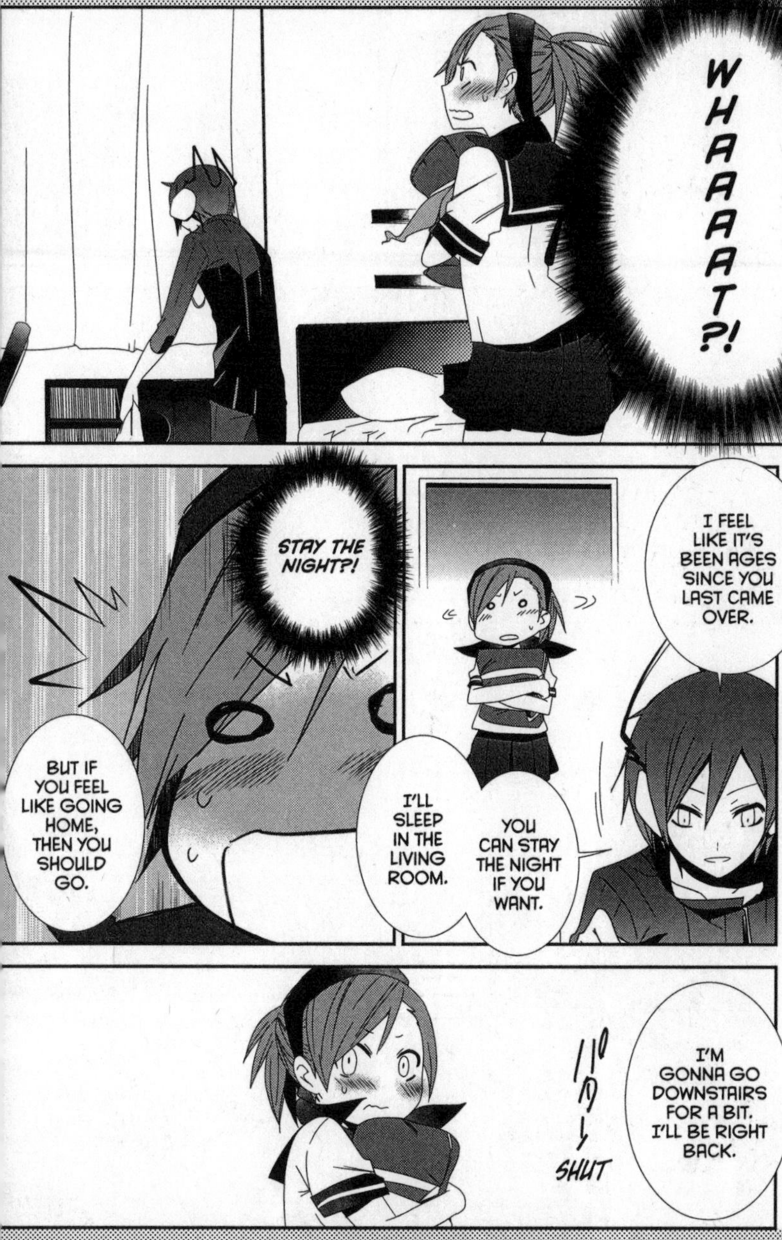
WHAAAAAT?!
I FEEL LIKE IT'S BEEN AGES SINCE YOU LAST CAME OVER.
YOU CAN STAY THE NIGHT IF YOU WANT.
I'LL SLEEP IN THE LIVING ROOM.
STAY THE NIGHT?!
BUT IF YOU FEEL LIKE GOING HOME, THEN YOU SHOULD GO.
I'M GONNA GO DOWNSTAIRS FOR A BIT. I'LL BE RIGHT BACK.
SHUT

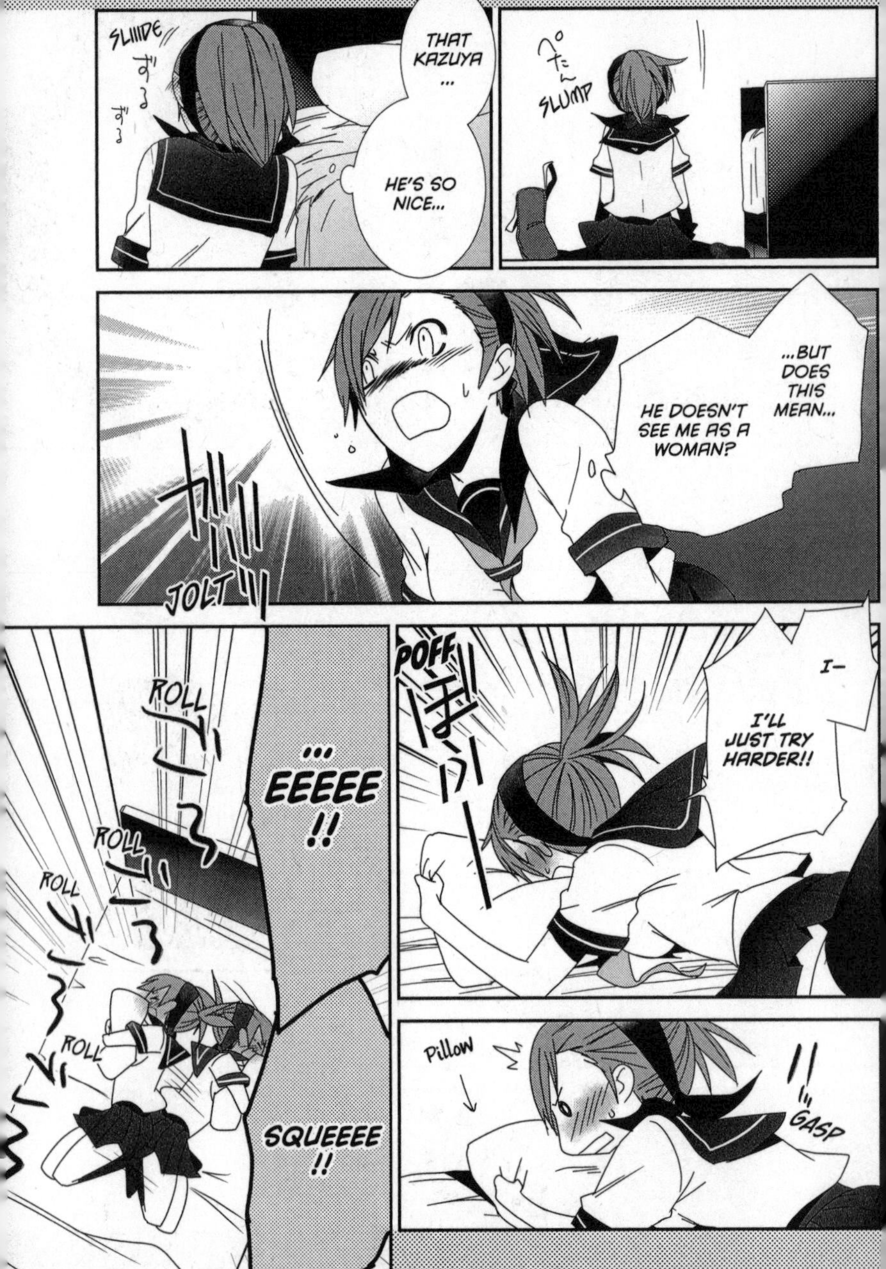
ぺたん
SLUMP
SLIIIDE
ずる
ずる
THAT KAZUYA...
HE'S SO NICE...
...BUT DOES THIS MEAN...
HE DOESN'T SEE ME AS A WOMAN?
JOLT
I—
I'LL JUST TRY HARDER!!
POFF
Pillow
GASP
ROLL
ROLL
ROLL
ROLL
...EEEEEE!!
SQUEEEE!!

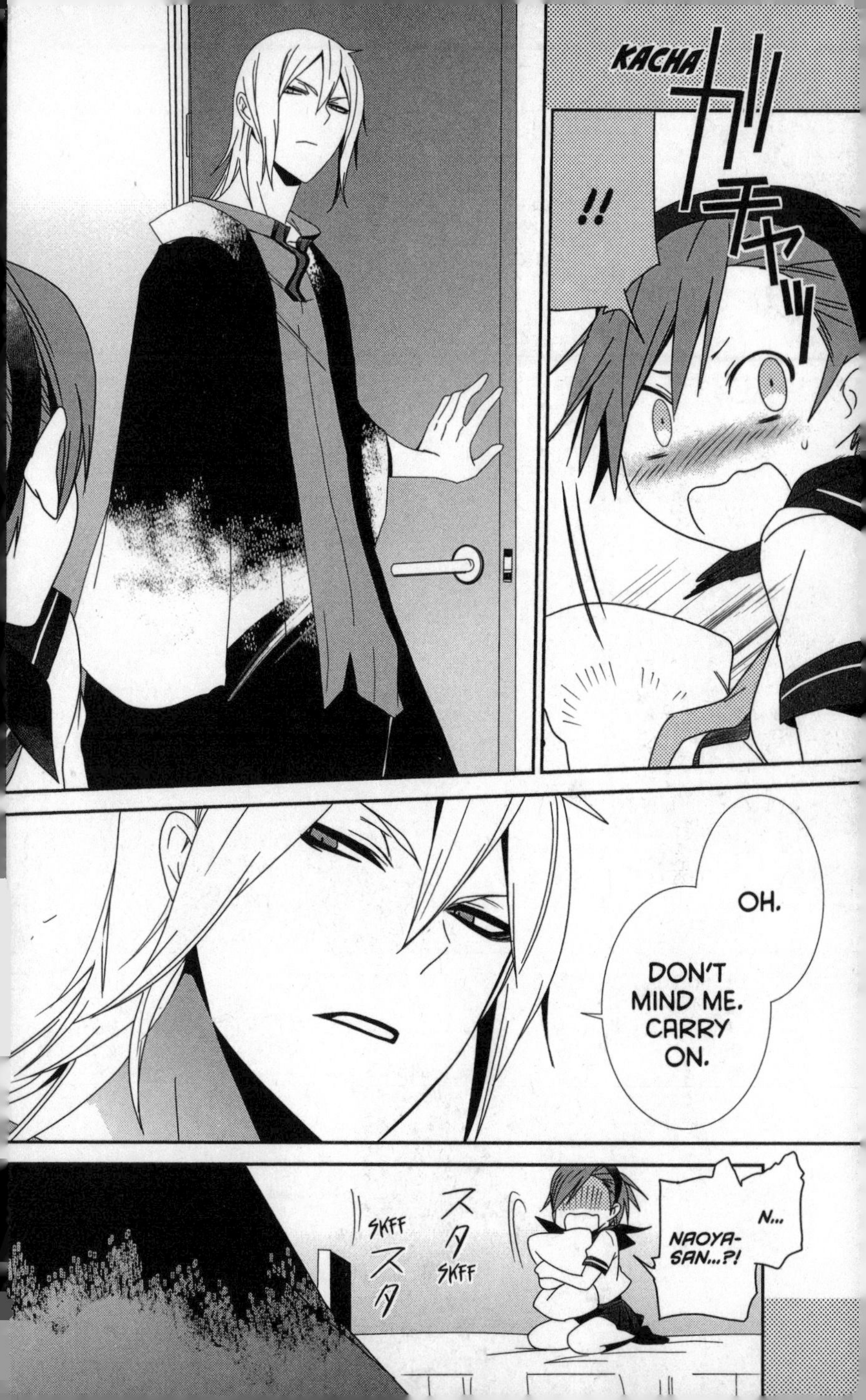
KACHA
ガチャッ
!!
OH.
DON'T MIND ME. CARRY ON.
N...
NAOYA-SAN...?!
スタ SKFF
スタ SKFF

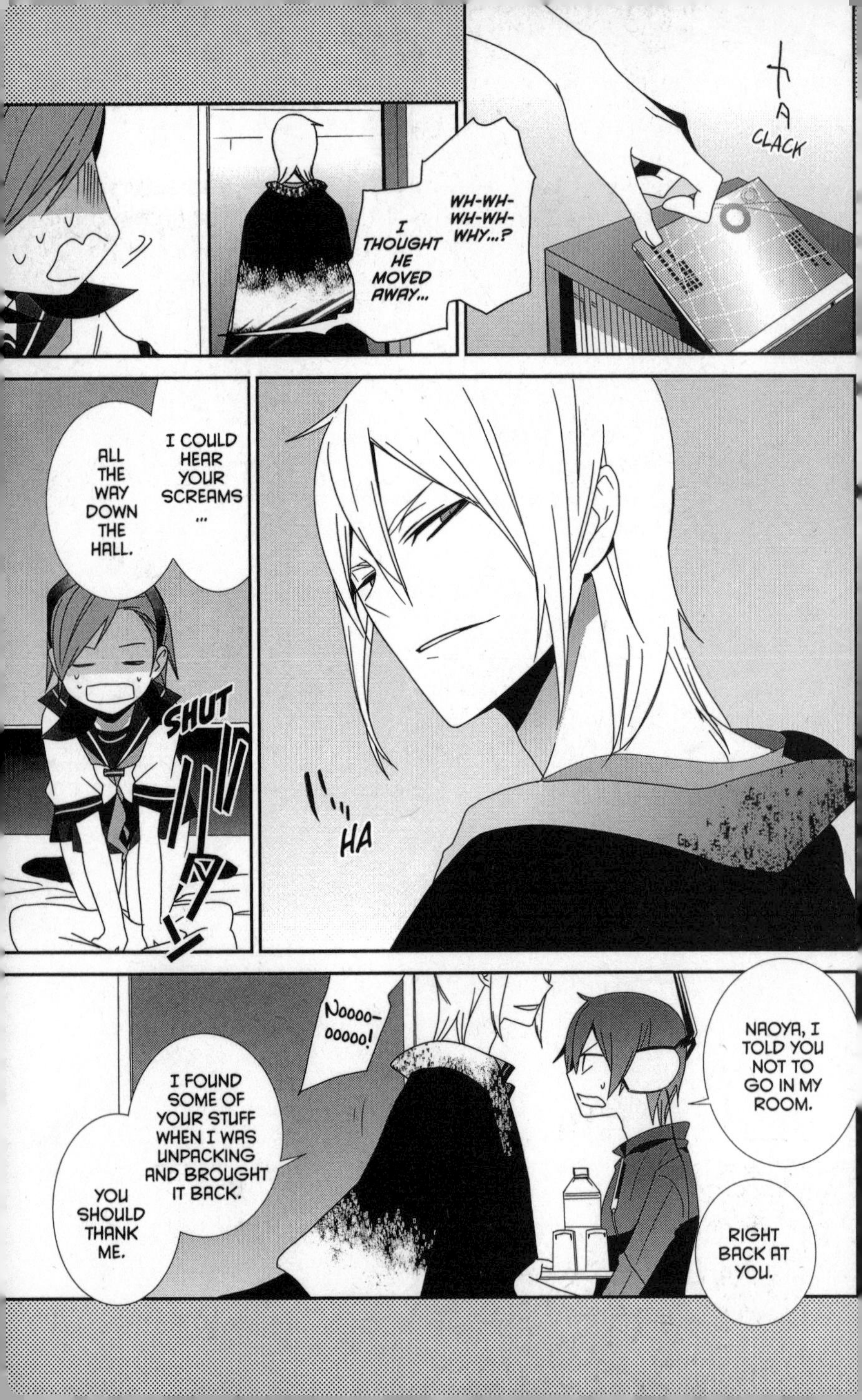

CLACK
WH-WH-WH-WH-WHY...?
I THOUGHT HE MOVED AWAY...
HA
I COULD HEAR YOUR SCREAMS ...
ALL THE WAY DOWN THE HALL.
SHUT
NAOYA, I TOLD YOU NOT TO GO IN MY ROOM.
RIGHT BACK AT YOU.
Noooo-ooooo!
I FOUND SOME OF YOUR STUFF WHEN I WAS UNPACKING AND BROUGHT IT BACK.
YOU SHOULD THANK ME.

Devil Survivor volume 2 is a work of fict
places, and incidents are the products of the author's imagination or are used fictitiously. Any resemblance to actual events, locales, or persons, living or dead, is entirely coincidental.

A Kodansha Comics Trade Paperback Original.

©Index Corp.

Published in the United States by Kodansha Comics, an imprint of Kodansha USA Publishing, LLC, New York.

Publication rights for this English edition arranged through Kodansha Ltd., Tokyo.

First published in Japan in 2013 by Kodansha Ltd., Tokyo.

ISBN 978-1-63236-192-9

Printed in the United States of America.

www.kodanshacomics.com

9 8 7 6 5 4 3 2 1

Editor: Lauren Scanlan
Translator: Alethea Nibley & Athena Nibley
Lettering: AndWorld Design